Wolfgang Mieder
& George B. Bryan

Proverbs in World Literature

A Bibliography

PETER LANG
New York • Washington, D.C./Baltimore
Bern • Frankfurt am Main • Berlin • Vienna • Paris

Library of Congress Cataloging-in-Publication Data

Mieder, Wolfgang.
Proverbs in world literature: a bibliography /
Wolfgang Mieder & George B. Bryan.
p. cm.
Includes bibliographical references and index.
1. Proverbs in literature—Bibliography. I. Bryan, George B. II. Title.
Z6514.P76M535 [PN56.P75] 016.80888'2—dc20 96-25570
ISBN 0-8204-3499-X

Die Deutsche Bibliothek-CIP-Einheitsaufnahme

Mieder, Wolfgang.
Proverbs in world literature: a bibliography / Wolfgang Mieder &
George B. Bryan. –New York; Washington, D.C./Baltimore;
Bern; Frankfurt am Main; Berlin; Vienna; Paris: Lang.
ISBN 0-8204-3499-X
NE: Mieder, Wolfgang [Hrsg.]; HST

Cover design by James F. Brisson.

The paper in this book meets the guidelines for permanence and durability
of the Committee on Production Guidelines for Book Longevity
of the Council of Library Resources.

Printed in the United States of America.

Proverbs in World Literature

Upon her retirement from teaching at the University of Vermont,

we lovingly dedicate this book to

VERONICA C. RICHEL,

a valued friend and colleague.

Change in everything is sweet. EURIPIDES

TABLE OF CONTENTS

PREFACE

Literary critics and folklorists have long been interested in the use and function of proverbial language in literature. As this bibliography indicates, the scholarship is voluminous, and the time has surely come to apprise scholars and students of the extent of research on this fascinating subject. This book enables the reader to establish what has been published on proverbs, proverbial expressions, proverbial comparisons, proverbial exaggerations, and wellerisms in the works of numerous authors throughout the world. With this information at hand, new research endeavors that build on previous research and avoid unnecessary duplication can be mapped out.

For this international bibliography, we have collected and organized extensive materials from many languages and cultures. Our interest in foreign languages, folklore, and literature has enabled us to cast our bibliographical nets rather widely. The bibliography thus includes not only proverb studies regarding the major authors of world literature, but also those investigations that deal with regional writers. In addition, we have also included analyses of proverbial diction in anonymous literary works as well as in folk literature.

While we have labored together for many strenuous yet joyful hours on this volume, we have also benefitted from and greatly appreciated the assistance of Patricia E. Mardeusz, Amy Beth, Barbara Lambert, Karen McGregor, and Daryl Purvee of the Interlibrary Loan Department of the Bailey-Howe Library at the University of Vermont. Because of their help, we were able to inspect almost every publication listed in this bibliography. Our work-study student Eric Doane also deserves our thanks for his dependable and efficient services.

March 1996   WM
                                                                           GBB

INTRODUCTION

The study of literature and folklore has a long and significant scholarly tradition behind it. Literary historians and folklorists have long been interested in the role played in literary texts by folkloristic elements and have established that many writers base their works on folk narratives or at least allude to segments of them. Quite naturally, they have also employed proverbial language in their literary texts. Although authors differ in the frequency with which they use proverbs, proverbial expressions, proverbial comparisons, proverbial exaggerations, and wellerisms, they nevertheless do at least sporadically employ such formulaic language. Literary works thus become important repositories for verbal folklore, and it behooves the literary critic as well as the folklorist to pay attention to its use and function.

Whatever the number of proverbial texts in a literary work, locating them and interpreting their meaning can be a revealing bipartite task. Identification serves primarily paremiographical goals in that it deals only with the texts. Since the oral use of proverbs in former centuries can no longer be investigated through actual field research, scholars depend on the written word as sources of them. Every literary investigation should, ideally, include an index of all proverbial material. Obviously, precise references must accompany the texts, and proper verification of their proverbiality (as far as possible) by means of standard proverb dictionaries is also desirable. Such annotated proverb lists are of great importance for the preparation of both expanded and new historical proverb dictionaries. In fact, one obvious task for the lexicographically-oriented paremiographer is to take the numerous lists that have been assembled for a particular language or culture and merge them into a comprehensive dictionary. Unfortunately, numerous literary proverb studies do not include such indexes and thus do not contribute to the long overdue aggrandizements of historical proverb collections of textual variants throughout the centuries.

Settling for simply listing proverbs in the works of an author, all too many scholars provide only a bare minimum of annotations and no interpretive comments. This purely lexicographical approach is not particularly satisfactory, for in addition to the identification of proverbial locutions, there should also be a detailed interpretation of their contextual function. Critics, folklorists, and paremiologists want to know when, why, how, by whom, and to whom proverbs are used in literary works. They will thus consider each example in its context to determine what effect it has on the style and message of the entire work. Of great interest also is whether introductory formulas are used to integrate the proverb into the texts, whether the formulaic structure of the proverb has been changed for stylistic effect, whether a proverb is merely alluded to in an ironic twist, whether a proverb is intentionally parodied or questioned, etc. The answers to such questions reveal the function and meaning of proverbial wisdom in literary works.

Ideally, then, a literary proverb investigation consists of a proverb index and an interpretive essay. Most studies thus far have tended to go in one or the other direction, i. e., they are either purely paremiographical or exclusively paremiological. The former is significant for the lexicographical database needed to assemble historical proverb dictionaries; the latter is crucial to a complete interpretation of a literary work. An analysis of the semantic function of proverbs in a Shakespearean play does not require yet another proverb index since a number of excellent reference works on Shakespeare's proverbs already exist. Such annotated indexes of proverbs in the works of authors for whom such standard compilations have not been made (and that is usually the case) would be of inestimable value. Sadly, journal editors are often reluctant to provide the space for these indexes, which has resulted in excellent interpretive essays at the expense of lexicographically-oriented lists of proverbs. In the case of dissertations and book-length studies, however, a plea must be made for the inclusion of indexes of proverbs.

A perusal of the present bibliography shows that some internationally-known authors have definitely been overworked, viz., there is a multitude of superb proverb studies (both indexes and interpretations) of Geoffrey Chaucer, William Shakespeare, François Rabelais, Hans Sachs, Miguel de Cervantes Saavedra, Chinua Achebe, etc. Authors of the Middle Ages as well as the sixteenth and seventeenth centuries have often been excerpted and studied. Scholars should now also consider the literature of other periods, such as the Enlightenment and modern experimental literature. The writings of many regional authors have been examined, but primarily only to find proverb texts and possible variants. Only recently have scholars investigated such major twentieth-century figures as George Bernard Shaw, Eugene O'Neill, and Agatha Christie, but there are many others whose proverbial language awaits a serious look. Nobody has, for example, explored the complete works of such significant writers as Thomas Mann, James Joyce, Marcel Proust, and Bertolt Brecht. One of the aims of this bibliography is to lead scholars in new directions by showing them what has already been done.

Literary proverb studies must not be limited to investigations of *belles lettres*. It is high time to look at proverbial language in sermons, letters, diaries, travel journals, songs, and the mass media. Recently there have been studies of such major political figures as Winston S. Churchill, Adolf Hitler, and Harry S. Truman, but much remains to be done. And why not investigate the use of proverbial language in the transcripts of the Nuremberg Trials and the McCarthy and Watergate investigative hearings? There has been an overemphasis on prose narrative and dramatic literature at the expense of the richness of proverbs in poetry that ranges from medieval proverb ballads to Emily Dickinson and beyond. Popular songs also are worthy of proverb investigation. Proverbs play a large role in folk songs, but they are also conspicuous in popular music, country and western, and even rock 'n' roll. The connection of proverbs and fables has been studied, but we need further explanation of how proverbs and folk narratives, such as fairy tales and jokes, interrelate.

The rich and impressive contents of this bibliography serve as a clear indication that the study of proverbs in literature is an established scholarly phenomenon. Much has been accomplished, but literally dozens of important projects await execution. To tackle the works of extremely prolific authors is a major undertaking, but in such a project, scholars of the arts and humanities can join forces as colleagues in the social and natural sciences have long been accustomed to do. We, a paremiologist-folklorist and a theatre historian, have found that sharing the load not only halves the work, but it also adds to the enjoyment of the scholarly task and enhances the product. We are presently at work on a proverb investigation of the collected writings of Charles Dickens (including letters, speeches, etc.), something that neither one of us would have undertaken alone. Such team efforts would enable scholars to analyze the works of other prolific writers, from Johann Wolfgang von Goethe to Vladimir Ilich Lenin. We hope that this bibliography will inspire others to join us on this proverbial bandwagon.

A few comments about the organization of this bibliography are in order. It contains 2,654 entries, of which Nos. 1-284 comprise a section of General Studies. Here we list proverb dictionaries based on texts collected from literary works, books and articles about numerous authors (also listed under individual names in the major body of this bibliography), studies of the interrelationship of proverbs and folk literature (fairy tales, legends, tall tales, folk songs, etc.), and theoretical writings on the integration and function of proverbs in literature in general.

The second part of the bibliography is arranged alphabetically according to the last name of the literary author whose proverbial usage has been investigated. If there is more than one study of any particular author, they are listed alphabetically according to the scholars' last names. If a scholar has published more than one study of a particular author, the entries are arranged chronologically. Anonymous literary works are also listed alphabetically. Finally, there is a name index of the scholars cited. The numbers after individual names refer to the specific items in the bibliography and not to page numbers.

Since this bibliography is meant for international scholars and students interested in proverbs and literature, the use of abbreviations is kept to an absolute minimum. All journal titles are cited in their entirety, and the only abbreviations are the standard "c." (circa), "Diss." (dissertation), "Ed(s)." (Editor[s]), "fl." (flourished), "M. A." (Master of Arts), "ns" (new series), "No(s)" (Number[s]), and "ser." (series).

PROVERBS IN WORLD LITERATURE:

A BIBLIOGRAPHY

GENERAL STUDIES

1. Abrahams, Roger D., and Barbara A. Babcock. "The Literary Use of Proverbs." *Journal of American Folklore* 90 (1977): 414-429. Also in *Wise Words: Essays on the Proverb.* Ed. Wolfgang Mieder. New York: Garland Publishing, 1994. 415-437.

2. Adeeko, Adeleke. "Words' Horse, or The Proverb as a Paradigm of Literary Understanding." Diss. University of Florida, 1991. 229 pp.

3. Alster, Bendt. "Early Dynastic Proverbs and Other Contributions to the Study of Literary Texts from Abu Salabikh." *Archiv für Orientforschung* 38-39 (1991-1992): 1-51. 17 illus.

4. Arthurs, Jeffrey D. "Proverbs in Inspirational Literature: Sanctioning the American Dream." *Journal of Communication and Religion* 17, 2 (1994): 1-15.

5. Baar, Adolf. *Sprichwörter und Sentenzen aus den griechischen Idyllendichtern.* Görz: Selbstverlag des Staatsgymnasiums, 1887. 41 pp.

6. Bass, Josef. *Sprichwörtliche Redensarten aus Sage, Geschichte und Mythologie.* Wien: Steyermühl, 1926. 98 pp.

7. Bautier, Anne-Marie. "Peuples, provinces et villes dans la littérature proverbiale latine du Moyen Âge." *Richesse du proverbe*, 2 vols. Eds. François Suard and Claude Buridant. Lille: Université de Lille, 1984. I, 1-22.

8. Bean, Sue McEachern. "The Use of Proverbs in Pre-Shakespearean Drama." M. A. Thesis. Stetson University, 1936. 165 pp.

9. Berthold, Luise. "Mittelalterliche Sprichwörter und das moderne Mundartwörterbuch." *Hessische Blätter für Volkskunde* 39 (1940): 64-67.

10. Bizzarri, Hugo Oscar. "La palabra y el silencio en la literatura sapiencial de la edad media castellana." *Incipit* 13 (1993): 21-49.

11. Bizzarri, Hugo Oscar. "Oralidad y escritura en el refranero medieval." *Proverbium: Yearbook of International Proverb Scholarship* 12 (1995): 27-66.

12.   Bouchet, Émile. "Les proverbes dans l'épopée française." *Revue des traditions populaires* 9 (1894): 384-391.

13.   Bouchet, Émile. "Maximes et proverbes tirés des chansons de geste." *Mémoires de la Société d'Agriculture, Sciences, Belles-lettres et Arts d'Orléans* 31 (1892): 81-130.

14.   Božinova, Dragica. "Le local et l'universel dans un monde merveilleux: Les formes parémiologiques dans les contes populaires macédoniens." *Cahiers balkaniques* No. 16 (1990): 183-192.

15.   Braun, Peter. "Sprichwörter—Redensarten—Zitate—Titel: Oder die Tendenz zur Abwandlung von Formeln." *Tendenzen in der deutschen Gegenwartssprache.* Stuttgart: W. Kohlhammer, 1979. 159-164.

16.   Brenner, Clarence D. *Le développement du proverbe dramatique en France et sa vogue au XVIIIe siècle avec un Proverbe inédit de Carmontelle.* Berkeley: University of California Press, 1937. 68 pp.

17.   Broek, Marinus A. van den. "'Lieb reden macht guot freund': Zum Sprichwortgebrauch in der frühreformatorischen Flugschriftenliteratur." *Wirkendes Wort* 40, 2 (1990): 164-178.

18.   Broek, Marinus A. van den. "Sprachliche Vergleiche in der frühreformatorischen Flugschriftenliteratur." *Proverbium: Yearbook of International Proverb Scholarship* 8 (1991): 29-53.

19.   Brunvand, Jan Harold. *A Dictionary of Proverbs and Proverbial Phrases from Books Published by Indiana Authors before 1890.* Bloomington: Indiana University Press, 1961. 168 pp.

20.   Buezo, Catalina. "El empleo paródico de refranes y frases proverbiales en la mojiganga paródica dramática." *Paremia* No. 2 (1993): 109-115.

21.   Bulbena y Tosell, Antoni. "Obres teyatrals catalanesques ab titol paremiólogica." *Assaig de Bibliografia paremiologica catalana.* Barcelona: Llibreria Antiga y Moderna, 1915. 83-93.

22.   Burger, Harald, Annelies Buhofer, and Ambros Sialm. *Handbuch der Phraseologie.* Berlin: Walter de Gruyter, 1982. 435 pp.

23.	Buridant, Claude. "Les proverbes et la prédication au Moyen Age: De l'utilisation des proverbes vulgaires dans les sermons." *Richesse du proverbe*. Eds. François Suard and C. Buridant. Lille: Université de Lille, 1984. I, 23-54.

24.	Carion, Flavia de. "Some Florida Proverbs and Their Literary Background." M. A. Thesis. University of Florida, 1948. 191 pp.

25.	Carnes, Pack, ed. *Proverbia in Fabula: Essays on the Relationship of the Fable and the Proverb*. Bern: Peter Lang, 1988. 343 pp.

26.	Carnes, Pack. "The Fable and the Proverb: Intertexts and Reception." *Proverbium: Yearbook of International Proverb Scholarship* 8 (1991): 55-76. Also in *Wise Words: Essays on the Proverb*. Ed. Wolfgang Mieder. New York: Garland Publishing, 1994. 467-493.

27.	Chevalier, Maxime. "Conte, proverbe, romance: Trois formes traditionelles en question au siècle d'or." *Bulletin Hispanique* 95, 1 (1993): 237-264.

28.	Cirese, Alberto M. "Wellérismes et micro-récits." *Proverbium* No. 14 (1969): 384-390. Also as "Wellerismi et microrécits." *Lingua e stile* 5 (1970): 283-292.

29.	Clogan, Paul M. "Literary Genres in a Medieval Textbook." *Medievalia et Humanistica* 11 (1982): 199-209.

30.	Cnyrim, Eugen. *Sprichwörter, sprichwörtliche Redensarten und Sentenzen bei den provenzalischen Lyrikern*. Marburg: N. G. Elwert, 1888. 75 pp.

31.	Cohen, Helen Louise. "Proverbs and the Ballade." *The Ballade*. New York: Columbia University Press, 1915. 94-102.

32.	Costa, Hamilton. "La représentation du corps dans la littérature populaire portugaise: Le discours proverbial." *Littérature orale traditionelle populaire: Actes du colloque Paris, 20-22 novembre 1986*. Ed. D. Alcoforado et al. Paris: Fondation Calouste Gulbenkian, 1987. 561-576.

33.	Crusius, Otto. "Märchenreminiscenzen im antiken Sprichwort." *Verhandlungen der Görlitzer Philologenversammlung* (1889): 31-47.

34.   Cuscoy, Luis Diego. "Paremiologia y literatura." *Archivos Venezolanos de Folklore* 1 (1952): 81-91.

35.   Dal, Erik. "Proverbs in Danish Prosodies and Grammars before 1700." *Proverbium* No. 15 (1970): 436-438.

36.   Davis, Natalie Zemon. "Proverbial Wisdom and Popular Error." *Society and Culture in Early Modern France*. Stanford, California: Stanford University Press, 1975. 227-267, 336-348 (notes). Also as "Sagesse proverbiale et erreurs populaires." *Les cultures du peuple: Rituels, savoirs et résistances au XVIe siècle*. Paris: Aubier, 1979. 366-425. Also as "Spruchweisheiten und populäre Irrleh-ren." *Volkskultur: Zur Wiederentdeckung des vergessenen Alltags (16.-20. Jahrhundert)*. Eds. Richard van Dülmen and Norbert Schindler. Frankfurt am Main: Fischer, 1984. 78-116, 394-406 (notes).

37.   De Caro, Francis A. "Proverbs and Originality in Modern Short Fiction." *Western Folklore* 37 (1978): 30-38.

38.   Dent, Robert William. *Proverbial Language in English Drama Exclusive of Shakespeare, 1495-1616: An Index*. Berkeley: University of California Press, 1984. 797 pp.

39.   Desaivre, Léo. "Les traditions populaires chez les auteurs poitevins." *Revue des traditions populaires* 20 (1905): 226-236, 302-313; 21 (1906): 149-155, 210-217; 22 (1907): 373-381, 417-425; 23 (1908): 358-366.

40.   Dobesch, Gerhard. "Die Sprichwörter der griechischen Sagengeschich-te." Diss. Wien, 1962. 362 pp.

41.   Doctor, Raymond. "Mutant Proverbs or the Tale of the Shaggy Dog." *Proverbium: Yearbook of International Proverb Scholarship* 12 (1995): 119-139.

42.   Doyle, Charles Clay. "On Some Paremiological Verses." *Proverbium* No. 25 (1975): 979-982.

43.   Dreeßen, Wulf-Otto. "Zur Signifikanz des Sprichwörtlichen in Teilen der altjiddischen Literatur." *Proverbium: Yearbook of International Proverb Scholarship* 12 (1995): 141-155.

44. Eastman, Carol M. "The Proverb in Modern Written Swahili Literature: An Aid to Proverb Elicitation." *African Folklore*. Ed. Richard M. Dorson. Garden City, N. Y.: Anchor Books, 1972. 193-207.

45. Eberhard, Wolfram. "Some Notes on the Use of Proverbs in Chinese Novels." *Proverbium* No. 9 (1967): 201-209. Also in *Studies in Chinese Folklore and Related Essays*. Bloomington: Indiana University Press, 1970. 176-181.

46. Eberhard, Wolfram. "Proverbs in Selected Chinese Novels." *Proverbium: Yearbook of International Proverb Scholarship* 2 (1985): 21-57.

47. Ebert, Emil. *Die Sprichwörter der altfranzösischen Karlsepen*. Marburg: N. G. Elwert, 1884. 52 pp.

48. Egudu, R. N. "Social Values and Thought in Traditional Literature: The Case of the Igbo Proverb and Poetry." *Nigerian Libraries* 8 (1972): 63-84.

49. Eiselein, Josua. *Die reimhaften, anklingenden und ablautartigen Formeln der hochdeutschen Sprache in alter und neuer Zeit*. Leipzig: F. Fleischer, 1841. 68 pp.

50. Fabian, Johannes. *Power and Performance: Ethnographic Explorations through Proverbial Wisdom and Theater in Shaba, Zaire*. Madison: University of Wisconsin Press, 1990. 314 pp.

51. Fechter, Werner. "Galle und Honig: Eine Kontrastformel in der mittelhochdeutschen Literatur." *Beiträge zur Geschichte der deutschen Sprache und Literatur* (Tübingen) 80 (1958): 107-142.

52. Fedler, Stephan. "[Aphorismus]: Anspielung—Kontrafaktur—Antithese." *Der Aphorismus: Begriffsspiel zwischen Philosophie und Poesie*. Stuttgart: M und P Verlag für Wissenschaft und Forschung, 1992. 114-127.

53. Foley, John Miles. "Proverbs and Proverbial Function in South Slavic and Com-parative Epic." *Proverbium: Yearbook of International Proverb Scholarship* 11 (1994): 77-92.

54. Folsom, Steven. "Proverbs in Recent Country Music: Form and Function in Three Hits from 1991." *Proceedings for the 1992 Annual*

Conference of the Southwest/Texas Popular Culture Association. Ed. Sue Poor. Stillwater, Oklahoma: Southwest/Texas Popular Culture Association, 1992. 178-181.

55.   Folsom, Steven. "A Discography of American Country Music Hits Employing Proverbs: Covering the Years 1986-1992." *Proceedings for the 1993 Annual Conference of the Southwest/Texas Popular Culture Association.* Ed. Sue Poor. Stillwater, Oklahoma: The Association, 1993. 31-42.

56.   Folsom, Steven. "Form and Function of Proverbs in Four Country Music Hits from 1992." *Proceedings for the 1993 Annual Conference of the Southwest/Texas Popular Culture Association.* Ed. Sue Poor. Stillwater, Oklahoma: The Association, 1993. 27-31.

57.   Folsom, Steven. "Proverbs in Recent American Country Music: Form and Function in the Hits of 1986-87." *Proverbium: Yearbook of International Proverb Scholarship* 10 (1993), 65-88.

58.   Frank, Grace. "Proverbs in Medieval Literature." *Modern Language Notes* 58 (1943): 508-515.

59.   Franke, Margarete. "Der Stabreim in der neudeutschen Literatur." Diss. Rostock, 1930. 152 pp.

60.   Frenk Alatorre, Margit. "Refranes cantados y cantares proverbializados." *Nueva Revista de Filologia Hispanica* 15 (1961): 155-168.

61.   Frizzel, John Henry. "Proverbial Philosophy in American Literature." M. A. Thesis. Pennsylvania State University, 1912. 48 pp.

62.   Fukuchi, Michael. "Gnomic Statements in Old English Poetry." *Neuphilologus* 59 (1975): 610-613.

63.   Ganßert, Erwin. "Das formelhafte Element in der nachwaltherischen Spruchdichtung und im frühen Minnesang." Diss. Mainz, 1955. 752 pp.

64.   Garbe, Burckhard. "Vogel und Schlange: Variation eines Motivs in Redensart, Fabel, Märchen und Mythos." *Zeitschrift für Volkskunde* 75 (1979): 52-56. Also in Pack Carnes, ed. *Proverbia in Fabula: Essays on the Relationship of the Fable and the Proverb.* Bern: Peter Lang, 1988. 277-283.

65. Gilly, Carlos. "Das Sprichwort 'Die Gelehrten, die Verkehrten' in der Toleranzliteratur des 16. Jahrhunderts." *Anabaptistes et dissidents au XVIe siècle: Actes du Colloque international d'histoire anabaptiste du XVIe siècle tenu à l'occasion de la XIe Conférence Mennonite mondiale à Strasbourg, juillet 1984.* Eds. Jean-Georges Rott and Simon L. Verheus. Baden-Baden: Editions Körner, 1987. 159-172.

66. Gilly, Carlos. "Das Sprichwort 'Die Gelehrten, die Verkehrten' oder der Verrat der Intellektuellen im Zeitalter der Glaubensspaltung." *Forme e destinazione del messaggio religioso: Aspetti della propaganda religiosa nel cinquecento.* Ed. An-tonio Rotondo. Firenze: Leo S. Olschki, 1991. 229-375.

67. Girvin, William H. "The Medieval German Proverb as Reflected in the *Gesammtabenteuer.*" Diss. Michigan State University, 1972. 94 pp.

68. Goldberg, Harriet. "The Proverb in 'Cuaderna via' Poetry: A Procedure for Identification." *Hispanic Studies in Honor of Alan D. Deyermond: A North American Tribute.* Ed. John S. Miletich. Madison, Wisconsin: Hispanic Seminary of Medieval Studies, 1986. 119-133.

69. Grzybek, Peter. "Sprichwort und Fabel: Überlegungen zur Beschreibung von Sinnstrukturen in Texten." *Proverbium: Yearbook of International Proverb Scholarship* 5 (1988): 39-67.

70. Grzybek, Peter. "Invariant Meaning Structures in Texts: Proverb and Fable." *Issues in Slavic Literary and Cultural Theory.* Eds. Karl Eimermacher, P. Grzybek, and Georg Witte. Bochum: Norbert Brockmeyer, 1989. 349-389.

71. Grzybek, Peter. "Das Sprichwort im literarischen Text." *Sprichwörter und Redensarten im interkulturellen Vergleich.* Eds. Annette Sabban and Jan Wirrer. Opladen: Westdeutscher Verlag, 1991. 187-205.

72. Grzybek, Peter. "Winged Word." *Simple Forms: An Encyclopaedia of Simple Text-Types in Lore and Literature.* Ed. Walter A. Koch. Bochum: Norbert Brockmeyer, 1994. 293-298.

73. Gueunier, Nicole. "Une forme brève: La parémie d'origine évangelique et son usage dans les titres littéraires en français." *Cahiers de l'Institut de Linguistique de Louvain* 17, 4 (1991): 77-95.

74.   Haller, Joseph. *Altspanische Sprichwörter und sprichwörtliche Redens-arten aus den Zeiten vor Cervantes*, 2 vols. Regensburg: G. J. Manz, 1883. 652 pp.; 304 pp.

75.   Halpert, Herbert. "Folktale and Wellerism: A Note." *Southern Folklore Quarterly* 7 (1943): 75-76.

76.   Hasan-Rokem, Galit. "Proverbs in Folk Tales: A Structural Semantic Model for Folklore in Context." *Proverbium Paratum* 1 (1980): 36-45.

77.   Hasan-Rokem, Galit. *Proverbs in Israeli Folk Narratives: A Structural Semantic Analysis*. Helsinki: Suomalainen Tiedeakatemia, 1982. 107 pp.

78.   Hayes, Francis Clement. "The Use of Proverbs in the 'Siglo de Oro' Drama: An Introductory Study." Diss. University of North Carolina, 1936. 227 pp.

79.   Hayes, Francis Clement. "The Collecting of Proverbs in Spain before 1650." *Hispania* 20 (1937): 85-94.

80.   Heft, David. *Proverbs and Sentences in Fifteenth Century French Poetry*. Diss. New York University, 1941. Chapter 2. New York: Washington Square Press, 1942 (abridged to 12 pp.).

81.   Hernandez, José Luis Alonso. "Interprétation psychoanalytique de l'utilisation des parémies dans la littérature espagnole." *Richesse du proverbe*. Eds. François Suard and Claude Buridant. Lille: Université de Lille, 1984. II, 213-225.

82.   Hess-Lüttich, Ernest W. B. "Sprichwörter und Redensarten als Übersetzungsproblem: Am Beispiel deutscher Übersetzungen spanischer und türkischer Literatur." *Mehrsprachigkeit und Gesellschaft: Akten des 17. Linguistischen Kolloquiums Brüssel 1982*. Eds. René Jongen, Sabine De Knop, Peter H. Nelde, and Marie-Paule Quix. Tübingen: Max Niemeyer, 1983. II, 222-236.

83.   Hofmann, Liselotte. "Volks- und Spruchweisheit." *Der volkskundliche Gehalt der mittelhochdeutschen Epen von 1100 bis gegen 1250*. Zeulenroda: Bernhard Sporn, 1939. 52-82.

84.   Hofmeister, Wernfried. "Das Sprichwort im historisch-literarischen Kontext: Vorschläge zur Erfassung und Beschreibung sprichwortartiger

Mikrotexte." *Proverbium: Yearbook of International Proverb Scholarship* 9 (1992): 43-65.

85. Hofmeister, Wernfried. *Sprichwortartige Mikrotexte als literarische Medien, dargestellt an der hochdeutschen politischen Lyrik des Mittelalters*. Bochum: Norbert Brockmeyer, 1995. 574 pp.

86. Homann, Carl. "Beiträge zur Kenntnis des Wortschatzes der altfranzösischen Sprichwörter." Diss. Greifswald, 1900. Greifswald: F. W. Kunike, 1900. 55 pp.

87. Hulme, F. Edward. *Proverb Lore: Being a Historical Study of the Similarities, Contrasts, Topics, Meanings, and Other Facets of Proverbs, Truisms, and Pithy Sayings, as Expressed by the Peoples of Many Lands and Times*. London: Elliot Stock, 1902; rpt. Detroit, Michigan: Gale Research Company, 1968. Especially 65-89.

88. Hüttig, Ernst. *Der Vergleich im mittelhochdeutschen Heldenepos*. Halle: Eduard Klinz, 1930. 82 pp.

89. Jäger, Dietrich. "Der Gebrauch formelhafter zweigliedriger Ausdrücke in der vor-, früh- und hochhöfischen Epik." Diss. Kiel, 1960. 277 pp.

90. Jarosh, Jiri. "Zu der Funktion der Phrasen, Redensarten und Sprüche bei den Ortschronisten, Bibelleser[n] und Versemacher[n] in Mittelmähren." *Proverbium Paratum* 3 (1982): 241-250.

91. Johnson, James Henry. "The Proverb in the Medieval Spanish 'Exempla.'" Diss. University of North Carolina, 1958. 246 pp.

92. Jokinen, Ulla. "Observations sur les locutions françaises dans les farces et dans les sotties." *La locution: Actes du colloque international Université McGill, Montréal, 15-16 octobre 1984*. Eds. Giuseppe Di Stefano and Russell G. McGillivray. Montréal: Editions CERES, 1984. 302-322.

93. Kadler, Alfred. *Sprichwörter und Sentenzen der altfranzösischen Artus- und Abenteuerromane*. Marburg: N. G. Elwert, 1886. 106 pp.

94. Kellner, Leon. *Altenglische Spruchweisheit: Alt- und mittelenglischen Autoren entnommen*. Wien: Verlag der Staatsrealschule, 1897. 26 pp.

95.   Kim, Du Gyu. "Sprichwörter." *Volkstümlichkeit und Realismus: Unter-suchungen zu Geschichte, Motiven und Typologien der Erzählgattung "Dorfgeschichte."* Bielefeld: Aisthesis Verlag, 1991. 120-123.

96.   Kindstrand, Jan Fredrik. "The Greek Concept of Proverbs." *Eranos: Acta Philologica Suecana* 76 (1978): 71-85. Also in Pack Carnes, ed. *Proverbia in Fabula: Essays on the Relationship of the Fable and the Proverb.* Bern: Peter Lang, 1988. 233-275.

97.   Knappert, Jan. "Swahili Proverb Songs." *Afrika und Übersee* 59 (1976): 105-112.

98.   Koinakov, Ivan. "Poslovitsi i pogovorki ot literaturni iztochnitsi v bulgarskiia folklor." *Folklorat i narodnite traditsii v savremennata natsionalna kultura.* Ed. Veselin Khadzhinikolov. Sofia: BAN, 1976. 115-122.

99.   Koller, Werner. "Redensarten in gesprochener Sprache, in Leserbriefen, in der Trivialliteratur und bei F. X. Kroetz." *Redensarten: Linguistische Aspekte, Vor-kommensanalysen, Sprachspiel.* Tübingen: Max Niemeyer, 1977. 73-87.

100.   Koller, Werner. "Redensartenspiel in der schönen Literatur." *Redens-arten: Linguistische Aspekte, Vorkommensanalysen, Sprachspiel.* Tübingen: Max Niemeyer, 1977. 197-210.

101.   Krohn, Kaarle. "Die Entwicklung eines Sprichwortes zum lyrischen Liede." *Mélanges publiés en l'honneur de Vaclav Tille.* Eds. Jiri Polivka, Jan Frcek, Jiri Jezek, and Jiri Horak. Prague: Editions "Orbis," 1927. 109-112.

102.   Krzyżanowski, Julian. "Sprichwort und Märchen in der polnischen Volkserzählung." *Volksüberlieferung: Festschrift für Kurt Ranke.* Eds. Fritz Harkort, Karel C. Peeters, and Robert Wildhaber. Göttingen: Otto Schwartz, 1968. 151-158.

103.   Kuusi, Matti. *Parömiologische Betrachtungen.* Helsinki: Suomalainen Tiedeakatemia, 1957. Especially 17-18.

104.   La Curne de Sainte-Palaye, Jean Baptiste. "Proverbes qui se trouvent dans nos poètes des XIIe, XIIIe et XIVe siècles." *Dictionnaire historique*

de l'ancien langage françois. . . . , 10 vols. Paris: H. Champion, 1875-1882.

105.	Le Roux de Lincy, M. "De l'emploi des proverbes par les auteurs français depuis le XIIe jusqu'au XVIIe siècle." *Le Livre des Proverbes Français*, 2 vols. 2nd ed. Paris: A. Delahays, 1859; rpt. Genève: Slatkine, 1968. I, xlvii-lxiv.

106.	Le Roux de Lincy, M. "De l'emploi des proverbes par les auteurs français des XVIIe et XVIIIe siècles." *Le Livre des Proverbes Français*, 2 vols. 2nd ed. Paris: A. Delahays, 1859; rpt. Genève: Slatkine, 1968. I, lxiv-lxxxiv.

107.	Le Roux de Lincy, M. "Proverbes récueillis dans les auteurs français du XIIe au XVIIIe siècle." *Le Livre des Proverbes Français*, 2 vols. 2nd ed. Paris: A. Dela-hays, 1859; rpt. Genève: Slatkine, 1968. II, 485-546.

108.	Łabno-Falecka, Ewa. *Phraseologie und Übersetzen: Eine Untersuchung der Übersetzbarkeit kreativ-innovativ gebrauchter wiederholter Rede anhand von Beispielen aus der polnischen und deutschen Gegenwartsliteratur.* Frankfurt am Main: Peter Lang, 1995. 542 pp.

109.	Lardinois, André Pierre. "Wisdom in Context: The Use of Gnomic Statements in Archaic Greek Poetry." Diss. Princeton University, 1995. 386 pp.

110.	Leino, Pentti. "Dialogsprichwort oder Replikenanekdote?" *Proverbium* No. 23 (1974): 904-908.

111.	Lewent, K. "Zu einigen Sprichwörtern in der provenzalischen Dichtung." *Neuphilologische Mitteilungen* 38 (1937): 47-60.

112.	Lieres und Wilkau, Marianne von. *Sprachformeln in der mittelhochdeutschen Lyrik bis zu Walther von der Vogelweide.* München: C. H. Beck, 1965. Especially 1-29.

113.	Lindemann, Johannes. *Über die Alliteration als Kunstform im Volks- und Spielmannsepos.* Diss. Breslau, 1914. Breslau: A. Favorke, 1914. 62 pp.

114.	Lindfors, Bernth. "Perverted Proverbs in Nigerian Chapbooks." *Proverbium* No. 15 (1970): 482-487.

115. Lindow, Wolfgang. "Volkstümliches Sprachgut in der neuniederdeutschen Dialektdichtung." Diss. Kiel, 1961. Part I, 268 pp.; Part II, 171 pp.

116. Loomis, C. Grant. "Random Proverbs in Popular Literature." *Western Folklore* 16 (1957): 133-135.

117. Loth, Johannes. "Die Sprichwörter und Sentenzen der altfranzösischen Fabliaux, nach ihrem Inhalte zusammengestellt." *Königliches Friedrich-Wilhelms-Gymnasium zu Greifenberg in Pommern.* Greifenberg: Lempcke, 1895. 1-15.

118. Louis, Cameron. "Proverbs, Precepts, and Monitory Pieces." *A Manual of the Writings in Middle English 1050-1500.* Ed. Albert E. Hartung. New Haven, Connecticut: The Connecticut Academy of Arts and Sciences, 1993. Vol. 9, 2957-3048 (commentary); 3349-3404 (bibliography).

119. Loukatos, Démétrios. "Le proverbe dans le conte." *IV. International Congress for Folk-Narrative Research in Athens 1964: Lectures and Reports.* Ed. Georgios A. Megas. Athens: Laographia, 1965. 229-233.

120. Luomala, Katharine. "The Narrative Source of a Hawaiian Proverb and Related Problems." *Proverbium* No. 21 (1973): 783-787.

121. Mampell, Klaus. "Schriftsteller bereichern die Sprache." *Sprachspiegel* 43 (1987): 148.

122. Mauch, Thomas Karl. 'The Proverb in the Late Middle Ages: A Brief Survey.' "The Role of the Proverb in Early Tudor Literature." Diss. University of California at Los Angeles, 1963. 19-40.

123. Mauch, Thomas Karl. "The Role of the Proverb in Early Tudor Literature." Diss. University of California at Los Angeles, 1963. 361 pp.

124. McKenna, John F. "The Proverb in Humanistic Studies: Language, Literature and Culture: Theory and Classroom Practice." *The French Review* 48 (1974): 377-391.

125. Mckenzie, Alyce M. "The Preacher as Subversive Sage: Preaching on Biblical Proverbs." *Proverbium: Yearbook of International Proverb Scholarship* 12 (1995): 169-193.

126. McNeil, W. K. "Proverbs Used in New York Autograph Albums 1820-1900." *Southern Folklore Quarterly* 33 (1969): 352-359.

127. Meherremova, R. Dzh. "XVIII esr azerbajdzhan edebi dilinde dzhanly danyshyg dili khisusijjetleri." *Izvestiia Akademii Nauk Azerbaidzhanskoi SSR, Seriia literatury, iazyka i iskusstva* No. 3 (1978): 67-74.

128. Mettmann, Walter. "Spruchweisheit und Spruchdichtung in der spanischen und katalanischen Literatur des Mittelalters." *Zeitschrift für romanische Philologie* 76 (1960): 94-117. Also in Pack Carnes, ed. *Proverbia in Fabula: Essays on the Relationship of the Fable and the Proverb*. Bern: Peter Lang, 1988. 165-193.

129. Meyer, Richard M. "Sprichwörter." *Die altgermanische Poesie nach ihren formelhaften Elementen beschrieben*. Berlin: Wilhelm Hertz, 1889; rpt. Hildesheim: Georg Olms, 1985. 452-460.

130. Michel, F. "Proverbes recueillis dans les auteurs français du XIIe au XVIIIe siècle." In M. Le Roux de Lincy. *Le Livre des Proverbes Français*, 2nd ed. Paris: A. Delahays, 1859; rpt. Genève: Slatkine, 1968. II, 485-498.

131. Mieder, Wolfgang. "Das Sprichwort und die deutsche Literatur." *Fabula* 13 (1972): 135-149. Expanded version in *Ergebnisse der Sprichwörterforschung*. Ed. Wolfgang Mieder. Bern: Peter Lang, 1978. 179-200.

132. Mieder, Wolfgang. "The Essence of Literary Proverb Studies." *Proverbium* No. 23 (1974): 888-894. Also in *New York Folklore Quarterly* 30 (1974): 66-76.

133. Mieder, Wolfgang. "The Proverb and Anglo-American Literature." *Southern Folklore Quarterly* 38 (1974): 49-62.

134. Mieder, Wolfgang. "The Proverb and Romance Literature." *Romance Notes* 15 (1974): 610-621.

135. Mieder, Wolfgang. "Buchtitel als Schlagzeile." *Sprachspiegel* 31 (1975): 36-43. Also in *Sprichwort, Redensart, Zitat: Tradierte Formelsprache in der Moderne*. Bern: Peter Lang, 1985. 115-123.

136.   Mieder, Wolfgang. *Das Sprichwort in unserer Zeit*. Frauenfeld: Huber, 1975. Especially 51-61, 82-91.

137.   Mieder, Wolfgang. "Sprichwörter im modernen Sprachgebrauch." *Muttersprache* 85 (1975): 65-88, especially 71-77. Also in *Ergebnisse der Sprichwörterforschung*. Bern: Peter Lang, 1978. 213-238.

138.   Mieder, Wolfgang. *Das Sprichwort in der deutschen Prosaliteratur des neunzehnten Jahrhunderts*. München: Wilhelm Fink, 1976. 197 pp.

139.   Mieder, Wolfgang. "Sprichwort und Volkslied: Eine Untersuchung des Ambraser Liederbuches vom Jahre 1582." *Jahrbuch für Volksliedforschung* 22 (1977): 23-35. Also in *Sprichwort—Wahrwort!? Studien zur Geschichte, Bedeutung und Funktion deutscher Sprichwörter*. Frankfurt am Main: Peter Lang, 1992. 87-102.

140.   Mieder, Wolfgang. *Proverbs in Literature: An International Bibliography*. Bern: Peter Lang, 1978. 150 pp.

141.   Mieder, Wolfgang. "Das Sprichwort im Volkslied: Eine Untersuchung des *Deutschen Liederhortes* von Erk/Böhme." *Jahrbuch des österreichischen Volksliedwerkes* 27 (1978): 44-71.

142.   Mieder, Wolfgang. *Deutsche Sprichwörter und Redensarten*. Stuttgart: Reclam, 1979. 199 pp.

143.   Mieder, Wolfgang. "Moderne deutsche Sprichwortgedichte." *Fabula* 21 (1980): 247-260. Also in *Sprichwort, Redensart, Zitat: Tradierte Formelsprache in der Moderne*. Bern: Peter Lang, 1985. 73-90; *Deutsche Sprichwörter in Literatur, Politik, Presse und Werbung*. Hamburg: Helmut Buske, 1983. 53-76.

144.   Mieder, Wolfgang. "A Sampler of Anglo-American Proverb Poetry." *Folklore Forum* 13 (1980): 39-53.

145.   Mieder, Wolfgang. "Traditional and Innovative Proverb Use in Lyric Poetry." *Proverbium Paratum* 1 (1980): 16-27.

146.   Mieder, Wolfgang. "*International Bibliography of Literary Proverb Studies*." *Motif: International Newsletter of Research in Folklore and Literature* No. 1 (October 1981): 3-7.

147. Mieder, Wolfgang. *Deutsche Sprichwörter in Literatur, Politik, Presse und Werbung.* Hamburg: Helmut Buske, 1983. 230 pp.

148. Mieder, Wolfgang. *Sprichwort, Redensart, Zitat: Tradierte Formelsprache in der Moderne.* Bern: Peter Lang, 1985. 203 pp.

149. Mieder, Wolfgang. *American Proverbs: A Study of Texts and Contexts.* Bern: Peter Lang, 1989. 394 pp.

150. Mieder, Wolfgang. "Moderne Sprichwörterforschung zwischen Mündlichkeit und Schriftlichkeit." *Volksdichtung zwischen Mündlichkeit und Schriftlichkeit.* Eds. Lutz Rörich and Erika Lindig. Tübingen: Gunter Narr, 1989. 187-208.

151. Mieder, Wolfgang, ed. *"Kommt Zeit-kommt Rat!?" Moderne Sprichwortgedichte von Erich Fried bis Ulla Hahn.* Frankfurt am Main: Rita G. Fischer, 1990. 139 pp.

152. Mieder, Wolfgang. "'Des vielen Büchermachens ist kein Ende': Traditionelle und manipulierte Sprachformeln als Buchtitel." *Der Sprachdienst* 35 (1991) 105-114. Also in *Sprichwörtliches und Geflügeltes: Sprachstudien von Martin Luther bis Karl Marx.* Bochum: Norbert Brockmeyer, 1995. 87-102.

153. Mieder, Wolfgang, ed. *"Deutsch reden": Moderne Redensartengedichte von Rose Ausländer bis Yaak Karsunke.* Frankfurt am Main: Rita G. Fischer, 1992. 190 pp.

154. Mieder, Wolfgang. *Sprichwort—Wahrwort!? Studien zur Geschichte, Bedeutung und Funktion deutscher Sprichwörter.* Frankfurt am Main: Peter Lang, 1992. 297 pp.

155. Mieder, Wolfgang. *Proverbs Are Never Out of Season: Popular Wisdom in the Modern Age.* New York: Oxford University Press, 1993. 284 pp.

156. Mieder, Wolfgang. *Deutsche Redensarten, Sprichwörter und Zitate: Studien zu ihrer Herkunft, Überlieferung und Verwendung.* Vienna: Edition Praesens, 1995. 232 pp.

157. Mieder, Wolfgang, ed. *"Hasen im Pfeffer": Sprichwörtliche Kurzprosatexte von Marie Luise Kaschnitz bis Martin Walser.* Frankfurt am Main: Rita G. Fischer Verlag, 1995. 151 pp.

158.   Mieder, Wolfgang. *Sprichwörtliches und Geflügeltes: Sprachstudien von Martin Luther bis Karl Marx.* Bochum: Norbert Brockmeyer, 1995. 197 pp.

159.   Militz, Hans-Manfred. "Sprichwörtliche Redewendungen im Französischen des 18. Jahrhunderts." *Proverbium: Yearbook of International Proverb Scholarship* 10 (1993): 185-198.

160.   Mokitimi, Makali Isabella Phomolo. "A Literary Analysis of Sesotho Proverbs (Maele)." Diss. University of South Africa, 1991. 248 pp.

161.   Mone, Franz Joseph. "Zur Literatur und Geschichte der Sprichwörter." *Quellen und Forschungen zur Geschichte der deutschen Literatur und Sprache* 1 (1830): 186-214.

162.   Mone, Franz Joseph. "Sprichwörter aus Dichtern: Eine Gruppe von 35 Fragmenten aus verschiedenen mittelhochdeutschen Dichtungen, die noch nicht in ihrem Ganzen herausgegeben sind." *Anzeiger für Kunde des deutschen Mittelalters* 3 (1834): 29-31.

163.   Monteiro, George. "The Literary Uses of a Proverb [Deus escreve direito por linkas tortas (God writes straight with crooked lines)]." *Folklore* (London) 87 (1976): 216-218.

164.   Morawski, Joseph. *Proverbes français antérieurs au XVe siècle.* Paris: Champion, 1925. 146 pp.

165.   Morgan, Frances Elnora Williams. "Proverbs from Four Didactic Works of the Thirteenth Century." Diss. University of Kentucky, 1968. 492 pp.

166.   Moya, Ismael. "El refranero en las coplas criollas." *Refranero. . . formas paremiólogicas tradicionales en la República Argentina.* Buenos Aires: Imprenta de la Universidad, 1944. 199-206.

167.   Myrick, Leslie Diane. "The Deployment of Irish Proverbial Phrases in Medieval Irish Adaptations of Greco-Roman Epics." *Proverbium: Yearbook of International Proverb Scholarship* 11 (1994): 175-187.

168.   Neumann, Siegfried. "Sagwörter im Schwank—Schwankstoffe im Sagwort." *Volksüberlieferung: Festschrift für Kurt Ranke.* Eds. Fritz

Harkort, Karel C. Peeters, and Robert Wildhaber. Göttingen: Schwartz, 1968. 249-266.

169. Neumann, Siegfried. "Sagwort und Schwank." *Lětopis: Jahresschrift des Instituts für sorbische Volksforschung* Reihe C, No. 11/12 (1968/69): 147-158.

170. Neumeister, Sebastian. "Geschichten vor und nach dem Sprichwort." *Kleinstformen der Literatur.* Eds. Walter Haug und Burghart Wachinger. Tübingen: Max Niemeyer, 1994. 205-215.

171. Neuss, Paula. "The Sixteenth-Century English 'Proverb' Play." *Comparative Drama* 18, 1 (1984): 1-18.

172. Nicklas, Friedrich. *Untersuchung über Stil und Geschichte des deutschen Tageliedes.* Berlin: Emil Ebering, 1929; rpt. Nendeln, Liechtenstein: Kraus Reprint, 1967. For proverbs see especially pp. 78-79, 142, 186.

173. Oberman, Heiko A. "'Die Gelehrten, die Verkehrten': Popular Response to Learned Culture in the Renaissance and Reformation." *Religion and Culture in the Renaissance and Reformation.* Ed. Steven Ozment. Kirksville, Missouri: Six-teenth Century Journal Publishers, 1989. 43-63 (=*Sixteenth Century Essays & Studies* 11 [1989]: 43-63).

174. Obiechina, Emmanuel. "Narrative Proverbs in the African Novel." *Oral Tradition* 7, 2 (1992): 197-230. Also in *Research in African Literatures* 24, 4 (1993): 123-140.

175. Odell, George Clinton. "Simile and Metaphor in the English and Scottish Ballads." M. A. Thesis. Columbia University, 1892. 107 pp.

176. Ohly, Friedrich. "'Du bist mein, ich bin dein, du in mir, ich in dir, ich du, du ich.'" *Kritische Bewahrung: Beiträge zur deutschen Philologie: Festschrift für Werner Schröder zum 60. Geburtstag.* Ed. Ernst-Joachim Schmidt. Berlin: Erich Schmidt, 1975. 371-415.

177. O'Kane, Eleanor. "A Dictionary of Medieval Spanish Proverbs and Proverbial Phrases." Diss. Bryn Mawr, 1947. 477 pp.

178. Paczolay, Gyula. "Proverbs in Hungarian Literature: A Bibliography." *Proverbium: Yearbook of International Proverb Scholarship* 5 (1988): 207-211.

179. Peil, Dietmar. "Beziehungen zwischen Fabel und Sprichwort." *Germanica Wratislaviensia* 85 (1989): 74-87.

180. Peretz, Bernhard. *Altprovenzalische Sprichwörter mit einem kurzen Hinblick auf den mittelhochdeutschen Freidank.* Erlangen: Andreas Deichert, 1887. Also in *Romanische Forschungen* 3 (1887): 415-457.

181. Perry, B. E. "Fable." *Studium generale* 12 (1959): 17-37. Also in Pack Carnes, ed. *Proverbia in Fabula: Essays on the Relationship of the Fable and the Proverb.* Bern: Peter Lang, 1988. 65-116.

182. Petkanova-Toteva, Donka. "Poslovitsata i sententsiiata v starobalgarskata knizhnina i folklora." *Problemi na Balgarskiia Folklor* 1 (1972): 295-325.

183. Pétropoulos, Demetrios. *La comparison dans la chanson populaire grecque.* Athens: L'Institut Français d'Athènes, 1954. 167 pp.

184. Petsch, Robert. "'Geflügelte Worte' und Verwandtes: Aus der Formenwelt der menschlichen Rede." *Deutsche Literaturwissenschaft: Aufsätze zur Begründung der Methode.* Berlin: Emil Ebering, 1940. 230-238.

185. Pillet, Alfred. *Die neuprovenzalischen Sprichwörter der jüngeren Cheltenhamer Liederhandschrift.* Diss. Breslau, 1897. Berlin: C. Vogt, 1897. 38 pp.

186. Pineaux, Jacques. "L'utilisation du proverbe dans la littérature." *Proverbes et dictons français*, 6th ed. Paris: Presses Universitaires de France, 1973. 41-66.

187. Pipping, Rolf. "En visa och ett ordspråk (A ballad and a proverb)." *Acta Philologica Scandinavica* 23 (1955): 117-138.

188. Pop, Mihai, and Pavel Ruxandoiu. "Literatura aforistica si enigmatica." *Folclor literar românesc.* Bucuresti: Editura didactica si pedagogica, 1976. 230-248.

189. Prahlad, Sw. Anand [Dennis Folly]. "Persona and Proverb Meaning in Roots Reggae: Proverbs of the Itals Reggae Group." *Proverbium: Yearbook of International Proverb Scholarship* 12 (1995): 275-293.

190. Predota, Stanisław. "Over Nederlandse spreekwoorden in boektitels." *Neerlandica Wratislaviensia* 7 (1994): 211-216.

191. Priest, John F. "'The Dog in the Manger': In Quest of a Fable." *The Classical Journal* 81, 1 (1985): 49-58.

192. Prittwitz-Gaffron, Erich von. *Das Sprichwort im griechischen Epigramm.* Diss. München, 1912. Gießen: Alfred Töpelmann, 1912. 68 pp.

193. Redfern, V. S. "Metaphor and Simile in 'Storm and Stress' Drama." M. A. Thesis. University of North Carolina, 1939. 77 pp.

194. Reyes de la Rosa, José. "La misoginia de refranes y frases proverbiales en los relatos trágicos del siglo XVII en Francia y en España." *Paremia* No. 2 (1993): 199-203.

195. Riffaterre, Michael. "Fonction du cliché dans la prose littéraire." *Essais de stylistique structurale.* Paris: Flammarion, 1971. 161-181. Also in German as "Die Funktion des Klischees in der literarischen Form." *Strukturale Stilistik.* München: List Taschenbuch, 1973. 139-156.

196. Röhrich, Lutz. "Sprichwörtliche Redensarten aus Volkserzählungen." *Volk, Sprache, Dichtung: Festgabe für Kurt Wagner.* Eds. Karl Bischoff and Lutz Röhrich. Gießen: Wilhelm Schmitz, 1960. 247-275. Also in *Ergebnisse der Sprichwörterforschung.* Ed. Wolfgang Mieder. Bern: Peter Lang, 1978. 121-141.

197. Röhrich, Lutz, and Wolfgang Mieder. *Sprichwort.* Stuttgart: Metzler, 1977. Especially 26-51, 83-89, 90-95.

198. Rosières, Raoul. "Quelques proverbes français du XVe siècle." *Revue des traditions populaires* 5 (1890): 449-462.

199. Rowlands, E. C. "The Illustration of a Yoruba Proverb." *Journal of the Folklore Institute* 4 (1967): 250-264.

200. Russo, Joseph. "The Poetics of the Ancient Greek Proverb." *Journal of Folklore Research* 20 (1983): 121-130.

201. S., M. S. "Old Words and Phrases from the Puritan Writers." *Notes and Queries* 2nd ser. 6 (1858): 321-322.

202. Sackett, S. J. "Simile in Folksong." *Midwest Folklore* 13 (1963): 5-12.

203. Salomone-Marino, S. "La onnipotenza dei proverbj dimonstrata da una noveletta popolare siciliana." *Archivo per lo Studio delle Tradizioni Popolari* 10 (1891): 228-234.

204. Saulnier, Verdun L. "Proverbe et paradoxe du XVe et XVIe siècle: Un aspect majeur de l'antithèse: Moyen Age—Renaissance." *Pensée humaniste et tradition chrétienne aux XVe et XVIe siècles.* Ed. Henri Bédarida. Paris: Boivin, 1950. 87-104.

205. Schepp, Fritz. *Altfranzösische Sprichwörter und Sentenzen aus den höfischen Kunstepen über antike Sagenstoffe und aus einigen didaktischen Dichtungen nebst einer Untersuchung über Sprichwörtervarianten.* Diss. Greifswald, 1905. Leipzig: Robert Noske, 1905. 78 pp.

206. Schmidt, Leopold. "Singen, nicht sagen: Zwischen Redensart und Schwank." *Volkslied, Volkstanz, Volksmusik* 49 (1948): 67-68.

207. Schmidt-Hidding, Wolfgang. "Deutsche Sprichwörter und Redewendungen." *Deutschunterricht für Ausländer* 13 (1963): 13-26, especially 13-15.

208. Schmidt-Hidding, Wolfgang. *Englische Idiomatik in Stillehre und Literatur.* München: Max Hueber, 1962. 95 pp.

209. Schröder, C. "Hundert niederdeutsche Sprichwörter, gesammelt aus mittelniederdeutschen und niederrheinischen Dichtungen." *Archiv für das Studium der neueren Sprachen und Literaturen* 43 (1868): 411-420; 44 (1869): 337-344.

210. Schulze-Busacker, Elisabeth. "Proverbes et expressions proverbiales dans les Fabliaux." *Marche romane* 28 (1978): 163-174.

211. Schulze-Busacker, Elisabeth. "Eléments de culture populaire dans la littérature courtoise." *La culture populaire au Moyen Ages: Etudes présentés au Quatrième colloque de l'Institut d'études médiévales de l'Université de Montréal 2-3 avril 1977.* Ed. Pierre Boglioni. Montréal: L'Aurora, 1979. 81-101.

212. Schulze-Busacker, Elisabeth. "La moralité des fabliaux: Considérations stylistiques." *Epopée animale, fable, fabliau: Actes du IVe Colloque de*

la Société Internationale Renardienne, Evreux, 7-11 septembre 1981. Eds. Gabriel Bianciotto and Michel Salvat. Paris: Presses Universitaires de France, 1984. 525-547.

213. Schulze-Busacker, Elisabeth. *Proverbes et expressions proverbiales dans la littérature narrative du moyen âge français: Recueil et analyse.* Paris: Librairie Honoré Champion, 1985. 356 pp.

214. Schulze-Busacker, Elisabeth. "Proverbs and Maxims in Medieval French Literature." *Proverbium: Yearbook of International Proverb Scholarship* 9 (1992): 205-220.

215. Schützeichel, Rudolf. "Genitiv und Possessiv: Zum Tegernseer 'Du bist min.'" *Sprachwissenschaft* 4 (1979): 109-120.

216. Sébillot, Paul. "Les traditions populaires et les écrivains français." *Revue des traditions populaires* 3 (1888): 465-473; 4 (1889): 476-479; 5 (1890): 150, 242-243, 396-412, 487-499, 712-716; 6 (1891): 470-473, 551-559; 8 (1893): 99-111, 182-193, 453-454; 9 (1894): 582-587; 10 (1895): 286-292, 341-346; 11 (1896): 33-34, 372-379, 562-566; 16 (1901): 400, 454-456; 18 (1903): 10, 211-212, 598; 19 (1904): 90-91; 20 (1905): 98-102, 190-191, 268-269; 21 (1906): 58-62; 22 (1907): 34; 24 (1909): 291-292; 26 (1911): 343-344.

217. Seiler, Friedrich. *Das deutsche Sprichwort.* Straßburg: Karl J. Trübner, 1918. Especially 12-15.

218. Seiler, Friedrich. *Deutsche Sprichwörterkunde.* München: C. H. Beck, 1922, 1967. Especially 46-56.

219. Shippey, T. A. "Maxims in Old English Narrative: Literary Art or Traditional Wisdom?" *Oral Tradition—Literary Tradition: A Symposium.* Eds. Hans Bekker-Nielsen, Peter Foote, Andreas Haarder, and Hans Frede Nielsen. Odense: Odense University Press, 1977. 28-46.

220. Shippey, T. A. "Approaches to Truth in Old English Poetry." *University of Leeds Review* 25 (1982): 171-189.

221. Sinclair, K. V. "The Proverbial Question in French Literature." *New Zealand Journal of French Studies* 1, 2 (1980): 5-25.

222.   Singer, Samuel. "Alte schweizerische Sprichwörter." *Schweizerisches Archiv für Volkskunde* 20 (1916): 389-419; 21 (1917): 235-236.

223.   Singer, Samuel. *Sprichwörter des Mittelalters*, 3 vols. Bern: Herbert Lang, 1944-1947. 198 pp.; 203 pp.; 162 pp.

224.   Skeat, Walter William. *Early English Proverbs, Chiefly of the Thirteenth and Fourteenth Centuries*. Oxford: Clarendon Press, 1910; rpt. Darby, Pennsylvania: Folcroft Library Editions, 1974. 147 pp.

225.   Souto Marques, António José. "Histoire(s) de sobriquets: du populaire au littéraire." *Paremia* No. 2 (1993): 183-186.

226.   Soyter, G. "Die neugriechischen Sprichwörter in der Volkslieder-sammlung Werner von Haxthausens." *Byzantinisch-Neugriechische Jahrbücher* 16 (1939-1940): 171-189.

227.   Spanke, H. "Volkstümliches in der altfranzosischen Lyrik." *Zeitschrift für romanische Philologie* 53 (1933): 258-286.

228.   Spicker, Friedemann. "Aphorismen über Aphorismen: Fragen über Fragen: Zur Gattungsreflexion der Aphoristiker." *Zeitschrift für deutsche Philologie* 113 (1994): 161-198.

229.   Stackmann, Karl. "Gold, Glas und Ziegel: Über einige Vergleiche in mittelhochdeutschen Dichtungen." *Teilnahme und Spiegelung: Festschrift für Horst Rüdiger*. Eds. Beda Allemann, Erwin Koppen, and Dieter Gutzen. Berlin: Walter de Gruyter, 1975. 120-129.

230.   Steiner, Arpad. "The Vernacular Proverb in Mediaeval Latin Prose." *American Journal of Philology* 65 (1944): 37-68.

231.   Suard, François. "La fonction des proverbes dans les chansons de geste des XIVe et XVe siècles." *Richesse du proverbe*. Eds. F. Suard and Claude Buridant. Lille: Université de Lille, 1984. I, 131-144.

232.   Sweterlitsch, Richard. "Reexamining the Proverb in the Child Ballad." *Proverbium: Yearbook of International Proverb Scholarship* 2 (1985): 233-256.

233. Taft, Michael. "Proverbs in the Blues: How Frequent Is Frequent?" *Proverbium: Yearbook of International Proverb Scholarship* 11 (1994): 227-258.

234. Tarbé, Louis Hardouin Prosper. *Poètes de Champagne antérieurs au siècle de François 1er (Proverbes champenois avant le XVIe siècle).* Reims: Régnier, 1851. 3-48.

235. Taylor, Archer. *The Proverb.* Cambridge, Massachusetts: Harvard University Press, 1931; rpt. as *The Proverb and an Index to The Proverb.* Hatboro, Pa.: Folklore Associates, 1962 (also Copenhagen: Rosenkilde and Bagger, 1962); rpt. with an introduction and bibliography by Wolfgang Mieder. Bern: Peter Lang, 1985. Especially 27-34, 171-183.

236. Taylor, Archer. "The Proverb 'The Black Ox Has not Trod on His Foot' in Renaissance Literature." *Philological Quarterly* 20 (1941): 266-278. Also in *Selected Writings on Proverbs by Archer Taylor.* Ed. Wolfgang Mieder. Helsinki: Suomalainen Tiedeakatemia, 1975. 152-164.

237. Taylor, Archer, and Bartlett Jere Whiting. *A Dictionary of American Proverbs and Proverbial Phrases, 1820-1880.* Cambridge, Massachusetts: Harvard University Press, 1958. 418 pp.

238. Taylor, Archer. *Selected Writings on Proverbs.* Ed. Wolfgang Mieder. Helsinki: Suomalainen Tiedeakatemia, 1975. Especially 106-114, 152-164.

239. Thiel, Helmut van. "Sprichwörter in Fabeln." *Antike und Abendland* 17 (1971): 105-118. Also in Pack Carnes, ed. *Proverbia in Fabula: Essays on the Relationship of the Fable and the Proverb.* Bern: Peter Lang, 1988. 209-232.

240. Thiolier-Méjean, Suzanne. "Les proverbes et dictons dans la poésie morale des troubadours." *Mélanges d'histoire, de linguistique et de philologie romanes offerts à Charles Rostaing.* Liège: Association Intercommunale de Mécanographie, 1974. II, 1117-1128.

241. Tilavov, Bozor. "O roli literatury v razvitii Tadzhikskikh poslovits i pogovorok." *Proverbium* No. 16 (1971): 557-563.

242.   Tilley, Morris Palmer. *A Dictionary of the Proverbs in England in the Sixteenth and Seventeenth Centuries*. Ann Arbor: University of Michigan Press, 1950. 854 pp.

243.   Tolman, Ruth B. "Proverbs and Sayings in Eighteenth-Century Almanacs." *Western Folklore* 21 (1962): 35-42.

244.   Trencsényi-Waldapfel, I. "Sprichwort oder geflügeltes Wort?" *Acta Antiqua Academiae Scientiarum Hungaricae* 12 (1964): 365-371.

245.   Trevor, J. Robert, and Paul M. Zall. "The Story." *Proverb to Poem*. New York: McGraw-Hill, 1970. 11-20.

246.   Vial'tseva, S. I. "Okkazional'noe ispol'zovanie angliiskikh poslovits." *Issledovaniia leksicheskoi sochetaemosti i frazeologii: Sbornik trudov*. Ed. N. A. Popova. Moskva: MGPI, 1975. 245-270.

247.   Vinken, P. J. "Some Observations on the Symbolism of the Broken Pot in Art and Literature." *American Imago* 15 (1958): 149-174.

248.   Vlach, John M. "The Functions of Proverbs in Yoruba Folktales." *Studies in Yoruba Folklore*. Bloomington, Indiana: Folklore Forum, 1973. 31-41.

249.   Walker, Carolyn Brasher. "A Catalogue of the Proverbs in Selected Medieval Spanish Works." M. A. Thesis. University of Texas, 1964. 110 pp.

250.   Wallrabe, Herbert. "Bedeutungsgeschichte der Worte liebe, trût, friedel, wine, minnaere, senedaere nebst einem eingeschalteten Kapitel über die Formeln von liebe und leide." Diss. Leipzig, 1925. Especially pp. 48-83.

251.   Wandelt, Oswin. *Sprichwörter und Sentenzen des altfranzösischen Dramas (1100-1400)*. Diss. Marburg, 1887. Marburg: Fr. Sömmering, 1887. 75 pp.

252.   Weinreich, Otto. "Das Märchen von Amor und Psyche und andere Volksmärchen im Altertum." In Ludwig Friedländer, *Darstellungen aus der Sittengeschichte Roms*, 4 vols. 9th and 10th ed. by Georg Wissowa. Leipzig: S. Hirzel, 1921; rpt. Aalen: Scientia, 1964. IV, 89-132, especially 91-97.

253. Werner, Richard. *Zur Geschichte der "Proverbes dramatiques."* Berlin: R. Gaertner, 1887. 24 pp.

254. Wesselski, Albert. *Erlesenes*. Prag: Gesellschaft deutscher Bücherfreunde in Böhmen, 1928. 165 pp.

255. Westcott, Roger W. "From Proverb to Aphorism: The Evolution of a Verbal Art Form." *Forum Linguisticum* 5, 3 (1981): 213-225.

256. Whiting, Bartlett Jere. "Studies in the Middle English Proverb," 3 vols. Diss. Harvard University, 1932. 1386 pp.

257. Whiting, Bartlett Jere. "Proverbs in Certain Middle English Romances in Relation to Their French Sources." *Harvard Studies and Notes in Philology and Literature* 15 (1933): 75-126.

258. Whiting, Bartlett Jere. "Proverbial Material in the Popular Ballads." *Journal of American Folklore* 47 (1934): 22-44.

259. Whiting, Bartlett Jere. "Proverbs in the Fabliaux." *Chaucer's Use of Proverbs*. Cambridge, Massachusetts: Harvard University Press, 1934. 243-264.

260. Whiting, Bartlett Jere. "The Devil and Hell in Current English Literary Idiom." *Harvard Studies and Notes in Philology and Literature* 20 (1938): 201-247.

261. Whiting, Bartlett Jere. "French Biblical Plays." *Proverbs in the Earlier English Drama, with Illustrations from Contemporary French Plays*. Cambridge, Massachusetts: Harvard University Press, 1938; rpt. New York: Octagon Books, 1969. 55-64.

262. Whiting, Bartlett Jere. "French Interludes." *Proverbs in the Earlier English Drama, with Illustrations from Contemporary French Plays*. Cambridge, Massachusetts: Harvard University Press, 1938; rpt. New York: Octagon Books, 1969. 202-208.

263. Whiting, Bartlett Jere. "French Moralities." *Proverbs in the Earlier English Drama, with Illustrations from Contemporary French Plays*. Cambridge, Massachusetts: Harvard University Press, 1938; rpt. New York: Octagon Books, 1969. 168-169.

264.   Whiting, Bartlett Jere. *Proverbs in the Earlier English Drama, with Illustrations from Contemporary French Sources.* Cambridge, Massachusetts: Harvard University Press, 1938; rpt. New York: Octagon Books, 1969. 505 pp.

265.   Whiting, Bartlett Jere. "Proverbs and Proverbial Sayings from Scottish Writings before 1600." *Mediaeval Studies* 11 (1949): 123-205; 13 (1951): 87-164.

266.   Whiting, Bartlett Jere. *Proverbs, Sentences, and Proverbial Phrases from English Writings Mainly before 1500.* Cambridge, Massachusetts: Harvard University Press, 1968. 733 pp.

267.   Whiting, Bartlett Jere. *Early American Proverbs and Proverbial Phrases.* Cambridge, Massachusetts: Harvard University Press, 1977. 555 pp.

268.   Whiting, Bartlett Jere. *Modern Proverbs and Proverbial Sayings.* Cambridge, Massachusetts: Harvard University Press, 1989. 710 pp.

269.   Wienert, Walter. *Die Typen der griechisch-römischen Fabel: Mit einer Einleitung über das Wesen der Fabel.* Helsinki: Suomalainen Tiedeakatemia, 1925. Especially 6-25. Also in Pack Carnes, ed. *Proverbia in Fabula: Essays on the Relationship of the Fable and the Proverb.* Bern: Peter Lang, 1988. 47-64.

270.   Wildhaber, Robert. *Das Sündenregister auf der Kuhhaut.* Helsinki: Suomalainen Tiedeakatemia, 1955. 36 pp.

271.   Williams, Harry F. "French Proverbs in Fifteenth-Century Literature: A Sampling." *Fifteenth-Century Studies* 5 (1982): 223-232.

272.   Wirrer, Jan. "Phraseologismen in der erzählenden niederdeutschen Literatur." *Sprachbilder zwischen Theorie und Praxis.* Eds. Christoph Chlosta, Peter Grzybek, and Elisabeth Piirainen. Bochum: Norbert Brockmeyer, 1994. 273-303.

273.   Witt, Arthur. "Siebzig sprichwörtliche Redewendungen aus niederdeutschen politischen Flugschriften des Jahres 1644." *Zeitschrift für Volkskunde* 26 (1917): 355-357.

274.   Woodburn, Roland Rickey. "Proverbs in Health Books of the English Renaissance." Diss. Texas Technological University, 1975. 99 pp.

275. Wotjak, Barbara. "Fuchs, die hast du ganz gestohlen: Zu auffälligen Vernetzungen von Phraseologismen in der Textsorte Anekdote." *Europhras 92: Tendenzen der Phraseologieforschung.* Ed. Barbara Sandig. Bochum: Norbert Brockmeyer, 1994. 619-650.

276. Wyss, Wilhelm von. "Die Sprichwörter bei den römischen Komikern." Diss. Zürich, 1889. 114 pp.

277. Yates, Irene. "A Collection of Proverbs and Proverbial Sayings from South Carolina Literature." *Southern Folklore Quarterly* 11 (1947): 187-199.

278. Zholkovski, Alexandr K. "At the Intersection of Linguistics, Paremiology and Poetics: On the Literary Structure of Proverbs." *Poetics* 7 (1978): 309-332.

279. Zick, Gisela. "Der zerbrochene Krug als Bildmotiv des 18. Jahrhunderts." *Wallraf-Richartz Jahrbuch* 31 (1969): 149-204.

280. Ziltener, Werner. "Parömiologie und provenzalische Philologie." *Proverbium* No. 15 (1970): 548-550.

281. Zimmer, Wolfgang. "Les chevaux de la conversation, le miel de la tradition et l'or des paroles: Emploi et fonction des proverbes dans le théâtre burkinabè." *Anthropos* 89, 1-3 (1994): 15-27.

282. Zingerle, Ignaz V. "Die Alliteration bei mittelhochdeutschen Dichtern." *Sitzungsberichte der philosophisch-historischen Classe der Kaiserlichen Akademie der Wissenschaften Wien* 47 (1864): 103-174.

283. Zoozmann, Richard. *Unsere Klassiker im Volksmund: Ein kleiner Zitatenschatz.* Leipzig: Hesse und Becker, 1911. 186 pp.

284. Zumthor, Paul. "L'épiphonème proverbial." *Revue des sciences humaines* 41, 163 (1976): 313-328.

SPECIFIC STUDIES

A

ABRAHAM A SANTA CLARA (1644-1709)

285. Blanckenburg, Curt. *Studien über die Sprache Abrahams a Santa Clara.* Diss. Halle, 1897. Halle: Niemeyer, 1897. 87 pp.

286. Fleckenstein, Sister Mary Thecla. "Das Sprichwort, sprichwörtliche und eigenartige bildliche Redensarten und Wortspiele in den Predigten 'Auf, auf ihr Christen' von Abraham a Sancta [*sic*] Clara." Diss. University of Pittsburgh, 1942. 86 pp.

287. Hoffmann, Hellmut. *Die Metaphern in Predigten und Schriften Abrahams a Santa Clara.*" Diss. Köln, 1933. Düsseldorf: Express Druckerei, 1933. 102 pp.

288. Lauchert, Friedrich. "Sprichwörter und sprichwörtliche Redensarten bei P. Abraham à S. Clara." *Alemannia* 20 (1892): 213-254.

289. Schmidt, Leopold. "Wiener Redensarten. III: 'Schabab' und 'Schlecka-bartl.'" *Das deutsche Volkslied* 43 (1941): 119-121.

290. Seiler, Friedrich. *Deutsche Sprichwörterkunde.* München: C. H. Beck, 1922, 1967. 58-59.

291. Wander, Karl Friedrich Wilhelm. *Abrahamisches Parömiakon.* Breslau: Ignaz Kohn, 1838. 412 pp.

ABRAHAM AND ISAAC (c. 1458)

292. Whiting, Bartlett Jere. "The Dublin and Brome *Abraham and Isaac* Plays." *Proverbs in the Earlier English Drama.* Cambridge, Massachusetts: Harvard University Press, 1938; rpt. New York: Octagon Books, 1969. 32-33.

ACCA (died 740)

293. Babcock, Robert G. "The 'proverbium antiquum' in Acca's Letter to Bede." *Mittellateinisches Jahrbuch,* 22 (1987): 53-55.

ACHEBE, CHINUA [Albert Chinualumogo] (1931—)

294.   Adeeko, Adeleke. "Words' Horse, or The Proverb as a Paradigm of Literary Understanding." Diss. University of Florida, 1991. 140-168.

295.   Adeeko, Adeleke. "Contests of Text and Context in Chinua Achebe's *Arrow of God*." *Ariel: A Review of International English Literature* 23, 2 (1992): 7-22.

296.   Ferris, William R. "Folklore and the African Novelist: Achebe and Tutuola." *Journal of American Folklore* 86 (1973): 25-36.

297.   Lindfors, Bernth. "The Palm Oil with Which Achebe's Words Are Eaten." *Afri-can Literature Today* 1 (1968): 3-18.

298.   Lindfors, Bernth. "Chinua Achebe's Proverbs." *Nigerian Field* 35 (1970): 180- 181; 36 (1971): 45-48, 90-96, 139-143.

299.   Lindfors, Bernth. "Perverted Proverbs in Nigerian Chapbooks." *Proverbium* No. 15 (1970): 482-487.

300.   Nwachukwu-Agbada, J. O. J. "Chinua Achebe's Literary Proverbs as Reflections of Igbo Culture and Philosophical Tenets." *Proverbium: Yearbook of International Proverb Scholarship* 10 (1993): 215-235.

301.   Okoye, Chukwuma. "Achebe: The Literary Function of Proverbs and Proverbial Sayings in Two Novels." *Lore and Language* 2, 10 (1979): 45-63.

302.   Patnaik, Eira. "Proverbs as Cosmic Truths and Chinua Achebe's *No Longer at Ease*." *Africana Journal* 13, 1-4 (1982): 98-103.

303.   Seitel, Peter. "Proverbs: A Social Use of Metaphor." *Genre* 2 (1969): 143-161, especially 145-150.

304.   Shelton, Austin J. "The 'Palm-Oil' of Language: Proverbs in Chinua Achebe's Novels." *Modern Language Quarterly* 30 (1969): 86-111.

305.   Workman, Mark E. "Proverbs for the Pious and the Paranoid: The Social Use of Metaphor." *Proverbium: Yearbook for International Proverb Scholarship* 4 (1987): 225-241.

ADAMS, ANDY (1859-1935)

306. Taylor, Archer. "Americanisms in *The Log of a Cowboy*." *Western Folklore* 8 (1959): 39-41.

ADAMS, EDWARD CLARKSON (1876-1946)

307. Yates, Irene. "A Collection of Proverbs and Proverbial Sayings from South Carolina Literature." *Southern Folklore Quarterly* 11 (1947): 187-199.

ADELUNG, JOHANN CHRISTOPH (1732-1806)

308. Pape, Walter. "Zwischen Sprachspiel und Sprachkritik: Zum literarischen Spiel mit der wörtlichen Bedeutung von Idiomen." *Sprache und Literatur in Wissenschaft und Unterricht* 16, 56 (1985): 2-13.

ADRIEN DE MONTLUC (1589-1646)

309. Perrin-Naffakh, Anne-Marie. "Locutions et proverbes dans les 'Fables' de La Fontaine." *L'information littéraire* 31 (1979): 151-155. Also in *Proverbia in Fabula: Essays on the Relationship of the Fable and the Proverb*. Ed. Pack Carnes. Bern: Peter Lang, 1988. 285-294.

AELIAN [Claudius Aelianus] (c. 170-c. 235)

310. Tsirimbas, Dimitrios. "Sprichwörter und sprichwörtliche Redensarten bei den Epistolographen der zweiten Sophistik, Alkiphron—Cl. Aelianus." Diss. München, 1936. 66-87.

AESCHYLUS (525/24-456/55 B. C.)

311. Koch, Joh. Georg. E. "Quaestionum de Proverbiis apud Aeschylum, Sophoclem, Euripidem." Diss. Königsberg, 1877. 92 pp.

312. Robertson, H. G. "Legal Expressions and Ideas of Justice in Aeschylus." *Classical Philology* 34 (1939): 209-219.

AFYANI, ALI MOHAMMADE (1925—)

313. Vahman, F. "Some Rare and Hitherto Unknown Proverbs in Ali Mohammade Afyani's *Souhare Ahu-Xanom*." *Acta Orientalia* 30 (1966): 195-212.

AGRICOLA, ERHARD (1921—)

314. Militz, Hans-Manfred. "Phraseologische Wendungen in der Klassifikation und im Text." *Sprachpflege* 37, 6 (1988): 77-79.

AGRICOLA, JOHANNES (1494-1566)

315.   Pfeifer, Wolfgang. "Volkstümliche Metaphorik." *Zur Literatursprache im Zeitalter der frühbürgerlichen Revolution: Untersuchungen zu ihrer Verwendung in der Agitationsliteratur.* Eds. Gerhard Kettmann and Joachim Schildt. Berlin: Akademie-Verlag, 1978. 87-217.

AGRICOLA, MICHAEL (1509-1557)

316.   Tarkiainen, Viljo. "Agricolan suhde sananlaskuihin." *Kalevalaseuran Vuosikirja* 31 (1951): 55-63. Also in *Tarkiainen Tutkielmia.* Forssa: Suomalaisen Kirjallisuuden Seura, 1958. 233-244.

AIMERIC DE PEGUILHAN (c. 1175-c. 1220)

317.   Pfeffer, Wendy. "'Eu l'auzi dir en un ver reprovier': Aimeric de Peguilhan's Use of the Proverb." *Neophilologus* 70 (1986): 520-527.

ALBION KNIGHT (c. 1566)

318.   Whiting, Bartlett Jere. "*Albion Knight.*" *Proverbs in the Earlier English Drama.* Cambridge, Massachusetts: Harvard University Press, 1938; rpt. New York: Octagon Books, 1969. 132-133.

ALBRECHT VON EYB (1420-1475)

319.   Cowie, Murray A. "Proverbs and Proverbial Phrases in the German Works of Albrecht von Eyb." Diss. University of Chicago, 1942. 106 pp.

ALBRECHT VON HALBERSTADT (13th cent.)

320.   Hofmann, Liselotte. *Der volkskundliche Gehalt der mittelhochdeutschen Epen von 1100 bis gegen 1250.* Zeulenroda: Bernhard Sporn, 1939. 77-78.

ALCOTT, LOUISA MAY (1832-1888)

321.   Monteiro, George. "Louisa May Alcott's Proverb Stories." *Tennessee Folklore Society Bulletin* 42 (1976): 103-107.

ALEKSEEV, MIKHAIL NIKOLAEVICH (1918—)

322.   Godenko, Mikhail. "The Main Book." *Soviet Literature* No. 1 (1981): 143-150.

ALEMAN, MATEO (1547-1610)

323.   Feliciano Rivera, José Raúl. "El refrán como estrategia discursiva en *Guzman de Alfarache.*" Diss. Tulane University, 1993. 226 pp.

324. Joly, Monique. "Aspectos del refrán en Mateo Alemán y Cervantes." *Nueva Revista de Filologia Hispánica* 20 (1971): 95-106.

ALEXANDER, Meister (13th cent.)
325. Seibicke, Wilfried. "'Über Stock und Stein.'" *Der Sprachdienst* 22 (1978): 9-10.

ALEXANDERLIED (12th cent.)
326. Hofmann, Liselotte. *Der volkskundliche Gehalt der mittelhochdeutschen Epen von 1100 bis gegen 1250*. Zeulenroda: Bernhard Sporn, 1939. 75.

ALEXIS, GUILLAUME (15th cent.)
327. Heft, David. *Proverbs and Sentences in Fifteenth Century French Poetry*. Diss. New York University, 1941. Chapter 2. New York: Washington Square Press, 1942 (abridged to 12 pp.).

ALGREN, NELSON (1909-1981)
328. Olinick, Stanley L. "On Proverbs: Creativity, Communication, and Community." *Contemporary Psychoanalysis* 23 (1987): 463-468.

ALKIPHRON (170-229)
329. Tsirimbas, Dimitrios. "Sprichwörter und sprichwörtliche Redensarten bei den Epistolographen der zweiten Sophistik, Alkiphron—Cl. Aelianus." Diss. München 1936. 3-65.

AMAN Y MORDOCHAY, COMEDIA DE (1699)
330. Selig, Karl-Ludwig. "Spanish Proverbs and the *Comedia de Aman y Mordochay*." *Proverbium* No. 15 (1970): 530.

ANCREN RIWLE (13th cent.)
331. Ives, D. Y. "Proverbs in the *Ancren Riwle*." *Modern Language Review* 29 (1934): 257-266.

332. Prins, A. A. "On Two Proverbs in the *Ancren Riwle*." *English Studies* 29 (1948): 146-150.

333. Skeat, Walter William. "*Ancren Riwle*." *Early English Proverbs, Chiefly of the Thirteenth and Fourteenth Centuries*. Oxford: Clarendon Press, 1910; rpt. Darby, Pennsylvania: Folcroft Library Editions, 1974. 8-12.

334. Whiting, Bartlett Jere. "Proverbs in the *Ancren Riwle* and the *Recluse*." *Modern Language Review* 30 (1935): 502-505.

ANDERSCH, ALFRED (1914-1980)

335.   Higi-Wydler, Melanie. *Zur Übersetzung von Idiomen: Eine Beschreibung und Klassifizierung deutscher Idiome und ihrer französischen Übersetzungen.* Bern: Peter Lang, 1989. 335 pp.

ANDRESEN, INGEBORG (1878-1955)

336.   Lindow, Wolfgang. "Volkstümliches Sprachgut in der neuniederdeutschen Dialektdichtung." Diss. Kiel, 1960. Part I, 100-104.

ANDRIC, IVO (1892-1975)

337.   Zhukovic, Ljubomir. "Narodne izreke i poslovice u djelu Ive Andrica." *Izraz: Casopis za knjizevnu i umjetnicku kritiku* 22 (1978): 1497-1516.

ANEGENGE (c. 1160-70)

338.   Hofmann, Liselotte. *Der volkskundliche Gehalt der mittelhochdeutschen Epen von 1100 bis gegen 1250.* Zeulenroda: Bernhard Sporn, 1939. 79.

ANNA SOPHIA, Countess (1619-1680)

339.   Schulze, Carl. "Spruchbuch der jungen Pfalzgräffin Anna Sophia, nachherigen Aebtissin von Quedlinburg, vom Jahre 1630." *Archiv für das Studium der neuren Sprachen und Literaturen* 59 (1878): 318-338.

ANTIPATER OF SIDON (2nd cent. B. C.)

340.   Prittwitz-Gaffron, Erich von. *Das Sprichwort im griechischen Epigramm.* Diss. München, 1912. Gießen: Alfred Töpelmann, 1912. 28-34.

ANULUS, BARPTOLEMAEUS (1500-1565)

341.   Dittrich, Lothar. "Emblematische Weisheit und naturwissenschaftliche Realität." *Die Sprache der Bilder: Realität und Bedeutung in der niederländischen Malerei des 17. Jahrhunderts.* Eds. Wolfgang J. Müller, Konrad Renger, and Rüdiger Klessmann. Braunschweig: ACO Druck, 1978. 21-33. Also in *Jahrbuch für Internationale Germanistik* 13 (1981): 36-60.

ANZENGRUBER, LUDWIG (1839-1889)

342.   Mieder, Wolfgang. "Das Sprichwort in den Dorf- und Kalendergeschichten von Ludwig Anzengruber." *Österreichische Zeitschrift für Volkskunde* 76 (1973): 219-242. Also in *Das Sprichwort in der deutschen Prosaliteratur des neunzehnten Jahrhunderts.* München: Wilhelm Fink, 1976. 129-151.

APIUS AND VIRGINIA (1575)

343. Whiting, Bartlett Jere. *"Apius and Virginia."* Proverbs in the Earlier English Drama. Cambridge, Massachusetts: Harvard University Press, 1938; rpt. New York: Octagon Books, 1969. 294-297.

APOLLINARIUS [Gaius Sulpitius Apollinarius] (2nd cent. A. D.)

344. Prittwitz-Gaffron, Erich von. *Das Sprichwort im griechischen Epigramm.* Diss. München, 1912. Gießen: Alfred Töpelmann, 1912. 59.

APOLLONIUS (c. 295-c. 215 B. C.)

345. Kellogg, George Dwight. *"Study of a Proverb Attributed to the Rhetor Apollonius."* American Journal of Philology 28 (1907): 301-310.

APOSTOLIUS, MICHAEL (born c. 1422)

346. Geisler, Eugen. *"Beiträge zur Geschichte des griechischen Sprichwortes im Anschluß an Planades und Michael Apostolius."* Diss. Breslau, 1908. 40 pp.

AQUINAS, THOMAS (c. 1225-1274)

347. Meichsner, Irene. *Die Logik von Gemeinplätzen: Vorgeführt an Steuermannstopos und Schiffsmetapher.* Bonn: Bouvier, 1983. 263 pp.

ARCHIAS, AULUS LICINIUS (120-after 61 B. C.)

348. Prittwitz-Gaffron, Erich von. *Das Sprichwort im griechischen Epigramm.* Diss. München, 1912. Gießen: Alfred Töpelmann, 1912. 29-30.

ARCHILOCHUS (c. 700-c. 645 B. C.)

349. Moran, William L. *"Puppies in Proverbs: From Samsi-Adad I to Archilochus?"* Eretz-Israel 14 (1978): 32-37.

ARCIPRESTE DE HITA [Juan Ruiz] (1283-c. 1350)

350. Aguilera, Miguel. *"Rica fuente del refranero español."* Boletin de la Academia Columbiana 14, 55 (1964): 252-259.

351. Gella Iturriaga, José. *"Refranero del Arcipreste de Hita."* Arcipreste de Hita: Actas del I Congreso Internacional sobre el Arcipreste de Hita. Ed. M. Criado de Val. Barcelona: Jorge Casas, 1973. 251-269.

352. Hernandez, José Luis Alonso. *"Interprétation psychoanalytique de l'utilisation des parémies dans la littérature espagnole."* Richesse du

proverbe. Eds. François Suard and Claude Buridant. Lille: Université de Lille, 1984. II, 213-225.

ARGENTARIUS, MARCUS (1st cent. A. D.)
353. Prittwitz-Gaffron, Erich von. *Das Sprichwort im griechischen Epigramm.* Diss. München, 1912. Gießen: Alfred Töpelmann, 1912. 41-43.

ARISTOPHANES (c. 445-c. 385 B. C.)
354. Bauck, Ludovicus. "De Proverbiis aliisque locutionibus ex usu vitae communis petitis apud Aristophanem comicum." Diss. Königsberg, 1880. 88 pp.

355. Crusius, Otto, and Leopold Cohn. "Zur handschriftlichen Überlieferung der Paroemiographen." *Philologus* 6 (1891-1893): 201-324.

356. Ewbank, Joseph Boothroyd. "Fable and Proverb in Aristophanes." Diss. University of North Carolina, 1980. 302 pp.

357. Kostakis, P. "Proverbes et expressions proverbiales dans l'oeuvre d'Aristophane (en grec)." *Revue Laografia* 24 (1966): 113-227.

358. Newiger, Hans-Joachim. *Metapher und Allegorie: Studien zu Aristophanes.* Kiel, 1953. München: Beck, 1957. 185 pp.

359. Rohdewald, Wilhelm. *De usu proverbiorum apud Aristophanem.* Burgsteinfurt: Programm des Gymnasiums zu Burgsteinfurt, 1857.

ARISTOTLE (384-322 B. C.)
360. Crane, Mary Thomas. "Proverbial and Aphoristic Sayings: Sources of Authority in the English Renaissance." Diss. Harvard University, 1986. 464 pp.

361. Tarán, Leonardo. "'Amicus Plato sed magis amica veritas': From Plato and Aristotle to Cervantes." *Antike und Abendland* 30 (1984): 93-124.

362. Wilson, Edward. "An Aristotelian Commonplace in Chaucer's *Franklin's Tale*." *Notes and Queries* 230 ns 32 (1985): 303-305.

363. Wilkins, Eliza Gregory. *"Know Thyself" in Greek and Latin Literature.* Diss. University of Chicago, 1917. Chicago: University of Chicago Libraries, 1917. 104 pp.

ARP, BILL [Charles Henry Smith] (1826-1903)

364. Figh, Margaret Gillis. "Tall Talks and Folk Sayings in Bill Arp's Works." *Southern Folklore Quarterly* 13 (1949): 206-212.

ARTMANN, HANS CARL (1921—)

365. Riha, Karl. "Balla Balla, Balla Basta: Zur Poetik kleiner literarischer Formen." *Akzente* 21 (1974): 265-287.

ASHBY, GEORGE (died 1475)

366. Bühler, C. F. "The *Liber de dictis philosophorum antiquorum* and Common Proverbs in George Ashby's Poems." *Publications of the Modern Language Association of America* 65 (1950): 282-289.

ASKLEPIADES OF SAMOS (3rd cent. B. C.)

367. Prittwitz-Gaffron, Erich von. *Das Sprichwort im griechischen Epigramm.* Diss. München, 1912. Gießen: Alfred Töpelmann, 1912. 24-25.

ASTEL, ARNFRID (1933—)

368. Hess, Peter. *Epigramm.* Stuttgart: Metzler, 1989. 14-15.

ATLAKVIDA (c. 1240)

369. Hill, Thomas D. "The Foreseen Wolf and the Path of Wisdom: Proverbial and Beast Lore in *Atlakvida*." *Neophilologus* 77, 4 (1993): 675-677.

AUBIGNÉ, THÉODORE AGRIPPA d' (1552-1630)

370. Desaivre, Léo. "Théodore Agrippa d'Aubigné." *Revue des traditions populaires* 20 (1905): 302.

AUDEN, W. H. [Wystan Hugh Auden] (1907-1973)

371. Mieder, Wolfgang. "The Proverb in the Modern Age: Old Wisdom in New Clothing." *Tradition and Innovation in Folk Literature.* Hanover, New Hampshire: University Press of New England. 1987. 118-156, 248-255 (notes).

AUERBACH, BERTHOLD (1812-1882)

372. Frelander, Allen Edwin. "The Proverb and Proverbial Expression in Berthold Auerbach's *Dorfgeschichten*." M. A. Thesis. Michigan State University, 1953.

373. Mieder, Wolfgang. "Das Sprichwort in den *Schwarzwälder Dorfge-schichten* von Berthold Auerbach." *Ländliche Kulturformen im deutschen*

Südwesten: Festschrift für Heiner Heimberger. Ed. Peter Assion. Stuttgart: W. Kohlhammer, 1971. 123-147. Also in *Das Sprichwort in der deutschen Prosaliteratur des neunzehnten Jahrhunderts.* München: Wilhelm Fink, 1976. 48-67.

374.   Schewe, Harry. "'Ihr gebt mir ja nichts dazu': Eine Redeformel der Volkssprache, ein Volkstanzlied und Goethes Ballade *Vor Gericht.*" *Beiträge zur sprachlichen Volksüberlieferung.* Eds. Ingeborg Weber-Kellermann and Wolfgang Stei-nitz. Berlin [East]: Akademie-Verlag, 1953. 28-38.

AUGUSTINE OF HIPPO (354-430)

375.   Crane, Mary Thomas. "Proverbial and Aphoristic Sayings: Sources of Authority in the English Renaissance." Diss. Harvard University, 1986. 464 pp.

376.   Oroz Reta, José. "El genio paremiológico de san Agustin." *Augustinus* 33 (1988): 93-125.

377.   Szöverffy, Joseph. "St. Augustine and an Irish Saying." *Eigse: A Journal of Irish Studies* 7 (1957): 197-203.

AUGUSTUS [Gaius Julius Caesar Octavianus] (27 B. C.-A. D. 14)

378.   Meichsner, Irene. *Die Logik von Gemeinplätzen: Vorgeführt an Steuermannstopos und Schiffsmetapher.* Bonn: Bouvier, 1983. 263 pp.

AUTOMEDON (1st cent. A. D.)

379.   Prittwitz-Gaffron, Erich von. *Das Sprichwort im griechischen Epigramm.* Diss. München, 1912. Gießen: Alfred Töpelmann, 1912. 39-41.

AYCKBOURN, ALAN (1939—)

380.   Glaap, Albert-Reiner. "Idiomatisches Englisch=Besseres English? Zu einem vernachlässigten Bereich des fremdsprachlichen Unterrichts." *Sprache und Literatur in Wissenschaft und Unterricht* 16, 56 (1985): 95-104.

B

BA, AMADOU HAMPATÉ (1899—)
381. Emeto-Agbasière, Julie. "Le proverbe dans le roman africain." *Présence francophone* No. 29 (1986): 27-41.

BAALAWY, SULEIMAN OMAN SAID (1945—)
382. Parker, Carolyn Ann. "The Advice of Elders, a Broken Leg, and a Swahili Proverb Story." *Artist and Audience: African Literature as a Shared Experience.* Eds. Richard K. Priebe and Thomas A. Hale. Washington, D. C.: Three Continents Press, 1979. 49-59.

383. Parker, Carolyn Ann. "Techniques and Problems in Swahili Proverb Stories: The Case of Baalawy." *Design and Intent in African Literature.* Eds. David F. Dorsey, Phanuel A. Egejuru, and Stephen H. Arnold. Washington, D. C.: Three Continents, 1982. 71-80.

BACHAUMONT, FRANÇOIS (1624-1702)
384. Sébillot, Paul. "Chapelle et Bachaumont." *Revue des traditions populaires* 11 (1896): 34.

BACON, Sir FRANCIS (1561-1626)
385. Bensly, Edward. "Bacon, Essay XII: Mohammed and the Mountain." *Notes and Queries* 12th ser. 4 (1918): 325.

386. Crane, Mary Thomas. "Proverbial and Aphoristic Sayings: Sources of Authority in the English Renaissance." Diss. Harvard University, 1986. 325-377.

387. Preis, A. "Shakespeare, Bacon, and English Proverbs." *Notes and Queries* 190 (1946): 146.

388. Whiting, Bartlett Jere. "Studies in the Middle English Proverb," 3 vols. Diss. Harvard University, 1932. 1386 pp.

389. Wilcox, Stewart C. "Hazlitt's Aphorisms." *Modern Language Notes* 9 (1948): 418-423.

BAKER, Sir RICHARD (1568-1645)
390. Whiting, Bartlett Jere. "Sir Richard Baker's *Cato Variegatus* (1636)." *Humaniora: Essays Honoring Archer Taylor.* Eds. Wayland D. Hand and Gustave O. Arlt. Locust Valley, New York: J. J. Augustin, 1960. 8-16.

BALDWIN, WILLIAM (died c. 1564)

391.　Bühler, Curt F. "A Survival from the Middle Ages: William Baldwin's Use of the *Dictes and Sayings.*" *Speculum* 23 (1948): 76-80.

BALE, JOHN (1495-1563)

392.　Whiting, Bartlett Jere. "John Bale." *Proverbs in the Earlier English Drama.* Cambridge, Massachusetts: Harvard University Press, 1938; rpt. New York: Octagon Books, 1969. 46-48.

393.　Whiting, Bartlett Jere. "John Bale's *The Three Laws.*" *Proverbs in the Earlier English Drama.* Cambridge, Massachusetts: Harvard University Press, 1938; rpt. New York: Octagon Books, 1969. 97-99.

394.　Whiting, Bartlett Jere. "John Bale's *King Johan.*" *Proverbs in the Earlier English Drama.* Cambridge, Massachusetts: Harvard University Press, 1938; rpt. New York: Octagon Books, 1969. 99-102.

BAL[L]HORN, JOHANN (1530-1603)

395.　Wiese, Ursula von. "Aus Namen werden Begriffe [Johann Balhorn]." *Sprachspiegel* 41 (1985): 51.

A BALLAD OF OLD PROVERBS (1707)

396.　Doyle, Charles Clay. "On Some Paremiological Verses." *Proverbium* No. 25 (1975): 979-982.

BALZAC, HONORÉ de (1799-1850)

397.　Juillard, Alain. "Discours proverbial et écriture romanesque dans *La Comédie Humaine*: Le cas de *Un début dans la vie.*" *Richesse du proverbe.* Eds. François Suard and Claude Buridant. Lille: Université de Lille, 1984. II, 261-272.

BALZAC, JEAN LOUIS (1597-1654)

398.　Lafond, Jean. "Des formes brèves de la littérature morale aux XVIe et XVIIe siècles." *Les formes brèves de la prose et le discours discontinu (XVIe-XVIIe siècles).* Paris: Librairie Philosophique J. Vrin, 1984. 101-122.

BARBOUR, JOHN (c. 1316-1395)

399.　Skeat, Walter William. "*The Bruce*: by John Barbour." *Early English Proverbs, Chiefly of the Thirteenth and Fourteenth Centuries.* Oxford: Clarendon Press, 1910; rpt. Darby, Pennsylvania: Folcroft Library Editions, 1974. 52-53.

BARCLAY, ALEXANDER (c. 1475-1552)

400. Mauch, Thomas Karl. "The Role of the Proverb in Early Tudor Literature." Diss. University of California at Los Angeles, 1963. 43-48, 99-101, 263-265.

BARKER, JAMES NELSON (1784-1858)

401. Montgomery, Evelyn. "Proverbial Materials in *The Politician Out-Witted* and Other Comedies of Early American Drama 1789-1829." *Midwest Folklore* 11 (1961-1962): 215-224.

BASILE, GIAMBATTISTA (1575-1632)

402. Speroni, Charles. "Proverbs and Proverbial Phrases in Basile's *Pentameron.*" *University of California Publications in Modern Philology* 24, 2 (1941): 181-288.

BAST, JOHANNA DE (17th cent.)

403. Hameyde, Jan van der. "Uit Oude Memorieboeken: Van hop, wol en vlas: Uit het Memorieboek van Johanna de Bast, 1667." *Eigen Schoon en de Brabander* 19 (1936): 360.

BAUDE, HENRI (c. 1430-c. 1495)

404. Heft, David. *Proverbs and Sentences in Fifteenth Century French Poetry.* Diss. New York University, 1941. Chapter 2. New York: Washington Square Press, 1942 (abridged to 12 pp.).

405. Vandenbroeck, Paul. "Dits illustrés et emblèmes moraux: Contribution à l'étude de l'iconographie profane et de la pensée sociale vers 1500 (Paris, B. N., ms. fr. 24461)." *Jaarboek van het koninklijk Museum voor Schone Kunsten (Antwerpen)* (1988): 23-94.

BAUDELAIRE, CHARLES (1821-67)

406. Riffaterre, Michael. "Fonction du cliché dans la prose littéraire." *Essais de stylistique structurale.* Paris: Flammarion, 1971. 161-181. Also in German as "Die Funktion des Klischees in der literarischen Form." *Strukturale Stilistik.* München: List Taschenbuch, 1973. 139-156.

BAUDOUIN DE CONDÉ (13th cent.)

407. Whiting, Bartlett Jere. "Proverbial Material in the Poems of Baudouin and Jean de Condé." *Romanic Review* 27 (1936): 204-223.

BEAUMARCHAIS [Pierre Augustin Caron] (1732-1799)

408. Morel, Jacques. "'Clocher devant les boiteux' (*Mariage de Figaro*, I, 2)." *Revue des sciences humaines* 30 (1965): 127-128.

409. Pineaux, Jacques. "Beaumarchais." *Proverbes et dictons français*, 6th ed. Paris: Presses Universitaires de France, 1973. 65.

410. Sébillot, Paul. "Beaumarchais." *Revue des traditions populaires* 24 (1909): 291-292.

BEAUMONT, FRANCIS (1584-1616)

411. Marshall, Ed. "Proverbial Phrases in Beaumont and Fletcher: 'To Write in Water.'" *Notes and Queries* 7th ser. 12 (1891): 14.

412. Pierpoint, Robert. "Proverbial Phrases in Beaumont and Fletcher." *Notes and Queries* 8th ser. 1 (1892): 74.

413. Prideaux, W. F. "Proverbial Phrases in Beaumont and Fletcher." *Notes and Queries* 7th ser. 10 (1890): 361-362.

414. Smith, I. E. "Proverbial Phrases in Beaumont and Fletcher." *Notes and Queries* 7th ser. 11 (1891): 274.

415. Taylor, Archer. "Proverbial Comparisons in the Plays of Beaumont and Fletcher." *Journal of American Folklore* 70 (1957): 25-36.

416. Taylor, Archer. "Proverbial Phrases in the Plays of Beaumont and Fletcher." *Bulletin of the Tennessee Folklore Society* 23 (1957): 39-59.

417. Taylor, Archer. "Proverbs in the Plays of Beaumont and Fletcher." *Southern Folklore Quarterly*, 24 (1960): 77-100.

418. Terry, F. C. Birkbeck. "Proverbial Phrases in Beaumont and Fletcher." *Notes and Queries* 7th ser. 10 (1891): 53.

419. Yardley, E. "Proverbial Phrases in Beaumont and Fletcher." *Notes and Queries* 7th ser. 10 (1890): 431.

THE BEAUTY AND GOOD PROPERTIES OF WOMEN (c. 1530)

420. Whiting, Bartlett Jere. "*The Beauty and Good Properties of Women: or Calisto and Melibaea.*" *Proverbs in the Earlier English Drama*. Cam-

bridge, Massachusetts: Harvard University Press, 1938; rpt. New York: Octagon Books, 1969. 184-187.

BECKETT, SAMUEL (1906-89)

421. Sherzer, Dina. "Saying Is Inventing: Gnomic Expressions in *Molloy*." *Speech Play: Research and Resources for Studying Linguistic Creativity.* Ed. Barbara Kirshenblatt-Gimblett. Philadelphia: University of Pennsylvania Press, 1976. 163-171.

BEDE, The Venerable (673-735)

422. Babcock, Robert G. "The 'proverbium antiquum' in Acca's Letter to Bede." *Mittellateinisches Jahrbuch* 22 (1987): 53-55.

423. Crane, Mary Thomas. "Proverbial and Aphoristic Sayings: Sources of Authority in the English Renaissance." Diss. Harvard University, 1986. 464 pp.

424. Whiting, Bartlett Jere. "The Earliest Recorded English Wellerism." *Philological Quarterly*, 15 (1936): 310-311.

BEHEIM, MICHEL (1416-1474)

425. Hofmeister, Wernfried. *Sprichwortartige Mikrotexte als literarische Medien, dargestellt an der hochdeutschen politischen Lyrik des Mittelalters.* Bochum: Norbert Brockmeyer, 1995. 395-429.

BEHNKEN, HEINRICH (1880-1960)

426. Lindow, Wolfgang. "Volkstümliches Sprachgut in der neuniederdeutschen Dialektdichtung." Diss. Kiel, 1960. Part I, pp. 104-107.

BELLAY, JOACHIM du (1522-1560)

427. Screech, Michael. "Commonplaces of Law, Proverbial Wisdom and Philosophy: Their Importance in Renaissance Scholarship." *Classical Influences on European Culture, A. D. 1500-1700.* Ed. R. R. Bolgar. Cambridge: Cambridge University Press, 1976. 127-134.

BENICZKY, PÉTER (1606-1664)

428. Csanda, Sándor. "Beniczky Péter magyar és szlovak verses példabeszédei." *Irodalomtörteneti kozlemények* 89, 3 (1985): 259-270.

BENYOËTZ, ELAZAR (1937—)

429.   Grubitz, Christoph. "Die Verknüpfung von Redensarten zu Priameln." *Der israelische Aphoristiker Elazar Benyoëtz.* Tübingen: Max Niemeyer, 1994. 16-25.

BEOWULF (10th-12th cent.)

430.   Burlin, Robert B. "Gnomic Indirection in *Beowulf.*" *Anglo-Saxon Poetry: Essays in Appreciation for John C. McGalliard.* Eds. Lewis E. Nicholson and Dolores Warwick Frese. Notre Dame, Indiana: University of Notre Dame Press, 1975. 41-49.

431.   Deskis, Susan Elizabeth. "Proverbial Backgrounds to the 'Sententiae' of *Beowulf.*" Diss. Harvard University, 1991. 176 pp.

432.   Malone, Kemp. "Words of Wisdom in *Beowulf.*" *Humaniora: Essays Honoring Archer Taylor.* Eds. Wayland D. Hand and Gustave Arlt. New York: J. J. Augustin, 1960. 180-194.

433.   Shippey, T. A. "Maxims in Old English Narrative: Literary Art or Traditional Wisdom?" *Oral Tradition—Literary Tradition: A Symposium.* Eds. Hans Bekker-Nielsen, Peter Foote, Andreas Haarder, and Hans Frede Nielsen. Odense: Odense University Press, 1977. 28-46.

BERNANOS, GEORGES (1888-1948)

434.   Gosselin, Monique. "De la maxime au proverbe: Fragments du discours sentencieux dans les textes de fiction de G. Bernanos." *Richesse du proverbe.* Eds. François Suard and Claude Buridant. Lille: Université de Lille, 1984. II, 227-243.

BIERMANN, WOLF (1936—)

435.   Mieder, Wolfgang. "'It's Five Minutes to Twelve': Folklore and Saving Life on Earth." *International Folklore Review* 7 (1989): 10-21.

BILLINGS, JOSH [Henry Wheeler Shaw] (1818-1885)

436.   Grimes, Geoffrey Allan. "'Mules,' 'Owls' and Other Things: Folk Material in the Tobacco Philosophy of Josh Billings." *New York Folklore Quarterly* 26 (1970): 283-296.

BION (2nd cent. B. C.)

437.   Baar, Adolf. *Sprichwörter und Sentenzen aus den griechischen Idyllendichtern.* Görz: Selbstverlag des Staatsgymnasiums, 1887. 1-41.

BISMARCK, OTTO VON (1815-1898)

438. Blümmer, Hugo. *Der bildliche Ausdruck in den Reden des Fürsten Bismarck.* Leipzig: S. Hirzel, 1891. Especially 182-186.

439. Blümmer, Hugo. "Der bildliche Ausdruck in den Briefen des Fürsten Bismarck." *Euphorion* 1 (1894): 590-603, 771-787.

440. Blümmer, Hugo. "Der bildliche Ausdruck in den Ansprachen des Fürsten Bismarck." *Zeitschrift des allgemeinen deutschen Sprachvereins* 10 (1895): 78-87.

BLACKMORE, RICHARD DODDRIDGE (1825-1900)

441. Kirwin, William. "Blackmore—Creator of Proverbs." *Lore and Language* 1, 8 (1973): 26-28.

BLAKE, WILLIAM (1757-1827)

442. Blondel, Jacques. "Les *Proverbes d'Enfer* de William Blake." *Études Anglaises* 40, 4 (1987): 448-454.

443. Cox, Philip. "Blake, Marvell, and Milton: A Possible Source for a Proverb of Hell." *Notes and Queries* 236 ns 38 (1991): 292-293.

444. Cox, Philip. "Blake, Marvell, Milton, and Young: A Further Possible Source for a 'Proverb of Hell.'" *Notes and Queries* 238 ns 40, 1 (1993): 37-38.

445. Edwards, Gavin. "Repeating the Same Dull Round." *Unnam'd Forms: Blake and Textuality.* Eds. Nelson Hilton and Thomas A. Vogler. Berkeley: University of California Press, 1986. 26-48.

446. Helms, Randel. "Proverbs of Heaven and Proverbs of Hell." *Paunch* 38 (1974): 51-58.

447. Holstein, Michael E. "Crooked Roads without Improvement: Blake's *Proverbs of Hell.*" *Genre* 8 (1975): 26-41.

448. Lansverk, Marvin Duane. *The Wisdom of Many, the Vision of One: The Proverbs of William Blake.* Diss. University of Washington, 1988. 242 pp. New York: Peter Lang, 1994. 215 pp.

449. Meister, Barbara. "The Interaction of Music and Poetry: A Study of the Poems of Paul Verlaine as Set to Music by Claude Debussy and of the

Song Cycle *Songs and Proverbs of William Blake* by Benjamin Britten."
Diss. City University of New York, 1987. 273 pp.

450. Obelkevich, James. "Proverbs and Social History." *The Social History of Language*. Eds. Peter Burke and Roy Porter. Cambridge: Cambridge University Press, 1987. 43-72. Also in *Wise Words: Essays on the Proverb*. Ed. Wolfgang Mieder. New York: Garland Publishing, 1994. 211-252.

451. Villalobos, John. "William Blake's *Proverbs of Hell* and the Tradition of Wisdom Literature." *Studies in Philology* 87, 2 (1990): 246-259.

452. Williams, Porter. "Blake's 'An Ancient Proverb' and a Dash of 'Blood.'" *Philological Quarterly* 60 (1981): 264-269.

BLOCH, ERNST (1885-1977)
453. Küntzel, Heinrich. "'Mich wundert, daß ich fröhlich bin': Marginalien zu einem alten Spruch." *Deutsche Vierteljahrsschrift für Literaturwissenschaft und Geistesgeschichte* 61 (1987): 399-418.

BOBROWSKI, JOHANNES (1917-1965)
454. Mieder, Wolfgang. "Sprichwörter im modernen Sprachgebrauch." *Muttersprache* 85 (1975): 65-88. Also in *Ergebnisse der Sprichwörterforschung*. Bern: Peter Lang, 1978. 213-238; *Deutsche Sprichwörter in Literatur, Politik, Presse und Werbung*. Hamburg: Helmut Buske, 1983. 53-76.

455. Stegner, Margarete. "Volkstümliche Sprachelemente in Johannes Bobrowskis *Levins Mühle*: Ein Beitrag zur Interpretation." M. A. Thesis. University of Vermont, 1976. 107 pp.

BOCADOS DE ORO (13th cent.)
456. Morgan, Frances Elnora Williams. "Proverbs from Four Didactic Works of the Thirteenth Century." Diss. University of Kentucky, 1968. 492 pp.

BOCCACCIO, GIOVANNI (1313-1375)
457. Ageno, Franca. "Ispirazione proverbiale del *Trecentonovelle*." *Lettere Italiane* 51 (1958): 288-305.

458. Chiecchi, Giuseppe. "Sentenze e Proverbi nel *Decameron*." *Studi sul Boccaccio* 9 (1975-1976): 119-168.

459. Pittaluga, Stefano. "Proverbi e facezie di Antonio Cornazzano." *Res Publica Litterarum* 9 (1986): 231-239.

BÖLL, HEINRICH (1917-1985)
460. Higi-Wydler, Melanie. *Zur Übersetzung von Idiomen: Eine Beschreibung und Klassifizierung deutscher Idiome und ihrer französischen Übersetzungen*. Bern: Peter Lang, 1989. 335 pp.

461. Mieder, Wolfgang. "Sprichwörter im moderen Sprachgebrauch." *Muttersprache* 85 (1975): 65-88. Also in *Ergebnisse der Sprichwörterforschung*. Bern: Peter Lang, 1978. 213-238; *Deutsche Sprichwörter in Literatur, Politik, Presse und Werbung*. Hamburg: Helmut Buske, 1983. 53-76.

462. Mieder, Wolfgang. "Einer fehlt beim Gruppenbild: 'Geflügelter' Abschied von Heinrich Böll." *Der Sprachdienst* 29 (1985): 167-172.

BÖSCH, ALEXANDER (17th cent.)
463. Singer, Samuel. "Das Exempelbuch des Alexander Bösch." *Schweizerisches Archiv für Volkskunde* 42 (1945): 58-62.

BOETHIUS, ANNICIUS MANLIUS SEVERINUS (c. 475-525)
464. Crane, Mary Thomas. "Proverbial and Aphoristic Sayings: Sources of Authority in the English Renaissance." Diss. Harvard University, 1986. 464 pp.

465. Holloway, Julia Bolton. "'The Asse to the Harpe': Boethian Music in Chaucer." *Boethius and the Liberal Arts: A Collection of Essays*. Ed. Michael Masi. Bern: Peter Lang, 1981. 175-188.

466. Wilson, Edward. "An Aristotelian Commonplace in Chaucer's *Franklin's Tale*." *Notes and Queries* 230 ns 32 (1985): 303-305.

BOILEAU, NICOLAS (1636-1711)
467. Sébillot, Paul. "Boileau." *Revue des traditions populaires* 6 (1891): 556-559.

BOJARDO, MATTEO MARIA (c. 1440-1494)
468. Matzke, John E. "On the Source of the Italian and English Idioms Meaning 'To Take Time by the Forelock,' with Special Reference to Bojardo's *Orlando Innamorato*, Book II, Cantos VII-IX." *Publications of the Modern Language Association* 8 (1893): 303-334.

BONAVENTURA [Giovanni di Fidanza] (1221-1274)

469.   Crane, Mary Thomas. "Proverbial and Aphoristic Sayings: Sources of Authority in the English Renaissance." Diss. Harvard University, 1986. 464 pp.

LE BONE FLORENCE OF ROME (13th cent.)

470.   Whiting, Bartlett Jere. "Proverbs in Certain Middle English Romances in Relation to Their French Sources." *Harvard Studies and Notes in Philology and Literature* 15 (1933): 75-126, especially 118-121.

BOOK OF MARGERY KEMPE (1436)

471.   Robinson, J. W. "'As Small as Flesh to Pot.'" *Folklore (London)* 80 (1969): 197-198.

BORCHARDT, RUDOLF (1877-1945)

472.   Schmidt-Hidding, Wolfgang. "Deutsche Sprichwörter und Redewendungen." *Deutschunterricht für Ausländer* 13 (1963): 13-26, especially 14-15.

BOSSDORF, HERMANN (1877-1921)

473.   Lindow, Wolfgang. "Volkstümliches Sprachgut in der neuniederdeutschen Dialektdichtung." Diss. Kiel, 1960. Part I, 108-114.

474.   Lindow, Wolfgang. "Das Sprichwort als stilistisches und dramatisches Mittel in der Schauspieldichtung Stavenhagens, Boßdorfs und Schureks." *Niederdeutsches Jahrbuch* 84 (1961): 97-116.

BOSWELL, JAMES (1740-1795)

475.   Barnes, Daniel R. "Boswell, Johnson, and a Proverbial Candlestick." *Midwestern Journal of Language and Folklore* 8, 2 (1982): 120-122.

BOTE, HERMANN (1460-1520)

476.   Cordes, Gerhard. "Hermann Bote und sein *Köker.*" *Festschrift für Ludwig Wolff zum 70. Geburtstag.* Ed. Werner Schröder. Neumünster: Karl Wachholtz, 1962. 287-319.

477.   Marinus, Albert. "Thyl Ulenspiegel dans la sculpture satirique." *Folklore Brabançon* 7 (1927-1928): 42-58.

478.   Mieder, Wolfgang. "'Eulenspiegel macht seine Mitbürger durch Schaden klug': Sprichwörtliches im *Dil Ulenspiegel* von 1515." *Eulenspiegel-Jahrbuch* 29 (1989): 27-50. Also in *Sprichwort—Wahr-*

wort!? Studien zur Geschichte, Bedeutung und Funktion deutscher Sprichwörter. Frankfurt am Main: Peter Lang, 1992. 59-85.

479. Rusterholz, Peter. "Till Eulenspiegel als Sprachkritiker." *Wirkendes Wort* 27 (1977): 18-26.

480. Uther, Hans-Jörg. "Eulenspiegel und die Landesverweisung (Historie 25, 26): Einige Betrachtungen zur Stoff- und Motivgeschichte." *Eulenspiegel-Jahrbuch* 25 (1985): 60-74.

BOTTOMLEY, GORDON (1874-1948)
481. Burns, D. A. "A Potpourri of Parasites in Poetry and Proverbs." *British Medical Journal* 303 (December 21-28, 1991): 1611-1614.

BOUCHET, GUILLAUME (1526-1606)
482. Desaivre, Léo. "Guillaume Bouchet." *Revue des traditions populaires* 23 (1908): 365-366.

BOUCIQUAUT [Jean le Meingre] (1365-1421)
483. Gaucher, E. "Les proverbes dans une biographie du XVe siècle: *Le Livre des faits de Bouciquaut.*" *Moyen Age* 99, 1 (1993): 61-81.

BOURGET, PAUL (1852-1935)
484. Brenner, Clarence D. *The French Dramatic Proverb.* Berkeley, California: Privately printed, 1977. 68 pp.

BRAAK, MENNO TER (1902-1940)
485. Lindow, Wolfgang. "Volkstümliches Sprachgut in der neuniederdeutschen Dialektdichtung." Diss. Kiel, 1960. Part I, 114-117.

BRAHMS, JOHANNES (1833-1897)
486. Bozarth, George S. "Johannes Brahms's Collection of *Deutsche Sprichworte* (German Proverbs)." *Brahms Studies.* Ed. David Brodbeck. Lincoln: University of Nebraska Press, 1994. I, 1-29.

BRAINE, JOHN (1922-1986)
487. Breitkreuz, Hartmut. "John Braine's Proverbs." *Western Folklore* 31 (1972): 130-131.

488. Taylor, Archer. "John Braine's Proverbs." *Western Folklore* 23 (1964): 42-43.

BRANDT, WILLY [Karl Herbert Frahm] (1913-1992)

489. Kühn, Peter. "Phraseologismen und ihr semantischer Mehrwert: 'Jemandem auf die Finger gucken' in einer Bundestagsrede." *Sprache und Literatur in Wissenschaft und Unterricht* 16, 56 (1985): 37-46.

BRANT, SEBASTIAN (1458-1521)

490. Eberth, Hans Henrich [*sic*]. *Die Sprichwörter in Sebastian Brants "Narrenschiff": Ein Beitrag zur deutschen Sprichwortgeschichte.* Greifswald: L. Bamberg, 1933. 110 pp.

491. Pfister, Guenter Georg. "Das Sprichwort als didaktisches Werkzeug in Sebastian Brants *Narrenschiff.*" M. A. Thesis. Michigan State University, 1965.

492. Rosenfeld, Hellmut. "Sebastian Brants *Narrenschiff* und die Tradition der Ständesatire, Narrenbilderbogen und Flugblätter des 15. Jahrhunderts." *Gutenberg-Jahrbuch* (1965): 242-248.

493. Vredeveld, Harry. "The Motto and Woodcut to Chapter 32 of Sebastian Brant's *Narrenschiff.*" *Modern Language Notes* 103, 3 (1988): 648-651.

494. Zarncke, Friedrich. "Bemalte Holzschüssel vom 15. Jahrhundert." *Anzeiger für Kunde der deutschen Vorzeit* ns 6 (1859): 413-416.

BRATHWAIT, RICHARD (1588-1673)

495. Morton, Gerald W. "An Addendum to Apperson." *Notes and Queries* 228 ns 30 (1983): 437.

BRECHT, BERTOLT (1898-1956)

496. Bänziger, Hans. "'Zuerst kommt das Fressen, dann kommt die Moral': Zu einem Motiv Bert Brechts." *Reformatio* 11 (1962): 496-503.

497. Bernath, Peter. *Die Sentenz im Drama von Kleist, Büchner und Brecht: Wesensbestimmung und Funktionswandel.* Bonn: Bouvier, 1976. Especially pp. 230-233, 244-247.

498. Goy, Eva-Maria S. "'Erst kommt das Fressen, dann kommt die Moral': A Proverbial Analysis of Bertolt Brecht's *Mutter Courage und ihre Kinder.*" M. A. Thesis. University of Vermont, 1990. 84 pp.

499. Hess, Peter. *Epigramm.* Stuttgart: Metzler, 1989. 24-25, 155-160.

500. Hess-Lüttich, Ernest W. B. "Kontrastive Phraseologie im DaF-Unterricht anhand arabischer und niederländischer Brecht-Übersetzungen." *Textproduktion und Textrezeption.* Tübingen: Gunter Narr, 1983. 25-39; rpt. in *Sprichwörter und Redensarten im interkulturellen Vergleich.* Eds. Annette Sabban and Jan Wirrer. Opladen: Westdeutscher Verlag, 1991. 109-127.

501. Hilmi, Aladin. "Zum Problem der Übersetzung von Sprichwörtern und Redensarten." *Sprache im technischen Zeitalter* No. 96 (1985): 283-285.

502. Jung, Paul. "Sprichwörter (Weisheit und Lüge)." *Sprachgebrauch, Sprachautorität, Sprachideologie.* Heidelberg: Quelle and Meyer, 1974. 99-109.

503. Kanzog, Klaus. "Spruch." *Reallexikon der deutschen Literaturgeschichte.* Eds. K. Kanzog, Achim Masser, and Dorothea Kanzog. Berlin: Walter de Gruyter, 1979. IV, 151-160.

504. Knopf, Jan. "Sprachformeln und eingreifende Sätze." *Geschichten zur Geschichte: Kritische Tradition des "Volkstümlichen" in den Kalendergeschichten Hebels und Brechts.* Stuttgart: Metzler, 1973. 186-211.

505. Mieder, Wolfgang. "Sprichwörter im moderen Sprachgebrauch." *Muttersprache* 85 (1975): 65-88. Also in *Ergebnisse der Sprichwörterforschung.* Bern: Peter Lang, 1978. 213-238; *Deutsche Sprichwörter in Literatur, Politik, Presse und Werbung.* Hamburg: Helmut Buske, 1983. 53-76.

506. Mieder, Wolfgang. "Sprichwörter unterm Hakenkreuz." *Muttersprache* 93 (1983): 1-30. Also in *Deutsche Sprichwörter in Literatur, Politik, Presse und Werbung.* Hamburg: Helmut Buske, 1983. 181-210.

507. Pohl, Rainer. "Entwertete und neugeformte Sprichwörter." *Strukturelemente und Entwicklung von Pathosformen in der Dramensprache Bertold Brechts.* Bonn: Bouvier, 1969. 24-27.

508. Rundell, Richard J. "Aphoristic Formulations in the Works of Bertolt Brecht." Diss. University of Colorado, 1971. 173 pp.

509. Schärer, Bruno. *Zitat und Zitierbarkeit: "Mutter Courage und ihre Kinder": Bertolt Brechts Theater, Sprache und Bühne.* Diss. Zürich, 1964. Zürich: Juris-Verlag, 1964. 94-102, 119 (notes).

510. Schaffner, Emil. "Spiel mit Wortfügungen und Wendungen." *Es rumpelt und stilzt im Sprach-Spülkasten*. Frauenfeld: Huber, 1982. 92-99.

511. Schmidt-Hidding, Wolfgang. "Deutsche Sprichwörter und Redewendungen." *Deutschunterricht für Ausländer* 13 (1963): 13-26.

512. Schneider, Angelika. "Verarbeitung von Zitaten und Redensarten." *Brecht-Dramen auf Russisch: Problematik der Dramenübersetzung*. Neuried: Hieronymus, 1984. 38-41, 59-72.

513. Woods, Barbara Allen. "English Sayings in Brecht's Plays: A Preliminary Study." *Proverbium* No. 6 (1966): 121-129.

514. Woods, Barbara Allen. "Perverted Proverbs in Brecht and 'Verfremdungssprache.'" *Germanic Review* 43 (1968): 100-108.

515. Woods, Barbara Allen. "The Function of Proverbs in Brecht." *Monatshefte* 61 (1969): 49-57.

516. Woods, Barbara Allen. "A Man of Two Minds." *German Quarterly* 42 (1969): 44-51.

517. Woods, Barbara Allen. "English Sayings in Brecht: An Addendum." *Proverbium* No. 15 (1970): 129-131.

518. Woods, Barbara Allen. "Unfamiliar Quotations in Brecht's Plays." *Germanic Review* 46 (1971): 26-42.

BREMER, FREDRIKA (1801-1865)
519. Pipping, Rolf. "Ordspråkstudier." *Studier i nordisk filologi* 28 (1938): 1-82.

BRENTANO, CLEMENS (1778-1842)
520. Rölleke, Heinz. "'Zeit bringt Rosen': Anmerkungen zu einem Sprichwort in Brentanos Gedicht 'Die Einsiedlerin.'" *Aurora* 37 (1977): 107-114. Also in *Nebeninschriften. "Brüder Grimm—Arnim und Brentano—Droste-Hülshoff: Literarische Studien*. Bonn: Bouvier, 1980. 106-115.

521. Rölleke, Heinz. "'Warteinweil': Zur Genealogie eines überirdischen Begriffs." *Jahrbuch des Freien Deutschen Hochstifts* (1991): 131-138.

BRENZ, JOHANNES (1498-1570)

522. Danner, Berthilde. "Dem Volk aufs Maul geschaut: Gleichnisse, Redensarten und Sprichwörter im Salomokommentar des Johannes Brenz." *Festschrift für Gerd Wunder*. Editor unknown. Schwäbisch Hall: Historischer Verein für Württembergisch Franken, 1974. 167-199.

BRETON, NICHOLAS (c. 1545-c. 1626)

523. Collier, John Payne. "Nicholas Breton's *Crossing of Proverbs*." *Notes and Queries* 1st ser. 1 (1849/50): 364.

524. Robertson, Jean. "Nicholas Breton's Collection of Proverbs." *Huntington Literary Quarterly* 7 (1944): 307-315.

BRIE, ANDRÉ (1950—)

525. Mieder, Wolfgang. "'Eigener Unruheherd ist Goldes wert': Zu den sprichwörtlichen Aphorismen von André Brie." *Sprachpflege und Sprachkultur* 40 (1991): 8-11. Also in *Sprichwörtliches und Geflügeltes: Sprachstudien von Martin Luther bis Karl Marx*. Bochum: Norbert Brockmeyer, 1995. 103-110.

BRINCKMAN, JOHN (1814-1870)

526. Neumann, Siegfried. "John Brinckman und das mecklenburgische Sprichwort." *Wissenschaftliche Zeitschrift das Pädagogischen Instituts Güstrow* 2 (1963-1964): 23-24. Also in *Festschrift zum 150. Geburtstag von John Brinckman*. Ed. Hans-Jürgen Klug. Güstrow: Stad Güstrow, 1964. 21-25.

527. Neumann, Siegfried. "Das Sagwort in Mecklenburg um die Mitte des 19. Jahrhunderts im Spiegel der Mundartdichtungen Reuters und Brinckmans." *Deutsches Jahrbuch für Volkskunde* 12 (1966): 50-66.

528. Römer, A. "Eine Sammlung plattdeutscher Sprichwörter und Kernsprüche nebst Erzählungsbruchstücken von John Brinckman." *Jahrbuch des Vereins für niederdeutsche Sprachforschung* 31 (1905): 20-35.

BRONTË, CHARLOTTE (1816-1855)

529. Shvydkaia, L. I. "Sinonimicheskie otnosheniia poslovits i aforizmov v angliiskom iazyke." *Leksikologicheskie osnovy stilistiki (Sbornik nauchnykh trudov)*. Ed. I. V. Arnol'd. Leningrad: Gosudarstvennyi pedagogicheskii institut im. A. I. Gertsena, 1973. 167-175.

BROUGHTON, RHODA (1840-1920)

530. Shvydkaia, L. I. "Sinonimicheskie otnosheniia poslovits i aforizmov v angliiskom iazyke." *Leksikologicheskie osnovy stilistiki (Sbornik nauchnykh trudov).* Ed. I. V. Arnol'd. Leningrad: Gosudarstvennyi pedagogicheskii institut im. A. I. Gertsena, 1973. 167-175.

BROWN, LEW (1893-1958)

531. Mieder, Wolfgang. "Proverbs in American Popular Songs." *Proverbium: Yearbook of International Proverb Scholarship* 5 (1988): 85-101.

BROWNING, ROBERT (1812-1889)

532. Mieder, Wolfgang. "'To Pay the Piper' and the Legend of 'The Pied Piper of Hamelin.'" *Proverbium: Yearbook of International Proverb Scholarship* 2 (1985): 263-270.

533. Smith, Cornelia Marshall. "Proverb Lore in *The Ring and the Book.*" *Publications of the Modern Language Association* 56 (1941): 219-229.

534. Smith, Cornelia Marshall. *Browning's Proverb Lore.* Waco, Texas: Baylor University, 1989. 124 pp.

BRUEYS, DAVID AUGUSTIN (1640-1723)

535. Sébillot, Paul. "Brueys." *Revue des traditions populaires* 11 (1896): 33-34.

BRUNE, JOHAN DE (1588-1658)

536. Brune, J. D. "Oud goud: Uit banketwerk van Mr. Johan de Brune." *Leesmuseum* 4, 7 (1859): 57-60, 128.

537. Meertens, Pieter Jacobus. "Proverbs and Emblem Literature." *Proverbium* No. 15 (1970): 498-499.

538. Schilling, Michael. "Die literarischen Vorbilder der Ludwigsburger und Gaarzer Embleme." *Außerliterarische Wirkungen barocker Emblembücher: Emblematik in Ludwigsburg, Gaarz und Pommersfelden.* Eds. Wolfgang Harms and Hartmut Freytag. München: Wilhelm Fink, 1975. 41-71.

539. Selig, Karl-Ludwig. "Los proverbios españoles en el Banket-Werk de Johan de Brune." *Beiträge zur französischen Aufklärung und zur spanischen Literatur: Festgabe für Werner Krauss zum 70. Geburtstag.* Ed. Werner Bahner. Berlin [East]: Akademie-Verlag, 1971. 591-613.

BRUNFELS, OTTO (1488-1543)

540. Weigelt, Sylvia. "Predigt als Flugschrift—untersucht am Beispiel der Zehntenschrift von Otto Brunfels." *Wissenschaftliche Zeitschrift der Friedrich Schiller Universität Jena*, Gesellschaftswissenschaftliche Reihe, Sprachwissenschaftliche Beiträge 34, 1 (1985): 91-96.

BUDAI-DELEANU, ION (1760-1820)

541. Negreanu, Constantin. "Valentele educative si stilistice ale expresiilor si proverbelor în limba literaturii artistice." *Scoala Mehedintiului* 3 (1978): 23-26.

BÜCHNER, GEORG (1813-1837)

542. Bernath, Peter. *Die Sentenz im Drama von Kleist, Büchner und Brecht: Wesensbestimmung und Funktionswandel*. Bonn: Bouvier, 1976. Especially pp. 230-233, 244-247.

543. Hölter, Achim. "'Blau pfeifen'—Rätsel um eine Redensart bei Büchner und Grimm." *Proverbium: Yearbook of International Proverb Scholarship* 9 (1992): 67-80.

544. Scheichl, Sigurd Paul. "Feste Syntagmen im dramatischen Dialog: Materialien zur Geschichte eines Stilmittels zwischen Goethe und Kroetz." *Tradition und Entwicklung: Festschrift Eugen Thurnher*. Eds. Werner Bauer, Achim Masser, and Guntram Plangg. Innsbruck: Institut für Germanistik der Universität Innsbruck, 1982. 383-407.

THE BUGBEARS (1564-1565)

545. Whiting, Bartlett Jere. "*The Bugbears*." *Proverbs in the Earlier English Drama*. Cambridge, Massachusetts: Harvard University Press, 1938; rpt. New York: Octagon Books, 1969. 218-224.

THE BUIK OF ALEXANDER (c. 1300)

546. Whiting, Bartlett Jere. "Proverbs in Certain Middle English Romances in Relation to Their French Sources." *Harvard Studies and Notes in Philology and Literature*, 15 (1933): 75-126, especially 85-93.

BUNYAN, JOHN (1628-1688)

547. Lansverk, Marvin Duane. "The Wisdom of Many, the Vision of One: The Proverbs of William Blake." Diss. University of Washington, 1988. 40-65.

548.   Walton, George William. "The Function of Proverbs in Certain Works by John Bunyan," 2 vols. Diss. Texas Technological University, 1976. 507 pp.

BURNS, ROBERT (1759-1796)

549.   Burns, D. A. "A Potpourri of Parasites in Poetry and Proverbs." *British Medical Journal* 303 (December 21-28, 1991): 1611-1614.

BURTON, Sir RICHARD FRANCIS (1821-1890)

550.   Taylor, Archer. "'Feed a Cold and Starve a Fever.'" *Journal of American Folklore* 71 (1958): 190.

BUSCH, WILHELM (1832-1908)

551.   Balzer, Hans. *Buschs Wesen und Werk im Spiegel seiner Spruchweisheit.* Leipzig: E. Weibezahl, 1941. 223 pp.

552.   Riha, Karl. "Balla Balla, Balla Basta: Zur Poetik kleiner literarischer Formen." *Akzente* 21 (1974): 265-287.

BYRON, GEORGE GORDON, 6th Baron (1788-1824)

553.   Sawyer, Frederick E. "Scottish Proverbs in *Don Juan.*" *Notes and Queries* 7th ser. 4 (1887): 293.

C

CABALLERO, FERNÁN [Cecilia Francisca Josefa de Arrom] (1796-1877)

554. Altura, Yvonne. "Proverbs in Fernán Caballero's *Cuadros de costumbres*." M. A. Thesis. Washington University, 1953. 38 pp.

CABALLERO CIFAR (1512)

555. Gella Iturriaga, José. "Los proverbios del *Caballero Cifar*." *Homenaje a Julio Caro Baroja*. Eds. Antonio Carreira, Jesús Antonio Cid, Manuel Guttiérez Esteve, and Rogelio Rubio. Madrid: Centro de Investigaciones Sociologicas, 1978. 449-469.

CABRERA, ALONSO DE (1546-1598)

556. Ramirez, Alejandro. "Los *Adagia* de Erasmo en los sermones de Fr. Alonso de Cabrera." *Hispano* 11 (1961): 29-38.

CABRERA INFANTE, GUILLERMO (1929—)

557. Fernandez, Roberto. "El refranero en *T. T. T. [Tres tristes tigres]*." *Revista iberoamericana* 57, 154 (1991): 265-272.

CAESAR, JULIUS [Gaius Julius Caesar] (100-44 B. C.)

558. Deutsch, Monroe E. "'Veni, Vidi, Vici.'" *Philological Quarterly* 4 (1925): 151-156.

559. Mieder, Wolfgang. "'Veni, Vidi, Vici': Zum heutigen Leben eines klassischen Zitats." *Sprachpflege und Sprachkultur* 40 (1991): 97-102. Also in *Sprichwörtliches und Geflügeltes: Sprachstudien von Martin Luther bis Karl Marx*. Bochum: Norbert Brockmeyer, 1995. 111-124.

CALDERÓN DE LA BARCA, PEDRO (1600-1681)

560. Canavaggio, Jean. "Calderón entre refranero y comedia: De refrán a enredo." *Aureum Saeculum Hispanum: Beiträge zu Texten des Siglo de Oro: Festschrift für Hans Flasche*. Eds. Karl-Hermann Korner and Dietrich Briesemeister. Wiesbaden: Steiner, 1983. 27-36. Also in *Calderón: Actas del Congreso internacional sobre Calderón y el teatro español del Siglo de Oro*. Ed. Luciano Garcia Lorenzo. Madrid: Consejo Superior de Investigaciones Cientificas, 1983. I, 381-392.

561. Gates, Eunice Joiner. "Proverbs in the Plays of Calderón." *Romanic Review* 38 (1947): 203-215.

562. Gates, Eunice Joiner. "A Tentative List of the Proverbs and Proverb Allusions in the Plays of Calderón." *Publications of the Modern Language Association of America* 64 (1949): 1027-1048.

563. Hayes, Francis Clement. "The Use of Proverbs in the 'Siglo de Oro' Drama: An Introductory Study." Diss. University of North Carolina, 1936. 117-154.

564. Hayes, Francis Clement. "The Use of Proverbs as Titles and Motives in the 'Siglo de Oro' Drama: Calderón." *Hispanic Review* 15 (1947): 453-463.

565. Soufas, Teresa S. "Calderón's Charlatan of Honor: 'Refranero' Wisdom and Its Condemnation of Gutierre." *Bulletin of the Comediantes* 38 (1986): 165-176.

CALISTO AND MELIBEA (c. 1530)

566. Castells, Ricardo. "Los refranes y la problemática autoria de la *Comedia de Calisto y Melibea.*" *Celestinesca* 16, 1 (1992): 15-23.

CALVO-SOTELO, JOAQUIN (1905—)

567. Sevilla Muñoz, Julia. "Joaquin Calvo-Sotelo y los refranes." *Paremia* No. 1 (1993): 7-9.

CAMDEN, WILLIAM (1551-1623)

568. Dunn, Robert D. "English Proverbs from William Camden's *Remains Concerning Britain.*" *The Huntington Library Quarterly* 49 (1986): 271-275.

CAMERARIUS, JOACHIM (1534-1598)

569. Dittrich, Lothar. "Emblematische Weisheit und naturwissenschaftliche Realität." *Die Sprache der Bilder: Realität und Bedeutung in der niederländischen Malerei des 17. Jahrhunderts.* Eds. Wolfgang J. Müller, Konrad Renger, and Rüdiger Klessmann. Braunschweig: ACO Druck, 1978. 21-33. Also in *Jarbuch für Internationale Germanistik* 13 (1981): 36-60.

570. Schilling, Michael. "Die literarischen Vorbilder der Ludwigsburger und Gaarzer Embleme." *Außerliterarische Wirkungen barocker Emblembücher: Emblematik in Ludwigsburg, Gaarz und Pommersfelden.* Eds. Wolfgang Harms and Hartmut Freytag. München: Wilhelm Fink, 1975. 41-71.

CAMOËNS, LUIS VAZ de (1524-1580)

571. Caseudo, Luis. "Folclore nos autos camoneanos." *Revista de Etnografia* 16 (1972): 17-29.

CANETTI, ELIAS (1905-1994)

572. Beckmann, Susanne, and Peter-Paul König. "'Ich zähle bis drei. . .'—'Zählen kann jeder': Überlegungen zur pragmatischen Funktion von Phraseologismen am Beispiel einiger Dialogsequenzen aus Elias Canettis Roman *Die Blendung*." *Dialoganalyse III: Referate der 3. Arbeitstagung, Bologna 1990*. Eds. Sorin Stati, Edda Weigand, and Franz Hundsnurscher. Tübingen: Max Niemeyer, 1991. II, 263-273.

573. Fricke, Harald. *Aphorismus*. Stuttgart: Metzler, 1984. 32-33, 60-61, 132-139, 153-155.

574. Higi-Wydler, Melanie. *Zur Übersetzung von Idiomen: Eine Beschreibung und Klassifizierung deutscher Idiome und ihrer französischen Übersetzungen*. Bern: Peter Lang, 1989. 335 pp.

575. Mieder, Wolfgang. "'Die falschesten Redensarten haben den größten Reiz': Zu Elias Canettis Sprachaphorismen." *Der Sprachdienst* 38, 6 (1994): 173-180. Also in *Sprichwörtliches und Geflügeltes: Sprachstudien von Martin Luther bis Karl Marx*. Bochum: Norbert Brockmeyer, 1995. 175-186.

CANTEMIR, DIMITRIE (1673-1723)

576. Negreanu, Constantin. "Valentele educative si stilistice ale expresiilor si proverbelor în limba literaturii artistice." *Scoala Mehedintiului* 3 (1978): 23-26.

CARMONTELLE, LOUIS [Louis Carrogis] (1717-1806)

577. Brahmer, Miecyzslaw. "Le vicende del proverbio dramatico." *XIV. Congresso internazionale di linguistica e filologia romanza*. Ed. Alberto Várvaro. Naples: Macchiaroli, 1981. V, 509-511.

578. Brenner, Clarence D. *Le développement du proverbe dramatique en France et sa vogue au XVIIIe siècle*. Berkeley: University of California Press, 1937. 12-18.

579. Brenner, Clarence D. *The French Dramatic Proverb*. Berkeley, California: Privately printed, 1977. 68 pp.

580. Hermann, Michael. *Das Gesellschaftstheater des Louis Carrogis de Carmontelle.* Meisenheim am Glan: Hain, 1968. 175 pp.

581. Holz, Karl. "Mussets frühe 'Proverbe'-Dichtung (1834-1836): Zum Wandel einer Gattung." *Zeitschrift für französische Sprache und Literatur* 85 (1975): 128-144.

582. Le Roux de Lincy, M. *Le Livre des Proverbes Français*, 2 vols. 2nd ed. Paris: A. Delahays, 1859; rpt. Genève: Slatkine, 1968. I, lxxix-lxxxii.

583. Masson, Alain. "Eric Rohmer: Le Capricorne souverain de l'onde occidentale sur les *Comédies et proverbes.*" *Positif* No. 307 (1986): 43-45.

584. Méry, M. C. de. *Proverbes dramatiques de Carmontelle, précédés de sa vie, d'une dissertation historique et morale sur les proverbes*, 4 vols. Paris: Delongchamps, 1822.

585. Shaw, Marjorie. "Les proverbes dramatiques de Carmontelle, Leclercq et Alfred de Musset." *Revue des sciences humaines* (1959): 56-76.

586. Urschlechter, Hans. "Die vornehme französische Frau des XVIII. Jahrhunderts nach den *Proverbes dramatiques* Carmontelle's [sic]." *Zeitschrift für französische Sprache und Literatur* 37 (1911): 1-82.

587. Werner, Richard. *Geschichte der "Proverbes dramatiques."* Berlin: R. Gaertner, 1887. 3-24.

CARPENTIER Y VALMONT, ALEJO (1904-1980)
588. Zuluaga O. [sic], Alberto. "Empleo de locuciones y refranes en *La consagración de la primavera*, de Alejo Carpentier." *Aspekte der Hispania im 19. und 20. Jahrhundert: Akten des Deutschen Hispanistentages 1983*. Ed. Dieter Kremer. Hamburg: Helmut Buske, 1983. 97-112.

CARTER, ANGELA (1940-1992)
589. Haase, Donald P. "Is Seeing Believing? Proverbs and the Film Adaptation of a Fairy Tale." *Proverbium: Yearbook of International Proverb Scholarship* 7 (1990): 89-104.

CARY, ALICE (1820-1871)
590. Mieder, Wolfgang. "The Proverb in the Modern Age: Old Wisdom in New Clothing." *Tradition and Innovation in Folk Literature.* Hanover, New Hampshire: University Press of New England, 1987. 118-156, 248-255 (notes).

CASSILL, RONALD VERLIN (1919—)
591. Monteiro, George. "Derisive Adjectives: Two Notes and a List." *Western Folklore* 34 (1975): 244-246.

CASTELLAIN, GEORGE (c. 1405-1475)
592. Heft, David. *Proverbs and Sentences in Fifteenth Century French Poetry.* Diss. New York University, 1941. Chapter 2. New York: Washington Square Press, 1942 (abridged to 12 pp.).

CASTELLANOS, Don JOAN DE (1522-1607)
593. Romero, Mario German. "Aspecto literarios de la orba de don Joan de Castellanos: Refranes y frases proverbiales." *Boletin Cultural y Bibliográfico* 10 (1967): 100-105.

THE CASTLE OF PERSEVERANCE (c. 1425)
594. Whiting, Bartlett Jere. "*The Castle of Perseverance.*" *Proverbs in the Earlier English Drama.* Cambridge, Massachusetts: Harvard University Press, 1938; rpt. New York: Octagon Books, 1969. 68-72.

CASTRO, GUILLEN DE (1569-1631)
595. Hayes, Francis Clement. "The Use Proverbs in the 'Siglo de Oro' Drama: An Introductory Study." Diss. University of North Carolina, 1936. 75-88.

CATS, JACOB (1577-1660)
596. Meertens, Pieter Jacobus. "Proverbs and Emblem Literature." *Proverbium* No. 15 (1970): 498-499.

597. Ozenfant, E. "Les proverbes de Jacob Cats." *La Tradition* 6 (1892): 33-38, 86-88, 186-190, 335-339; 7 (1893): 24-26, 101-104, 147-149, 211-215, 275-280; 8 (1894): 37-41, 71-77, 214-222.

598. Schilling, Michael. "Die literarischen Vorbilder der Ludwigsburger und Gaarzer Embleme." *Außerliterarische Wirkungen barocker Emblembücher: Emblematik in Ludwigsburg, Gaarz und Pommersfelden.* Eds.

Wolfgang Harms and Hartmut Freytag. München: Wilhelm Fink, 1975. 41-71.

599.   Sleeckx. "Jacob Cats en zijn invloed op Zuid-Nederland (Spreekwoord: elk meent zijn uil een valk te zijn)." *Jaarboek van het Willems-Fond* 6 (1874): 138-162.

600.   Vinken, P. J. "Some Observations on the Symbolism of 'The Broken Pot' in Art and Literature." *American Imago* 15 (1958): 149-174.

CAVASSICO, BARTOLOMEO (1480-1555)

601.   Zanenga, Bartolomeo. "Proverbi e detti popolari nel dialetto Bellunese del cinquecento." *Archivio Storico di Belluno Feltre e Cadore* 42 (1971): 52-65.

CAZOTTE, JACQUES (1628-1703)

602.   Hudde, Hinrich. "'Conte à dormir debout': Eine Redensart als Bezeichnung für parodistische Märchen des 18. Jahrhunderts." *Romanische Forschungen* 97, 1 (1985): 15-35.

ČELAKOVSKY, FRANTIŠEK (1799-1832)

603.   Mukařovský, Jan. "Přislovi jako součást kontextu." *Cestami poetiky a estetiky*. Praha: Edice Dilna, 1971. 277-359.

LA CELESTINA (c. 1499)

604.   Barrick, Mac E. "El 446. refran de *Celestina*." *Celestinesca: Boletin Informativo Internacional* 7, 2 (1983), 13-15.

605.   Behiels, Lieve. "¿Como se tradujeron los proverbios de *La Celestina* en neerlandés y alemán?" *Paremia* No. 2 (1993): 189-194.

606.   Cantalapiedra, Fernando. "Los refranes en *Celestina* y el problema de su autoria." *Celestinesca: Boletin Informativo Internacional* 8, 1 (1984): 49-53.

607.   Castillo de Lucas, Antonio. "Refranes de interès médico en *La Celestina*." *Actas do Congresso Internacional de Etnografia, promovido pela Câmara Municipal de Santo Tirso de 10 a 18 de Julho de 1963*. Lisboa: Imprensa Portuguesa, 1965. III, 147-1966.

608.   Chevalier, Jean-Claude. "Proverbes et traduction (La traduction italienne de la *Célestine*, par Alphonso Hordoñez, Rome, 1506)." *Bulletin Hispanique* 90, 1-2 (1988): 59-89.

609.   Dubno, Barbara Riss, and John K. Walsh. "Pero Diaz de Toledo's *Proverbios de Seneca* and the Composition of *Celestina*, Act IV." *Celestinesca* 11, 1 (1987): 3-12.

610.   Ernouf, Anita Bonilla. "Proverbs and Proverbial Phrases in the *Celestina*." Diss. Columbia University, 1970. 743 pp.

611.   Gella Iturriaga, José. "444 refranes de *La Celestina*." *La Celestina y su contorno social*. Ed. Manuel Criado de Val. Barcelona: Borrás, 1977. 245-268.

612.   Hernandez, José Luis Alonso. "Interprétation psychoanalytique de l'utilisation des parémies dans la littérature espagnole." *Richesse du proverbe*. Eds. François Suard and Claude Buridant. Lille: Université de Lille, 1984. II, 213-225.

613.   Martin-Aragón, Julián. "Vocabulario popular de *La Puebla de Montalbán*." *La Celestina y su contorno social: Actas del I Congresso Internacional sobre La Celestina*. Ed. Manuel Criado de Val. Barcelona: Borrás, 1977. 269-271.

614.   O'Donnell, Kathleen Palatucci. "Sentencias and Refranes in *La Celestina*: A Compilation, Analysis, and Examination of Their Function." Diss. University of California at Los Angeles, 1993. 322 pp.

615.   Shipley, George A. "El natural de la raposa: Un proverbio estratégico de *La Celestina*." *Nueva Revista de Filologia Hispanica* 23 (1974): 35-64.

616.   Shipley, George A. "Usos y abusos de la autoridad del refrán en *La Celestina*." *La Celestina y su contorno social: Actas del I Congreso Internacional sobre La Celestina*. Ed. Manuel Criado de Val. Barcelona: Borrás, 1977. 231-244.

CERVANTES SAAVEDRA, MIGUEL de (1547-1616)

617.   Arco, López del. *Refranes de Sancho Panza: Aventuras desventuras, malicias y agudezas del eseudero de Don Quijote*. Madrid: López del Arco, 1905. 132 pp.

618. Aulnaye, Ed. "Proverbes et sentences tirés de l'Histoire de Don Quixote." *L'Ingénieux Chevalier Don Quixote de la Manche.* Paris: Desoer, 1821. IV, 401-440.

619. Axnick, Margarete. "Probleme der deutschen Sprichwortübersetzungen aus Miguel de Cervantes' *Don Quijote*—eine vergleichende sprachliche und literarische Untersuchung." M. A. Thesis. University of Bonn, 1984. 139 pp.

620. Baird-Smith, David. "One Shrewd Wife in All the World." *Moreana: Bulletin Thomas More* 21, 83-84 (1984): 93-94.

621. Burke, Ulick Ralph. *Sancho Panza's Proverbs, and Others Which Occur in Don Quixote: With a Literal English Translation, Notes, and an Introduction.* London: Pickering, 1872, 1892. 116 pp.

622. Burke, Ulick Ralph. *Spanish Salt: A Collection of All the Proverbs Which Are to Be Found in Don Quixote.* London: Pickering, 1877. 99 pp.

623. Cárzer y de Sobies, Enrique de. *Las frases del "Quijote": Su exposición, ordenación y commentarios, y su versión a las lenguas francesca, portuguesa, italiana, catalana, inglesa y alemanna.* Lerida: Artes Gráficas de Sol y Benet, 1916. 660 pp.

624. Coll y Vehí, José. "Máximas y refranes del Quijote entresacados y compilados." *Revista Popular* 3 (1873): 115-117, 131, 147, 207-208, 231-232, 245-246.

625. Coll y Vehí, José. *Los refranes del Quijote, ordenados por materias y glosados.* Barcelona: Diario de Barcelona, 1874. 248 pp.

626. Colombi, Maria Cecilia. "Los refranes en *Don Quijote.*" Diss. University of California at Santa Barbara, 1988. 236 pp.; published as *Los refranes en el Quijote: texto y contexto.* Potomac, Maryland: Scripta Humanistica, 1989. 142 pp.

627. Colombi, Maria Cecilia. "'Al buen callar llaman Sancho.'" *Speculum historiographiae linguisticae.* Ed. Klaus D. Dutz. Münster: Modus Publikationen, 1989. 243-252.

628. Colombi, Maria Cecilia. "Los refranes en el Quijote: Discurso autoritario y des-autoritario." *Proverbium: Yearbook of International Proverb Scholarship* 7 (1991): 37-55.

629. Diaz Isaacs, Gloria. "Los Refranes del Quijote." *Loteria* (Panama) No. 220 (1974): 20-38.

630. Garci-Gómez, Miguel. "La tradición del león reverente: Glosas para los episodios en *Mio Cid, Palmerin de Oliva, Don Quijote* y otras." *Kentucky Romance Quarterly* 19 (1972): 255-284.

631. Hansen, Terrence L. "Folk Narrative Motifs, Beliefs and Proverbs in Cervantes' Exemplary Novels." *Journal of American Folklore* 72 (1959): 24-29.

632. Hernandez, José Luis Alonso. "Interprétation psychoanalytique de l'utilisation des parémies dans la littérature espagnole." *Richesse du proverbe.* Eds. François Suard and Claude Buridant. Lille: Université de Lille, 1984. II, 213-225.

633. Hess-Lüttich, Ernest W. B. "Sprichwörter und Redensarten als Übersetzungsproblem: Am Beispiel deutscher Übersetzungen spanischer und türkischer Literatur." *Mehrsprachigkeit und Gesellschaft: Akten des 17. Linguistischen Kolloquiums Brüssel 1982.* Eds. René Jongen, Sabine De Knop, Peter H. Nelde, and Marie-Paule Quix. Tübingen: Max Niemeyer, 1983. II, 222-236.

634. Joly, Monique. "Aspectos del refrán en Mateo Alemán y Cervantes." *Nueva Revista de Filologia Hispánica* 20 (1971): 95-106.

635. Joly, Monique. "Le discours métaparémique dans *Don Quichotte*." *Richesse du proverbe.* Eds. François Suard and Claude Buridant. Lille: Université de Lille, 1984. II, 245-260.

636. Jullien, Auguste. *Le véritable Sancho Panza: ou, Choix de proverbes, dictons, adages, colligés pour l'agrément de son neveu E. L.* Paris: Librairie Hachette, 1856. 240 pp.

637. Krauss, Werner. *Die Welt im spanischen Sprichwort.* Wiesbaden: Limes, 1946. 3rd ed. Leipzig: Reclam, 1975. 117 pp.

638.   Krauss, Werner. "Die Welt im spanischen Sprichwort." *Studien und Aufsätze*. Berlin: Rütten and Loening, 1959. 73-91.

639.   Lacosta, Francisco. "El infinito mundo de los proverbios: *Don Quijote*." *Universidad* (Santa Fé) 65 (1965): 135-151.

640.   Lucas, Castillo de. "Aphorisms of Cervantes." *El siglo médico* 115 (May 10, 1947): 577-582.

641.   Morel-Fatio, Alfred. "Al buen callar llaman sancho." *Romania* 11 (1882): 114-119.

642.   O'Kane, Eleanor. "The Proverb: Rabelais and Cervantes." *Comparative Literature* 2 (1950): 360-369.

643.   *Pensamientos, sentencias, consejos y refranes, de Miguel de Cervantes Saavedra*. Madrid: Biblioteca Enciclopédica Mundial, 1932. 122 pp.

644.   Rockwood, Stanley Walker. "The Proverbs in the *Novelas Ejemplares* of Cervantes." M. A. Thesis. University of Chicago, 1920. 18 pp.

645.   Rodríguez Marín, Francisco, and Louis Montoto y Rautenstrauch. *Discursos leídos ante la Real Academia Sevillana de Buenas Letras el 8 dicembre de 1895*. Sevilla: E. Rasco, 1895. 99 pp.

646.   Sbarbi, José M. "Colección de los refranes, adagios, proverbios y frases proverbiales que se hallan en el Quijote." *El Refranero General Espanol*, 10 vols. Madrid: Fuentenebro, 1874-78. VI, 198-291.

647.   *Sentencias de Don Quijote y agudezas de Sancho*. Madrid: Moya y Plaza, 1863. 88 pp.

648.   Sune Benages, Juan. *Fraseologia de Cervantes: Colección de frases, refranes, proverbios, aforismos, adagios, expressiones y modos adverbiales que se leen en las obras cervantinas, recopilados y ordenados*. Barcelona: Editorial Lux, 1929. 323 pp.

649.   Tarán, Leonardo. "'Amicus Plato sed magis amica veritas': From Plato and Aristotle to Cervantes." *Antike und Abendland* 30 (1984): 93-124.

650. Thompson, Emma, trans. and comp. *Wit and Wisdom of Don Quixote.* New York: D. Appleton and Company, 1867, 1882. 161 pp., 288 pp.; Boston: Roberts Brothers, 1882. 288 pp.

651. Vidal y Valenciano, Cayetano. *El entremés de refranes les de Cervantes? Ensayo de sa traducción al catalán: Estudio critico-literario.* Barcelona: Bastinos, 1883. 78 pp.

652. Vrtunski, Dushko. "O prevodenju poslovitsa u Servantesovom Don Kikhotu." *Mostovi* 16, 63 (1985): 225-228.

653. Woodward, Katherine Burchell. "Proverbs in *Don Quixote.*" M. A. Thesis. Stanford University, 1930. 44 pp.

CHAMFORT, SÉBASTIAN (1741-1794)
654. Fink, Arthur-Hermann. *Maxime und Fragment: Grenzmöglichkeiten einer Kunstform: Zur Morphologie des Aphorismus.* München: Max Huber, 1934. 115 pp.

CHANSON DE ROLAND (12th cent.)
655. Taylor, Archer. "'All Is not Gold That Glitters' and *Rolandslied,* 1956." *Romance Philology* 11 (1958): 370-371.

CHAPELLE, CLAUDE (1626-1686)
656. Sébillot, Paul. "Chapelle et Bachaumont." *Revue des traditions populaires,* 11 (1896): 34.

CHARLES D'ORLÉANS (1394-1465)
657. Arn, Mary-Jo. "Charles of Orleans and the Poems of B[ritish] L[ibrary] MS, Harley 682." *English Studies* 74, 3 (1993): 222-235.

658. Céard, Jean, and Jean-Claude Margolin. "Rébus et proverbes." *Rébus de la renaissance: Des images qui parlent.* Paris: Maisonneuve et Larose, 1986. I, 135-162.

659. Heft, David. *Proverbs and Sentences in Fifteenth Century French Poetry.* Diss. New York University, 1941. Chapter 2. New York: Washington Square Press, 1942 (abridged to 12 pp.).

660. Le Roux de Lincy, M. *Le Livre des Proverbes Français,* 2 vols. 2nd ed. Paris: A. Delahays, 1859; rpt. Genève: Slatkine, 1968. I, lv.

661.   Pinkernell, Gert. "Une réplique haineuse à la *Ballade des proverbes*, de François Villon, émanant du cercle de Charles d'Orléans." *Archiv für das Studium der neueren Sprachen und Literaturen* 224 (1987): 110-116.

ELISABETH CHARLOTTE VON ORLEANS (1652-1722)

662.   Bodemann, Eduard, ed. *Aus den Briefen der Elisabeth Charlotte von Orleans an die Kurfürstin Sophie von Hannover*, 2 vols. Hannover: Hahn, 1891. 439 pp., 412 pp. (References to individual proverbs appear in the index.)

663.   Bodemann, Eduard, ed. *Briefe der Herzogin Elisabeth Charlotte und A. K. von Harling*. Hannover: Hahn, 1895. 234 pp. (References to individual proverbs appear in the index.)

664.   Bolte, Johannes. "Aus den Briefen der Herzogin Elisabeth Charlotte von Orleans." *Alemannia* 15 (1887): 50-62, especially 56-61.

665.   Holland, Wilhelm Ludwig, ed. *Briefe der Herzogin Elisabeth Charlotte von Orleans*, 6 vols. (Publikationen des literarischen Vereins in Stuttgart, vols. 88, 107, 122, 132, 144, 157.) Stuttgart: Bibliothek des literarischen Vereins, 1867-1881. (References to individual proverbs appear in the index.)

666.   Seiler, Friedrich. *Deutsche Sprichwörterkunde*. München: C. H. Beck, 1922, 1967. 61.

667.   Urbach, A. "Über die Sprache in den deutschen Briefen der Herzogin Elisabeth Charlotte von Orleans." Diss. Greifswald, 1899. 26-28.

CHARTIER, ALAIN (c. 1385-c. 1430)

668.   Heft, David. *Proverbs and Sentences in Fifteenth Century French Poetry*. Diss. New York University, 1941. Chapter 2. New York: Washington Square Press, 1942 (abridged to 12 pp.).

CHASTELLAIN, GEORGE (1404/05-1475)

669.   Heft, David. *Proverbs and Sentences in Fifteenth Century French Poetry*. Diss. New York University, 1941. Chapter 2. New York: Washington Square Press, 1942 (abridged to 12 pp.).

CHATEAUBRIAND, FRANÇOIS RENÉ, Vicomte de (1768-1848)

670.   Sébillot, Paul. "Les traditions populaires dans les mémoires d'outre-tombe." *Revue des traditions populaires* 11 (1896): 372-379, 562-566.

CHAUCER, GEOFFREY (c. 1340-1400)

671. Andrae, A. "Noch einmal Chaucer's [*sic*] Sprichwörter." *Beiblatt zur Anglia* 3 (1893): 276-282.

672. Andrae, A. "Sprichwörtliches bei Chaucer." *Beiblatt zur Anglia* 4 (1894): 330-341.

673. Andrew, Malcolm. "January's Knife: Sexual Morality and Proverbial Wisdom in the *Merchant's Tale.*" *English Language Notes* 16 (1979): 273-277.

674. Bowden, Betsy. "Fluctuating Proverbs in Three Eighteenth Century Modernizations of Chaucer's *Miller's Tale.*" *Proverbium: Yearbook of International Proverb Scholarship* 9 (1992): 11-29.

675. Bowers, R. H. "Impingham's Borrowings from Chaucer." *Modern Language Notes* 73 (1958): 327-329.

676. Brosnahan, Leger. "Now (This), Now (That) and BD 646." *Harvard English Studies* 5 (1974): 11-18 (= *The Learned and the Lewd: Studies in Chaucer and Medieval Literature.* Ed. Larry D. Benson. Cambridge, Massachusetts: Harvard University Press, 1974. 11-18.

677. Brown, Calvin S., and Robert H. West. "As by the Whelp Chastised Is the Leon." *Modern Language Notes* 55 (1940): 209-210.

678. C., M. A. "The Proverbs of Chaucer, with Illustrations from Other Sources." *Scottish Notes and Queries* 6 (1893): 51-52, 69-70, 81-83, 113-115, 147-149, 178-180.

679. Davis, Norman. "Chaucer's *Gentilesse*: A Forgotten Manuscript with Some Proverbs." *Review of English Studies* 20 (1969): 43-50.

680. Dunbar, Leila Lusila. "Chaucer's Use of Proverbs." M. A. Thesis. Indiana University, 1933. 211 pp.

681. Faulkner, Esther. "An Index of Chaucer's Proverbs and Proverbial Phrases." M. A. Thesis. Stetson University, 1940. 242 pp.

682. Fleavy, Frederick Gard. "Some Folklore from Chaucer." *Folk-Lore Record* 2 (1879): 136-142.

683. Gillmeister, Heiner. "Chaucer's 'Kan Ke Dort' (*Troilus*, II, 1752), and the 'Sleeping Dogs' of the Trouvères." *English Studies* 59 (1978): 310-323.

684. Grauls, Jan, and Jan F. Vanderheijden. "Two Flemish Proverbs in Chaucer's *Canterbury Tales*." *Revue Belge de Philologie et d'Histoire* 13 (1934): 745-749.

685. Haeckel, Willibald. *Das Sprichwort bei Chaucer: Zugleich ein Beitrag zur vergleichenden Sprichwörterkunde.* Erlangen: A. Deichert, 1890. 77 pp.

686. Hall, Ann C. "Educating Reader: Chaucer's Use of Proverbs in *Troilus and Criseyde*." *Proverbium: Yearbook of International Proverb Scholarship* 3 (1986): 47-58.

687. Hendrickson, Rhoda Miller Martin. "Chaucer's Proverbs: Of Medicyne and of Compleynte." Diss. Emory University, 1980. 281 pp.

688. Holloway, Julia Bolton. "'The Asse to the Harpe': Boethian Music in Chaucer." *Boethius and the Liberal Arts: A Collection of Essays.* Ed. Michael Masi. Bern: Peter Lang, 1981. 175-188.

689. Kittredge, George L. "Chauceriana." *Modern Philology* 7 (1910): 465-483, especially 478-479.

690. Klaeber, Friedrich. *Das Bild bei Chaucer.* Berlin: Richard Heinrich, 1893. 454 pp.

691. Koeppel, E. "Das Sprichwort bei Chaucer." *Beiblatt zur Anglia* 2 (1892): 169-173.

692. Lumiansky, R. M. "The Function of the Proverbial Monitory Elements in Chaucer's *Troilus and Criseyde*." *Tulane Studies in English* 2 (1950): 5-48.

693. Luxon, Thomas H. "'Sentence' and 'Solaas': Proverbs and Consolation in the *Knight's Tale*." *The Chaucer Review* 22, 2 (1987): 94-111.

694. MacDonald, Donald. "Chaucer's Influence on Henryson's *Fables*: The Use of Proverbs and Sententiae." *Medium Aevum* 39 (1970): 21-27.

695. MacDonald, Donald. "Proverbs, Sententiae, and Exempla in Chaucer's Comic Tales: The Function of Comic Misapplication." *Speculum* 41 (1966): 453-465.

696. McKenna, Steven R. "Orality, Literacy, and Chaucer: A Study of Performance, Textual Authority, and Proverbs in the Major Poetry." Diss. University of Rhode Island, 1988. 272 pp.

697. Obelkevich, James. "Proverbs and Social History." *The Social History of Language*. Eds. Peter Burke and Roy Porter. Cambridge: Cambridge University Press, 1987. 43-72. Also in *Wise Words: Essays on the Proverb*. Ed. Wolfgang Mieder. New York: Garland Publishing, 1994. 211-252.

698. Pace, George B. "The Chaucerian 'Proverbs.'" *Studies in Bibliography* 18 (1965): 41-48.

699. Pazdziora, Marian. "The Sapiential Aspect of the *Canterbury Tales*." *Kwartalnik Neofilologiczny* 27 (1980): 413-426.

700. Perry, Mary Agnes. "Chaucer's Use of Proverbs." M. A. Thesis. University of Washington (Seattle), 1927. 41 pp.

701. Philo-Chaucer. "Flemish Proverb Quoted by Chaucer." *Notes and Queries* 1st ser. 5 (1852): 466.

702. Puhvel, Martin. "Chaucer's *Troilus and Criseyde*: III, 890; V, 505; V, 1174-5." *Explicator* 42, 4 (1984): 7-9.

703. Ragen, Brian Abel. "Chaucer, Jean de Meun, and Proverbs 30:20." *Notes and Queries* 233 ns 35 (1988): 295-296.

704. Renoir, Alain. "Bayard and Troilus: Chaucerian Non-Paradox in the Reader." *Orbis Litterarum* 36 (1981): 116-140.

705. Rutherford, Charles S. "Troilus' Farewell of Criseyde: The Idealist as Clairvoyant and Rhetorician." *Papers on Language and Literature* 17 (1981): 245-254.

706. Sartoris, Brenda Eve. "Chaucer's Use of Proverbs as an Artistic Device." M. A. Thesis. Louisiana State University, 1964. 91 pp.

707. Scattergood, John. *"Chaucer a Bukton* and Proverbs." *Nottingham Medieval Studies* 31 (1987): 98-107.

708. Schmidt-Hidding, Wolfgang. "Geoffrey Chaucer." *Englische Idiomatik in Stillehre und Literatur.* München: Max Hueber, 1962. 20-26.

709. Skeat, Walter William. "Geoffrey Chaucer." *Early English Proverbs, Chiefly of the Thirteenth and Fourteenth Centuries.* Oxford: Clarendon Press, 1910; rpt. Darby, Pennsylvania: Folcroft Library Editions, 1974. 57-126.

710. Smith, Roland M. "Chaucer's 'Castle in Spain' (HF 1117)." *Modern Language Notes* 60 (1945): 39-40.

711. Smith, Roland M. "Three Obscure English Proverbs [The game is not worth the candle; He that will swear will lie; Life is a pilgrimage]." *Modern Language Notes* 65 (1950): 441- 447.

712. Smith, Sarah Stanbury. "'Game in Myn Hood': The Tradition of a Comic Proverb." *Studies in Iconography* 9 (1983): 1-12.

713. Strohn, Paul. "The Allegory of the *Tale of Melibee.*" *Chaucer Review* 2 (1967): 32-42.

714. Tatlock, John S. P. "Chaucer's Whelp and Lion." *Modern Language Notes* 38 (1923): 506-507.

715. Taylor, Karla. "Proverbs and the Authentication of Convention in *Troilus and Criseyde.*" *Chaucer's Troilus: Essays in Criticism.* Ed. Stephen A. Barney. Hamden, Connecticut: Archon Books, 1980. 277-296.

716. Utley, Francis Lee. "Chaucer's Way with a Proverb: 'Allas! Allas! That Evere Love Was Synne!'" *North Carolina Folklore* 21 (1973): 98-104.

717. Walker, Hazel Pearl. "A Study of the Use of Proverbs as an Artistic Device in Geoffrey Chaucer's *Troilus and Cresside.*" M. A. Thesis. University of Iowa, 1932. 62 pp.

718. Weekley, Ernest. "Proverbs Considered." *The Atlantic Monthly* 145 (1930): 504-512, especially 507-508.

719. Weidenbrück, Adolf. "Chaucers Sprichwortpraxis: Eine Form- und Funktionsanalyse." Diss. Bonn, 1970. 185 pp.

720. Wentersdorf, Karl P. "Chaucer's Worthless Butterfly." *English Language Notes* 14 (1977): 167-172.

721. Whiting, Bartlett Jere. "Studies in the Middle English Proverb," 3 vols. Diss. Harvard University, 1932. 1386 pp.

722. Whiting, Bartlett Jere. *Chaucer's Use of Proverbs*. Cambridge, Massachusetts: Harvard University Press, 1934; New York: AMS Press, 1973. 297 pp.

723. Wilson, Edward. "An Aristotelian Commonplace in Chaucer's *Franklin's Tale*." *Notes and Queries* 230 ns 32 (1985): 303-305.

724. Winick, Stephen D. "Proverbial Strategy and Proverbial Wisdom in *The Canterbury Tales*." *Proverbium: Yearbook of International Proverb Scholarship* 11 (1994): 259-281.

725. Wright, Louis B. "William Painter and the Vogue of Chaucer as a Moral Teacher." *Modern Philology* 31 (1933): 165-174.

726. Young, Karl. "Chaucer's Aphorisms from Ptolemy." *Studies in Philology* 34 (1937): 1-7.

727. Zupitza, Julius. "*The Prouerbis of Wysdom*." *Archiv für das Studium der neuren Sprachen und Literaturen* 90 (1893): 241-268.

CHEKHOV, ANTON (1860-1904)

728. Eckert, Rainer. "Zum Einsatz von Phraseologismen im schöngeistigen Text (A. Čechovs Kurzerzählung *O ljubvi*)." *Z problemów frazeologii polskiej i slowianskiej* 6 (1994): 89-92.

CHELTENHAMER LIEDERHANDSCHRIFT (14th cent.)

729. Pillet, Alfred. *Die neuprovenzalischen Sprichwörter der jüngeren Cheltenhamer Liederhandschrift: Mit Einleitung und Übersetzung zum ersten Mal herausgegeben*. Berlin: C. Vogt, 1897. 38 pp.

THE CHESTER CYCLE OF MYSTERY PLAYS (14th cent.)

730.   Whiting, Bartlett Jere. "*The Chester Plays*." *Proverbs in the Earlier English Drama*. Cambridge, Massachusetts: Harvard University Press 1938; rpt. New York: Octagon Books, 1969. 5-8.

CHEVALIER, PIERRE (15th cent.)

731.   Pinkernell, Gert. "Une réplique haineuse à la *Ballade des proverbes*, de François Villon, émanant du cercle de Charles d'Orléans." *Archiv für das Studium der neueren Sprachen und Literaturen* 224 (1987): 110-116.

CHING-KUAN-TSE (20th cent.)

732.   Eberhard, Wolfram. "Some Notes on the Use of Proverbs in Chinese Novels." *Proverbium* No. 9 (1967): 201-209. Also in *Studies in Chinese Folklore and Related Essays*. Bloomington: Indiana University Press, 1970. 176-181.

CHOLIÈRES, NICOLAS (1509-1592)

733.   Aliberti, Luisella. "Proverbi ed espressioni proverbiali nell' opera di Cholières." *La nouvelle française à la Renaissance*. Ed. Lionello Sozzi. Geneva: Slatkine, 1981. 607-625.

CHRÉTIEN DE TROYES (c. 1150-c. 1190)

734.   Altieri, Marcelle B. "Les romans de Chrétien de Troyes vus dans la perspective de leur contenu proverbial et gnomique." Diss. New York University, 1972. 315 pp.; published as *Les romans de Chrétien de Troyes: Leur perspective proverbiale et gnomique*. Paris: Editions A.-G. Nizet, 1976. 224 pp.

735.   Ellis, Margery Alice. "A Catalogue of the Proverbs of Chrétien de Troyes with an Introduction." M. A. Thesis. University of Chicago, 1927. 40 pp.

736.   Holland, Wilhelm Ludwig. *Chrestien von Troies: Eine litteraturge-schichtliche Untersuchung*. Tübingen: L. F. Fues, 1854. 264-271.

737.   Le Roux de Lincy, M. *Le Livre des Proverbes Français*, 2 vols. 2nd ed. Paris: A. Delahays, 1859; rpt. Genève: Slatkine, 1968. I, xlvii-xlviii.

738.   Nitze, W. A. "'Or est venuz qui aunera': A Medieval Dictum." *Modern Language Notes* 56 (1941): 405-409.

739. Ollier, Marie-Louise. "Proverbe et sentence—le discours d'autorité chez Chrétien de Troyes." *Revue des sciences humaines* 41, 163 (1976): 329-357.

740. Ollier, Marie-Louise. "Specificité discursive d'une locution: 'Si m'aist dex' vs. 'Se dex m'ait.'" *La locution: Actes du colloque international Université McGill, Montréal, 15-16 octobre 1984*. Eds. Giuseppe Di Stefano and Russell G. McGillivray. Montréal: Éditions CERES, 1984. 323-367.

741. Schulze-Busacker, Elisabeth. "Proverbes et expressions proverbiales chez Chrétien de Troyes, Gautier d'Arras et Hue de Rotelande." *Incidences* 5 (1981): 7-16.

742. Schulze-Busacker, Elisabeth. "Proverbes et expressions proverbiales dans les romans de Chrétien de Troyes." *Chrétien de Troyes et le Graal: Colloque arthurien belge de Bruges*. Eds. Juliette De Caluwé-Dor and Herman Bract. Paris: Éditions Nizet, 1984. 107-119.

743. Schulze-Busacker, Elisabeth. *Proverbes et expressions proverbiales dans la littérature narrative du moyen âge français: Recueil et analyse*. Paris: Librairie Honoré Champion, 1985. 46-64.

CHRISTINE DE PISAN (1365-c. 1429)

744. Cohen, Helen Louise. "Proverbs and the Ballade." *The Ballade*. New York: Columbia University Press, 1915. 94-102.

745. Fehse, Erich. *Sprichwort und Sentenz bei Eustache Deschamps und Dichtern seiner Zeit*. Diss. Berlin, 1905. Erlangen: Universitäts-Buchdrucherei, 1905. 44. Also in *Romanische Forschungen* 19 (1906): 588.

746. Le Roux de Lincy, M. *Le Livre des Proverbes Français*, 2 vols. 2nd ed. Paris: A. Delahays, 1859; rpt. Genève: Slatkine, 1968. I, liv-lv.

747. Roques, Gilles. "'Sans rime et sans raison.'" *La locution: Actes du colloque international Université McGill, Montréal, 15-16 octobre 1984*. Eds. Giuseppe Di Stefano and Russell G. McGillivray. Montréal: Editions CERES, 1984. 419-436.

CHRISTIE, AGATHA (1890-1976)

748. Bryan, George B. *Black Sheep, Red Herrings, and Blue Murder: The Proverbial Agatha Christie.* Bern: Peter Lang, 1993. 482 pp.

749. Shvydkaia, L. I. "Sinonimicheskie otnosheniia poslovits i aforizmov v angliiskom iazyke." *Leksikologicheskie osnovy stilistiki (Sbornik nauchnykh trudov).* Ed. I. V. Arnol'd. Leningrad: Gosudarstvennyi pedagogicheskii institut im. A. I. Gertsena, 1973. 167-175.

750. Taylor, Archer. "'Hell,' said the Duchess." *Proverbium* No. 2 (1965): 32.

CHRONIQUE DE RAINS (13th cent.)

751. Le Roux de Lincy, M. *Le Livre des Proverbes Français,* 2 vols. 2nd ed. Paris: A. Delahays, 1859; rpt. Genève: Slatkine, 1968. I, lii-liii.

CHURCHILL, Sir WINSTON S. (1874-1965)

752. Crum, Richard Henry. "'Blood, Sweat and Tears.'" *The Classical Journal* 42 (1947): 299-300.

753. Mieder, Wolfgang. "Bibliographische Skizze zur Überlieferung des Ausdrucks 'Iron Curtain'/'Eiserner Vorhang.'" *Muttersprache* 91 (1981): 1-14. Also in *Deutsche Sprichwörter in Literatur, Politik, Presse und Werbung.* Hamburg: Helmut Buske, 1983. 144-157.

754. Mieder, Wolfgang. "'Make Hell While the Sun Shines': Proverbial Rhetoric in Winston Churchill's *The Second World War.*" *Folklore* (London) 106 (1995): 57-69.

755. Mieder, Wolfgang, and George B. Bryan. *The Proverbial Winston S. Churchill: An Index to Proverbs in the Works of Sir Winston Churchill.* Westport, Connecticut: Greenwood Press, 1995. 448 pp.

756. Miller, Edd, and Jesse J. Villareal. "The Use of Clichés by Four Contemporary Speakers." *Quarterly Journal of Speech* 31 (1945): 151-155.

757. Underhill, W. R. "Fulton's Finest Hour." *Quarterly Journal of Speech* 52 (1966): 155-163.

758. Weidhorn, Manfred. "Churchill the Phrase Forger." *Quarterly Journal of Speech* 58, 2 (1972): 161-174.

CI-NOUS-DIT (13th cent.)

759. Blangez, Gérard. "Proverbes dans le *Ci-nous-dit.*" *Bulletin du Centre d'Étude médiévales et dialectales de l'Université Lille III* 1 (1978): 68-78.

CICERO [Marcus Tullius Cicero] (143-106 B. C.)

760. Büchner, Karl. "'Summum ius summa iniuria.'" *Humanitas Romana: Studien über Werke und Wesen der Römer.* Heidelberg: Carl Winter, 1957. 80-105.

761. Crane, Mary Thomas. "Proverbial and Aphoristic Sayings: Sources of Authority in the English Renaissance." Diss. Harvard University, 1986. 464 pp.

762. Crum, Richard Henry. "'Blood, Sweat and Tears.'" *The Classical Journal* 42 (1947): 299-300.

763. Genthe, Hermann. "De proverbiis a Cicerone adhibitis." *Commentationes philol. in honorem Theodori Mommseni scripservnt amici: Adiecta est Tabula.* Berlin: Weidmann, 1887. 1-8.

764. Meichsner, Irene. *Die Logik von Gemeinplätzen: Vorgeführt an Steuermannstopos und Schiffsmetapher.* Bonn: Bouvier, 1983. 263 pp.

765. Mieder, Wolfgang. "'Wir sitzen alle in einem Boot': Herkunft, Geschichte und Verwendung einer neueren deutschen Redensart." *Muttersprache* 100 (1990): 18-37. Also in *Deutsche Redensarten, Sprichwörter und Zitate: Studien zu ihrer Herkunft, Überlieferung und Verwendung.* Vienna: Edition Praesens, 1995. 140-159.

766. Nestle, Wilhelm. "'Wer nicht mit mir ist, der ist wider mich.'" *Zeitschrift für die neutestamentliche Wissenschaft und die Kunde des Urchristentums* 13 (1912): 84-87.

767. Peil, Dietmar. "'Im selben Boot': Variationen über ein metaphorisches Argument." *Archiv für Kulturgeschichte* 68, 2 (1986): 269-293.

768. Puccioni, Giulio. "Recupero di un'espressione proverbiale romana [Etiam capillus unus habet umbram suam (Even a hair has its shadow)]." *Maia: Rivista di Letterature classiche* 19 (1967): 176-178.

769. Roos, Paolo. *Sentenza e proverbio nell'antichità e i "Distici di Catone":
Il testo latino e i volgarizzamenti italiani.* Brescia: Morcelliana, 1984.
254 pp.

770. Schumacher, Meinolf. "'. . . ist menschlich': Mittelalterliche Variationen einer antiken Sentenz." *Zeitschrift für deutsches Altertum und
deutsche Literatur* 119 (1990): 163-170.

771. Wilkins, Eliza Gregory. *"Know Thyself" in Greek and Latin Literature.*
Diss. University of Chicago, 1917. Chicago: University of Chicago
Libraries, 1917. 104 pp.

772. Zholkovskii, Aleksandr K., and Iu. K. Tseglov. "Razbor odnoi
avtorskoi paremii." *Paremiologischeskii Sbornik.* Ed. Grigorii L'vovich
Permiakov. Moskva: Nauka, 1978. 163-210.

CANTAR DE MIO CID (c. 1140)
773. Garci-Gómez, Miguel. "La tradición del león reverente: Glosas para los
episodios en *Mio Cid, Palmerin de Oliva, Don Quijote* y otros." *Kentucky Romance Quarterly* 19 (1972): 255-284.

CLAUDEL, PAUL (1868-1955)
774. Monteiro, George. "The Literary Use of a Proverb." *Folklore* 87
(1976): 216-218.

CLAUDIUS, MATTHIAS (1740-1815)
775. Burger, Heinz Otto. "Luther im Spiegel der Tischreden: Wer nicht liebt
Wein, Weib und Gesang, | Der bleibt ein Narr sein Lebenlang.'" *Ger-
manisch-Romanische Monatsschrift* 54 ns 23 (1973): 385-403.

776. Mieder, Wolfgang. "'Wine, Women and Song': From Martin Luther to
American T-Shirts." *Kentucky Folklore Record* 29 (1983): 89-101. Also
in *Folk Groups and Folklore Genres: A Reader.* Ed. Elliott Oring.
Logan: Utah State University Press, 1989. 279-290.

777. Mieder, Wolfgang. "'Wer nicht liebt Wein, Weib und Gesang, der
bleibt ein Narr sein Leben lang': Zur Herkunft, Überlieferung und
Verwendung eines angeblichen Luther-Spruches." *Muttersprache* 94
(Sonderheft, 1983-1984): 68-103.

778. Mieder, Wolfgang. "'Wine, Women and Song': Zur anglo-amerikani-schen Überlieferung eines angeblichen Lutherspruches." *Germanisch-Romanische Monatsschrift* 65 ns 34 (1984): 385-403.

COLERIDGE, SAMUEL TAYLOR (1772-1834)
779. Mieder, Wolfgang. "The Proverb in the Modern Age: Old Wisdom in New Clothing." *Tradition and Innovation in Folk Literature*. Hanover, New Hampshire: University Press of New England. 1987. 118-156, 248-255 (notes).

COLLODI, CARLO (1826-1890)
780. Brissoni, Armando. "Un modello linguistico attuale: la parlata 'pinocchiesca.'" *I Problemi della Pedagogia* 27, 5-6 (1981): 777- 782.

COLOMBO, [JOHN] ROBERT (1936—)
781. Mieder, Wolfgang. "The Proverb in the Modern Age: Old Wisdom in New Clothing." *Tradition and Innovation in Folk Literature*. Hanover, New Hampshire: University Press of New England, 1987. 118-156, 248-255 (notes).

COMMON CONDITIONS (c. 1576)
782. Whiting, Bartlett Jere. "*Common Conditions.*" *Proverbs in the Earlier English Drama*. Cambridge, Massachusetts: Harvard University Press, 1938; rpt. New York: Octagon Books, 1969. 249-253.

CONRAD, JOSEPH (1857-1924)
783. Schmidt-Hidding, Wolfgang. "Joseph Conrad." *Englische Idiomatik in Stillehre und Literatur*. München: Max Hueber, 1962. 80-81.

COOK, ELIZA (1818-1889)
784. Mieder, Wolfgang. "The Proverb in the Modern Age: Old Wisdom in New Clothing." *Tradition and Innovation in Folk Literature*. Hanover, New Hampshire: University Press of New England. 1987. 118-156, 248-255 (notes).

COOPER, JAMES FENIMORE (1789-1851)
785. French, Florence Healy. "Cooper's Use of Proverbs in the Anti-Rent Novels." *New York Folklore Quarterly* 26 (1970): 42-49.

786. French, Florence Healy. "Cooper the Tinkerer." *New York Folklore Quarterly* 26 (1970): 229-239.

787.   Slater, Joseph.   "'The Dutch Treat' in Cooper's *Satanstoe*." *American Speech* 26 (1951): 153-154.

788.   Walker, Warren S. "Folk Elements in the Novels of James Fenimore Cooper." Diss. Cornell University, 1951. 213 pp.

789.   Walker, Warren S. "Proverbs in the Novels of James Fenimore Cooper." *Midwest Folklore* 3 (1953): 99-107.

COQUILLART, GUILLAUME (c. 1421-c. 1490)
790.   Heft, David. *Proverbs and Sentences in Fifteenth Century French Poetry.* Diss. New York University, 1941. Chapter 2. New York: Washington Square Press, 1942 (abridged to 12 pp.).

CORNAZZANO, ANTONIO (1429-1484)
791.   Pittaluga, Stefano. "Proverbi e facezie di Antonio Cornazzano." *Res Publica Litterarum* 9 (1986): 231-239.

CORNEILLE, PIERRE (1606-1684)
792.   Le Roux de Lincy, M. *Le Livre des Proverbes Français*, 2 vols. 2nd ed. Paris: A. Delahays, 1859; rpt. Genève: Slatkine, 1968. I, lxx-lxxii.

793.   Sébillot, Paul. "Cornellle." *Revue des traditions populaires* 6 (1891): 551-556, especially 553-556.

COSBUC, GHEORGHE (1866-1918)
794.   Negreanu, Constantin. "Valentele educative si stilistice ale expresiilor si proverbelor în limba literaturii artistice." *Scoala Mehedintiului* 3 (1978): 23-26.

COSTA, JUAN (1548-1597)
795.   Ubach Medina, Antonio. "El uso del refrán en la obra de Juan Costa." *Paremia* No. 2 (1993): 65-71.

COSTER, CHARLES de (1827-1879)
796.   Marinus, Albert. "Le folklore dans l'oeuvre de Charles de Coster." *Le Folklore Brabançon* 7 (1927): 1-153.

COTA, RODRIGO (died c. 1470)
797.   Gillet, Joseph E. "'Las ochavas en cadena': A Proverb in Rodrigo Cota and Diego Sánchez de Badajoz." *Romance Philology* 6 (1952-1953): 264-267.

THE COVENTRY PLAYS [*The Weavers' Play*; *The Shearmen and the Taylors' Play*] (1392)

798. Ishii, Mikiko. "Joseph's Proverbs in the *Coventry Plays.*" *Folklore* (London) 93, 1 (1982): 47-60.

799. Whiting, Bartlett Jere. "*The Coventry Plays.*" *Proverbs in the Earlier English Drama*. Cambridge, Massachusetts: Harvard University Press, 1938; rpt. New York: Octagon Books, 1969. 29-32.

CRANE, STEPHEN (1871-1900)

800. Peck, Richard. "'Out of Sight' Is Back in View." *American Speech* 41 (1966): 78-79.

CREANGA, ION (1837-1889)

801. Bîrlea, Ovidiu. *Proverbes et dictons roumains—Proverbe si zicatori românesti*. Bucaresti: Editura didactia si pedagogica, 1966. 55 pp.

802. Negreanu, Constantin. "Valentele educative si stilistice ale expresiilor si proverbelor în limba literaturii artistice." *Scoala Mehedintiului* 3 (1978): 23-26.

803. Negreanu, Constantin. "Observatii asupra elementelor paremiologice din opera lui Ion Creanga." *Revista de etnografie si folclor* 34, 6 (1989): 525-541.

CROWLEY, ROBERT (c. 1518-1588)

804. Crane, Mary Thomas. "Proverbial and Aphoristic Sayings: Sources of Authority in the English Renaissance." Diss. Harvard University, 1986. 464 pp.

THE CROXTON PLAY OF THE SACRAMENT (15th cent.)

805. Whiting, Bartlett Jere. "*The Croxton Play of the Sacrament.*" *Proverbs in the Earlier English Drama*. Cambridge, Massachusetts: Harvard University Press, 1938; rpt. New York: Octagon Books, 1969. 33.

CULMAN, LEONHARD (c. 1497-1562)

806. Senger, Matthias W. "The Fate of an Early American School Book: Leonhard Culmann's [sic] Sententiae Pueriles." *Harvard Library Bulletin* 32 (1984): 256-273.

807. Senger, Matthias W. "Leonhard Culmanns [sic] Sententiae Pueriles: Zur Sentenz als einer prägenden Denkform vom 16. bis 18. Jahrhundert."

Literatur und Volk im 17. Jahrhundert: Probleme populärer Kultur in Deutschland. Eds. Wolfgang Brückner et al. Wiesbaden: Otto Harrassowitz, 1985. II, 777-795.

808. Smith, Charles George. *Shakespeare's Proverb Lore: His Use of Sententiae of Leonard Culman and Publilius Syrus*. Cambridge, Massachusetts: Harvard University Press, 1963. 181 pp.

809. Smith, Charles George. *Spenser's Proverb Lore: With Special Reference to His Use of the Sententiae of Leonard Culman and Publilius Syrus*. Cambridge, Massachusetts: Harvard University Press, 1970. 365 pp.

CURSOR MUNDI (c. 1300)

810. Skeat, Walter William. *"Cursor Mundi." Early English Proverbs, Chiefly of the Thirteenth and Fourteenth Centuries*. Oxford: Clarendon Press, 1910; rpt. Darby, Pennsylvania: Folcroft Library Editions, 1974. 20-21.

CUVELIER (14th cent.)

811. Faucon, Jean-Claude. "La sagesse populaire au service du roi: De l'utilisation des proverbes par un chroniqueur du XIVe siècle." *Richesse du proverbe*. Eds. François Suard and Claude Buridant. Lille: Université de Lille, 1984. I, 87-111.

CYRANO DE BERGERAC, SAVINIEN (1619-1655)

812. Le Roux de Lincy, M. *Le Livre des Proverbes Français*, 2 vols. 2nd ed. Paris: A. Delahays, 1859; rpt. Genève: Slatkine, 1968. I, lxix-lxx.

813. Sébillot, Paul. "Cyrano de Bergerac." *Revue des traditions populaires* 4 (1889): 476-479.

D

DANSE MACABRE (1425)

814. Taylor, Jane H. M. "Poésie et prédication: La fonction du discours proverbial dans la *Danse macabre.*" *Medioevo Romanzo* 14, 2 (1989): 215-226.

DANTE ALIGHIERI (1265-1321)

815. Bronzini, Giovanni B. "Nota sulla 'popolarita' dei proverbi della *Divina Commedia.*" *Lares* 38 (1972): 9-18.

816. Cariddi, Caterina. *Attualità di Dante attraverso massime, proverbi e sentenze della "Divina Commedia."* Bari: Editoriale Universitaria, 1969. 82 pp.

817. Liver, Ricarda. "Sprichwörter in der *Divina Commedia.*" *Deutsches Dante Jahrbuch* 53-54 (1978-1979): 46-60.

818. Speroni, Charles. "Folklore in the *Divine Comedy.*" Diss. University of California at Berkeley, 1938. 339 pp.

DARWIN, CHARLES (1809-1882)

819. Angenot, Marc. "'La lutte pour la vie': Migrations et usages d'un idéologème." *La locution: Actes du colloque international Université McGill, Montréal, 15-16 octobre 1984.* Eds. Giuseppe Di Stefano and Russell G. McGillivray. Montréal: Editions CERES, 1984. 171-190.

DAUDET, ALPHONSE (1841-1897)

820. Angenot, Marc. "'La lutte pour la vie': Migrations et usages d'un idéologème." *La locution: Actes du colloque international Université McGill, Montréal, 15-16 octobre 1984.* Eds. Giuseppe Di Stefano and Russell G. McGillivray. Montréal: Editions CERES, 1984. 171-190.

DAVI, HANS LEOPOLD (1928—)

821. Mieder, Wolfgang. "'Wenige jedoch rudern gegen den Strom': Zu den sprichwörtlichen Aphorismen von Hans Leopold Davi." *Sprachspiegel* 46 (1990): 97-104. Also in *Sprichwörtliches und Geflügeltes: Sprachstudien von Martin Luther bis Karl Marx.* Bochum: Norbert Brockmeyer, 1995. 79-86.

DAVID, P. JAN (17th cent.)

822. "Spreekwoorden (Uit een zeldzaam boekje: *Lot van Wijsheid ende Goed Geluck*, P. Jan David, Antwerpen, 1606)." *Biekorf* 42 (1936): 134-136.

DAVIES, Sir JOHN (1569-1626)
823. Manley, Lawrence. "Proverbs, Epigrams, and Urbanity in Renaissance London." *English Literary Renaissance* 15 (1985): 247-276.

DAVIS, BURKE (1913—)
824. Clark, Joseph D. "Burke Davis as Folklorist." *North Carolina Folklore* 19 (1971): 59-65.

DEFFRANCS, CHRISTOPHE (16th cent.)
825. Desaivre, Léo. "Christophe Deffrancs." *Revue des traditions populaires* 20 (1905): 235-236.

DEFOE, DANIEL (c. 1659-1731)
826. Steensma, Robert C. "A Legal Proverb in Defoe, Swift, and Shenstone." *Proverbium* No. 10 (1968): 248.

DEKKER, THOMAS (c. 1570-1632)
827. Bruster, Douglas. "The Horn of Plenty: Cuckoldry and Capital in the Drama of the Age of Shakespeare." *Studies in English Literature 1500-1900* 30, 2 (1990): 195-215.

828. Prager, Carolyn. "'If I Be Devil': English Renaissance Response to the Proverbial and Ecumenical Ethiopian." *Journal of Medieval and Renaissance Studies* 17, 2 (1987): 257-279.

829. Rice, Warner G. "'To Turn Turk.'" *Modern Language Notes* 46 (1931): 153-154.

DELAVRANCEA, BARBU (1858-1918)
830. Negreanu, Constantin. "Valentele educative si stilistice ale expresiilor si proverbelor în limba literaturii artistice." *Scoala Mehedintiului* 3 (1978): 23-26.

DELICADO, FRANCISCO (died after 1527)
831. Gella Iturriaga, José. "Los refranes de *La Lozana Andaluza*." *Libro Homenaje a Antonio Pérez Gómez*, 2 vols. Ed. Damaso Alonso. Cieza (Murcia): La Fonte que Mana y Corre, 1978. I, 255-268.

832. Vigier, Françoise. "Quelques exemples de manipulation littéraire des proverbes dans le *Retrato de Lozana Andaluza* de Francisco Delicado." *Paremia* No. 2 (1993): 97-102.

DELONEY, THOMAS (c. 1543-1600)

833. Reuter, O. R. *Proverbs, Proverbial Sentences and Phrases in Thomas Deloney's Works*. Helsinki: The Finnish Society of Sciences and Letters, 1986. 146 pp.

834. Reuter, O. R. "Some Notes on Thomas Deloney's Indebtedness to Shakespeare." *Neuphilologische Mitteilungen* 87 (1986): 255-261.

DENNIS, JOHN (1657-1733)

835. Wilkins, A. N. "John Dennis' Stolen Thunder." *Notes and Queries* 201 ns 3 (1956): 425-428.

DEOR (9th-10th cent.)

836. Harris, Joseph. "*Deor* and Its Refrain: Preliminaries to an Interpretation." *Traditio: Studies in Ancient and Medieval History, Thought, and Religion* 43 (1987): 23-53.

DEPLAZES, GION (1918—)

837. Roman, Thomas. "Proverbis e locuziones proverbialas en duas ovras da Gion Deplazes *Paun casa* e *La Bargia dil tschéss*: Specia e funcziun." *Annalas de la Società Retorumantscha* 101 (1988): 7-48.

DEPPERT, FRITZ (1932—)

838. Mieder, Wolfgang. "'It's Five Minutes to Twelve': Folklore and Saving Life on Earth." *International Folklore Review* 7 (1989): 10-21.

DESCARTES, RENÉ (1596-1650)

839. Brands, Hartmut. "*Cogito ergo sum*": *Interpretationen von Kant bis Nietzsche*. München: Karl Alber, 1982. 318 pp.

840. Kann, Hans-Joachim. "Zu den Quellen von Spontisprüchen." *Der Sprachdienst* 29 (1985): 75-79.

841. Mieder, Wolfgang. "'Cogito, ergo sum': Zum Weiterleben eines berühmten Zitats." *Der Sprachdienst* 28 (1984): 161-167. Also in *Sprichwort, Redensart, Zitat: Tradierte Formelsprache in der Moderne*. Bern: Peter Lang, 1985. 163-173.

842. Suter, Beat. "Verbale Sprache." *Graffiti: Rebellion der Zeichen*. Frankfurt am Main: Rita G. Fischer, 1988. 31-49.

DESCHAMPS, EUSTACHE [a.k.a. Morel] (c. 1346-c. 1406)

843. Céard, Jean, and Jean-Claude Margolin. "Rébus et proverbes." *Rébus de la renaissance: Des images qui parlent.* Paris: Maisonneuve et Larose, 1986. I, 135-162.

844. Cerquiglini, Jacqueline and Bernard. "L'écriture proverbiale." *Revue des sciences humaines* 41, 163 (1976): 359-375.

845. Cohen, Helen Louise. "Proverbs and the Ballade." *The Ballade.* New York: Columbia University Press, 1915. 94-102.

846. Fehse, Erich. *Sprichwort und Sentenz bei Eustache Deschamps und Dichtern seiner Zeit.* Diss. Berlin, 1905. Erlangen: Universitäts-Buchdrucherei, 1905. Also in *Romanische Forschungen* 19 (1906): 545-594.

847. Roques, Gilles. "'Sans rime et sans raison.'" *La locution: Actes du colloque international Université McGill, Montréal, 15-16 octobre 1984.* Eds. Giuseppe Di Stefano and Russell G. McGillivray. Montréal: Editions CERES, 1984. 419-436.

848. Smith, Roland M. "Three Obscure English Proverbs [The game is not worth the candle; He that will swear will lie; Life is a pilgrimage]." *Modern Language Notes* 65 (1950): 441- 447.

849. Whiting, Bartlett Jere. "Proverbs in Deschamps." *Chaucer's Use of Proverbs.* Cambridge, Massachusetts: Harvard University Press, 1934; rpt. Cambridge, Massachusetts, AMS Press, 1973. 207-242.

DESPÉRIERS, BONAVENTURE (c. 1510-c. 1543)

850. Desaivre, Léo. "Bonaventure des Perriers." *Revue des traditions populaires,* 20 (1905): 227-229.

851. Hassell, J. Woodrow. "The Proverb in Bonaventure des Périers' Short Stories." *Journal of American Folklore* 75 (1962): 35-57.

852. Hassell, J. Woodrow. "A Wellerism in the Tales of Des Périers." *Romance Notes* 5 (1963/64): 66-71.

853. Hassell, J. Woodrow. "Proverbs in the Writings of Bonaventure des Périers." *Journal of American Folklore* 77 (1964): 53-57.

854. Hassell, J. Woodrow. "The Proverbs and Proverbial Expressions in the Works of Bonaventure des Périers." *Journal of American Folklore* 77 (1964): 58-68.

855. Kasprzyk, Krystyna. "Un exemple de comique subversif: L'emploi du proverbe dans les *Nouvelles Récréations* de B. Des Périers." *Le comique verbal en France au XVIe siècle.* Ed. Halina Lewicka. Warsaw: Editions de l'Université de Varsovie, 1981. 219-232.

DICKENS, CHARLES (1811-1870)

856. Baer, Florence E. "Wellerisms in *The Pickwick Papers*." *Folklore* (London), 94 (1983): 173-183.

857. Bailey, William H. "Wellerisms and Wit." *The Dickensian* 1 (1905), 31-34.

858. Bede, Cuthbert. "Sam Vale and Sam Weller." *Notes and Queries* 6th ser. 5 (April 29, 1882): 326; 6th ser. 5 (May 20, 1882): 338-389.

859. Boquera Matarredona, María. "La traducción al español de paremias en *The Pickwick Papers*: refranes y proverbios." *Paremia* No. 3 (1994): 89-96.

860. Bryan, George B., and Wolfgang Mieder. "'As Sam Weller Said, When Finding Himself on the Stage': Wellerisms in Dramatizations of Charles Dickens' *Pickwick Papers*." *Proverbium: Yearbook of International Proverb Scholarship* 11 (1994): 57-76.

861. Edgecombe, R. S. "Locution and Authority in *Martin Chuzzlewit*." *English Studies* 74, 2 (1993): 143-153.

862. Haupt, Moriz. "[Anglicis plurimis utitur vel unus ille Dickensii Samuel Wellerus]." *Opuscula.* Leipzig: Salomon Hirzel, 1876. II, 395-406.

863. Hogan, Rebecca S. H. "The Wisdom of Many, the Wit of One: The Narrative Function of the Proverb in Tolstoy's *Anna Karenina* and Trollope's *Orley Farm*." Diss. University of Colorado, 1984. 1-68.

864. Maass, M. "39 Old Similes aus dem Pickwick Papers von Charles Dickens." *Archiv für das Studium der neueren Sprachen und Literaturen* 41 (1867): 207-215.

865. McGowan, Mary Teresa. "Pickwick and the Pirates: A Study of Some Early Imitations, Dramatisations and Plagiarisms of Pickwick Papers." Diss. University of London, 1975. 284-296.

866. Mieder, Wolfgang. "Wellerism Bibliography." In W. Mieder and Stewart A. Kingsbury. *A Dictionary of Wellerisms*. New York: Oxford University Press, 1994. 153-166.

867. Salveit, Laurits. "Beobachtungen zu einem Sonderfall der Parataxe in deutschen Sprichwörtern." *Aspekte der Germanistik: Festschrift für Hans-Friedrich Rosenfeld zum 90. Geburtstag*. Ed. Walter Tauber. Göppingen: Kümmerle, 1989. 657-670.

868. Schmidt-Hidding, Wolfgang. "Charles Dickens." *Englische Idiomatik in Stillehre und Literatur*. München: Max Hueber, 1962. 60-69.

869. Williams, Gwenllian L. "Sam Weller." *Trivium* 1 (1966): 88-101, especially 92-95.

870. Wood, Frederick T. "Sam Weller's Cockneyisms." *Notes and Queries* 190 (1946): 234-235.

DICKINSON, EMILY (1830-1886)
871. Barnes, Daniel R. "Telling It Slant: Emily Dickinson and Proverb." *Genre* 12 (1979): 219-241. Also in *Wise Words: Essays on the Proverb*. Ed. Wolfgang Mieder. New York: Garland Publishing, 1994. 439-465.

DIDEROT, DENIS (1713-1784)
872. Militz, Hans-Manfred. "Redewendungen im Dialog: Diderots *Neveu de Rameau*." *Proverbium: Yearbook of International Proverb Scholarship* 12 (1995): 239-250.

DIETRICH, VEIT (1506-1549)
873. Broek, Marinus A. van den. "Sprichwort und Redensart in Veit Dietrichs *Etliche Schrifften für den gemeinen man*." *Leuvense bijdragen* 75, 3 (1986): 307-334.

THE DIGBY PLAYS (15th cent.)
874. Whiting, Bartlett Jere. "*The Digby Plays*." *Proverbs in the Earlier English Drama*. Cambridge, Massachusetts: Harvard University Press, 1938; rpt. New York: Octagon Books, 1969. 33-35.

DIOSCURIDES (3rd cent. B. C.)
875. Prittwitz-Gaffron, Erich von. *Das Sprichwort im griechischen Epigramm.* Diss. München, 1912. Gießen: Alfred Töpelmann, 1912. 25-26.

DOBROLIUBOV, NIKOLAI A. (1836-1861)
876. Shakhnovich, Mikh. "Kratkaia istoriia sobiraniia i izucheniia russkikh poslovits i pogovorok." *Sovetskii fol'klor: Sbornik statei i materialov* 4-5 (1936): 299-368.

DÖBLIN, ALFRED (1878-1957)
877. Grésillon, Almuth, and Dominique Maingueneau. "Polyphonie, proverbe et détournement, ou un proverbe peut en cacher un autre." *Langages* 19, 73 (1984): 112-125.

878. Mieder, Wolfgang. "Das Sprichwort als Ausdruck kollektiven Sprechens in Alfred Döblins *Berlin Alexanderplatz.*" *Muttersprache* 83 (1973): 405-415. Also in *Deutsche Sprichwörter in Literatur, Politik, Presse und Werbung.* Hamburg: Helmut Buske, 1983. 42-52.

879. Mieder, Wolfgang. "Sprichwörter im modernen Sprachgebrauch." *Muttersprache* 85 (1975): 65-88. Also in *Ergebnisse der Sprichwörtforschung.* Bern: Peter Lang, 1978. 213-238; *Deutsche Sprichwörter in Literatur, Politik, Presse und Werbung.* Hamburg: Helmut Buske, 1983. 53-76.

DÖHL, REINHARD (1934—)
880. Mieder, Wolfgang. "Sprichwörter unterm Hakenkreuz." *Muttersprache* 93 (1983): 1-30. Also in *Deutsche Sprichwörter in Literatur, Politik, Presse und Werbung.* Hamburg: Helmut Buske, 1983. 181-210.

DONNE, JOHN (1572-1631)
881. Mathews, Ernst G. "A Spanish Proverb (Probable Spanish Source for Passage in One of Donne's Letters)." *The Times (London) Literary Supplement* September 12, 1936: 729.

882. Pitts, Arthur William. "John Donne's Use of Proverbs in His Poetry." Diss. Louisiana State University, 1966. 213 pp.

883. Pitts, Arthur William. "Proverbs as Testimony in Donne's Style." *Essays in Honor of Esmond Linworth Marilla.* Eds. Thomas Austin Kirby and William John Olive. Baton Rouge: Louisiana State University Press, 1970. 43-55.

DOSTOEVSKY, FEODOR (1821-1881)

884.   Levinton, G. A. "Dostoevsky i 'nizkie' zhanry fol'klora." *Wiener Slawistischer Almanach* 9 (1982): 63-82.

885.   Rice, James L. "Raskol'nikov and Tsar Gorox." *Slavic and East European Journal* 25 (1981): 38-53.

886.   Workman, Mark E. "Proverbs for the Pious and the Paranoid: The Social Use of Metaphor." *Proverbium: Yearbook for International Proverb Scholarship* 4 (1987): 225-241.

DOYLE, Sir ARTHUR CONAN (1859-1930)

887.   Bryan, George B. "The Proverbial Sherlock Holmes." *Proverbium: Yearbook of International Proverb Scholarship* 13 (1996): forthcoming.

888.   Waterhouse, William C. "The Case of the Persian Proverb." *The Baker Street Journal: An Irregular Quarterly of Sherlockiana* 40, 3 (1990): 135-136.

DRAYTON, MICHAEL (1563-1631)

889.   "The Folklore of (Michael) Drayton." *Folk-Lore Journal* 3 (1885): 88-90.

DREISER, THEODORE (1871-1945)

890.   Shvydkaia, L. I. "Sinonimicheskie otnosheniia poslovits i aforizmov v angliiskom iazyke." *Leksikologicheskie osnovy stilistiki (Sbornik nauchnykh trudov)*. Ed. I. V. Arnol'd. Leningrad: Gosudarstvennyi pedagogicheskii institut im. A. I. Gertsena, 1973. 167-175.

DRESCHER, HORST (1929—)

891.   Mieder, Wolfgang. "Sprachliche Entfesselungskünst: zu den sprichwörtlichen *Notizen* des Leipzigers Horst Drescher." *Der Sprachdienst* 40, 2 (1996): forth-coming.

DROSTE-HÜLSHOFF, ANNETTE, Baroness von (1797-1848)

892.   Bluhm, Lothar. "'Er ist ihr zu dick, er hat kein Geschick': Zu einem Spruch in Annette von Droste-Hülshoffs *Westphälische Schilderungen aus einer westphälischen Feder* und den *Kinder- und Hausmärchen* der Brüder Grimm." *Wirkendes Wort* 37 (1987): 181-183.

893.   Mieder, Wolfgang. "Das Sprichwort in den Prosawerken Annette von Droste-Hülshoffs." *Rheinisches Jahrbuch für Volkskunde*, 21 (1973):

329-346. Also in *Das Sprichwort in der deutschen Prosaliteratur des neunzehnten Jahrhunderts*. München: Wilhelm Finks, 1976. 93-106.

894. Rölleke, Heinz. "Miszelle zur *Judenbuche.*" *Kleine Beiträge zur Droste-Forschung*. Ed. Winfried Woesler. Münster Laumann, 1973. 139-140.

895. Sprenger, R. "Eine Shakespearesche Redewendung bei Annette von Droste-Hülshoff." *Archiv für das Studium der neueren Sprachen und Literaturen* 115 (1905): 176-177.

DROUHET, JEAN (1617-1681)
896. Desaivre, Léo. "Jean Drouhet." *Revue des traditions populaires* 20 (1905): 304-305.

DUCLOS, CHARLES (1704-1772)
897. Silverblatt, B. G. "The Maxims in the Novels of Duclos." Diss. Case Western Reserve University, 1971. 263 pp.

DÜRRENMATT, FRIEDRICH (1921—1990)
898. Burger, Harald. "'Die Achseln zucken'—Zur sprachlichen Kodierung nichtsprachlicher Kommunikation." *Wirkendes Wort* 26 (1976): 311-334.

DUFRESNY, CHARLES (1648-1724)
899. Sébillot, Paul. "Dufresny." *Revue des traditions populaires* 9 (1894): 582-587.

DUKAKIS, MICHAEL S. (1933—)
900. Arora, Shirley L. "On the Importance of Rotting Fish: A Proverb and Its Audience." *Western Folklore* 48 (1989): 271-288.

DUNBAR, WILLIAM (c. 1465-c. 1530)
901. Burrow, John Anthony. "'Young Saint, Old Devil': Reflections on a Medieval Proverb." *Review of English Studies* 30 (1979): 385-396. Also in *Essays on Medieval Literature*. Oxford: Oxford University Press, 1984. 177-191.

DUNNE, FINLEY PETER [a.k.a. Mr. Dooley] (1867-1936)
902. Jones, Joseph. "Wellerisms: Some Further Evidence." *American Speech* 20 (1945): 235-236.

DUNTON, JOHN (1659-1733)

903. Ray, Robert H. "John Dunton and the Origin of 'A Penny Saved Is a Penny Earned.'" *Notes and Queries* 229 ns 31 (1984): 372-373.

DURRELL, LAWRENCE (1912-1990)

904. Schmidt-Hidding, Wolfgang. "Lawrence Durrell." *Englische Idiomatik in Stillehre und Literatur*. München: Max Hueber, 1962. 90.

DYLAN, BOB [Robert Zimmerman] (1941—)

905. Bowden, Betsy. "[Like a Rolling Stone]." *Performed Literature: Words and Music by Bob Dylan*. Bloomington: Indiana University Press, 1982. 77-80, 193-195 (text).

906. Mieder, Wolfgang. "Proverbs in American Popular Songs." *Proverbium: Yearbook of International Proverb Scholarship* 5 (1988): 85-101.

E

EBERHARD VON CERSNE (14th/15th cent.)

907. Leitzmann, Albert. "Studien zu Eberhard von Cersne." *Beiträge zur Geschichte der deutschen Sprache und Literatur* 71 (1949) 306-330.

EBERLIN VON GÜNZBURG, JOHANN (1468-1533)

908. Broek, Marinus A. van den. "Das Sprichwort in den Schriften Johann Eberlins von Günzburg." *Proverbium: Yearbook of International Proverb Scholarship* 10 (1993): 37-50.

EBNER-ESCHENBACH, MARIE VON (1830-1916)

909. Mautner, Franz H. "Der Aphorismus als literarische Gattung." *Zeitschrift für Ästhetik und allgemeine Kunstwissenschaft* 27 (1933): 132-175.

910. Mautner, Franz H. "Maxim(e)s, Sentences, Fragmente, Aphorismen." *Actes du 4e Congrès de l'Association Internationale de Littérature Comparée, Fribourg 1964.* Ed. François Jost. The Hague: Mouton, 1966. II, 812-819.

911. Mieder, Wolfgang. "'Ausnahmen können auch die Vorboten einer neuen Regel sein': Zu den sprichwörtlichen Aphorismen von Marie von Ebner-Eschenbach." *Sprachspiegel* 45 (1989): 66-73. Also in *Sprichwort—Wahrwort!? Studien zur Geschichte, Bedeutung und Funktion deutscher Sprichwörter.* Frankfurt am Main: Peter Lang, 1992. 159-167.

912. Mieder, Wolfgang. "'Ausnahmen Können auch die Vorboten einer neuen Regel sein': Marie von Ebner-Eschenbach's Proverbial Aphorisms." *Modern Austrian Literature* 26, 1 (1993): 105-114.

913. Stasiewski, Bernhard. "'Polnische Wirtschaft' und Johann Georg Forster, eine wortgeschichtliche Studie." *Deutsche wissenschaftliche Zeitschrift im Wartheland* 2 (1941): 207-216.

914. Winterling, Gisela. "Aphorismen von Frauen: Marie von Ebner-Eschenbach und moderne Autorinnen." M. A. Thesis. University of Mainz, 1995. 126 pp.

ECK, JOHANN (1486-1543)

915. Brandt, Gisela. "Feste Wendungen." In Erwin Arndt and G. Brandt. *Luther und die deutsche Sprache.* Leipzig: VEB Bibliographisches Institut, 1983. 215-219.

916.   Pfeifer, Wolfgang. "Volkstümliche Metaphorik." *Zur Literatursprache im Zeitalter der frühbürgerlichen Revolution: Untersuchungen zu ihrer Verwendung in der Agitationsliteratur.* Eds. Gerhard Kettmann and Joachim Schildt. Berlin: Akademie-Verlag, 1978. 87-217.

EDDA SONGS (c. 1240)

917.   Delpire, L. "De Edda en hare Zedeleer (Spreekwoorden)." *De Toekomst: Tijdschrift voor onderwijzers* 26 (1882): 174-180, 213-215.

918.   Heusler, Andreas. "Sprichwörter in den eddischen Sittengedichten." *Zeitschrift des Vereins für Volkskunde* 25 (1915): 108-115; 26 (1916), 42-57.

919.   Heusler, Andreas. "Altgermanische Sittenlehre und Lebensweisheit." *Germanische Wiedererstehung.* Ed. Hermann Nollau. Heidelberg: Carl Winter, 1926. 156-204.

920.   Kanzog, Klaus. "Spruch." *Reallexikon der deutschen Literaturgeschichte.* Eds. K. Kanzog, Achim Masser, and Dorothea Kanzog. Berlin: Walter de Gruyter, 1979. IV, 151-160.

921.   Meyn, Ludwig. "Germanische Wesensart in altländischen Sprichwörtern und Sprüchen." *Zeitschrift für deutsche Bildung* 11 (1935): 566-574.

922.   Mittelstädt, Hartmut. "Die isländischen Sprichwörter-Quellen, Bildgehalt, Klassifikation, Funktion im Text." *Nordeuropa-Studien* (special issue) 14 (1981): 85-94.

923.   Nordland, Odd. "Ordtak, Sosial Funksjon og Kultursamanheng." *Norveg* 7 (1960): 49-90.

924.   Singer, Samuel. *Sprichwörter des Mittelalters*, 3 vols. Bern: Herbert Lang, 1944-1947. I, 6-30.

925.   Spieß, Gisela. "Die Stellung der Frau in den Sprichwörtern isländischer Sprichwörtersammlungen und in isländischen Sagas." *Proverbium: Yearbook of International Proverb Scholarship* 8 (1991): 159-178.

926.   Vrátny, K. "Noch einiges zu den altisländischen Sprichwörtern." *Arkiv för Nordisk Filologi* 33 (1916): 58-63.

927. Wessén, Elias. "Ordspråk och lärodikt: Några stilformer: Hávamál." *Vitterhets, historie och antikvitets akademien* 91 (1959): 455-473.

EDEN, ANTHONY, 1st Earl of Avon (1897-1977)
928. Miller, Edd, and Jesse J. Villareal. "The Use of Clichés by Four Contemporary Speakers." *Quarterly Journal of Speech* 31 (1945): 151-155.

EDWARD I, King of England (1239-1307)
929. Sinclair, K. V. "An Anglo-Norman Proverb of the Chase [Tant come li chin s'en vet le leu a bois (While the hound pauses to defecate, the hare heads for the woods)]." *Notes and Queries* 220 ns 22 (1975): 436-437.

EDWARD [or Edwardes], RICHARD (c. 1523-1566)
930. Landon, Sydney Ann. "'Sundry Pithie and Learned Inventions': *The Paradise of Dainty Devices* and Sixteenth Century Poetic Traditions." Diss. University of Washington, 1986. 144 pp.

931. Whiting, Bartlett Jere. "Richard Edward's *Damon and Pithias*." *Proverbs in the Earlier English Drama.* Cambridge, Massachusetts: Harvard University Press, 1938; rpt. New York: Octagon Books, 1969. 230-236.

EGGLESTON, EDWARD (1837-1902)
932. Taylor, Archer. "Proverbial Materials in Edward Eggleston *The Hoosier Schoolmaster.*" *Studies in Honor of Stith Thompson.* Ed. G. W. Edson Richmond. Bloomington: Indiana University Press, 1957. 262-270.

EGILS SAGA (13th cent.)
933. Janus, Louis Elliot. "The Phraseology of *Egils saga.*" Diss. University of Minnesota, 1994. 195 pp.

EHRKE, HANS (1898-1975)
934. Lindow, Wolfgang. "Volkstümliches Sprachgut in der neuniederdeutschen Dialektdichtung." Diss. Kiel, 1960. Part I, 117-120.

EIKE VON REPGOW (1180/90-c. 1233)
935. Grimm, Jacob. "Von der Poesie im Recht." *Zeitschrift für geschichtliche Rechtswissenschaft* 2 (1815): 25-99. Also in *Kleinere Schriften.* Berlin: Ferdinand Dümmler, 1882. VI, 152-191.

936. Janz, Brigitte. *Rechtssprichwörter im "Sachsenspiegel": Eine Unter-suchung zur Text-Bild-Relation in den Codices picturati.* Frankfurt am Main: Peter Lang, 1989. 586 pp.

937. Leiser, Wolfgang. "'Im Namen des Volkes!' Eine Formel und ihre Geschichte." *Vierteljahrschrift für Sozial- und Wirtschaftsgeschichte* 55 (1968): 501-515.

938. Schmidt-Wiegand, Ruth. "Rechtssprichwörter und ihre Wiedergabe in den Bilderhandschriften des *Sachsenspiegels*." *Text und Bild: Aspekte des Zusammenwirkens zweier Künste in Mittelalter und früher Neuzeit.* Eds. Christel Meier and Uwe Ruberg. Wiesbaden: Ludwig Reichert, 1980. 593-629.

EIXIMENIS (1340-1409)

939. Lassen, Regine. "'Wer der Gemeinschaft dient, der dient niemandem': Welche Funktionen haben Sprichwörter in Eiximenis *Regiment de la cosa publica*?" *Zeitschrift für romanische Philologie* 105, 3-4 (1989): 313-321.

ELIOT, GEORGE [Mary Ann Evans] (1819-1880)

940. Hogan, Rebecca S. H. "The Wisdom of Many, the Wit of One: The Narrative Function of the Proverb in Tolstoy's *Anna Karenina* and Trollope's *Orley Farm*." Diss. University of Colorado, 1984. 1-68.

941. Obelkevich, James. "Proverbs and Social History." *The Social History of Language.* Eds. Peter Burke and Roy Porter. Cambridge: Cambridge University Press, 1987. 43-72. Also in *Wise Words: Essays on the Proverb.* Ed. Wolfgang Mieder. New York: Garland Publishing, 1994. 211-252.

ELLIS, WILLIAM (c. 1700-1758)

942. Britten, James. "Proverbs and Folklore from William Ellis's *Modern Husband* (1750)." *Folklore Record* 3 (1880): 80-86, 287-288.

ÉLUARD, PAUL [Eugène Grindal] (1895-1952)

943. Baudouin, Dominique. "Jeux de mots surréalistes: L'expérience du *Proverbe*." *Symposium* 24 (1970): 293-302.

944. Éluard, Paul, and Benjamin Péret. *152 proverbes mis au goût du jour.* Paris: Bureau de recherches surréealistes, 1925; *152 Sprichwörter auf den neuesten Stand gebracht.* Ed. and translated and with an afterword

by Unda Hörner and Wolfram Kiepe. Gießen: Anabas Verlag, 1995. 168 pp.

945. Grésillon, Almuth, and Dominique Maingueneau. "Polyphonie, proverbe et détournement, ou un proverbe peut en cacher un autre." *Langages* 19, 73 (1984): 112-125.

EMERSON, RALPH WALDO (1803-1882)

946. Anderson, John Q. "Emerson and the Language of the Folk." *Folk Travelers: Ballads, Tales, and Talk.* Eds. Mody C. Boatright, Wilson M. Hudson, and Allen Maxwell. Dallas: Southern Methodist University Press, 1953. 152-159.

947. Cameron, Kenneth Walter. "Emerson, Thoreau, *Elegant Extracts*, and Proverb Lore." *Emerson Society Quarterly* No. 6 (1957): 28-39.

948. Cameron, Kenneth Walter. "Emerson's Arabian Proverbs." *Emerson Society Quarterly* 13 (1958): 50.

949. D'Avanzo, Mario L. "Emerson's *Days* and Proverbs." *American Transcendental Quarterly* No. 1 (1969): 83-85.

950. La Rosa, Ralph Charles. "Emerson's Proverbial Rhetoric: 1818-1838." Diss. University of Wisconsin, 1969. 259 pp.

951. La Rosa, Ralph Charles. "Emerson's 'Sententiae' in *Nature*." *Emerson Society Quarterly* No. 58 (1970): 153-157.

952. La Rosa, Ralph Charles. "Invention and Imitation in Emerson's Early Lectures." *American Literature* 44 (1972): 13-30.

953. La Rosa, Ralph Charles. "Necessary Truths: The Poetics of Emerson's Proverbs." *George Eliot, De Quincey, and Emerson.* Ed. Eric Rothstein. Madison: University of Wisconsin Press, 1976. 129-192.

954. Loomis, C. Grant. "Emerson's Proverbs." *Western Folklore* 17 (1958): 257-262.

955. Mieder, Wolfgang. *American Proverbs: A Study of Texts and Contexts.* Bern: Peter Lang, 1989. 143-169.

956.   Reaver, J. Russell. "Emerson's Use of Proverbs." *Southern Folklore Quarterly* 28 (1963): 280-299.

EMSER, HIERONYMUS (1478-1527)
957.   Brandt, Gisela. "Feste Wendungen." In Erwin Arndt and G. Brandt. *Luther und die deutsche Sprache*. Leipzig: VEB Bibliographisches Institut, 1983. 215-219.

958.   Pfeifer, Wolfgang. "Volkstümliche Metaphorik." *Zur Literatursprache im Zeitalter der frühbürgerlichen Revolution: Untersuchungen zu ihrer Verwendung in der Agitationsliteratur*. Eds. Gerhard Kettmann and Joachim Schildt. Berlin: Akademie-Verlag, 1978. 87-217.

ENCINA, JUAN DEL (c. 1468-c. 1529)
959.   Hayes, Francis Clement. "The Use of Proverbs in the 'Siglo de Oro' Drama: An Introductory Study." Diss. University of North Carolina, 1936. 17-18.

ENGELS, FRIEDRICH (1820-1895)
960.   Mieder, Wolfgang. "'Proletarier aller Länder, vereinigt euch!' —Wozu? Geflügelter Abschied vom Marxismus." *Sprachspiegel* 47 (1991): 69-77. Also in *Sprichwörtliches und Geflügeltes: Sprachstudien von Martin Luther bis Karl Marx*. Bochum: Norbert Brockmeyer, 1995. 125-136.

ENZENSBERGER, HANS MAGNUS (1929—)
961.   Horn, Katalin. "Grimmsche Märchen als Quellen für Metaphern und Vergleiche in der Sprache der Werbung, des Journalismus und der Literatur." *Muttersprache* 91 (1981): 106-115.

EPICHARMOS (c. 550-c. 460 B. C.)
962.   Crusius, Otto. "Epicharm bei den Paroemiographen." *Corpus Paroemiographorum Graecum (Supplementum)*. Hildesheim: Georg Olms, 1961. 281-294.

EPISTOLAE OBSCURORUM VIRORUM (1515)
963.   Steiner, Arpad. "The Vernacular Proverb in Mediaeval Latin Prose." *American Journal of Philology* 65 (1944): 37-68.

EPISTULA APOSTOLORUM (A. D. 2nd cent.)
964.   Hills, Julian. "Proverbs as Sayings of Jesus in the *Epistula Apostolorum*." *Semeia* 49 (1990): 7-34.

ERASMUS OF ROTTERDAM (1469-1536)

965. Appelt, Theodore Charles. *Studies in the Contents and Sources of Erasmus' "Adagia" with Particular Reference to the First Edition.* Diss. University of Chicago, 1942. Chicago: The University of Chicago Libraries, 1942. 155 pp.

966. Balavoine, Claudie. "Les principes de la parémiographie Érasmienne." *Richesse du proverbe.* Eds. François Suard and Claude Buridant. Lille: Université de Lille, 1984. II, 9-23.

967. Bebermeyer, Renate. "'Wie ein Pferd, das die Grammatik nicht beherrscht, keineswegs unglücklich ist. . .': Zum 450. Todestag des Erasmus von Rotterdam." *Sprachspiegel* 42 (1986): 109-112.

968. Crane, Mary Thomas. "Proverbial and Aphoristic Sayings: Sources of Authority in the English Renaissance." Diss. Harvard University, 1986. 168-248.

969. Czegle, Imre. "Szaraszi Ferenc, mint Erasmus Adagia-janak magyarra ültetöje." *A Raday Gyüjtemény Evkönyve* 4-5 (1984-1985): 122-137.

970. Hannemann, Brigitte, ed. *Erasmus von Rotterdam: "Süß scheint der Krieg den Unerfahrenen"—"Dulce bellum inexpertis."* München: Chr. Kaiser, 1987. 202 pp.

971. Heironimus, John Paul. "On Calling a Spade 'An Agricultural Implement' in Latin." *The Classical Journal* 33 (1938): 426- 427.

972. Kinney, Daniel. "Erasmus' *Adagia*: Midwife to the Rebirth of Learning." *Journal of Medieval and Renaissance Studies* 11 (1981): 169- 192.

973. Knops, Mathieu. "*Das Sprichwort, Man musz entweder ein König, oder aber ein Narr geborn werden: Außgeleget vnd beschrieben von Herrn Erasmo Roterodamo, von den Tugenden einem Christlichen Fürsten vnd Herren zuständig, verdeutschet. Anno 1638.*" *Erasmus und Europa: Vorträge.* Ed. August Buck. Wiesbaden: Otto Harrassowitz, 1988. 149-161.

974. Kuiper, Gerdien C. "An Erasmian Adage as 'Fortune's Fool': Martial's 'Oleum in auricula ferre.'" *Humanistica Lovaniensia* 39 (1990): 67-84.

975.   Metzger, Bruce M. "'To Call a Spade a Spade' in Greek and Latin."
        The Classical Journal 33 (1938): 229-231.

976.   Mieder, Wolfgang. "'Wir sitzen alle in einem Boot': Herkunft, Ge-
        schichte und Verwendung einer neueren deutschen Redensart." *Mutter-
        sprache* 100 (1990): 18-37. Also in *Deutsche Redensarten, Sprichwörter
        und Zitate: Studien zu ihrer Herkunft, Überlieferung und Verwendung.*
        Vienna: Edition Praesens, 1995. 140-159.

977.   Miller, Anthony. "A Reminiscence of Erasmus in *Hamlet*, III, ii, 92-
        95." *English Language Notes* 24 (1986): 19-22.

978.   Miller, Clarence H. "The Logic and Rhetoric of Proverbs in Erasmus's
        Praise of Folly." *Essays on the Works of Erasmus*. Ed. Richard L. De
        Molen. New Haven, Connecticut: Yale University Press, 1978. 83-98.

979.   Panofsky, Dora and Erwin. *Pandora's Box: The Changing Aspects of a
        Mythical Symbol*. New York: Pantheon Books, 1956, 1962. 185 pp.

980.   Peil, Dietmar. "'Im selben Boot': Variationen über ein metaphorisches
        Argument." *Archiv für Kulturgeschichte* 68, 2 (1986): 269-293.

981.   Phillips, Margaret Mann. *The "Adages" of Erasmus: A Study with
        Translations*. Cambridge: Cambridge University Press, 1964. 418 pp.

982.   Phillips, Margaret Mann. "Ways with Adages." *Essays on the Works of
        Erasmus*. Ed. Richard L. De Molen. New Haven, Connecticut: Yale
        University Press, 1978. 51-60.

983.   Ramirez, Alejandro. "Los *Adagia* de Erasmo en los sermones de Fr.
        Alonso de Cabrera." *Hispano* 11 (1961): 29-38.

984.   Sánchez y Escribano, F. Los *"Adagia"* de Erasmo en *"La Philosophia
        Vulgar"* de Juan de Mal Lara. New York: Hispanic Institute, 1944. 85
        pp.

985.   Suringar, Willem Hendrik Dominikus. *Erasmus over nederlandsche
        spreekwoorden en spreekwoordelijke uitdrukkingen van zijnen tijd, uit 's
        mans "Adagia" opgezameld en uit andere, meest nieuwere geschriften
        opgehelderd*. Utrecht: Kemink, 1873. 595 pp.

986. Vredeveld, Harry. "'That Familiar Proverb': Folly as the Elixir of Youth in Erasmus's *Moriae Encomium*." *Renaissance Quarterly* 42, 1 (1989): 78-91.

987. Wesseling, Ari. "Dutch Proverbs and Ancient Sources in Erasmus's *Praise of Folly*." *Renaissance Quarterly* 47, 2 (1994): 351-378.

ERMENGAUD, MATFRE (1288-1322)
988. Crespo, Roberto. "Una citazione di Matfre Ermengaud e il *Novellino*." *Lettere Italiane* 32 (1980): 232-234.

ESTIENNE, HENRI (c. 1528-1598)
989. Clément, C. "Henri Estienne et son oeuvre française." Diss. Paris, 1898. 149-183, 289-399.

990. McNeal, Doris Schuckler. "The Proverbs in the French Works of Henri Estienne." Diss. University of Georgia, 1972. 424 pp.

EURIPIDES (c. 480-406)
991. Koch, Joh. Georg E. "Quaestionum de proverbis apud Aeschylum, Sophoclem, Euripidem." Diss. Königsberg, 1877. 92 pp.

992. Stevens, Phillip T. *Colloquial Expressions in Euripides*. Wiesbaden: Franz Steiner, 1976. 76 pp.

EUSTATHIOS OF THESSALONIKE (1125-1193/98)
993. Crusius, Otto, and Leopold Cohn. "Zur handschriftlichen Überlieferung der Paroemiographen." *Philologus* 6 (1891-1893): 201-324.

994. Hotop, August. *De Eustathii proverbiis*. Leipzig: B. G. Teubner, 1888. 313 pp.

995. Karathanasis, Demetrius. *Sprichwörter und sprichwörtliche Redensarten des Altertums in den rhetorischen Schriften des Michael Psellos, des Eustathios und des Michael Choniates sowie in anderen rhetorischen Quellen des XII. Jahrhunderts*." Diss. München, 1936. Speyer am Rhein: Pilger, 1936. 128 pp.

996. Kurtz, Ed. "Die Sprichwörter bei Eustathios von Thessalonike." *Corpus Paroemiographorum Graecum (Supplementum)*. Hildesheim: Georg Olms, 1961. 307-321.

EVERSON, WILLIAM OLIVER (1912-1994)
997. Monteiro, George. "The Literary Use of a Proverb." *Folklore* 87 (1976): 216-218.

EVERYMAN (c. 1500)
998. Conley, John. "The Phrase 'The Oyle of Forgyuenes' in *Everyman*: A Reference to Extreme Unction." *Notes and Queries* 220 ns 22 (1975): 105- 106.

999. Whiting, Bartlett Jere. "*Everyman.*" *Proverbs in the Earlier English Drama*. Cambridge, Massachusetts: Harvard University Press, 1938; rpt. New York: Octagon Books, 1969. 92-94.

F

FANE, MILDMAY, 2nd Earl of Westmorland (c. 1602-1666)
1000. Morton, Gerald W. "An Addendum to Apperson." *Notes and Queries* 228 ns 30 (1983): 437.

FARQUHAR, GEORGE (1678-1707)
1001. Jones, Joseph. "Wellerisms: Some Further Evidence." *American Speech* 20 (1945): 235-236.

FAULKNER, WILLIAM (1897-1962)
1002. Boswell, George W. "Folkways in Faulkner." *Mississippi Folklore Register* 1 (1967): 83-90.

1003. Harder, Kelsie B. "Proverbial Snopeslore." *Tennessee Folklore Society Bulletin* 24 (1958): 89-95.

FAUSTBUCH (1587)
1004. Fränkel, Ludwig, and A. Bauer. "Entlehnungen im ältesten Faustbuch: Das Sprichwörterkapitel." *Vierteljahrschrift für Litteraturgeschichte* 4 (1888): 361-381.

1005. Seiler, Friedrich. *Deutsche Sprichwörterkunde*. München: C. H. Beck, 1922, 1967. 58.

FECHNER, GUSTAV THEODOR (1801-1887)
1006. Strube, Werner. "Zur Geschichte des Sprichworts 'Über den Geschmack läßt sich nicht streiten.'" *Zeitschrift für Ästhetik und Allgemeine Kunstwissenschaft* 30 (1985): 158-185.

FEDELE AND FORTUNIO (1584)
1007. Whiting, Bartlett Jere. "*Fedele and Fortunio, the Two Italian Gentlemen.*" *Proverbs in the Earlier English Drama*. Cambridge, Massachusetts: Harvard University Press, 1938; rpt. New York: Octagon Books, 1969. 270-276.

FED'KOVICH, IURII (1834-1888)
1008. Paziak, Mikhail Mikhailovich. "Transformatsiia narodnikh prisliv'iv i porivnian' u tvorchosti Iuriia Fed'kovicha." *Narodna Tvorchist' ta Etnografiia* No. 4 (1985): 12-22.

FEHRS, JOHANN HINRICH (1838-1916)
1009. Lindow, Wolfgang. "Volkstümliches Sprachgut in der neuniederdeutschen Dialektdichtung." Diss. Kiel, 1960. Part I, 120-126.

1010. Lindow, Wolfgang. "Das Sprichwort bei Johann Hinrich Fehrs." *Mitteilungen aus dem Quickborn* 52 (1962): 76-79.

FEIJOO Y MONTENEGRO, BENITO JERONIMO (1676-1764)
1011. Castillo de Lusas, Antonio. "Critica a la critica de los refranes del P. Feijóo." *Revista de Dialectologia y Tradiciones Populares* 22 (1966): 97-118.

1012. Köhler, Erich. "Der Padre Feijóo und das 'no sé qué.'" *Romanistisches Jahrbuch* 7 (1955-56): 272-290.

FÉNELON, FRANÇOIS de (1651-1715)
1013. Clark, John Edwards. "Sententious Sayings in the Writings of Fénelon." M. A. Thesis. University of North Carolina, 1954. 55 pp.

FERNANDEZ DE LIZARDI, JOSÉ JOAQUIN (1776-1827)
1014. O'Kane, Eleanor. "El refrán en las novelas de Fernández de Lizardi." *Anuario de la Sociedad folklórica de México* 6 (1945): 403-408.

FEUERBACH, LUDWIG (1804-1872)
1015. Hess, Peter. *Epigramm*. Stuttgart: Metzler, 1989. 142.

FEUILLET, OCTAVE (1821-1890)
1016. Brenner, Clarence D. *The French Dramatic Proverb*. Berkeley, California: Privately printed, 1977. 68 pp.

FIELD, NATHANIEL (1587-1619)
1017. Peery, William. "Proverbs and Proverbial Elements in the Plays of Nathan Field." *Southern Folklore Quarterly* 10 (1946): 1-16.

FIELDING, HENRY (1707-1754)
1018. Hamst, Olphar. "Fielding's Proverbs." *Notes and Queries* 5th ser. 2 (1874): 414.

1019. Jackson, Stephen. "Fielding's Proverbs." *Notes and Queries* 5th ser. 2 (1874): 209.

1020. Jackson, Stephen. "Fielding's Proverbs." *Notes and Queries* 5th ser. 3 (1875): 171-172.

1021. Rinehart, Hollis. "Fielding's Chapter 'Of Proverbs' (*Jonathan Wild* [1743], Book 2, Chapter 12): Sources, Allusions, and Interpretation." *Modern Philology* 77 (1980): 291-296.

1022. Rogers, Pat. "Tristram Shandy's *Polite Conversation.*" *Essays in Criticism* 32 (1982): 305-320.

1023. Schmidt-Hidding, Wolfgang. "Henry Fielding." *Englische Idiomatik in Stillehre und Literatur*. München: Max Hueber, 1962. 53-57.

FIELDS, W. C. [William Claude Dukenfield] (1880-1946)
1024. Olinick, Stanley L. "On Proverbs: Creativity, Communication, and Community." *Contemporary Psychoanalysis* 23 (1987): 463-468.

FILIMON, NICOLAE (1819-1865)
1025. Negreanu, Constantin. "Valentele educative si stilistice ale expresiilor si proverbelor în limba literaturii artistice." *Scoala Mehedintiului* 3 (1978): 23-26.

1026. Negreanu, Constantin. "Functiile proverbului in opera lui Nicolae Filimon." *Memoriile sectiei de stiinte filologice, literatura si arte* 4th ser. 9 (1987): 73-81.

1027. Negreanu, Constantin. "Aforistica lui Nicolae Filimon." *Limba si literatura română* 18, 1 (1989): 40-42.

1028. Negreanu, Constantin. "Nicolae Filimon and the Romanian Proverb." *Proverbium: Yearbook of International Proverb Scholarship* 9 (1992): 179-186.

FISCHART, JOHANN (1546-1590)
1029. "Alte deutsche Sprichwörter aus Fischart's [*sic*] Übersetzung von Rabelais." *Litterarisches Wochenblatt* 4 (1819): nos. 28, 30, 33.

1030. Gerke-Siefart, Hilde. "Sprichwörter und Redensarten bei Johann Fischart." Diss. München, 1953. 319 pp.

1031. Kelley, Edmond Morgan. "Fischart's Use of the Proverb as a Stylistic Device in His *Geschichtsklitterung*." Diss. Michigan State University, 1968. 230 pp.

1032. Prahl, August. "Sprichwörter und Redensarten bei Johann Fischart." M. A. Thesis. Washington University, 1928. 90 pp.

1033. Spengler, Walter Eckehart. *Johann Fischart gen. Mentzer: Studie zur Sprache und Literatur des ausgehenden 16. Jahrhunderts*. Göppingen: Alfred Kümmerle, 1969. Especially pp. 393-403.

1034. Sullivan, John F. "Das Sprichwort bei Johann Fischart (*Geschichtsklitterung*)." Diss. New York University, 1937. Abridgement published by the Graduate School of New York University, 1937. 33 pp.

FLAMANT, GUILLAUME (c. 1455-1510)
1035. Surdel, Alain-Julien. "Typologie et stylistique des locutions sentencieuses dans *Le Mystère de S. Didier de Langres* de Guillaume Flamant (1482)." *Richesse du proverbe*. Eds. François Suard and Claude Buridant. Lille: Université de Lille, 1984. I, 145-162.

FLAUBERT, GUSTAVE (1821-1880)
1036. Wesley, B. Josephine. "Similes and Metaphors in Flaubert's *Madame Bovary* and *Salammbo*." M. A. Thesis. University of Chicago, 1932. 191 pp.

FLECK, KONRAD (13th cent.)
1037. Hofmann, Liselotte. *Der volkskundliche Gehalt der mittelhochdeutschen Epen von 1100 bis gegen 1250*. Zeulenroda: Bernhard Sporn, 1939. 74.

FLETCHER, JOHN (1579-1625)
1038. Marshall, Ed. "Proverbial Phrases in Beaumont and Fletcher *To Write in Water*." *Notes and Queries* 7th ser. 12 (1891): 14.

1039. Pierpoint, Robert. "Proverbial Phrases in Beaumont and Fletcher." *Notes and Queries* 8th ser. 1 (1892): 74.

1040. Prager, Carolyn. "'If I Be Devil': English Renaissance Response to the Proverbial and Ecumenical Ethiopian." *Journal of Medieval and Renaissance Studies* 17, 2 (1987): 257-279.

1041. Prideaux, W. F. "Proverbial Phrases in Beaumont and Fletcher." *Notes and Queries* 7th ser. 10 (1890): 361-362.

1042. Smith, I. E. "Proverbial Phrases in Beaumont and Fletcher." *Notes and Queries*, 7th ser. 11 (1891): 274.

1043. Taylor, Archer. "Proverbial Comparisons in the Plays of Beaumont and Fletcher." *Journal of American Folklore* 70 (1957): 25-36.

1044. Taylor, Archer. "Proverbial Phrases in the Plays of Beaumont and Fletcher." *Bulletin of the Tennessee Folklore Society* 23 (1957): 39-59.

1045. Taylor, Archer. "Proverbs in the Plays of Beaumont and Fletcher." *Southern Folklore Quarterly* 24 (1960): 77-100.

1046. Terry, F. C. Birkbeck. "Proverbial Phrases in Beaumont and Fletcher." *Notes and Queries* 7th ser. 10 (1891): 53.

1047. Yardley, E. "Proverbial Phrases in Beaumont and Fletcher." *Notes and Queries* 7th ser. 10 (1890): 431.

FLORES DE FILOSOFIA (13th cent.)

1048. Bizzarri, Hugo Oscar. "Un testimonio mas papa tres capitulos del *Libro de los cien capitulos*." *Incipit* 9 (1989): 139-146.

1049. Morgan, Frances Elnora Williams. "Proverbs from Four Didactic Works of the Thirteenth Century." Diss. University of Kentucky, 1968. 492 pp.

FOLQUET DE MARSELHA (c. 1178-1231)

1050. Pfeffer, Wendy. "'Ben conosc e sai que merces vol so que razos dechai': L'emploi du proverbe chez Folquet de Marselha." *Actes du premier congrès international de l'association internationale d'études occitanes*. Ed. Peter T. Ricketts. London: Association Internationale d'Études Occitanes, Westfield College, 1987. 401-408.

FONTANE, THEODOR (1819-1898)

1051. Ester, Hans. "Über Redensart und Herzenssprache in Theodor Fontanes *Irrungen, Wirrungen*." *Acta Germanica* 7 (1972): 101-116.

1052. Fuchs, Hardy. "Die Funktion des Sprichwortes bei Theodor Fontane." Diss. Michigan State University, 1970. 250 pp.

1053. Kanzog, Klaus. "Spruch." *Reallexikon der deutschen Literaturgeschichte*. Eds. K. Kanzog, Achim Masser, and Dorothea Kanzog. Berlin: Walter de Gruyter, 1979. IV, 151-160.

1054. Khalil, Iman Osman. "Sprüche, Sentenzen und Zitate aus fremden Sprachen." *Das Fremdwort im Gesellschaftsroman Theodor Fontanes: Zur literarischen Untersuchung eines sprachlichen Phänomens*. Frankfurt am Main: Peter Lang, 1978. 322-329.

1055. Wenger, Marion R. "Redensarten in Theodor Fontanes *Irrungen, Wirrungen.*" *Semasia: Beiträge zur germanisch-romanischen Sprachforschung* 2 (1975): 325-331.

FORSTER, E. M. [Edward Morgan Forster] (1879-1970)
1056. De Caro, Francis A. "'A Mystery Is a Muddle': Gnomic Expressions in *A Passage to India.*" *Midwestern Journal of Language and Folklore* 12 (1986): 15-23.

1057. Gish, Robert. "Forster as Fabulist: Proverbs and Parables in *A Passage to India.*" *English Literature in Transition (1880-1920)* 15 (1972): 245-256.

FORSTER, JOHANN GEORG (1754-1794)
1058. Stasiewski, Bernhard. "'Polnische Wirtschaft' und Johann Georg Forster, eine wortgeschichtliche Studie." *Deutsche wissenschaftliche Zeitschrift im Wartheland* 2 (1941): 207-216.

1059. Wörster, Peter. "'Polnische Wirtschaft.'" *Der Sprachdienst* 28 (1984): 93-95.

FRANCK, SEBASTIAN (1499-1542)
1060. Bauer, Barbara. "Die Philosophie des Sprichworts bei Sebastian Franck." *Sebastian Franck (1499-1542)*. Ed. Jan-Dirk Müller. Wiesbaden: Harrassowitz, 1993. 181-221.

1061. Hub, Ignaz. *Die komische und humoristische Litteratur der deutschen Prosaisten des sechzehnten Jahrhunderts*, 2 vols. Nürnberg: Ebner, 1856-1857; rpt. Leipzig: Zentralantiquariat der Deutschen Demokratischen Republik, 1975. 214-223.

1062. Knauer, Peter Klaus. "Metapher und Sprichwort." *Der Buchstabe lebt: Schreibstrategien bei Sebastian Franck*. Bern: Peter Lang, 1993. 230-233.

1063. Kühlmann, Wilhelm. "Auslegungsinteresse und Auslegungsverfahren in der Sprichwortsammlung Sebastian Francks (1541)." *Kleinstformen der*

Literatur. Eds. Walter Haug and Burghart Wachinger. Tübingen: Max Niemeyer, 1994. 117-131.

1064. Meisser, Ulrich. *Die Sprichwörtersammlung Sebastian Francks von 1541*. Amsterdam: Rodopi, 1974. 536 pp.

1065. Peuckert, Will-Erich. "Die Sprichwörter." *Sebastian Franck: Ein deutscher Sucher*. München: R. Piper, 1943. 456-471.

1066. Stroszeck, Hauke. "Sebastian Francks Sprichwörtersammlung." *Pointe und poetische Dominante: Deutsche Kurzprosa im 16. Jahrhundert*. Frankfurt am Main: Thesen Verlag, 1970. 60-69.

FRANKLIN, BENJAMIN (1706-1790)

1067. Barbour, Frances M., ed. *A Concordance to the Sayings in Franklin's "Poor Richard."* Detroit, Michigan: Gale Research Company, 1974. 245 pp.

1068. Ford, Paul Leicester, ed. *"The Sayings of Poor Richard": The Preface, Proverbs and Poems of Benjamin Franklin Originally Printed in Poor Richard's Almanacs for 1733-1758*. New York: G. P. Putnam's Sons, 1890. 288 pp.

1069. Gallacher, Stuart A. "Franklin's *Way to Wealth*: A Florilegium of Proverbs and Wise Sayings." *Journal of English and Germanic Philology* 48 (1949): 229-251.

1070. Gallagher, Edward J. "The Rhetorical Strategy of Franklin's *Way to Wealth*." *Eighteenth Century Studies* 6 (1973): 475- 485.

1071. Meister, Charles W. "Franklin as a Proverb Stylist." *American Literature* 24 (1952-1953): 157-166.

1072. Mieder, Wolfgang. *American Proverbs: A Study of Texts and Contexts*. Bern: Peter Lang, 1989. 129-142.

1073. Newcomb, Robert. "Poor Richard's Debt to Lord Halifax." *Publications of the Modern Language Association* 70 (1955): 535-539.

1074. Newcomb, Robert. "Benjamin Franklin and Montaigne." *Modern Language Notes* 72 (1957): 489-491.

1075. Newcomb, Robert. "The Sources of Benjamin Franklin's Sayings of Poor Richard." Diss. University of Maryland, 1957. 399 pp.

1076. Newcomb, Robert. "Franklin and Richardson." *Journal of English and Germanic Philology* 57 (1958): 27-35.

1077. Newcomb, Robert. "Poor Richard and the English Epigram." *Philological Quarterly* 40 (1961): 270-280.

1078. Rendall, Vernon. "Proverbs and Popular Similes." *The Saturday Review* 148 (October 19, 1929): 443.

1079. Riley, Noël. "Benjamin Franklin's Maxims." *The History of Children's China. Part 1: 1790-1890*. Ilminster, England: Richard Dennis, 1991. 270-283 (with 83 ills.).

1080. Russell, Thomas H., comp. *The Sayings of Poor Richard: Wit, Wisdom and Humor of Benjamin Franklin in the Prefaces, Proverbs, Maxims, and Poems of Poor Richard's Almanacs for 1733-1758*. Chicago: E. T. Kelly, 1926. 47 pp.

1081. Schutz, Stephen, ed. *Poor Richard's Quotations: Being a Collection of Quotations from Poor Richard Almanacks Published by Benjamin Franklin in the Years of our Lord 1733 through 1758*. Boulder, Colorado: Blue Mountain Arts, 1975. 77 pp.

1082. Steele, Thomas J. "Orality and Literacy in Matter and Form: Ben Franklin's *Way to Wealth*." *Oral Tradition* 2, 1 (1987): 273-285.

1083. Sullivan, Patrick. "Benjamin Franklin, the Inveterate (and Crafty) Public Instructor: Instruction on Two Levels in *The Way to Wealth*." *Early American Literature* 21 (1986-1987): 248-259.

1084. Van Doren, Carl. "Poor Richard." *Benjamin Franklin*. New York: The Viking Press, 1938. 106-115, 149-151, 266-268.

1085. Webber, Eunice Lucille. "Proverbs and Proverbial Phrases in Volumes I-IV of the Works of Benjamin Franklin." M. A. Thesis. Stetson University, 1942. 69 pp.

FRAUENLOB [Heinrich von Meissen] (c. 1250-1318)

1086. Gallacher, Stuart A. "Frauenlob's Bits of Wisdom: Fruits of His Environment." *Middle Ages—Reformation—Volkskunde: Festschrift for John G. Kunstmann.* Editor unknown. Chapel Hill: University of North Carolina Press, 1959. 45-58.

1087. Hofmeister, Wernfried. *Sprichwortartige Mikrotexte als literarische Medien, dargestellt an der hochdeutschen politischen Lyrik des Mittelalters.* Bochum: Norbert Brockmeyer, 1995. 287-298.

1088. Saechtig, Oskar. "Über die Bilder und Vergleiche in den Sprüchen und Liedern Heinrichs von Meissen, genannt Frauenlob." Diss. Marburg, 1930. 86 pp.

FRAUENZUCHT-BERNKOPF (15th cent.)

1089. Hofmeister, Wernfried. *Sprichwortartige Mikrotexte als literarische Medien, dargestellt an der hochdeutschen politischen Lyrik des Mittelalters.* Bochum: Norbert Brockmeyer, 1995. 377-394.

FREDRO, ALEKSANDR (1793-1878)

1090. Połowniak-Wawrzonek, Dorota. "Stałe związki frazeologiczne i przysłowia w działach Aleksandra Fredry." *Poradnik Jezykowy* 5, 504 (1993): 259-273.

FREIDANK (died c. 1233)

1091. Eifler, Günter. "Volksmässige Tradition." *Die ethischen Anschauungen in "Freidanks Bescheidenheit."* Tübingen: Max Niemeyer, 1969. 15-27.

1092. Grubmüller, Klaus. "Freidank." *Kleinstformen der Literatur.* Eds. Walter Haug and Burghart Wachinger. Tübingen: Max Niemeyer, 1994. 38-55.

1093. Mieder, Wolfgang. *"Findet, so werdet ihr suchen!" Die Brüder Grimm und das Sprichwort.* Bern: Peter Lang, 1986. 53-63.

1094. Peretz, Bernhard. *Altprovenzalische Sprichwörter mit einem kurzen Hinblick auf den mittelhochdeutschen Freidank.* Erlangen: Andreas Deichert, 1887. Also in *Romanische Forschungen* 3 (1887): 415-457.

1095. Preuss, Richard. "Stilistische Untersuchungen über Gottfried von Straßburg." *Straßburger Studien: Zeitschrift für Geschichte, Sprache und Litteratur des Elsasses* 1 (1883): 1-75.

1096. Seiler, Friedrich. *Deutsche Sprichwörterkunde*. München: C. H. Beck, 1922, 1967. 49-50.

1097. Singer, Samuel. "Freidanks Bescheidenheit." *Sprichwörter des Mittelalters*, 3 vols. Bern: Herbert Lang, 1944-1947. II, 155-187; III, 7-119.

1098. *Vridanks Bescheidenheit*. Ed. Wilhelm Grimm. Göttingen: Dieterich, 1834. lxxiii-lxxvii, lxxxviii-cxi.

1099. Wagner, Eva. 'Das Sprichwort bei Freidank.' "Sprichwort und Sprichworthaftes als Gestaltungselemente im *Renner* Hugos von Trimberg." Diss. Würzburg, 1962. 153-164.

1100. Wilcke, Karin, and Lothar Bluhm. "Wilhelm Grimms Sammlung mittelhochdeutscher Sprichwörter." *Brüder Grimm Gedenken*. Ed. Ludwig Denecke. Marburg: N. G. Elwert, 1988. VIII, 81-122.

FRIED, ERICH (1921-1989)
1101. Mieder, Wolfgang. "'It's Five Minutes to Twelve': Folklore and Saving Life on Earth." *International Folklore Review* 7 (1989): 10-21.

FRISCH, MAX (1911-1991)
1102. Higi-Wydler, Melanie. *Zur Übersetzung von Idiomen: Eine Beschreibung und Klassifizierung deutscher Idiome und ihrer französischen Übersetzungen*. Bern: Peter Lang, 1989. 335 pp.

1103. Kantola, Markhu. "Zum phraseologischen Wortpaar in der deutschen Gegenwartssprache." *Beiträge zur allgemeinen und germanistischen Phraseologieforschung: Internationaler Symposium in Oulu 13.-15. Juni 1986*. Ed. Jarmo Kor-honen. Oulu: Oulun Yliopisto, 1987. 111-128.

FROISSART, JEAN (1337-c. 1410)
1104. Cohen, Helen Louise. "Proverbs and the Ballade." *The Ballade*. New York: Columbia University Press, 1915. 94-102.

1105. Fehse, Erich. *Sprichwort und Sentenz bei Eustache Deschamps und Dichtern seiner Zeit*. Diss. Berlin, 1905. Erlangen: Universitäts-Buchdruckerei, 1905. 43-44. Also in *Romanische Forschungen* 19 (1906): 587.

1106. Whiting, Bartlett Jere. "Proverbs in the Writings of Jean Froissart." *Speculum* 10 (1935): 291-321.

FROST, ROBERT (1875-1963)
1107. Airmet, Douglas Elliot. "The Saying: Snatches for a Poetic." Diss. University of Iowa, 1985. 339 pp.

1108. Barker, Addison. "'Good Fences Make Good Neighbors.'" *Journal of American Folklore* 64 (1951): 421.

1109. Monteiro, George. "'Good Fences Make Good Neighbors': A Proverb and a Poem." *Revista de Etnografia* 16 (1972): 83-88.

1110. Wilhelm, Albert E. "Robert Frost's Proverbial Promises: Indian Responses to *Stopping by Woods.*" *Motif: International Newsletter of Research in Folklore and Literature* No. 4 (1982): 7.

FÜHMANN, FRANZ (1922-1984)
1111. Mieder, Wolfgang. "Spiel mit Sprichwörtern: In memoriam Franz Fühmann (1922-1984)." *Sprachpflege* 34 (1985): 1-3. Also in *Sprichwörtliches und Geflügeltes: Sprachstudien von Martin Luther bis Karl Marx*. Bochum: Norbert Brockmeyer, 1995. 33-39.

FUERTES, GLORIA (1920—)
1112. Garcia-Page, Mario. "Texto paremiológico y discurso poético (el ejemplo de Gloria Fuertes)." *Paremia* No. 1 (1993): 45-53.

FULWELL, ULPIAN (1556-after 1579)
1113. Neuss, Paula. "The Sixteenth-Century English 'Proverb' Play." *Comparative Drama* 18, 1 (1984): 1-18.

1114. Whiting, Bartlett Jere. "Ulpian Fulwell's *Like Will to Like, Quoth the Devil to the Collier.*" *Proverbs in the Earlier English Drama*. Cambridge, Massachusetts: Harvard University Press, 1938; rpt. New York: Octagon Books, 1969. 127-130.

FURETIÈRE, ANTOINE (1619-1688)
1115. Perrin-Naffakh, Anne-Marie. "Locutions et proverbes dans les *Fables* de La Fontaine." *L'information littéraire* 31 (1979): 151-155. Also in *Proverbia in Fabula: Essays on the Relationship of the Fable and the Proverb*. Ed. Pack Carnes. Bern: Peter Lang, 1988. 285-294.

G

GADH, HEMMING (died 1520)

1116. Andersson, Thorsten. "'I saeng medh sko och hosor': En ordsprak-sallusion hos Hemming Gadh." *Arkiv for Nordisk Filologi* 83 (1968): 226-237.

GAETULICUS (A. D. 1st cent.)

1117. Prittwitz-Gaffron, Erich von. *Das Sprichwort im griechischen Epigramm.* Diss. München, 1912. Gießen: Alfred Töpelmann, 1912. 41.

GAMMER GURTON'S NEEDLE (c. 1579)

1118. Whiting, Bartlett Jere. "*Gammer Gurton's Needle.*" *Proverbs in the Earlier English Drama.* Cambridge, Massachusetts: Harvard University Press, 1938; rpt. New York: Octagon Books, 1969. 217-218.

GARASSE, LE P. FRANÇOIS (1585-1631)

1119. Duine, F. "Le P. Garasse." *Revue des traditions populaires* 18 (1903): 211-212.

GARCIA LORCA, FREDERICO (1898-1936)

1120. Molho, Mauricio. "Del poema como significante: refrán." *Homenaje al Professor Antonio Vilanova.* Ed. Marta Cristina Carbonell. Barcelona: Departamento de Filologia Española, Universidad de Barcelona, 1989. II, 427-432.

GARCIA MÁRQUEZ, GABRIEL (1928—)

1121. Wandruszka, Mario. "Sprache aus Bildern." *Die europäische Sprachengemeinschaft: Deutsch—Französisch—English—Italienisch—Spanisch im Vergleich.* Tübingen: A. Francke, 1990. 51-76.

GARDINER, JOHN (16th cent.)

1122. Mauch, Thomas Karl. "The Role of the Proverb in Early Tudor Literature." Diss. University of California at Los Angeles, 1963. 145-148.

GARNIER, ROBERT (1535-1590)

1123. Rech, Joseph. *Die Sentenzen und lehrhaften Stellen in den Tragödien Robert Garniers.* Diss. Straßburg, 1891. Metz: N. P., 1891. 62 pp.

GASCOIGNE, GEORGE (c. 1539/42-1577)

1124. Whiting, Bartlett Jere. "George Gascoigne's *Supposes.*" *Proverbs in the Earlier English Drama.* Cambridge, Massachusetts, 1938; rpt. New York: Octagon Books, 1969. 240-243.

1125. Whiting, Bartlett Jere. "George Gascoigne's *Glass of Government.*" *Proverbs in the Earlier English Drama*. Cambridge, Massachusetts: Harvard University Press, 1938; rpt. New York: Octagon Books, 1969. 244-249.

GASKELL, ELIZABETH (1810-1865)

1126. Hogan, Rebecca S. H. "The Wisdom of Many, the Wit of One: The Narrative Function of the Proverb in Tolstoy's *Anna Karenina* and Trollope's *Orley Farm.*" Diss. University of Colorado, 1984. 1-68.

1127. Nickel, Marjorie A. "The Dating of a Mrs. Gaskell Letter [Much would have more; Give him (her) an inch, and he (she) will take an ell]." *Notes and Queries* 220 ns 22 (1975): 113.

GAUTIER D'ARRAS (1135-1198)

1128. Schulze-Busacker, Elisabeth. "Proverbes et expressions proverbiales chez Chrétien de Troyes, Gautier d'Arras et Hue de Rotelande." *Incidences* 5 (1981): 7-16.

1129. Schulze-Busacker, Elisabeth. *Proverbes et expressions proverbiales dans la littérature narrative du moyen âge français: Recueil et analyse*. Paris: Librairie Honoré Champion, 1985. 64-75.

GAY, JOHN (1685-1732)

1130. Mieder, Wolfgang. "The Proverb in the Modern Age: Old Wisdom in New Clothing." *Tradition and Innovation in Folk Literature*. Hanover, New Hampshire: University Press of New England, 1987. 118-156, 248-255 (notes).

GEILER VON KAISERSBERG (1445-1510)

1131. Birlinger, Anton. "Alte gute Sprüche aus Geiler, Andern und Zimmern." *Alemannia* 1 (1873): 303-304.

1132. Birlinger, Anton. "Goldkörner aus Geiler von Kaisersberg." *Alemannia* 3 (1875): 13-15.

1133. Breitenstein, Eugen. "Sprichwörtliche Redensarten aus der *Emeis* Geiler von Kaisersbergs." *Archiv für elsässische Kirchengeschichte* 15 (1941): 147-148.

1134. Hub, Ignaz. "Sprüche, Gleichnisse, Zeitbilder." *Die komische und humoristische Litteratur der deutschen Prosaisten des sechzehnten*

Jahrhunderts, 2 vols. Nürnberg: Ebner, 1856-1857; rpt. Leipzig: Zentralantiquariat der Deutschen Demokratischen Republik, 1975. I, 36-58.

1135. Kurrelmeyer, William. "'Wes das Herz voll ist, des gehet der Mund über.'" *Modern Language Notes* 50 (1935): 380-382.

1136. Lambs, August. *Ein Dutzend elsässischer Sprichwörter aus Geyler's [sic] Schriften*. Strassburg: Heitz, 1890. 40 pp.

1137. Leffts, Joseph. "Altelsässische Spruchweisheit: Aus Geilers Predigten gesammelt." *Elsassland* 5 (1925): 333-337.

1138. Nelson, Timothy C. "'Ex abundantia cordis os loquitur': Ein Beitrag zur Rezeptionsgeschichte eines umstrittenen Sprichworts." *Proverbium: Yearbook of International Proverb Scholarship* 3 (1986): 101-123.

1139. Roeder von Diersberg, Elvire. "Sprichwörter, Sprüche, Redensarten." *Komik und Humor bei Geiler von Kaisersberg*. Berlin: Emil Ebering, 1921. 92-96.

1140. Seiler, Friedrich. *Deutsche Sprichwörterkunde*. München: C. H. Beck, 1922, 1967. 54-55.

1141. Stöber, August. "496 Sprichwörter und sprichwörtliche Redensarten aus den Schriften Geiler's [sic] von Kaisersberg." *Alsatia* (1862-1867): 131-162.

GENERYDES (15th cent.)
1142. Whiting, Bartlett Jere. "Proverbs in Certain Middle English Romances in Relation to Their French Sources." *Harvard Studies and Notes in Philology and Literature* 15 (1933): 75-126, especially 109-111.

LA GENTE POITEVINRIE (1572)
1143. Desaivre, Léo. "La gente Poitevinrie." *Revue des traditions populaires* 20 (1905): 229-235.

GERMANICUS CAESAR [Gaius Julius Caesar Germanicus] (15 B. C.-A. D. 19)
1144. Prittwitz-Gaffron, Erich von. *Das Sprichwort im griechischen Epigramm*. Diss. München, 1912. Gießen: Alfred Töpelmann, 1912. 39-40.

GESAMMTABENTEUER (12th-14th cent.)

1145. Girvin, William H. "The Medieval German Proverb as Reflected in the *Gesammtabenteuer*." Diss. Michigan State University, 1972. 94 pp.

GEZELLE, GUIDO (1830-1899)

1146. Jacob-Bekaert, Arthur. "De duivel-zeispreuken bij Guido Gezelle." *Wetenschappelijke Tijdingen* 24 (1965): 289-308.

GIELÉE, JACQUEMART (13th-14th cent.)

1147. Roberts, John G. "Proverbs and Ambiguous Locutions in *Renart le Nouvel*." *Kentucky Foreign Language Quarterly* 11 (1964): 218-225.

GIL DE BIEDMA, JAIME (1929—)

1148. Le Bigot, Claude. "La deconstrucción de la frase hecha en algunos poetas sociales." *Paremia* No. 2 (1993): 151-155.

GILBERT, Sir WILLIAM SCHWENCK (1836-1911)

1149. Mieder, Wolfgang. "Proverbs in American Popular Songs." *Proverbium: Yearbook of International Proverb Scholarship* 5 (1988): 85-101.

GILGAMESH (c. 2000 B. C.)

1150. Hallo, William W. "Proverbs Quoted in Epic." *Lingering over Words: Studies in Ancient Near Eastern Literature in Honor of W. L. Moran*. Eds. Tzvi Abusch, John Huehnergard, and Piotr Steinkeller. Atlanta, Georgia: Scholars Press, 1990. 203-217 (=*Harvard Semitic Studies* 37 [1990], 203-217).

GILLET DE LA TESSONNERIE (1620-1660)

1151. Duine, F. "*Le Campagnard*, Comédie, par Monsieur Gillet, Paris 1657." *Revue des traditions populaires* 16 (1901): 400.

GINGLAIN (13th cent.)

1152. Pineaux, Jacques. "Un roman de chevalerie: *Ginglain*." *Proverbes et dictons français*, 6th ed. Paris: Presses Universitaires de France, 1973. 52-55.

GIRART D'AMIENS (13th cent.)

1153. Saly, Antoinette. "Les proverbes dans le *Meliacin* de Girart d'Amiens: Aspect et fonction." *Richesse du proverbe*. Eds. François Suard and Claude Buridant. Lille: Université de Lille, 1984. I, 121-129.

GISLA SAGA SÚRSSONAR (13th cent.)

1154. Nelson, Timothy C. "'Ordhskvidhir' in der *Gisla saga Súrssonar*: Form und Funktion." *Proverbium: Yearbook of International Proverb Scholarship* 4 (1987): 143-172.

GISMOND OF SALERNE IN LOVE (1567/1568)

1155. Whiting, Bartlett Jere. "*Gismond of Salerne in Love*." *Proverbs in the Earlier English Drama*. Cambridge, Massachusetts: Harvard University Press, 1938; rpt. New York: Octagon Books, 1969. 285-289.

GLAUBRECHT, OTTO (1807-1859)

1156. Müller-Salget, Klaus. "Volkslied, Sprichwort, Bibel, Gesangbuch: Geistliches und Weltliches im Dienste der Bekräftigung und Vergewisserung." *Erzählungen für das Volk: Evangelische Pfarrer als Volksschriftsteller im Deutschland des 19. Jahrhunderts*. Berlin: Erich Schmidt, 1984. 314-326.

GODEFRID OF WINCHESTER (c. 1050-1107)

1157. Gerhard, Hartwig. *Der "Liber Proverbiorum" des Godefrid von Winchester*. Diss. Würzburg, 1971. Würzburg: Selbstverlag, 1974. 130 pp.

GODLY QUEEN HESTER (1525/1529)

1158. Whiting, Bartlett Jere. "*Godly Queen Hester*." *Proverbs in the Earlier English Drama*. Cambridge, Massachusetts: Harvard University Press, 1938; rpt. New York: Octagon Books, 1969. 43-45.

GOETHE, JOHANN WOLFGANG VON (1749-1832)

1159. Bertin, Robert. "Etwas vom Sprichwort bei Goethe." *Zeitschrift für den deutschen Unterricht* 24 (1910): 131-132.

1160. Dobel, Richard, ed. *Lexikon der Goethe-Zitate*. Zürich: Artemis, 1968; in paperback as *Dtv-Lexikon der Goethe-Zitate*, 2 vols. München: Deutscher Taschenbuch Verlag, 1972. 1308 cols.

1161. Ebrard, Wilhelm. *Alliterierende Wortverbindungen bei Goethe*, 2 vols. Nürnberg: U. E. Sebald, 1899, 1901. 42 pp.; 31 pp.

1162. Fasola, Carlo. "Questioncelle faustiane: Proverbi e canzoni nel *Faust* di Goethe." *Revista di Letteratura Tedesca* 3 (1909): 330-334.

1163. Frenken, J. "Till and Götz." *Eulenspiegel-Jahrbuch* 8 (1968): 12-16.

1164. Garbe, Joachim. "Das also war des Pudels Kern! 'Geflügelte Worte' und ihr Ursprung." *Praxis Deutsch* 16 (July 1989): 30-32, 37.

1165. Guthke, Karl S. *Letzte Worte: Variationen über ein Thema der Kulturgeschichte des Westens.* München: C. H. Beck, 1990. 225 pp.

1166. Guthke, Karl S. "'Gipsabgüsse von Leichenmasken'? Goethe und der Kult des letzten Worts." *Jahrbuch der deutschen Schillergesellschaft* 35 (1991): 73-95.

1167. Hecker, Max F. *Goethe Maximen und Reflexionen.* Weimar: Goethe-Gessellschaft, 1907. 411 pp.

1168. Hecker, Max F. *Goethes Sprüche in Reimen: Zahme Xenien und Invektiven.* Leipzig: Insel, 1908. 264 pp.

1169. Henkel, Arthur. "Die Quelle eines Goetheschen 'Spruchs' (Blasen ist nicht flöten, ihr müßt die Finger bewegen)." *Germanisch-Romanische Monatsschrift* 35 (1954): 68-69.

1170. Henkel, Hermann. "Sprichwörtliches bei Goethe." *Goethe-Jahrbuch* 11 (1890): 179-183.

1171. Hess, Peter. *Epigramm.* Stuttgart: Metzler, 1989. 20-21, 59-60, 62-63, 129-139.

1172. Kanzog, Klaus. "Spruch." *Reallexikon der deutschen Literaturgeschichte.* Eds. K. Kanzog, Achim Masser, and Dorothea Kanzog. Berlin: Walter de Gruyter, 1979. IV, 151-160.

1173. Lautenbach, Ernst. *Goethe: Zitate, Redensarten, Sprichwörter.* Hanau: Werner Dausien, 1986. 243 pp.

1174. Lefcourt, Charles R. "Goethe as a Folklorist." *Keystone Folklore Quarterly* 12 (1967): 175-176.

1175. Loeper, J. L. Gustav von. *Sprüche in Prosa: Zum ersten Mal erläutert und auf ihre Quellen zurückgeführt.* Berlin: G. Hempel, 1870. 259 pp.

1176. Mautner, Franz H. "Der Aphorismus als literarische Gattung." *Zeitschrift für Ästhetik und allgemeine Kunstwissenschaft* 27 (1933): 132-175.

1177. Mautner, Franz H. "Maxim(e)s, Sentences, Fragmente, Aphorismen." *Actes du 4e Congrès de l'Association Internationale de Littérature Comparée, Fribourg 1964.* Ed. François Jost. The Hague: Mouton, 1966. II, 812-819.

1178. Meyer, Richard M. "Zu Goethes Sprüchen." *Archiv für das Studium der neueren Sprachen und Literaturen* 106 (1901): 18-27.

1179. Mieder, Wolfgang. "'Nach Zitaten drängt, am Zitate hängt doch alles!' Zur modernen Verwendung von Goethe-Zitaten." *Muttersprache* 92 (1982): 76-98. Also in *Deutsche Sprichwörter in Literatur, Politik, Presse und Werbung.* Hamburg: Helmut Buske, 1983. 158-180.

1180. Mieder, Wolfgang. "Es 'kondomisiert' der Mensch, solang er strebt." *Der Sprachdienst* 31 (1987): 165-167.

1181. Novichkova, R. M. "Pro odnofrazovi teksti (na materiali nimets'koi movi)." *Movoznavstvo* 15, 3 (1981): 71-75.

1182. Pfeffer, J. Alan. *The Proverb in Goethe.* Diss. Columbia University, 1948. New York: King's Crown Press, 1948. 201 pp.

1183. Pfeffer, J. Alan. "The Identification of Proverbs in Goethe." *Modern Language Notes* 69 (1954): 596-598.

1184. Riha, Karl. "Balla Balla, Balla Basta: Zur Poetik kleiner literarischer Formen." *Akzente* 21 (1974): 265-287.

1185. Roche, Reinhard. "Floskeln im Gegenwartsdeutsch: 'Im Deutschen lügt man, wenn man höflich ist' (*Faust* V, 6771)." *Wirkendes Wort* 15 (1965): 385-405.

1186. Scheichl, Sigurd Paul. "Feste Syntagmen im dramatischen Dialog: Materialien zur Geschichte eines Stilmittels zwischen Goethe und Kroetz." *Tradition und Entwicklung: Festschrift Eugen Thurnher.* Eds. Werner Bauer, Achim Masser, and Guntram Plangg. Innsbruck: Institut für Germanistik der Universität Innsbruck, 1982. 383-407.

1187. Schewe, Harry. "'Ihr gebt mir ja nichts dazu': Eine Redeformel der Volkssprache, ein Volkstanzlied und Goethes Ballade *Vor Gericht.*" *Beiträge zur sprachlichen Volksüberlieferung.* Eds. Ingeborg Weber-

Kellermann and Wolfgang Steinitz. Berlin [East]: Akademie-Verlag, 1953. 28-38.

1188. Schoppe, Georg. "'Strohwitwe.'" *Germanisch-Romanische Monatsschrift* 26 (1938): 71-73.

1189. Seiler, Friedrich. "Ein 'alter Reim' bei Goethe (Es ist schlecht Wasser, sagte der Reiher und konnte nicht schwimmen)." *Zeitschrift für den deutschen Unterricht* 33 (1919): 383-386.

1190. Seiler, Friedrich. "Goethe und das deutsche Sprichwort." *Germanisch-Romanische Monatsschrift* 10 (1922): 328-340.

1191. Taylor, Archer. "'I Am Thine and Thou Art Mine.'" *Hommages à Georges Dumézil.* Bruxelles: Revue d'études latines, 1960. 201-208. Also in *Comparative Studies in Folklore: Asia—Europe—America.* Taipei: The Orient Cultural Service, 1972. 267-274.

1192. Thümmel, Julius. "Uber die Sentenz im Drama, namentlich bei Shakespeare, Goethe und Schiller." *Jahrbuch der deutschen Shakespeare Gesellschaft* 14 (1879): 97-114.

1193. Walz, John A. "'Einen Hasen laufen lassen' in Goethe's *Dichtung und Wahrheit.*" *Modern Language Notes* 23 (1908): 211-212.

1194. Zintl, Josef. "Prosodic Influences on the Meaning of 'Leck mich am Arsch' in Bavarian." *Maledicta* 4, 1 (1980): 91-95.

GOETHE, KATHARINA ELISABETH (1731-1808)
1195. Pfeffer, J. Alan. "The Proverbs in the Letters of the Frau Rath Goethe." *Journal of English and Germanic Philology* 47 (1948): 156-164.

GOGOL, NIKOLAI VASIL'EVICH (1809-1852)
1196. Gvozdarev, Iu. A. "Sem' piatnits na nedele: Istoki nekotoryykh izrechenii." *Russkaia Rech'* No. 4 (1981): 143-148.

1197. Hogan, Rebecca S. H. "The Wisdom of Many, the Wit of One: The Narrative Function of the Proverb in Tolstoy's *Anna Karenina* and Trollope's *Orley Farm.*" Diss. University of Colorado, 1984. 1-68.

1198. Voropaev, V. A. "'Mertvye dushi' v traditsii narodnoi kul'tury: N. V. Gogol' i I. M. Snegirev." *Russkaia Literatura* No. 2 (1981): 92-107.

GONZALES, AMBROSE E. (1857-1926)
1199. Yates, Irene. "A Collection of Proverbs and Proverbial Sayings from South Carolina Literature." *Southern Folklore Quarterly* 11 (1947): 187-199.

GONZÁLEZ, ANGEL (1925—)
1200. Le Bigot, Claude. "La deconstrucción de la frase hecha en algunos poetas sociales." *Paremia* No. 2 (1993): 151-155.

GORKI, MAXIM [Aleksei Maksimovich Peshkov] (1868-1936)
1201. Matveichuk, N. F. "Poslovitsy i pogovorki v povesti Gor'kogo *Foma Gordeev*." *Russkii Fol'klor* 1 (1956): 135-151.

1202. Shakhnovich, Mikh. "Kratkaia istoriia sobiraniia i izucheniia russkikh poslovits i pogovorok." *Sovetskii fol'klor: Sbornik statei i materialov* 4-5 (1936): 299-368.

GOTTFRIED VON STRASSBURG (12th/13th cent.)
1203. Jäger, Dietrich. "Der Gebrauch formelhafter zweigliedriger Ausdrücke in der vor-, früh- und hochhöfischen Epik." Diss. Kiel, 1960. 162-198.

1204. Hofmann, Liselotte. *Der volkskundliche Gehalt der mittelhochdeutschen Epen von 1100 bis gegen 1250*. Zeulenroda: Bernhard Sporn, 1939. 69-72.

1205. Mone, Franz Joseph. "Zur Literatur und Geschichte der Sprichwörter." *Quellen und Forschungen zur Geschichte der deutschen Literatur und Sprache* 1 (1830): 186-214, especially 208.

1206. Preuss, Richard. "Stilistische Untersuchungen über Gottfried von Straß-burg." *Straßburger Studien: Zeitschrift für Geschichte, Sprache und Litteratur des Elsasses* 1 (1883): 1-75.

1207. Täuber, Georg. *Die Bedeutung der Doppelformel für die Sprache und den Stil Gottfrieds von Strassburg*. Diss. Greifswald, 1912. Greifswald: Hans Adler, 1912. 108 pp.

1208. Wustmann, Rudolf. "Bildliche Redensarten in Gottfrieds *Tristan*." *Die Grenzboten* 64 (1905): 206-210.

GOTTHELF, JEREMIAS [Albert Bitzius] (1797-1854)

1209. Mieder, Wolfgang. "Das Sprichwort im Werke Jeremias Gotthelfs."
Diss. Michigan State University, 1970. 271 pp. Published as *Das Sprich-
wort im Werke Jeremias Gotthelfs: Eine volkskundlich literarische
Untersuchung*. Bern: Peter Lang, 1972. 167 pp.

1210. Mieder, Wolfgang. "Das Sprichwort in Jeremias Gotthelfs volkstümlichen Erzählungen." *Das Sprichwort in der deutschen Prosaliteratur des
neunzehnten Jahrhunderts*. München: Wilhelm Fink, 1976. 68-92.

1211. Mieder, Wolfgang. "Die Funktion des Sprichwortes als volkskundliches
Stilelement in den Werken Jeremias Gotthelfs." *Sprachspiegel* 29 (1973):
38-44, 68-74.

1212. Seiler, Friedrich. *Deutsche Sprichwörterkunde*. München: C. H. Beck,
1922, 1967. 62-63.

1213. Seiler, Friedrich. "Sonst nicht belegte Sprichwörter und sprichwörtliche
Redensarten aus Jeremias Gotthelf's [*sic*] (Bitzius) Schriften." *Germanisch-Romanische Monatsschrift* 13 (1925): 306-309.

GOTTSCHED, JOHANN CHRISTOPH (1700-66)

1214. Mieder, Wolfgang. "Die Einstellung der Grammatiker Schottelius und
Gottsched zum Sprichwort." *Sprachspiegel* 38 (1982): 70-75.

1215. Strube, Werner. "Zur Geschichte des Sprichworts 'Über den Geschmack
läßt sich nicht streiten.'" *Zeitschrift für Ästhetik und Allgemeine
Kunstwissenschaft* 30 (1985): 158-185.

GOWER, JOHN (1330-1408)

1216. Skeat, Walter William. "*Confessio Amantis*: by John Gower." *Early
English Proverbs, Chiefly of the Thirteenth and Fourteenth Centuries*.
Oxford: Clarendon Press, 1910; rpt. Darby, Pennsylvania: Folcroft
Library Editions, 1974. 54-56.

1217. Walz, Gotthard. *Das Sprichwort bei Gower, mit besonderem Hinweis auf
Quelle und Parallelen*. Nördlingen: C. H. Beck, 1907. 83 pp.

1218. Whiting, Bartlett Jere. "Chaucer and Gower." *Chaucer's Use of Proverbs*. Cambridge, Massachusetts: Harvard University Press, 1934; rpt.
New York: AMS Press, 1973. 134-154.

1219. Whiting, Bartlett Jere. "Proverbial Material in Gower's English and French Works." *Chaucer's Use of Proverbs*. Cambridge, Massachusetts: Harvard University Press, 1934; rpt. New York: AMS Press, 1973. 265-297.

GRABBE, CHRISTIAN (1801-1836)
1220. Porterfield, Allen W. "Seeing the Saw." *German Quarterly* 4 (1931): 175-187.

GRAF, OSKAR MARIA (1894-1967)
1221. Langston, Richard. "Proverbs and Self-Imposed Subjugation in Oskar Maria Graf's *Anton Sittinger*." *Proverbium: Yearbook of International Proverb Scholarship* 11 (1994): 125-142.

GRASS, GÜNTER (1927—)
1222. Angenendt, Thomas. "Die Verwendung 'vorgeprägter Sprachmuster.'" *"Wenn Wörter Schatten werfen": Untersuchungen zum Prosastil von Günter Grass*. Frankfurt am Main: Peter Lang, 1995. 50-79.

1223. Bebermeyer, Renate. "Formelabwandlung im *Butt*: Ein symptomatischer Vorgang der Alltagssprache und seine Spiegelung in einem unmittelbar aktuellen literarischen Werk." *Sprachspiegel* 34 (1978): 67-76.

1224. Hess-Lüttich, Ernest W. B. "Kontrastive Phraseologie im DaF-Unterricht—anhand arabischer und niederländischer Brecht-Übersetzungen." *Textproduktion und Textrezeption*. Tübingen: Gunter Narr, 1983. 25-39; rpt. in *Sprichwörter und Redensarten im interkulturellen Vergleich*. Eds. Annette Sabban and Jan Wirrer. Opladen: Westdeutscher Verlag, 1991. 109-127.

1225. Horn, Katalin. "Grimmsche Märchen als Quellen für Metaphern und Vergleiche in der Sprache der Werbung, des Journalismus und der Literatur." *Muttersprache* 91 (1981): 106-115.

1226. Koller, Werner. *Redensarten. Linguistische Aspekte, Vorkommensanalysen, Sprachspiel*. Tübingen: Max Niemeyer, 1977. 199-210.

1227. Mieder, Wolfgang. "Günter Grass und das Sprichwort." *Muttersprache* 83 (1973): 64-67. Also in *Sprichwort, Redensart, Zitat: Tradierte Formelsprache in der Moderne*. Bern: Peter Lang, 1985. 21-25.

1228. Mieder, Wolfgang. "Kulinarische und emanzipatorische Redensarten-verwendung in Günter Grass' *Der Butt.*" *Sprachspiegel* 34 (1978): 4-11. Also in *Sprichwort, Redensart, Zitat: Tradierte Formelsprache in der Moderne*. Bern: Peter Lang, 1985. 27-35.

1229. Mieder, Wolfgang. "Sprichwörter im moderen Sprachgebrauch." *Muttersprache* 85 (1975): 65-88. Also in *Ergebnisse der Sprichwörterforschung*. Bern: Peter Lang, 1978. 213-238; *Deutsche Sprichwörter in Literatur, Politik, Presse und Werbung*. Hamburg: Helmut Buske, 1983. 53-76.

1230. Schweitzer, Blanche-Marie. "Sprachspiel mit Idiomen: Eine Untersuchung am Prosawerk von Günter Grass." Diss. Zürich, 1978. 141 pp.

GRAY, WILLIAM (16th cent.)
1231. Mauch, Thomas Karl. "The Role of the Proverb in Early Tudor Literature." Diss. University of California at Los Angeles, 1963. 148-162.

GREBAN, ARNOUL (1420-1471)
1232. Heft, David. *Proverbs and Sentences in Fifteenth Century French Poetry*. Diss. New York University, 1941. Chapter 2. New York: Washington Square Press, 1942 (abridged to 12 pp.).

GREENE, GRAHAM (1904-1991)
1233. De Caro, Francis A. "Proverbs in Graham Greene's *The Power and the Glory*: Framing Thematic Concerns in a Modern Novel." *Proverbium: Yearbook of International Proverb Scholarship* 6 (1989): 1-7.

1234. Shvydkaia, L. I. "Sinonimicheskie otnosheniia poslovits i aforizmov v angliiskom iazyke." *Leksikologicheskie osnovy stilistiki (Sbornik nauchnykh trudov)*. Ed. I. V. Arnol'd. Leningrad: Gosudarstvennyi pedagogicheskii institut im. A. I. Gertsena, 1973. 167-175.

GREENE, ROBERT (1558-1592)
1235. Prager, Carolyn. "'If I Be Devil': English Renaissance Response to the Proverbial and Ecumenical Ethiopian." *Journal of Medieval and Renaissance Studies* 17, 2 (1987): 257-279.

GREGORY, Lady ISABELLA AUGUSTA (1852-1932)
1236. Bowen, Anne. "Lady Gregory's Use of Proverbs in Her Plays." *Southern Folklore Quarterly* 3 (1939): 231-243.

GRETTIS SAGA (14th cent.)

1237. Pipping, Rolf. "Ordspråkstudier." *Studier i nordisk filologi* 28 (1938): 1-82.

GRILLPARZER, FRANZ (1791-1882)

1238. Ochs, Franz. "'Wo Unrecht Gesetz ist, wird Widerstand Pflicht.'" *Der Sprachdienst* 31, 6 (1987): 178.

1239. Skreb, Zdenko. "Die Sentenz als stilbildendes Element." *Jahrbuch für Internationale Germanistik* 13 (1981): 76-84.

GRIMM, JACOB (1785-1863)

1240. Bluhm, Lothar. "Sprichwörter und Redensarten bei den Brüdern Grimm." *Sprichwörter und Redensarten im interkulturellen Vergleich.* Eds. Annette Sabban and Jan Wirrer. Opladen: Westdeutscher Verlag, 1991. 206-224.

1241. Mieder, Wolfgang. *"Findet, so werdet ihr suchen!": Die Brüder Grimm und das Sprichwort.* Bern: Peter Lang, 1986. 181 pp.

1242. Mieder, Wolfgang. "Sprichwörtliche Schwundstufen des Märchens: Zum 200. Geburtstag der Brüder Grimm." *Proverbium: Yearbook of International Proverb Scholarship* 3 (1986): 257-271.

1243. Rölleke, Heinz, ed. *"Redensarten des Volks, auf die ich immer horche":* *Das Sprichwort in den "Kinder- und Hausmärchen" der Brüder Grimm.* Eds. Heinz Rölleke and Lothar Bluhm. Bern: Peter Lang, 1988. 227 pp.

GRIMM, WILHELM (1786-1859)

1244. Bluhm, Lothar. "Sprichwörter und Redensarten bei den Brüdern Grimm." *Sprichwörter und Redensarten im interkulturellen Vergleich.* Eds. Annette Sabban and Jan Wirrer. Opladen: Westdeutscher Verlag, 1991. 206-224.

1245. Hölter, Achim. "'Blau pfeifen'—Rätsel um eine Redensart bei Büchner und Grimm." *Proverbium: Yearbook of International Proverb Scholarship* 9 (1992): 67-80.

1246. Mieder, Wolfgang. *"Findet, so werdet ihr suchen!": Die Brüder Grimm und das Sprichwort.* Bern: Peter Lang, 1986. 181 pp.

1247. Mieder, Wolfgang. "Wilhelm Grimm's Proverbial Additions in the Fairy Tales." *Proverbium: Yearbook of International Proverb Scholarship* 3 (1986): 59-83; slightly altered as "'Ever Eager to Incorporate Folk Proverbs': Wilhelm Grimm's Proverbial Additions in the Fairy Tales," *The Brothers Grimm and Folktale*. Eds. James McGlathery et al. Urbana: University of Illinois Press, 1988. 112-132.

1248. Mieder, Wolfgang. "Sprichwörtliche Schwundstufen des Märchens: Zum 200. Geburtstag der Brüder Grimm." *Proverbium: Yearbook of International Proverb Scholarship* 3 (1986): 257-271. Also in *Sprichwort—Wahrwort!? Studien zur Geschichte, Bedeutung und Funktion deutscher Sprichwörter*. Frankfurt am Main: Peter Lang, 1992. 103-111.

1249. Rölleke, Heinz, ed. *"Redensarten des Volks, auf die ich immer horche": Das Sprichwort in den "Kinder- und Hausmärchen" der Brüder Grimm*. Eds. Heinz Rölleke and Lothar Bluhm. Bern: Peter Lang, 1988. 227 pp.

1250. Wilcke, Karin, and Lothar Bluhm. "Wilhelm Grimms Sammlung mittelhochdeutscher Sprichwörter." *Brüder Grimm Gedenken*. Ed. Ludwig Denecke. Marburg: N. G. Elwert, 1988. VIII, 81-122.

GRIMMELSHAUSEN, HANS JAKOB CHRISTOFFEL VON (c. 1622-1676)

1251. Curtius, Ernst Robert. "Verkehrte Welt." *Europäische Literatur und lateinisches Mittelalter*. Bern: Francke, 1948, 1954, 1961. 104-108.

1252. Hiss, Albert. "Volksweisheit in den Sprichwörtern und Redensarten des *Simplicissimus* von Johann Jakob Christolph von Grimmelshausen." *Um Renchen und Grimmelshausen (= Grimmelshausen Archiv)* 1 (1976): 1-89.

1253. Lenschau, Martha. *Grimmelshausens Sprichwörter und Redensarten*. Frankfurt am Main: Moritz Diesterweg, 1924; rpt. Hildesheim: Gerstenberg, 1973. 155 pp.

1254. Schade, Richard E. "'Junge Soldaten, alte Bettler': Zur Ikonographie des Pikaresken am Beispiel des *Springinsfeld*-Titelkupfers." *Der deutsche Schelmenroman im europäischen Kontext: Rezeption, Interpretation, Bibliographie*. Ed. Gerhard Hoffmeister. Amsterdam: Rodopi, 1987. 93-112.

1255. Scholte, Jan Hendrik. *Johann Jacob Christoph von Grimmelshausen und die Illustrationen seiner Werke*. Leipzig: W. Drugulin, 1912. 1-8.

GRINGOIRE, PIERRE (c. 1475-c. 1540)

1256. Le Roux de Lincy, M. *Le Livre des Proverbes Français*, 2 vols. 2nd ed. Paris: A. Delahays, 1859; rpt. Genève: Slatkine, 1968. I, lv-lviii.

1257. Vignes, Jean, and B. Boudou. "Proverbes et dits sentencieux dans l'oeuvre de Pierre Gringore." *Bibliothèque d'Humanisme et Renaissance* 51, 2 (1989): 355-392.

GROTH, KLAUS (1819-1899)

1258. Böhme, Lothar. "Studien zu den Werken von Klaus Groth." *Zeitschrift für den deutschen Unterricht* 20 (1906): 172-181.

1259. Böhme, Lothar. "Studien zum Stil und Sprachgebrauch Klaus Groths." *Zeitschrift für den deutschen Unterricht* 25 (1911): 405-417.

GRYPHIUS, ANDREAS (1616-1664)

1260. Ade, Walter Frank Charles. "Das Sprichwort in den deutschen Werken des Andreas Gryphius." Diss. Northwestern University, 1949. 665 pp.

1261. Ottow, A. M. "Sprichwörter und sprichwörtliche Redensarten aus Andreae Gryphii *Seug-Amme, oder untreues Gesinde*, Lustspiel, Breslau 1663." *Deutscher Sprachwart* 6, 17 (1872): 269-271.

1262. Porter, Mary Gray. "Proverbs and Proverbial Expressions in the German Works of Andreas Gryphius." M. A. Thesis. University of North Carolina, 1955. Also in Kentucky Microcards, ser. A. Modern Language Series, No. 94 (3 cards). Lexington: University of Kentucky Press, 1962. 210 pp.

GRYSE, NICOLAUS (1543-1614)

1263. Hülsemann, Kurt. "Die niederdeutschen Sprichwörter in den Werken von Nicolaus Gryse." Diss. Hamburg, 1930. 125 pp.

GUILHEM DE TUDELA (12th/13th cent.)

1264. Pfeffer, Wendy. "Rotten Apples and Other Proverbs in *The Song of the Albigensian Crusade*." *Proverbium: Yearbook of International Proverb Scholarship* 8 (1991): 147-158.

GUILLAUME DE CLERC (12th-13th cent.)

1265. Haan, M. J. M. de. "Is Ferguut's geluk spreekwoordelijk?" *Taalen letterkundig gastenboek voor Prof. Dr. G.A. van Es*. Eds. G. Kazemier and P. P. J. van Caspel. Groningen: Archief foor de Nederlandse Syntaxis, 1975. 211-217.

GUILLAUME DE MACHAUT (c. 1300-1377)

1266. Cerquiglini, Jacqueline and Bernard. "L'écriture proverbiale." *Revue des sciences humaines* 41, 163 (1976): 359-375.

1267. Roques, Gilles. "'Sans rime et sans raison.'" *La locution: Actes du colloque international Université McGill, Montréal, 15-16 octobre 1984*. Eds. Giuseppe Di Stefano and Russell G. McGillivray. Montréal: Editions CERES, 1984. 419-436.

GUIMARAES ROSA, JOAO (1908-1967)

1268. Lima, Luiz Costa. "Mito e provérbio em Guimaraes Rosa." *Coloquio/ Letras* 17 (1974): 14-28.

GUITERMAN, ARTHUR (1871-1943)

1269. Mieder, Wolfgang. "The Proverb in the Modern Age: Old Wisdom in New Clothing." *Tradition and Innovation in Folk Literature*. Hanover, New Hampshire: University Press of New England, 1987. 118-156, 248-255 (notes).

GUTJAR, HENZE (15th. cent.)

1270. Hofmeister, Wernfried. *Sprichwortartige Mikrotexte als literarische Medien, dargestellt an der hochdeutschen politischen Lyrik des Mittelalters*. Bochum: Norbert Brockmeyer, 1995. 478-490.

GUYLEM DE CERVERA (13th cent.)

1271. Thomas, Antonio. "Les proverbes de Guylem de Cervera." *Romania* 15 (1886): 25-110.

H

HADLAUB, JOHANNES (c. 1300-c. 1340)

1272. Nicklas, Friedrich. *Untersuchung über Stil und Geschichte des deutschen Tageliedes*. Berlin: Emil Ebering, 1929; rpt. Nendeln, Liechtenstein: Kraus Reprint, 1967. 78-79.

HÄRTLING, PETER (1933—)

1273. Higi-Wydler, Melanie. *Zur Übersetzung von Idiomen: Eine Beschreibung und Klassifizierung deutscher Idiome und ihrer französischen Übersetzungen*. Bern: Peter Lang, 1989. 335 pp.

HALE, SUSAN (1833-1910)

1274. Coues, R. W. "Odd Terms in a Writer of Letters." *Dialect Notes* 6 (1928-1939): 1-6.

HALIFAX, GEORGE SAVILE, Marquis of (1633-1695)

1275. Newcomb, Robert. "Poor Richard's Debt to Lord Halifax." *Publications of the Modern Language Association* 70 (1955): 535-539.

HALL, EDWARD (c. 1498-1547)

1276. Mauch, Thomas Karl. "The Role of the Proverb in Early Tudor Literature." Diss. University of California at Los Angeles, 1963. 52-59, 101-105, 275.

HALL, JAMES (1793-1868)

1277. Taylor, Archer. "Some Americanisms in James Hall, *Legends of the West*." *Western Folklore* 18 (1959): 331.

HANDKE, PETER (1942—)

1278. Higi-Wydler, Melanie. *Zur Übersetzung von Idiomen: Eine Beschreibung und Klassifizierung deutscher Idiome und ihrer französischen Übersetzungen*. Bern: Peter Lang, 1989. 335 pp.

1279. Horn, Katalin. "Grimmsche Märchen als Quellen für Metaphern und Vergleiche in der Sprache der Werbung, des Journalismus und der Literatur." *Muttersprache* 91 (1981): 106-115.

HANSEN, MARTIN ALFRED (1909-1955)

1280. Houkjaer, Niels. "Ordsprog, der hjaelper: En proveniensanalyse af ordsprogsstoffet og dets litteraere funktion i Martin A. Hansens *Jonatans Rejse*." *Danske Studier* 73, 2 (1979): 24-38.

HARBARDSLIOD (13th cent.)

1281. Holtsmark, Anne. "An Old Norse Proverb." *Proverbium* No. 12 (1969): 319-321.

DER HARDEGGER (13th cent.)

1282. Hofmeister, Wernfried. *Sprichwortartige Mikrotexte als literarische Medien, dargestellt an der hochdeutschen politischen Lyrik des Mittelalters.* Bochum: Norbert Brockmeyer, 1995. 273-277.

HARDUYN, JUSTUS de (1582-1641)

1283. Duyse, P. van. "Justus de Harduyn." *Belgisch Museum* 10 (1846): 22-26.

HARDY, THOMAS (1840-1928)

1284. Firor, Ruth A. "Folk Wit and Wisdom." *Folkways in Thomas Hardy.* New York: Russell and Russell, 1931; rpt. New York: Russell and Russell, 1968. 211-228.

1285. Schmidt-Hidding, Wolfgang. "Thomas Hardy." *Englische Idiomatik in Stillehre und Literatur.* München: Max Hueber, 1962. 77-79.

1286. Smith, John B. "'Bees up Flues' and 'Chips in Porridge': Two Proverbial Sayings in Thomas Hardy's *The Return of the Native.*" *Proverbium: Yearbook of International Proverb Scholarship* 12 (1995): 315-322.

1287. Turner, E. M. "Thomas Hardy's Use of Proverbs and Proverbial Phrases." M. A. Thesis. Stetson University, 1936. 86 pp.

HARIG, LUDWIG (1927—)

1288. Lanzendörfer-Schmidt, Petra. "Sprachspiel mit Phraseologismen." *Die Sprache als Thema im Werk Ludwig Harigs: Eine sprachwissenschaftliche Analyse literarischer Schreibtechniken.* Tübingen: Max Niemeyer, 1990. 63-87.

1289. Seidel, Brigitte. "Redewendungen-Sprachschablonen (Unterrichtsmodell für die 10. Klasse/Baustein zu einem Kurs über Sprachverwendung für die 11. Klasse)." *Blätter für den Deutschlehrer* No. 2 (1980): 39-51.

HARRIS, JOEL CHANDLER (1848-1908)

1290. Brookes, Stella Brewer. "Proverbs and Folk-Say." *Joel Chandler Harris-Folklorist*. Athens: The University of Georgia Press, 1950, 1970. 97-110.

1291. Mieder, Wolfgang. *American Proverbs: A Study of Texts and Contexts*. Bern: Peter Lang, 1989. 111-128.

HARSDÖRFFER, GEORG PHILIPP (1607-1658)

1292. Hain, Mathilde. "Das Schauspiel Teutscher Sprichwörter." *Proverbium* No. 15 (1970): 46-47.

1293. Lennon, Moses. "Proverbs and Proverbial Phrases in Harsdörffer's *Das Schauspiel Teutscher Sprichwörter*." M. A. Thesis. University of Chicago, 1933. 54 pp.

1294. Meid, Volker. "Sprichwort und Predigt im Barock: Zu einem Erbauungsbuch Valerius Herbergers." *Zeitschrift für Volkskunde* 62 (1966): 209-234, especially 225-229.

1295. Mieder, Wolfgang. *"Das Schauspiel Teutscher Sprichwörter* oder Georg Philipp Harsdörffers Einstellung zum Sprichwort." *Daphnis* 3 (1974): 178-195.

1296. Mieder, Wolfgang. "Zwei Sprichwörterbriefe von Georg Philipp Harsdörffer." *Sprachspiegel* 31 (1975): 67-71.

HARTMANN VON AUE (c. 1165-c. 1215)

1297. Hofmann, Liselotte. *Der volkskundliche Gehalt der mittelhochdeutschen Epen von 1100 bis gegen 1250*. Zeulenroda: Bernhard Sporn, 1939. 55-60.

1298. Jäger, Dietrich. "Der Gebrauch formelhafter zweigliedriger Ausdrücke in der vor-, früh- und hochhöfischen Epik." Diss. Kiel, 1960. 90-122.

1299. Mone, Franz Joseph. "Zur Literatur und Geschichte der Sprichwörter." *Quellen und Forschungen zur Geschichte der deutschen Literatur und Sprache* 1 (1830): 186-214, especially 208.

1300. Singer, Samuel. "Sprichwortstudien." *Schweizerisches Archiv für Volkskunde* 37 (1939): 129-150, especially 139-145.

1301. Weise, Wilhelm. *Die Sentenz bei Hartmann von Aue*. Diss. University of Marburg, 1910. Bielefeld: A. von der Mühlen, 1910. 104 pp.

HAUPTMANN, GERHART (1862-1946)
1302. Küntzel, Heinrich. "'Mich wundert, daß ich fröhlich bin': Marginalien zu einem alten Spruch." *Deutsche Vierteljahrsschrift für Literaturwissenschaft und Geistesgeschichte* 61 (1987): 399-418.

1303. Scheichl, Sigurd Paul. "Feste Syntagmen im dramatischen Dialog: Materialien zur Geschichte eines Stilmittels zwischen Goethe und Kroetz." *Tradition und Entwicklung: Festschrift Eugen Thurnher*. Eds. Werner Bauer, Achim Masser, and Guntram Plangg. Innsbruck: Institut für Germanistik der Universität Innsbruck, 1982. 383-407.

1304. Schmidt-Hidding, Wolfgang. "Deutsche Sprichwörter und Redewendungen." *Deutschunterricht für Ausländer* 13 (1963): 13-26.

HAVAMAL (c. 1240)
1305. Singer, Samuel. "*Havamal.*" *Sprichwörter des Mittelalters*, 3 vols. Bern: Herbert Lang, 1946. I, 6-20.

1306. Spieß, Gisela. "Die Stellung der Frau in den Sprichwörtern isländischer Sprichwörtersammlungen und in isländischen Sagas." *Proverbium: Yearbook of International Proverb Scholarship* 8 (1991): 159-178.

1307. Wessén, Elias. "Ordspråk och lärodikt: Några stilformer: Hávamál." *Vitterhets, historie och antikvitets akademien* 91 (1959): 455-473.

HAVELOCK THE DANE (c. 1300)
1308. Skeat, Walter William. "*The Lay of Havelock the Dane.*" *Early English Proverbs, Chiefly of the Thirteenth and Fourteenth Centuries*. Oxford: Clarendon Press, 1910; rpt. Darby, Pennsylvania: Folcroft Library Editions, 1974. 22-24.

1309. Whiting, Bartlett Jere. "Proverbs in Certain Middle English Romances in Relation to Their French Sources." *Harvard Studies and Notes in Philology and Literature* 15 (1933): 75-126, especially 111-114.

HAZLITT, WILLIAM (1778-1830)
1310. Wilcox, Stewart C. "Hazlitt's Aphorisms." *Modern Language Notes* 9 (1948): 418-423.

HEBBEL, FRIEDRICH (1813-1863)

1311. Scheichl, Sigurd Paul. "Feste Syntagmen im dramatischen Dialog: Materialien zur Geschichte eines Stilmittels zwischen Goethe und Kroetz." *Tradition und Entwicklung: Festschrift Eugen Thurnher*. Eds. Werner Bauer, Achim Masser, and Guntram Plangg. Innsbruck: Institut für Germanistik der Universität Innsbruck, 1982. 383-407.

HEBEL, JOHANN PETER (1760-1826)

1312. Kahle, Hermann F. "Hebels Sprichwörterbearbeitungen: Benutzung und Behandlung des Sprichworts in der Schule: Werth, Wesen und Begriff desselben." *Claudius und Hebel: Hilfsbuch zum Studium deutscher volksthümlicher Sprache und Literatur*. Berlin: Wiegandt und Grieben, 1864. 204-223, especially 204-205.

1313. Knopf, Jan. "Sprachformeln und eingreifende Sätze." *Geschichten zur Geschichte: Kritische Tradition des "Volkstümlichen" in den Kalendergeschichten Hebels und Brechts*. Stuttgart: Metzler, 1973. 186-211.

1314. Leite, Rektor. "Sprichwörtliche Behandlung Hebelscher Sprichworterklärungen." *Evangelisches Schulblatt und Deutsche Schulzeitung* 44 (1900): 452-459.

1315. Mieder, Wolfgang. "Das Sprichwort in Johann Peter Hebels *Schatzkästlein des Rheinischen Hausfreundes*." *Forschungen und Berichte zur Volkskunde in Baden-Württemberg 1971-1973*. Eds. Irmgard Hampp and Peter Assion. Stuttgart: Müller und Gräff, 1973. 153-163. Also in *Das Sprichwort in der deutschen Prosaliteratur des neunzehnten Jahrhunderts*. München: Wilhelm Fink, 1976. 17-34.

1316. Röhrich, Lutz. *Johann Peter Hebels Kalendergeschichten zwischen Volksdichtung und Literatur*. Lörrach: Hebelbund, 1972. 14-16.

HEINE, HEINRICH (1797-1856)

1317. Bellmann, Werner. "'Cacatum non est pictum'—Ein Zitat in Heines *Wintermärchen*." *Wirkendes Wort* 33 (1983): 213-215.

HEINRICH VON MELK (12th cent.)

1318. Hofmann, Liselotte. *Der volkskundliche Gehalt der mittelhochdeutschen Epen von 1100 bis gegen 1250*. Zeulenroda: Bernhard Sporn, 1939. 80.

HEINRICH VON MÜGELN (c. 1320-1372)

1319. Hofmeister, Wernfried. *Sprichwortartige Mikrotexte als literarische Medien, dargestellt an der hochdeutschen politischen Lyrik des Mittelalters*. Bochum: Norbert Brockmeyer, 1995. 299-304.

HEINRICH VON TÜRLÎN (13th cent.)

1320. Hofmann, Liselotte. *Der volkskundliche Gehalt der mittelhochdeutschen Epen von 1100 bis gegen 1250*. Zeulenroda: Bernhard Sporn, 1939. 62-64.

1321. Wilcke, Karin, and Lothar Bluhm. "Wilhelm Grimms Sammlung mittelhochdeutscher Sprichwörter." *Brüder Grimm Gedenken*. Ed. Ludwig Denecke. Marburg: N. G. Elwert, 1988. VIII, 81-122.

HEINRICH VON VELDEKE (12th/13th cent.)

1322. Hofmann, Liselotte. *Der volkskundllche Gehalt der mittelhochdeutschen Epen von 1100 bis gegen 1250*. Zeulenroda: Bernhard Sporn, 1939. 77.

1323. Jäger, Dietrich. "Der Gebrauch formelhafter zweigliedriger Ausdrücke in der vor-, früh- und hochhöfischen Epik." Diss. Kiel, 1960. 70-89.

HEISSENBÜTTEL, HELMUT (1921—)

1324. Mieder, Wolfgang. "'Redensarten, Ausreden, Ansprüche': Zu Helmut Heissenbüttels Prosatext *Rollenverteilung* (1965)." *Sprachspiegel* 35 (1979): 70-76. Also in *Sprichwort, Redensart, Zitat: Tradierte Formelsprache in der Moderne*. Bern: Peter Lang, 1985. 37-44

1325. Mieder, Wolfgang. "Sprichwörter unterm Hakenkreuz." *Muttersprache* 93 (1983): 1-30. Also in *Deutsche Sprichwörter in Literatur, Politik, Presse und Werbung*. Hamburg: Helmut Buske, 1983. 181-210.

HELBLING, SEIFRIED (13th cent.)

1326. Wagner, Eva. 'Das Sprichwort bei Seifried Helbling.' "Sprichwort und Sprichworthaftes als Gestaltungselemente im *Renner* Hugos von Trimberg." Diss. Würzburg, 1962. 191 pp.

HEMINGWAY, ERNEST (1898-1961)

1327. Hand, Wayland D. "The Barn as a Haven, etc." *Proverbium* No. 2 (1965): 26.

1328. Stephens, Robert O. "Macomber and That Somali Proverb: The Matrix of Knowledge." *Fitzgerald-Hemingway Annual 1977*. Eds. Margaret M.

Duggan and Richard Layman. Detroit, Michigan: Gale Research Company, 1977. 137-147.

HENRYSON, ROBERT (c. 1424-1506)

1329. MacDonald, Donald. "Chaucer's Influence on Henryson's *Fables*: The Use of Proverbs and Sententiae." *Medium Aevum* 39 (1970): 21-27.

HENZE, WILHELM (1845-193?)

1330. Hülse, Horst. "Sprichwörter und Sinnsprüche im Werk Wilhelm Henzes." *Einbecker Jahrbuch* 32 (1981): 27-34.

HERBERGER, VALERIUS (1562-1627)

1331. Meid, Volker. "Sprichwort und Predigt im Barock: Zu einem Erbauungsbuch Valerius Herbergers." *Zeitschrift für Volkskunde* 62 (1966): 209-234.

HERBERT, GEORGE (1593-1633)

1332. Piret, Michael. "Herbert and Proverbs." *The Cambridge Quarterly* 17, 3 (1988): 222-243.

1333. Thorpe, James. "Reflections and Self-Reflections: *Outlandish Proverbs* as a Context for George Herbert's Other Writings." *Illustrious Evidence: Approaches to English Literature of the Early Seventeenth Century*. Ed. Earl Miner. Berkeley: University of California Press, 1975. 23-37.

HERBERT VON FRITZLAR (12th/13th cent.)

1334. Hofmann, Liselotte. *Der volkskundliche Gehalt der mittelhochdeutschen Epen von 1100 bis gegen 1250*. Zeulenroda: Bernhard Sporn, 1939. 73-74.

HERDER, JOHANN GOTTFRIED (1744-1803)

1335. Angress, Ruth K. "The Epigram as a Genre." *The Early German Epigram: A Study in Baroque Poetry*. Lexington: University Press of Kentucky, 1971. 19-40.

1336. Pape, Walter. "Zwischen Sprachspiel und Sprachkritik: Zum literarischen Spiel mit der wörtlichen Bedeutung von Idiomen." *Sprache und Literatur in Wissenschaft und Unterricht* 16, 56 (1985): 2-13.

1337. Novichkova, R. M. "Pro odnofrazovi teksti (na materiali nimets'koi movi)." *Movoznavstvo* 15, 3 (1981): 71-75.

HERMES, JOHANN (1738-1821)

1338. Cholevius, Johann Carl Leo. *Die Verkehrssprache in "Sophiens Reise von Memel nach Sachsen."* Königsberg: E. J. Dalkowski, 1873. 27 pp.

HERNANDEZ, JOSÉ (1834-1886)

1339. Drago, Mariano José. "Proverbios criollos tomados del poema gaucho *Martin Fierro* de José Hernandez." *Wit and Wisdom of the United Nations: Proverbs and Apothegms on Diplomacy.* Ed. V. S. M. de Guinzbourg. New York: United Nations, 1961. xxiii.

1340. Moya, Ismael. "El refranero de *Martin Fierro.*" *Refranero. . . formas paremiológicas tradicionales en la República Argentina.* Buenos Aires: Imprenta de la Universidad, 1944. 207-245.

1341. Moya, Ismael. "*Sententiae* de Publilius Syrus y el *Martin Fierro.*" *Anales de la Associación folklórica argentina* (1945): 67-70.

HERRICK, ROBERT (1591-1674)

1342. Crane, Mary Thomas. "Proverbial and Aphoristic Sayings: Sources of Authority in the English Renaissance." Diss. Harvard University, 1986. 378-442.

HERZOG ERNST (c. 1180)

1343. Hofmann, Liselotte. *Der volkskundliche Gehalt der mittelhochdeutschen Epen von 1100 bis gegen 1250.* Zeulenroda: Bernhard Sporn, 1939. 75.

HESIOD (8th cent. B. C.)

1344. Harrison, Jane E. "Pandora's Box." *Journal of Hellenic Studies* 20 (1900): 99-114.

1345. Panofsky, Dora and Erwin. *Pandora's Box: The Changing Aspects of a Mythical Symbol.* New York: Pantheon Books, 1956, 1962; rpt. Princeton, New Jersey: Princeton University Press, 1978, 1991. 185 pp.

HEYWOOD, JOHN (c. 1497-c. 1580)

1346. Crane, Mary Thomas. "Proverbial and Aphoristic Sayings: Sources of Authority in the English Renaissance." Diss. Harvard University, 1986. 249-324.

1347. Farmer, John. *The Proverbs, Epigrams, and Miscellanies of John Heywood.* London: Early English Drama Society, 1906; rpt. New York: Barnes and Noble, 1966. 466 pp.

1348. Habenicht, Rudolph E., ed. *John Heywood's "A Dialogue of Proverbs."* Berkeley: University of California Press, 1963. 300 pp.

1349. Holdsworth, R. V. "Two Proverbs in Middleton and Some Contemporaries." *Notes and Queries* 226 ns 28 (1981): 172-173.

1350. Landon, Sydney Ann. "'Sundry Pithie and Learned Inventions': *The Paradise of Dainty Devices* and Sixteenth Century Poetic Traditions." Diss. University of Washington, 1986. 144 pp.

1351. Manley, Lawrence. "Proverbs, Epigrams, and Urbanity in Renaissance London." *English Literary Renaissance* 15 (1985): 247-276.

1352. Mieder, Wolfgang. "The Proverb in the Modern Age: Old Wisdom in New Clothing." *Tradition and Innovation in Folk Literature.* Hanover, New Hampshire: University Press of New England, 1987. 118-156, 248-255 (notes).

1353. Sharman, Julian, ed. *The Proverbs of John Heywood.* London: George Bell and Sons, 1874; rpt. Darby, Pennsylvania: Folcroft Library Editions, 1972. 173 pp.

1354. Whiting, Bartlett Jere. "John Heywood's *Witty and Witless.*" *Proverbs in the Earlier English Drama.* Cambridge, Massachusetts: Harvard University Press, 1938; rpt. New York: Octagon Books, 1969. 171-172.

1355. Whiting, Bartlett Jere. "John Heywood's *A Play of Love.*" *Proverbs in the Earlier English Drama.* Cambridge, Massachusetts: Harvard University Press, 1938; rpt. New York: Octagon Books, 1969. 173-175.

1356. Whiting, Bartlett Jere. "John Heywood's *The Play of the Weather.*" *Proverbs in the Earlier English Drama.* Cambridge, Massachusetts: Harvard University Press, 1938; rpt. New York: Octagon Books, 1969. 175-177.

1357. Whiting, Bartlett Jere. "John Heywood's *The Pardoner and the Friar.*" *Proverbs in the Earlier English Drama.* Cambridge, Massachusetts: Harvard University Press 1938; rpt. New York: Octagon Books, 1969. 177.

1358.   Whiting, Bartlett Jere. "John Heywood's *The Four PP.*" *Proverbs in the Earlier English Drama.* Cambridge, Massachusetts: Harvard University Press, 1938; rpt. New York: Octagon Books, 1969. 178-180.

1359.   Whiting, Bartlett Jere. "John Heywood's *Johan Johan the Husband.*" *Proverbs in the Earlier English Drama.* Cambridge, Massachusetts: Harvard University Press, 1938; rpt. New York: Octagon Books, 1969. 180-181.

HEYWOOD, THOMAS (c. 1497-c. 1580)

1360.   Orkin, Martin R. "'He Shows a Fair Pair of Heels' in *1 Henry IV* and Elsewhere." *English Language Notes* 23, 1 (1985): 19-23.

HICKSCORNER (1497/1512)

1361.   Whiting, Bartlett Jere. "*Hickscorner.*" *Proverbs in the Earlier English Drama.* Cambridge, Massachusetts: Harvard University Press, 1938; rpt. New York: Octagon Books, 1969. 83-84.

HILDEBRANDSLIED (c. 810)

1362.   Lühr, Rosemarie. "'Mit geru scal man geba infahan, ort widar orte' V. 34, StD V. 37 f." *Studien zur Sprache des Hildebrandliedes* [sic], 2 vols. Bern: Peter Lang, 1982. I, 320; II, 588-596.

1363.   McDonald, William C. "'Too Softly a Gift of Treasure': A Rereading of the Old High German *Hildebrandslied.*" *Euphorion* 78 (1984): 1-16.

1364.   Singer, Samuel. *Sprichwörter des Mittelalters*, 3 vols. Bern: Herbert Lang, 1944-1947. I, 4-6.

HIPPEL, THEODOR GOTTLIEB (1741-1796)

1365.   Rixner, Thaddäus Anselm. *Weisheits-Sprüche und Witzreden, aus Theodor Gottlieb von Hippel's [sic] und Jean Paul Friedrich Richter's [sic] Schriften, auserlesen und alphabetisch geordnet mit den einleitenden Charakteristiken beider Männer und einem Anhang aus den deutschen Spruchdichtern des Mittelalters.* Amberg: Klöber, 1834. 232 pp.

HIPPOCRATES (c. 460-c. 377 B. C.)

1366.   Bar-Sela, Ariel, and Hebbel E. Hoff. "Maimonides' Interpretation of the First Aphorism of Hippocrates." *Bulletin of the History of Medicine* 37 (1963): 347-354.

1367. Richards, Dickinson W. "The First Aphorism of Hippocrates." *Perspectives in Biology and Medicine* 5 (1961): 61-64.

HITLER, ADOLF (1889-1945)

1368. Mieder, Wolfgang. "Proverbs in Nazi Germany: The Promulgation of Anti-Semitism and Stereotypes through Folklore." *Journal of American Folklore* 95 (1982): 435-464. Also in *Proverbs Are Never Out of Season: Popular Wisdom in the Modern Age*. New York: Oxford University Press, 1993. 225-255.

1369. Mieder, Wolfgang. "Sprichwörter unterm Hakenkreuz." *Muttersprache* 93 (1983): 1-30. Also in *Deutsche Sprichwörter in Literatur, Politik, Presse und Werbung*. Hamburg: Helmut Buske, 1983. 181-210.

1370. Mieder, Wolfgang. "'. . . als ob ich Herr der Lage würde': Zur Sprichwortmanipulation in Adolf Hitlers *Mein Kampf*." *Muttersprache* 104, 3 (1994): 193-218. Also in *Deutsche Redensarten, Sprichwörter und Zitate: Studien zu ihrer Herkunft, Überlieferung und Verwendung*. Vienna: Edition Praesens, 1995. 183-208.

1371. Mieder, Wolfgang. "Proverbs in Adolf Hitler's *Mein Kampf*." *Proverbium: Yearbook of International Proverb Scholarship* 11 (1994): 159-174.

1372. Mieder, Wolfgang. "Proverbial Manipulation in Adolf Hitler's *Mein Kampf*." *International Folklore Review* 10 (1995): 35-53.

HITOPADESA (c. 10th cent.)

1373. Wilkins, Charles, trans. *Fables and Proverbs from the Sanskrit: Being the "Hitopadesa."* 2nd ed. London: George Routledge and Sons, 1886. 277 pp.

HOBBES, THOMAS (1588-1657)

1374. Meichsner, Irene. *Die Logik von Gemeinplätzen: Vorgeführt an Steuermannstopos und Schiffsmetapher*. Bonn: Bouvier, 1983. 263 pp.

HOCHHUTH, ROLF (1931—)

1375. Horn, Katalin. "Grimmsche Märchen als Quellen für Metaphern und Vergleiche in der Sprache der Werbung, des Journalismus und der Literatur." *Muttersprache* 91 (1981): 106-115.

HÖSCHLE, OTTO (1952—)
1376. Mieder, Wolfgang. "'It's Five Minutes to Twelve': Folklore and Saving Life on Earth." *International Folklore Review* 7 (1989): 10-21.

HOFFMAN, AL (1902-1960)
1377. Mieder, Wolfgang. "Proverbs in American Popular Songs." *Proverbium: Yearbook of International Proverb Scholarship* 5 (1988): 85-101.

1378. Mieder, Wolfgang, and George B. Bryan. "'Zum Tango gehören zwei.'" *Der Sprachdienst* 27 (1983): 100-102, 181.

HOFMANNSTHAL, HUGO VON (1874-1929)
1379. Rölleke, Heinz. "Sprichwörtliche Redensarten in Hugo von Hofmannsthals *Jedermann.*" *Wirkendes Wort* 36 (1986): 347-353.

HOLTZWART, MATHIAS (1540-c. 1577)
1380. Peil, Dietmar. "Das Sprichwort in den *Emblematum Tyrocinia* des Mathias Holtzwart (1581)." *Kleinstformen der Literatur.* Eds. Walter Haug und Burghart Wachinger. Tübingen: Max Niemeyer, 1994. 132-164.

HOLZ, ARNO (1863-1929)
1381. Riha, Karl. "Balla Balla, Balla Basta: Zur Poetik kleiner literarischer Formen." *Akzente* 21 (1974): 265-287.

HOMER (8th cent. B. C.)
1382. Notopoulos, James A. "Homeric Similes in the Light of Oral Poetry." *The Classical Journal* 52 (1957): 323-328.

1383. Werner, Jürgen. "Blauer Himmel bei Homer." *Forschungen und Fortschritte* 33 (1959): 311-316.

HONESTUS (1st cent. B. C.)
1384. Prittwitz-Gaffron, Erich von. *Das Sprichwort im griechischen Epigramm.* Diss. München, 1912. Gießen: Alfred Töpelmann, 1912. 49.

HOOPER, JOHNSON JONES (c. 1815-1863)
1385. West, Harry C. "Simon Suggs and His Similes." *North Carolina Folklore* 16 (1968): 53-57.

HORN, W. O. VON [Wilhelm Oertel] (1798-1867)

1386. Müller-Salget, Klaus. "Volkslied, Sprichwort, Bibel, Gesangbuch: Geistliches und Weltliches im Dienste der Bekräftigung und Vergewisserung." *Erzählungen für das Volk: Evangelische Pfarrer als Volksschriftsteller im Deutschland des 19. Jahrhunderts*. Berlin: Erich Schmidt, 1984. 314-326.

DAS HORNBERGER SCHIESSEN (16th cent.)

1387. Tokofsky, Peter. "'Das Hornberger Schießen': Proverbial Expression, Narrative, and Drama." *Proverbium: Yearbook of International Proverb Scholarship* 10 (1993): 321-330.

HOROSZCO, SEBASTIÁN de (died 1568)

1388. Alonso Hernandez, José Luis. "Lexemas dependientes (diminutivos) y su función sociológica en el *Teatro Universal de Proverbios* de Sebastián de Horozco." *Actas del Quinto Congreso Internacional de Hispanistas (Bordeaux 1974)*. Eds. Maxime Chevalier, François Lopez, Joseph Perez, and Noël Salomon. Bordeaux: Instituto de Estudios Ibericos e Iberoamericanos, Universidad de Bordeaux, 1977. I, 131-144.

HORVÁTH, ÖDÖN VON (1901-1938)

1389. Goltschnigg, Dietmar. "Das Sprachklischee und seine Funktion im dramatischen Werk von Ödön von Horváths." *Wirkendes Wort* 25 (1975): 181-196.

1390. Küntzel, Heinrich. "'Mich wundert, daß ich fröhlich bin': Marginalien zu einem alten Spruch." *Deutsche Vierteljahrsschrift für Literaturwissenschaft und Geistesgeschichte* 61 (1987): 399-418.

HOSTROP, JENS CHRISTIAN (1818-1892)

1391. Holzapfel, Otto. "Stereotype Redensarten über 'den Deutschen' in der neueren dänischen Literatur." *Proverbium: Yearbook of International Proverb Scholarship* 4 (1987): 87-110.

HOUVILLE, GÉRARD d' (1875-1963)

1392. Brenner, Clarence D. *The French Dramatic Proverb*. Berkeley, California: Privately printed, 1977. 68 pp.

1393. Chaumeix, André. "La comédie proverbe." Rev. of *Je crois que je vous aime*, by G. d'Houville. *Revue des Deux Mondes* 40 (August 1, 1927): 698-708.

HOWARD, HENRY, Earl of Surrey (c. 1517-1547)

1394.   Daalder, Joost. "Wyatt's Proverbial 'Though the Wound Be Healed, Yet a Scar Remains.'" *Archiv für das Studium der neueren Sprachen und Literaturen* 138 (1986): 354-356.

HOWE, EDGAR WATSON (1853-1937)

1395.   Sackett, S. J. "E. W. Howe as Proverb Maker." *Journal of American Folklore* 85 (1972): 73-77.

HROTSVITHA VON GANDERSHEIM (c. 935-c. 973)

1396.   McEnerney, John I. "Proverbs in Hrotsvitha." *Mittellateinisches Jahrbuch* 21 (1986): 106-113.

HUE DE ROTELANDE (12th cent.)

1397.   Schulze-Busacker, Elisabeth. "Proverbes et expressions proverbiales chez Chrétien de Troyes, Gautier d'Arras et Hue de Rotelande." *Incidences* 5 (1981): 7-16.

1398.   Schulze-Busacker, Elisabeth. *Proverbes et expressions proverbiales dans la littérature narrative du moyen âge français: Recueil et analyse.* Paris: Librairie Honoré Champion, 1985. 356 pp.

1399.   Whiting, Bartlett Jere. "Proverbs in Certain Middle English Romances in Relation to Their French Sources." *Harvard Studies and Notes in Philology and Literature* 15 (1933): 75-126, especially 76-85.

HUGHES, THOMAS (fl. 1587)

1400.   Whiting, Bartlett Jere. "Thomas Hughes's *The Misfortunes of Arthur.*" *Proverbs in the Earlier English Drama.* Cambridge, Massachusetts: Harvard University Press, 1938; rpt. New York: Octagon Books, 1969. 297-302.

HUGO, VICTOR (1802-1885)

1401.   Riffaterre, Michael. "Fonction du cliché dans la prose littéraire." *Essais de stylistique structurale.* Paris: Flammarion, 1971. 161-181. Also in German as "Die Funktion des Klischees in der literarischen Form." *Strukturale Stilistik.* München: List Taschenbuch, 1973. 139-156.

HUGO VON MONFORT (1357-1423)

1402.   Nicklas, Friedrich. *Untersuchung über Stil und Geschichte des deutschen Tageliedes.* Berlin: Emil Ebering, 1929; rpt. Nendeln, Liechtenstein: Kraus Reprint, 1967. 142.

HUGO VON TRIMBERG (c. 1230-c. 1313)

1403. Schumacher, Meinolf. "'. . . ist menschlich': Mittelalterliche Variationen einer antiken Sentenz." *Zeitschrift für deutsches Altertum und deutsche Literatur* 119 (1990): 163-170.

1404. Seibicke, Wilfried. "'Über Stock und Stein.'" *Der Sprachdienst* 22 (1978): 9-10.

1405. Wagner, Eva. "Sprichwort und Sprichworthaftes als Gestaltungselemente im *Renner* Hugos von Trimberg." Diss. Würzburg, 1962. 191 pp.

1406. Wilcke, Karin, and Lothar Bluhm. "Wilhelm Grimms Sammlung mittelhochdeutscher Sprichwörter." *Brüder Grimm Gedenken.* Ed. Ludwig Denecke. Marburg: N. G. Elwert, 1988. VIII, 81-122.

HUME, DAVID (1771-1776)

1407. Strube, Werner. "Zur Geschichte des Sprichworts 'Über den Geschmack läßt sich nicht streiten.'" *Zeitschrift für Ästhetik und Allgemeine Kunstwissenschaft* 30 (1985): 158-185.

HUNNIS, WILLIAM (died 1597)

1408. Landon, Sydney Ann. "'Sundry Pithie and Learned Inventions': *The Paradise of Dainty Devices* and Sixteenth Century Poetic Traditions." Diss. University of Washington, 1986. 144 pp.

HUSSEIN, EBRAHIM N. (1943—)

1409. Eastman, Carol M. "The Proverb in Modern Written Swahili Literature: An Aid to Proverb Elicitation." *African Folklore.* Ed. Richard Dorson. Garden City, N. Y.: Anchor Books, 1972. 193-207.

HUTTEN, ULRICH VON (1488-1523)

1410. Brandt, Gisela. "Feste Wendungen." In Erwin Arndt and G. Brandt. *Luther und die deutsche Sprache.* Leipzig: VEB Bibliographisches Institut, 1983. 215-219.

1411. Pfeifer, Wolfgang. "Volkstümliche Metaphorik." *Zur Literatursprache im Zeitalter der frühbürgerlichen Revolution: Untersuchungen zu ihrer Verwendung in der Agitationsliteratur.* Eds. Gerhard Kettmann and Joachim Schildt. Berlin: Akademie-Verlag, 1978. 87-217.

HUYGENS, CONSTANTIN (1596-1687)

1412. Van Dam, C. F. A. "Un refranero espanol en Holanda a mediados del siglo XVII." *Romanistisches Jahrbuch* 5 (1952): 285-288.

HYSLOP, GRAHAM (1910—)

1413. Eastman, Carol M. "The Proverb in Modern Written Swahili Literature: An Aid to Proverb Elicitation." *African Folklore*. Ed. Richard Dorson. Garden City, N. Y.: Anchor Books, 1972. 193-207.

I

IBSEN, HENRIK (1828-1906)

1414. Anstensen, Ansten. "Notes on the Text of Ibsen's *Peer Gynt.*" *Journal of English and Germanic Philology* 29 (1930): 53-73.

1415. Anstensen, Ansten. *The Proverb in Ibsen: Proverbial Sayings and Citations as Elements in His Style.* Diss. Columbia University, 1936. New York: Columbia University Press, 1936. 255 pp.

ICHEGBEH, MICAH (20th cent.)

1416. Ogede, Ode S. "Proverb Usage in the Praise Songs of the Igede: *Adiyah* Poet Micah Ichegbeh." *Proverbium: Yearbook of International Proverb Scholarship* 10 (1993): 237-256.

IGBANG, ODE (20th cent.)

1417. Ogede, Ode S. "Songs from the Edge of Power: Interpreting Some Political Polemic of the Igede 'Etuh' (Proverbs) Poet Ode Igbang." *African Affairs* 93, 371 (1994): 219-231.

IMMERMANN, KARL (1796-1840)

1418. Knopf, Jan. "Sprachformeln und eingreifende Sätze." *Geschichten zur Geschichte: Kritische Tradition des "Volkstümlichen" in den Kalendergeschichten Hebels und Brechts.* Stuttgart: Metzler, 1973. 186-211.

1419. Mieder, Wolfgang. "Die Funktion des Sprichwortes in Karl Immermanns *Münchhausen.*" *Zeitschrift für deutsche Philologie* 90 (1971): 228-241. Also in *Das Sprichwort in der deutschen Prosaliteratur des neunzehnten Jahrhunderts.* München: Wilhelm Fink, 1976. 35-47.

IMPATIENT POVERTY (c. 1560)

1420. Whiting, Bartlett Jere. "*Impatient Poverty.*" *Proverbs in the Earlier English Drama.* Cambridge, Massachusetts: Harvard University Press, 1938; rpt. New York: Octagon Books, 1969. 125-127.

INGELEND, THOMAS (fl. 1560)

1421. Whiting, Bartlett Jere. "Thomas Ingelend's *The Disobedient Child.*" *Proverbs in the Earlier English Drama.* Cambridge, Massachusetts: Harvard University Press, 1938; rpt. New York: Octagon Books, 1969. 194-196.

IRVING, WASHINGTON (1783-1859)

1422. Forrest, Rex. "Irving and the 'Almighty Dollar.'" *American Speech* 15 (1940): 443-444.

1423.   Robinson, Frank K. 'Curtain Lecture.'" *American Notes and Queries* 10, 3 (1971): 40-41.

ISIDORE OF SÉVILLE (c. 560-636)

1424.   Cazier, Pierre. "Les 'sentences' d'Isidore de Séville, genre littéraire et procédés stylistiques." *Richesse du proverbe*. Eds. François Suard and Claude Buridant. Lille: Université de Lille, 1984. II, 61-72.

ISPIRESCU, PETRE (1838-1887)

1425.   Negreanu, Constantin. "Cîteva observatii asupra elementelor paremiologice din limba povestirilor lui Petre Ispirescu." *Proverbium Dacoromania* 4 (1989): 26-30.

1426.   Negreanu, Constantin. "Petre Ispirescu si limba popularia (Lucutiuni, expresii, proverbe)." *Revista de etnografie si folclor* 36, 3-4 (1991): 179-191.

ISSELBURG, PETER (c. 1580-c. 1630)

1427.   Dittrich, Lothar. "Emblematische Weisheit und naturwissenschaftliche Realität." *Die Sprache der Bilder: Realität und Bedeutung in der niederländischen Malerei des 17. Jahrhunderts*. Eds. Wolfgang J. Müller, Konrad Renger, and Rüdiger Klessmann. Braunschweig: ACO Druck, 1978. 21-33. Also in *Jahrbuch für Internationale Germanistik* 13 (1981): 36-60.

1428.   Schilling, Michael. "Die literarischen Vorbilder der Ludwigsburger und Gaarzer Embleme." *Außerliterarische Wirkungen barocker Emblembücher: Emblematik in Ludwigsburg, Gaarz und Pommersfelden*. Eds. Wolfgang Harms and Hartmut Freytag. München: Wilhelm Fink, 1975. 41-71.

J

JACK JUGGLER (1562)

1429. Whiting, Bartlett Jere. "*Jack Juggler.*" *Proverbs in the Earlier English Drama*. Cambridge, Massachusetts: Harvard University Press, 1938; rpt. New York: Octagon Books, 1969. 198-201.

JACOB AND ESAU (c. 1545)

1430. Whiting, Bartlett Jere. "*Jacob and Esau.*" *Proverbs in the Earlier English Drama*. Cambridge, Massachusetts: Harvard University Press, 1938; rpt. New York: Octagon Books, 1969. 48-51.

JEAN DE CONDÉ (died c. 1345)

1431. Whiting, Bartlett Jere. "Proverbial Material in the Poems of Baudouin and Jean de Condé." *Romanic Review* 27 (1936): 204- 223.

JEAN DE MEUN[G] (c. 1250-1305)

1432. Hicks, Eric. "Proverbe et polémique dans le *Roman de la Rose* de Jean de Meun." *Richesse du proverbe*. Eds. François Suard and Claude Buridant. Lille: Université de Lille, 1984. I, 113-120.

1433. Larsen, Judith Clark. "Proverbial Material in the *Roman de la Rose*." Diss. University of Georgia, 1978. 140 pp.

1434. Ragen, Brian Abel. "Chaucer, Jean de Meun, and Proverbs 30:20." *Notes and Queries* 233 ns 35 (1988): 295-296.

JEAN DE NIVELLE (1422-1477)

1435. Colson. "Le 'cycle' de Jean de Nivelle: Chansons, dictons, legendes et type populaire." *Wallonia* 8 (1900): 6-12.

JEAN PAUL [Jean Paul Friedrich Richter] (1763-1825)

1436. Pape, Walter. "Zwischen Sprachspiel und Sprachkritik: Zum literarischen Spiel mit der wörtlichen Bedeutung von Idiomen." *Sprache und Literatur in Wissenschaft und Unterricht* 16, 56 (1985): 2-13.

1437. Rixner, Thaddäus Anselm. *Weisheits-Sprüche und Witzreden, aus Theodor Gottlieb von Hippel's [sic] und Jean Paul Friedrich Richter's [sic] Schriften, auserlesen und alphabetisch geordnet mit den einleitenden Charakteristiken beider Männer und einem Anhang aus den deutschen Spruchdichtern des Mittelalters*. Amberg: Klöber, 1834. 232 pp.

JEUX-PARTIS (c. 1240-1310)

1438. Buridant, Claude. "Nature et fonction des proverbes dans les *Jeux-Partis*." *Revue des sciences humaines* 41, 163 (1976): 377-418.

1439. Pfeffer, Wendy. "The Riddle of the Proverb." *The Spirit of the Court: Selected Proceedings of the Fourth Congress of the International Courtly Literature Society (Toronto 1983)*. Eds. Glyn S. Burgess, Robert A. Taylor, Alan Deyermond, Dennis Green, and Beryl Rowland. Dover, New Hampshire: Brewer, 1985. 254-263.

JEWEL, JOHN (1522-1571)

1440. Cowgill. "Proverbial Philosophy." *Notes and Queries* 1st ser. 4 (1851): 81-82.

JOHANNES VON TEPL (c. 1350-c. 1414)

1441. Mieder, Wolfgang. "Streitgespräch und Sprichwort-Antithetik: Ein Beitrag zur *Ackermann aus Böhmen*-und Sprichwortforschung." *Daphnis* 2 (1973): 1-32. Also in *Sprichwort—Wahrwort!? Studien zur Geschichte, Bedeutung und Funktion deutscher Sprichwörter*. Frankfurt am Main: Peter Lang, 1992. 113-149.

JOHN THE EVANGELIST (c. 1557)

1442. Whiting, Bartlett Jere. "*John the Evangelist*." *Proverbs in the Earlier English Drama*. Cambridge, Massachusetts: Harvard University Press, 1938; rpt. New York: Octagon Books, 1969. 116.

JONSON, BEN (1572-1637)

1443. Crane, Mary Thomas. "Proverbial and Aphoristic Sayings: Sources of Authority in the English Renaissance." Diss. Harvard University, 1986. 378-442.

1444. Davidson, Mary Burdette. "Proverbs and Proverbial Phrases in Jonson's Plays." M. A. Thesis. Stetson University, 1938. 148 pp.

1445. Deckner, E. "Pfeffer's *Das elisabethanische Sprichwort bei Ben Jonson*." *Beiblatt zur Anglia* 46 (1935): 143-146.

1446. Doyle, Charles Clay. "The Homeless Ass in Jonson's *A Tale of a Tub*." *Notes and Queries* 229 ns 31 (1984): 241-242.

1447. Ellis, Marion. "Proverb Lore in Ben Jonson." M. A. Thesis. Northwestern University, 1934. 157 pp.

1448. Ezell, Carroll Paul. "Proverbs and Proverbial Phrases in Jonson's Non-Dramatic Works." M. A. Thesis. Stetson University, 1940. 74 pp.

1449. McKenzie, Kenneth. "Ben Jonson's Lombard Proverb [To get cold feet]." *Modern Language Notes* 27 (1912): 263.

1450. Nash, Ralph. "Milton, Jonson and Tiberius." *Classical Philology* 41 (1946): 164.

1451. Pfeffer, Karl. *Das elisabethanische Sprichwort in seiner Verwendung bei Ben Jonson*. Diss. Gießen, 1933. Gießen: Richard Glagow, 1933. 193 pp.

1452. Prager, Carolyn. "'If I Be Devil': English Renaissance Response to the Proverbial and Ecumenical Ethiopian." *Journal of Medieval and Renaissance Studies* 17, 2 (1987): 257-279.

JOYCE, GEORGE (c. 1495-1553)
1453. Mauch, Thomas Karl. "The Role of the Proverb in Early Tudor Literature." Diss. University of California at Los Angeles, 1963. 145-148.

JOYCE, JAMES (1882-1941)
1454. Aubert, Jacques. "Breton Proverbs in Notebook VI. B. 14." *A Wake Newsletter: Studies in James Joyce's "Finegan's Wake"* 15 (1978): 86-89.

1455. Dent, Robert William. *Colloquial Language in "Ulysses": A Reference Tool*. Newark: University of Delaware Press, 1994. 294 pp.

1456. Erzgräber, Willi. "The Narrative Presentation of Orality in James Joyce's *Finnegan's Wake*." *Oral Tradition* 7, 1 (1992): 150-170.

1457. Hart, Clive. "An Index of Motifs [and Proverbs] in *Finnegan's Wake*." *Structure and Motif in "Finnegan's Wake"*. Evanston, Illinois: Northwestern University Press, 1962. 211-247.

1458. Lobner, Corinna Del Greco. "James Joyce and the Italian Language." *Italica* 60, 2 (1983): 140-153.

1459. Stewart, James. "A Proverb in T. H. White [Horn of a bull, hoof of a horse, smile of a saxon]." *Notes and Queries* 220 ns 22 (1975): 561.

JUAN MANUEL, Infante Don (1282-1348)

1460. Michaelis de Vassoncellos, Carolina. "Zum Sprichwörterschatz des Don Juan Manuel." Ed. Elise Richter? *Bausteine zur romanischen Philologie: Festgabe für Adolfo Mussafia.* Halle: Niemeyer, 1905. 594-608.

JUAN DE LA CRUZ [Juan de Yepis Alvarez] (1542-1591)

1461. Fabry, Geneviève. "Sens et forme dans les 'dichos' de Saint Jean de la Croix." *Les Lettres Romanes* (1991): 25-36.

JUVENAL [Decimus Junius Juvenalis] (c. 60-140)

1462. Wilkins, Eliza Gregory. *"Know Thyself" in Greek and Latin Literature.* Diss. University of Chicago, 1917. Chicago: University of Chicago Libraries, 1917. 104 pp.

K

KÄSTNER, ERICH (1899-1974)
1463. Daniels, Karlheinz. "Text- und autorenspezifische Phraseologismen, am Beispiel von Erich Kästners Roman *Fabian.*" *Beiträge zur allgemeinen und germanistischen Phraseologieforschung.* Ed. Jarmo Korhonen. Oulu: Oulun Yliopisto, 1987. 207-219; revised as "Erich Kästner als Sprach- und Gesellschaftskritiker dargestellt an seiner Verwendung sprachlicher Schematismen." *Wörter: Schätze, Fugen und Fächer des Wissens: Festgabe für Theodor Lewandowski.* Ed. Hugo Aust. Tübingen: Gunther Narr, 1987. 191-206.

1464. Hess, Peter. *Epigramm.* Stuttgart: Metzler, 1989. 160-161.

KAFKA, FRANZ (1883-1924)
1465. Binder, Hartmut. "Geflügelte Bildreden: Zu Kafkas Umgang mit sprachlicher Fertigware." *Wirkendes Wort* 42, 3 (1992): 440-468.

1466. Gross, Ruth V. "Rich Text/Poor Text: A Kafka Confusion." *Publications of the Modern Language Association* 95 (1980): 168-182.

1467. Koelb, Clayton. "*In der Strafkolonie*: Kafka and the Scene of Reading." *German Quarterly* 55 (1982): 511-525.

KAISERCHRONIK (c. 1150)
1468. Hofmann, Liselotte. *Der volkskundliche Gehalt der mittelhochdeutschen Epen von 1100 bis gegen 1250.* Zeulenroda: Bernhard Sporn, 1939. 76-77.

1469. Jäger, Dietrich. "Der Gebrauch formelhafter zweigliedriger Ausdrücke in der vor-, früh- und hochhöfischen Epik." Diss. Kiel, 1960. 23-34.

KALEVALA (ed. 1835 by Elias Lonnröt [1802-1884])
1470. Kaukonen, Väinö. "Piirteitä Kalevalan sananlaskuista." *Kalevalaseuran Vuosikirja* 54 (1974): 197-200.

1471. Kuusi, Matti. "Kalevalakielen kysymyksiä." *Virittaja* 82 (1978): 209-225.

1472. Kuusi, Matti. *Suomalaista: karjalaista vai savokarjalaista? Vienan ja Pohjois-Aunuksen sananlaskut ja Kalevalan runojen alkuperäkiista.* Helsinki: Suomalaisen Kirjallisuuden Seura, 1978. 70 pp.

KALLIMACHOS (c. 310-c. 240 B. C.)

1473. Prittwitz-Gaffron, Erich von. *Das Sprichwort im griechischen Epigramm.* Diss. München, 1912. Gießen: Alfred Töpelmann, 1912. 9-24.

KANT, HERMANN (1926—)

1474. Mieder, Wolfgang. "Sprichwörter im moderen Sprachgebrauch." *Muttersprache* 85 (1975): 65-88. Also in *Ergebnisse der Sprichwörterforschung.* Bern: Peter Lang, 1978. 213-238; *Deutsche Sprichwörter in Literatur, Politik, Presse und Werbung.* Hamburg: Helmut Buske, 1983. 53-76.

KANT, IMMANUEL (1724-1804)

1475. Brands, Hartmut. "*Cogito ergo sum*": *Interpretationen von Kant bis Nietzsche.* München: Karl Alber, 1982. 318 pp.

1476. Soliva, Claudio. "Ein Bibelwort in Geschichte und Recht [Alles nun, was ihr wollt, daß euch die Leute tun sollen, das tut ihr ihnen auch (So whatever you wish that men would do to you, do so to them); Was du nicht willst, daß man dir tu, das füg auch keinem andern zu (What you don't want one to do to you, don't do that to another)]." "*Unser Weg.*" *Werkblatt der Schweizerischen Weggefährtinnen* Nos. 6-7 (1964): 51-57.

1477. Strube, Werner. "Zur Geschichte des Sprichworts 'Über den Geschmack läßt sich nicht streiten.'" *Zeitschrift für Ästhetik und Allgemeine Kunstwissenschaft* 30 (1985): 158-185.

KARADZIĆ, VUK (1787-1864)

1478. Polenaković, Haralampije. "Zwei Volkssprichwörter bei Dositej Obradović und Vuk Karadzić." *Stvaranje* 19 (1964): 1329-1331.

KARLSTADT, ANDREAS (1480-1541)

1479. Pfeifer, Wolfgang. "Volkstümliche Metaphorik." *Zur Literatursprache im Zeitalter der frühbürgerlichen Revolution: Untersuchungen zu ihrer Verwendung in der Agitationsliteratur.* Eds. Gerhard Kettmann and Joachim Schildt. Berlin: Akademie-Verlag, 1978. 87-217.

KASCHNITZ, MARIE LOUISE (1901-1974)

1480. Horn, Katalin. "Grimmsche Märchen als Quellen für Metaphern und Vergleiche in der Sprache der Werbung, des Journalismus und der Literatur." *Muttersprache* 91 (1981): 106-115.

KATHA-SARIT-SANGARA (1063/81)

1481. Sternbach, Leon. *Aphorisms and Proverbs in the Katha-sarit-sagara, I.* Lucknow: Akhila Bharatiya Sanskrit Parishad, 1980. 312 pp.

KEATS, JOHN (1795-1821)

1482. Partridge, Eric. "Clichés." *A Charm of Words: Essays and Papers on Language.* New York: The Macmillan Company, 1961. 44-54.

KELLER, GOTTFRIED (1819-1890)

1483. Mieder, Wolfgang. "Das Sprichwort in Gottfried Kellers *Die Leute von Seldwyla.*" *Das Sprichwort in der deutschen Prosaliteratur des neunzehnten Jahrhunderts.* München: Wilhelm Fink, 1976. 152-167.

1484. Schreiber, William. "Gottfried Keller's Use of Proverbs and Proverbial Expressions." *Journal of English and Germanic Philology* 53 (1954): 514-523.

1485. Seiler, Friedrich. *Deutsche Sprichwörterkunde.* München: C. H. Beck, 1922, 1967. 63-64.

KINDER- UND HAUSMÄRCHEN (1819)

1486. Bluhm, Lothar. "Sprichwörter und Redensarten bei den Brüdern Grimm." *Sprichwörter und Redensarten im interkulturellen Vergleich.* Eds. Annette Sabban and Jan Wirrer. Opladen: Westdeutscher Verlag, 1991. 206-224.

1487. Hölter, Achim. "'Blau pfeifen'—Rätsel um eine Redensart bei Büchner und Grimm." *Proverbium: Yearbook of International Proverb Scholarship* 9 (1992): 67-80.

1488. Horn, Katalin. "Grimmsche Märchen als Quellen für Metaphern und Vergleiche in der Sprache der Werbung, des Journalismus und der Literatur." *Muttersprache* 91 (1981): 106-115.

1489. Mieder, Wolfgang. "*Findet, so werdet ihr suchen!*": Die Brüder Grimm und das Sprichwort.* Bern: Peter Lang, 1986. 181 pp.

1490. Mieder, Wolfgang. "Wilhelm Grimm's Proverbial Additions in the Fairy Tales." *Proverbium: Yearbook of International Proverb Scholarship* 3 (1986): 59-83; slightly altered as "'Ever Eager to Incorporate Folk Proverbs': Wilhelm Grimm's Proverbial Additions in the Fairy

Tales," *The Brothers Grimm and Folktale*. Eds. James McGlathery et al. Urbana: University of Illinois Press, 1988. 112-132.

1491. Mieder, Wolfgang. "Sprichwörtliche Schwundstufen des Märchens: Zum 200. Geburtstag der Brüder Grimm." *Proverbium: Yearbook of International Proverb Scholarship* 3 (1986): 257-271. Also in *Sprichwort—Wahrwort!? Studien zur Geschichte, Bedeutung und Funktion deutscher Sprichwörter*. Frankfurt am Main: Peter Lang, 1992. 103-111.

1492. Mieder, Wolfgang. "Fairy-Tale Allusions in Modern German Aphorisms." *The Reception of Grimms' Fairy Tales: Responses, Reactions, Revisions*. Ed. Donald Haase. Detroit, Michigan: Wayne State University Press, 1993. 149-166.

1493. Rölleke, Heinz. "'Dû bist mîn, ich bin dîn': Ein mittelhochdeutscher Vers in den *Kinder- und Hausmärchen* der Brüder Grimm?" *Fabula* 23 (1982): 269-275. Also in *"Wo das Wünschen noch geholfen hat": Gesammelte Aufsätze zu den "Kinder- und Hausmärchen" der Brüder Grimm*. Bonn: Bouvier, 1985. 133-141.

1494. Rölleke, Heinz. "'Wie ein Lämmerschwänzchen': Zur Herkunft einer Redensart in Grimms Märchen." *Wirkendes Wort* 32 (1982): 233-234. Also in *"Wo das Wünschen noch geholfen hat": Gesammelte Aufsätze zu den "Kinder- und Hausmärchen" der Brüder Grimm*. Bonn: Bouvier, 1985. 142-144.

1495. Rölleke, Heinz, ed. *"Redensarten des Volks, auf die ich immer horche": Das Sprichwort in den "Kinder- und Hausmärchen" der Brüder Grimm*. Eds. Heinz Rölleke and Lothar Bluhm. Bern: Peter Lang, 1988. 227 pp.

KIND, JOHANN FRIEDRICH (1768-1843)

1496. Sokol, A. E. "'What the Sam Hill?'" *American Speech* 15 (1940): 106-109.

KING ALISAUNDER (c. 13th cent.)

1497. Skeat, Walter William. "*King Alisaunder*." *Early English Proverbs, Chiefly of the Thirteenth and Fourteenth Centuries*. Oxford: Clarendon Press, 1910; rpt. Darby, Pennsylvania: Folcroft Library Editions, 1974. 25-27.

KINWELMERSH, FRANCIS (died c. 1580)

1498. Landon, Sydney Ann. "'Sundry Pithie and Learned Inventions': *The Paradise of Dainty Devices* and Sixteenth Century Poetic Traditions.*" Diss. University of Washington, 1986. 144 pp.

KIRKMAN, FRANCIS (born 1661)

1499. Roberts, W. "Peculiar Words and Phrases in F. Kirkman's *The Wits.*" *Notes and Queries* 7th ser. 2 (1886): 83.

KIRSTEN, WULF (1934–)

1500. Militz, Hans-Manfred. "Wertende Konnotation in der Phraseologie.*" *Sprachpflege* 35, 8 (1986): 109-111.

KIVI, ALEKSIS (1834-1872)

1501. Kuusi, Anna-Leena. "Henkilöiden karakterisointi fraasien avulla Aleksis Kiven nummisuutareissa.*" *Kalevalaseuran Vuosikirja* 50 (1970): 169-196.

DIE KLAGE (13th cent.)

1502. Haase. *Über die Alliteration in der "Klage."* Neu-Ruppin: Gustav Kühn, 1875. 17 pp.

KLEIST, HEINRICH VON (1777-1811)

1503. Backenstoss, R. E. "Figures of Speech in Heinrich von Kleist's *Der zerbrochene Krug*: An Investigation into Kleist's Style.*" M. A. Thesis. University of North Carolina, 1937.

1504. Bernath, Peter. *Die Sentenz im Drama von Kleist, Büchner und Brecht: Wesensbestimmung und Funktionswandel.* Bonn: Bouvier, 1976. Especially pp. 230-233, 244-247.

1505. Mieder, Wolfgang. "Der Krieg um den Krug: Ein Sprichwortgefecht: Zum 200. Geburtstag Heinrich von Kleists.*" *Muttersprache* 87 (1977): 178-192. Also in *Deutsche Sprichwörter in Literatur, Politik, Presse und Werbung.* Hamburg: Helmut Buske, 1983. 77-91.

1506. Müller, Gernot. "'Die Gelegenheit beim Schopfergreifen.'—Geschwätz, gehauen nicht und nicht gestochen': Zur Verankerung zweier Phraseologismen im Werk Heinrich von Kleists.*" *Europhras 90: Akten der internationalen Tagung zur germanistischen Phraseologieforschung, Aske/ Schweden 12.-15. Juni 1990.* Ed. Christine Palm. Uppsala: Acta Universitatis Upsaliensis, 1991. 139-153.

1507. Stambaugh, Ria. "Proverbial and Human Corruption and Other Distortions of Popular Sayings." *Proverbium* No. 15 (1970): 531-535.

1508. Vinken, P. J. "Some Observations on the Symbolism of 'The Broken Pot' in Art and Literature." *American Imago* 15 (1958): 149-174.

1509. Zick, Gisela. "Der zerbrochene Krug als Bildmotiv des 18. Jahrhunderts." *Wallraf-Richartz Jahrbuch* 31 (1969): 149-204.

KLICPERA, VÁCLAV (1792-1859)
1510. Mukařovský, Jan. "Přislovi jako součást kontextu." *Cestami poetiky a estetiky*. Praha: Edice Dilna, 1971. 277-359.

KNOX, VICESIMUS (1752-1821)
1511. Cameron, Kenneth Walter. "Emerson, Thoreau, *Elegant Extracts*, and Proverb Lore." *Emerson Society Quarterly* No. 6 (1957): 28-39.

KÖNIG ROTHER (c. 1150/1160)
1512. Hofmann, Liselotte. *Der volkskundliche Gehalt der mittelhochdeutschen Epen von 1100 bis gegen 1250*. Zeulenroda: Bernhard Sporn, 1939. 75.

1513. Jäger, Dietrich. "Der Gebrauch formelhafter zweigliedriger Ausdrücke in der vor-, früh- und hochhöfischen Epik." Diss. Kiel, 1960. 42-48.

KÖNIGSDORF, HELGA (1938—)
1514. Militz, Hans-Manfred. "'Sich einen Kopf machen.'" *Sprachpflege* 32, 11 (1983): 168-169.

KÖSTLIN, KARL (1819-1894)
1515. Strube, Werner. "Zur Geschichte des Sprichworts 'Über den Geschmack läßt sich nicht streiten.'" *Zeitschrift für Ästhetik und Allgemeine Kunstwissenschaft* 30 (1985): 158-185.

KOHL, HELMUT (1930—)
1516. Mieder, Wolfgang. "'Die Hunde bellen, aber die Karawane zieht weiter': Zum türkischen Ursprung eines neuen deutschen Sprichwortes." *Der Sprachdienst* 32, 5 (1988): 129-134. Also in *Sprichwort— Wahrwort!? Studien zur Geschichte, Bedeutung und Funktion deutscher Sprichwörter*. Frankfurt am Main: Peter Lang, 1992. 203-210.

KONČIUS, IGNO (born 1886)

1517. Volotkiene, Lina. "Lietuviu patarles ir ju kontekstas Igno Končius Žemaičio šnekose." *Tautosakos Darbai* 2, 9 (1993): 110-114.

KONRAD VON WÜRZBURG (1220/1230-1287)

1518. Nicklas, Friedrich. *Untersuchung über Stil und Geschichte des deutschen Tageliedes.* Berlin: Emil Ebering, 1929; rpt. Nendeln, Liechtenstein: Kraus Reprint, 1967. 79.

1519. Stechow, Walter. *Sprichwörter, Redensarten und moralische Betrachtungen in den Werken Konrads von Würzburg.* Diss. Greifswald, 1921. Greifswald: Hans Adler, 1921. 117 pp.

KOUROUMA, AHMADOU (1940–)

1520. Emeto-Agbasière, Julie. "Le proverbe dans le roman africain." *Présence francophone* No. 29 (1986): 27-41.

KRAUS, KARL (1874-1936)

1521. Fricke, Harald. *Aphorismus.* Stuttgart: Metzler, 1984. 125-132.

1522. Grésillon, Almuth, and Dominique Maingueneau. "Polyphonie, proverbe et détournement, ou un proverbe peut en cacher un autre." *Langages* 19, 73 (1984): 112-125.

1523. Hess, Peter. *Epigramm.* Stuttgart: Metzler, 1989. 154-155.

1524. Mautner, Franz H. "Der Aphorismus als literarische Gattung." *Zeitschrift für Ästhetik und allgemeine Kunstwissenschaft* 27 (1933): 132-175.

1525. Mautner, Franz H. "Maxim(e)s, Sentences, Fragmente, Aphorismen." *Actes du 4e Congrès de l'Association Internationale de Littérature Comparée, Fribourg 1964.* Ed. François Jost. The Hague: Mouton, 1966. II, 812-819.

1526. Mieder, Wolfgang. "Sprichwörter im modernen Sprachgebrauch." *Muttersprache* 85 (1975): 65-88. Also in *Ergebnisse der Sprichwörterforschung.* Bern: Peter Lang, 1978. 213-238; *Deutsche Sprichwörter in Literatur, Politik, Presse und Werbung.* Hamburg: Helmut Buske, 1983. 53-76.

1527. Mieder, Wolfgang. "Karl Kraus und der sprichwörtliche Aphorismus."
      Muttersprache 89 (1979): 97-115. Also in *Deutsche Sprichwörter in
      Literatur, Politik, Presse und Werbung*. Hamburg: Helmut Buske, 1983.
      113-131.

1528. Mieder, Wolfgang. "Sprichwörter unterm Hakenkreuz." *Muttersprache*
      93 (1983): 1-30. Also in *Deutsche Sprichwörter in Literatur, Politik,
      Presse und Werbung*. Hamburg: Helmut Buske, 1983. 181-210.

1529. Schaffner, Emil. "Spiel mit Wortfügungen und Wendungen." *Es rumpelt
      und stilzt im Sprach-Spülkasten*. Frauenfeld: Huber, 1982. 92-99.

1530. Skreb, Zdenko. "Die Sentenz als stilbildendes Element." *Jahrbuch für
      Internationale Germanistik* 13 (1981): 76-84.

KRINAGORAS (1st cent. B. C.-1st cent. A. D.)
1531. Prittwitz-Gaffron, Erich von. *Das Sprichwort im griechischen Epigramm*.
      Diss. München, 1912. Gießen: Alfred Töpelmann, 1912. 34-36.

KROETZ, FRANZ XAVER (1946—)
1532. Koller, Werner. "Redensarten in gesprochener Sprache, in Leserbriefen,
      in der Trivialliteratur und bei F. X. Kroetz." *Redensarten: Linguistische
      Aspekte, Vorkommensanalysen, Sprachspiel*. Tübingen: Max Niemeyer,
      1977. 73-87, especially 84-87.

1533. Koller, Werner. "Die einfachen Wahrheiten der Redensarten." *Sprache
      und Literatur in Wissenschaft und Unterricht* 16, 56 (1985): 26-36.

1534. Pilipp, Frank. "Volksgut versus Volkswirtschaft: Zur Funktion von
      Sprichwort und Redensart in Franz Xaver Kroetz' Milieudrama *Mensch
      Meier*." *Proverbium: Yearbook of International Proverb Scholarship* 5
      (1988): 145-154.

1535. Scheichl, Sigurd Paul. "Feste Syntagmen im dramatischen Dialog:
      Materialien zur Geschichte eines Stilmittels zwischen Goethe und
      Kroetz." *Tradition und Entwicklung: Festschrift Eugen Thurnher*. Eds.
      Werner Bauer, Achim Masser, and Guntram Plangg. Innsbruck: Institut
      für Germanistik der Universität Innsbruck, 1982. 383-407.

KROLL, HARRY HARRISON (1888-1967)
1536. Kroll, Harry Harrison. "How I Collect Proverbial Material for My
      Novels." *Tennessee Folklore Society Bulletin* 23 (1957): 1-5.

1537. Taylor, Archer. "Proverbial Materials in Two Novels by Harry Harrison Kroll." *Tennessee Folklore Society Bulletin* 22 (1956): 39-52.

1538. Taylor, Archer. "Proverbial Materials in Two More Novels by Harry Harrison Kroll." *Tennessee Folklore Society Bulletin* 22 (1956): 73-84.

KRÜGER, FERDINAND (1843-1915)
1539. Zurhausen, Helene. "Sprichwörtliches in Ferdinand Krügers Romanen." *Beckumer Jahrbuch* (1950). No pp.

KRUSHCHEV, NIKITA (1894-1971)
1540. Breuillard, Jean. "Proverbes et pouvoir politique: Le cas de l'U. R. S. S." *Richesse du proverbe*. Eds. François Suard and Claude Buridant. Lille: Université de Lille, 1984. II, 155-166.

1541. Reynolds, Horace. "A Proverb in the Hand—Is Often Worth a Thousand Words: Herewith an Examination of a Much Used but Seldom Analyzed Form of Homely Literature." *New York Times Magazine* (September 13, 1959): 74.

KUDRUN (c. 1230/1240)
1542. Hofmann, Liselotte. *Der volkskundliche Gehalt der mittelhochdeutschen Epen von 1100 bis gegen 1250*. Zeulenroda: Bernhard Sporn, 1939. 79.

KYD, THOMAS (1558-1594)
1543. Prager, Carolyn. "'If I Be Devil': English Renaissance Response to the Proverbial and Ecumenical Ethiopian." *Journal of Medieval and Renaissance Studies* 17, 2 (1987): 257-279.

L

LA BRUYÈRE, JEAN DE (1645-1696)

1544. Lafond, Jean. "Des formes brèves de la littérature morale aux XVIe et XVIIe siècles." *Les formes brèves de la prose et le discours discontinu (XVIe-XVIIe siècles)*. Paris: Librairie Philosophique J. Vrin, 1984. 101-122.

LA FONTAINE, JEAN DE (1621-1695)

1545. García Peinado, Miguel Angel. "Le fonds populaire chez La Fontaine: proverbes et locutions proverbiales." *Paremia* No. 2 (1993): 195-198.

1546. Lang, George. "La Fontaine Transmogrified: Creole Proverbs and the *Cric? Crac!* of Georges Sylvain." *French Review* 63, 4 (1990): 679-693.

1547. Ott, Karl August. "Lessing und La Fontaine: Von dem Gebrauche der Tiere in der Fabel." *Germanisch-Romanische Monatsschrift* 9 (1959): 235-266. Also in *Proverbia in Fabula: Essays on the Relationship of the Fable and the Proverb*. Ed. Pack Carnes. Bern: Peter Lang, 1988. 117-163.

1548. Perrin-Naffakh, Anne-Marie. "Locutions et proverbes dans les *Fables* de La Fontaine." *L'information littéraire* 31 (1979): 151-155. Also in *Proverbia in Fabula: Essays on the Relationship of the Fable and the Proverb*. Ed. Pack Carnes. Bern: Peter Lang, 1988. 285-294.

1549. Pineaux, Jacques. "La Fontaine." *Proverbes et dictons français*, 6th ed. Paris: Presses Universitaires de France, 1973. 60-62.

1550. Le Roux de Lincy, M. *Le Livre des Proverbes Français*, 2 vols. 2nd ed. Paris: A. Delahays, 1859; rpt. Genève: Slatkine, 1968. I, lxv-lxvi.

1551. Le Roux de Lincy, M. "Proverbes cités par La Fontaine." *Le Livre des Proverbes Français*, 2 vols. 2nd ed. Paris: A. Delahays, 1859; rpt. Genève: Slatkine, 1968. II, 505-518.

LA MONNOYE, BERNARD de (1641-1728)

1552. Sébillot, Paul. "Des traditions populaires dans les *Noëls Bourguignons* de La Monnoye." *Revue des traditions populaires* 5 (1890): 487-499.

LA PERRIÈRE, GUILLAUME de (1499-1569)

1553. Dittrich, Lothar. "Emblematische Weisheit und naturwissenschaftliche Realität." *Die Sprache der Bilder: Realität und Bedeutung in der niederländischen Malerei des 17. Jahrhunderts*. Eds. Wolfgang J.

Müller, Konrad Renger, and Rüdiger Klessmann. Braunschweig: ACO Druck, 1978. 21-33. Also in *Jarbuch für Internationale Germanistik* 13 (1981): 36-60.

LA ROCHEFOUCAULD, FRANÇOIS (1613-1680)
1554. Fink, Arthur-Hermann. *Maxime und Fragment: Grenzmöglichkeiten einer Kunstform: Zur Morphologie des Aphorismus*. München: Max Huber, 1934. 15-33.

1555. Lafond, Jean. "Des formes brèves de la littérature morale aux XVIe et XVIIe siècles." *Les formes brèves de la prose et le discours discontinu (XVIe-XVIIe siècles)*. Paris: Librairie Philosophique J. Vrin, 1984. 101-122.

1556. Mautner, Franz H. "Der Aphorismus als literarische Gattung." *Zeitschrift für Ästhetik und allgemeine Kunstwissenschaft* 27 (1933): 132-175.

1557. Mautner, Franz H. "Maxim(e)s, Sentences, Fragmente, Aphorismen." *Actes du 4e Congrès de l'Association Internationale de Littérature Comparée, Fribourg 1964*. Ed. François Jost. The Hague: Mouton, 1966. II, 812-819.

1558. Wilcox, Stewart C. "Hazlitt's Aphorisms." *Modern Language Notes* 9 (1948): 418-423.

1559. Zholkovskii, Aleksandr K., and Iu. K. Tseglov. "Razbor odnoi avtorskoi paremii." *Paremiologischeskii Sbornik*. Ed. G. L. Permiakov. Moskva: Nauka, 1978. 163-210.

LALIC, MIHAILO (1914—)
1560. Pizhuritza, Krsto. "Poslovitse, izreke i aforizmi kod Lalica." *Stvaranje* 39 (1984): 81-91.

LANGLAND, WILLIAM (c. 1332-1400)
1561. Gray, Nick. "Langland's Quotations from the Penitential Tradition." *Modern Philology* 84 (1986): 53-60.

1562. Kaske, Robert Earl. "The Nature and Use of Figurative Expression in *Piers Plowman*." Diss. University of North Carolina, 1950. 554 pp.

1563. Sellert, F. "Das Bild in *Pierce the Plowman.*" Diss. Rostock, 1904. 152 pp.

1564. Skeat, Walter William. *"Piers the Plowman." Early English Proverbs, Chiefly of the Thirteenth and Fourteenth Centuries.* Oxford: Clarendon Press, 1910; rpt. Darby, Pennsylvania: Folcroft Library Editions, 1974. 42-51.

LAUB, GABRIEL (1928—)
1565. Mieder, Wolfgang. "'Gedankensplitter, die ins Auge gehen': Zu den sprichwörtlichen Aphorismen von Gabriel Laub." *Kairoer Germanistische Studien* 4 (1989): 141-158. Also in *Wirkendes Wort* 41 (1991): 228-239.

LAUBE, HEINRICH (1806-1884)
1566. Stasiewski, Bernhard. "'Polnische Wirtschaft' und Johann Georg Forster, eine wortgeschichtliche Studie." *Deutsche wissenschaftliche Zeitschrift im Wartheland* 2 (1941): 207-216.

LAWRENCE, D. H. [David Herbert Lawrence] (1885-1930)
1567. Schmidt-Hidding, Wolfgang. "D. H. Lawrence." *Englische Idiomatik in Stillehre und Literatur.* München: Max Hueber, 1962. 88-90.

1568. Shvydkaia, L. I. "Sinonimicheskie otnosheniia poslovits i aforizmov v angliiskom iazyke." *Leksikologicheskie osnovy stilistiki (Sbornik nauchnykh trudov).* Ed. I. V. Arnol'd. Leningrad: Gosudarstvennyi pedagogicheskii institut im. A. I. Gertsena, 1973. 167-175.

LAYAMON (fl. 1200)
1569. Deskis, Susan Elizabeth, and Thomas D. Hill. "The Wolf Doesn't Care: The Proverbial and Traditional Context of Layamon's *Brut*, Lines 10624-36." *Review of English Studies* 46, 181 (1995): 41-48.

1570. Skeat, Walter William. "Layamon." *Early English Proverbs, Chiefly of the Thirteenth and Fourteenth Centuries.* Oxford: Clarendon Press, 1910; rpt. Darby, Pennsylvania: Folcroft Library Editions, 1974. 3-7.

LE CARRÉ, JOHN (1931—)
1571. Mieder, Wolfgang. "Buchtitel als Schlagzeile." *Sprachspiegel* 31 (1975): 36-43. Also in *Sprichwort, Redensart, Zitat: Tradierte Formelsprache in der Moderne.* Bern: Peter Lang, 1985. 115-123.

LE FÈVRE, JEAN (c. 1326-1380/87)

1572. Hasenohr, Geneviève. "La locution verbale figurée dans l'oeuvre de Jean Le Fèvre." *La locution: Actes du colloque international Université McGill, Montréal, 15-16 octobre 1984.* Eds. Giuseppe Di Stefano and Russell G. McGillivray. Montréal: Editions CERES, 1984. 229-281.

LE FRANC, MARTIN (c. 1410-1461)

1573. Williams, Harry F. "French Proverbs in Fifteenth-Century Literature: A Sampling." *Fifteenth-Century Studies* 5 (1982): 223-232.

LEBEUS-BATILLIUS, DIONYSIUS (16th-17th cent.)

1574. Dittrich, Lothar. "Emblematische Weisheit und naturwissenschaftliche Realität." *Die Sprache der Bilder: Realität und Bedeutung in der niederländischen Malerei des 17. Jahrhunderts.* Eds. Wolfgang J. Müller, Konrad Renger, and Rüdiger Klessmann. Braunschweig: ACO Druck, 1978. 21-33. Also in *Jarbuch für Internationale Germanistik* 13 (1981): 36-60.

LEC, STANISLAW JERZY (1909-1966)

1575. Dedecius, Karl. "Letztes Geleit für den ersten Aphoristiker unserer Zeit: Lec." *Der Aphorismus: Zur Geschichte, zu den Formen und Möglichkeiten einer literarischen Gattung.* Ed. Gerhard Neumann. Darmstadt: Wissenschaftliche Buchgesellschaft, 1976. 452-477.

1576. Frackiewicz, Iwona. "Sprichwörtliche Aphorismen von Stanislaw Jerzy Lec." *Proverbium: Yearbook of International Proverb Scholarship* 7 (1990): 77-88.

1577. Skreb, Zdenko. "Die Sentenz als stilbildendes Element." *Jahrbuch für Internationale Germanistik* 13 (1981): 76-84.

LECLERCQ, MICHEL-THÉODORE (1777-1851)

1578. Brahmer, Miecyzslaw. "Le vicende del proverbio dramatico." *XIV. Congresso internazionale di linguistica e filologia romanza.* Ed. Alberto Várvaro. Naples: Macchiaroli, 1981. V, 509-511.

1579. Le Roux de Lincy, M. *Le Livre des Proverbes Français,* 2 vols. 2nd ed. Paris: A. Delahays, 1859; rpt. Genève: Slatkine, 1968. I, lxxxii-lxxxiv.

1580. Schmidt-Clausen, Uta. *Michel-Théodore Leclercq und das Proverbe dramatique der Restauration.* Braunschweig: Georg Westermann, 1971. 200 pp.

1581. Shaw, Marjorie. "Les proverbes dramatiques de Carmontelle, Leclercq et Alfred de Musset." *Revue des sciences humaines* (1959): 56-76.

1582. Siegel, Patricia J. "Political Proverbs and the French Revolution: The Landscape Observed by Théodore Leclercq and Auguste Romieu." *Re-Naming the Landscape*. Eds. Jürgen Kleist and Bruce A. Butterfield. New York: Peter Lang, 1994. 159-175.

LEHMANN, WILHELM (1882-1968)
1583. Horn, Katalin. "Grimmsche Märchen als Quellen für Metaphern und Vergleiche in der Sprache der Werbung, des Journalismus und der Literatur." *Muttersprache* 91 (1981): 106-115.

LEMAIRE DE BELGES, JEAN (1473-c. 1525)
1584. Zumthor, Paul. "L'épiphonème proverbial." *Revue des sciences humaines* 41, 163 (1976): 313-328.

LENIN, VLADIMIR ILICH (1870-1924)
1585. Breuillard, Jean. "Proverbes et pouvoir politique: Le cas de l'U. R. S. S." *Richesse du proverbe*. Eds. François Suard and Claude Buridant. Lille: Université de Lille, 1984. II, 155-166.

1586. Meshcherskii, N. A. "Traditsionno-knizhnye vyrazheniia v sovremennom russkom literaturnom iazyke (na materiale proizvedenii V. I. Lenina)." *Voprosy frazeologii* 9 (1975): 110-121. Also in German as "Traditionellbuchsprachliche Ausdrücke in der heutigen russischen Literatursprache (anhand der Werke V. I. Lenins)." *Reader zur sowjetischen Phraseologie*. Eds. Harald Jaksche, Ambros Sialm, and Harald Burger. New York: Walter de Gruyter, 1981. 131- 143.

1587. Morozova, L. A. "Upotreblenie V. I. Leninym poslovits." *Russkaia Rech'* No. 2 (1979): 10-14.

1588. Zhigulev, Aleksandr M. "Poslovitsy i pogovorki v bol'shevitskikh listovkakh." *Sovetskaia Etnografiia* 5 (1970): 124-131.

LENNEP, JACOB VAN (1802-1868)
1589. Es, J. van. "Over 'Zeispreuken' in *Ferdinand Huyck* van Jacob van Lennep." *Oostvlaamsche Zanten* 15 (1940): 55-57.

LEONIDAS OF TARENTUM (3rd cent. B. C.)

1590. Prittwitz-Gaffron, Erich von. *Das Sprichwort im griechischen Epigramm.* Diss. München, 1912. Gießen: Alfred Töpelmann, 1912. 26-27.

LESKOV, NIKOLAJ S. (1831-1895)

1591. Russell, James George. "Leskov and Folklore." Diss. Princeton University, 1971. 324 pp.

LESSING, GOTTHOLD EPHRAIM (1729-1781)

1592. Angress, Ruth K. "The Epigram as a Genre." *The Early German Epigram: A Study in Baroque Poetry.* Lexington: University Press of Kentucky, 1971. 19-40.

1593. Bebermeyer, Renate. "Lehnsprichwörter als Mittel zur Sprachbereicherung bei Lessing." *Sprachspiegel* 35 (1979): 99-103.

1594. Novichkova, R. M. "Pro odnofrazovi teksti (na materiali nimets'koi movi)." *Movoznavstvo* 15, 3 (1981): 71-75.

1595. Ott, Karl August. "Lessing und La Fontaine: Von dem Gebrauche der Tiere in der Fabel." *Germanisch-Romanische Monatsschrift* 9 (1959): 235-266. Also in *Proverbia in Fabula: Essays on the Relationship of the Fable and the Proverb.* Ed. Pack Carnes. Bern: Peter Lang, 1988. 117-163

1596. Pape, Walter. "Zwischen Sprachspiel und Sprachkritik: Zum literarischen Spiel mit der wörtlichen Bedeutung von Idiomen." *Sprache und Literatur in Wissenschaft und Unterricht* 16, 56 (1985): 2-13.

L'ESTRANGE, ROGER (1616-1704)

1597. Taylor, Archer. "Proverbs and Proverbial Phrases in Roger L'Estrange, *The Fables of Aesop.*" *Southern Folklore Quarterly* 26 (1962): 232-245.

LEVI, PRIMO (1919-1987)

1598. Gilman, Sander L. "To Quote Primo Levi: 'Redest keyn jiddisch, bist nit kejn jid' ['If you don't speak Yiddish, you're not a Jew']." *Prooftexts: A Journal of Jewish Literary History* 9, 2 (1989): 139-160.

LEVNĪ, RESSAM (died 1732)

1599. Macfie, A. L. and F. "A Proverb Poem by Levnī." *Asian Folklore Studies* 48, 2 (1989): 189-193.

1600. Theodoridis, Dimitri. "Zum türkischen Sprichwörtergedicht des Levnī." *Proverbium* No. 25 (1975): 983-984.

1601. Turková, Helena. "Über ein türkisches Sprichwörtergedicht." *Charisteria Orientalia praecipue ad Persiam pertinentia: Festschrift für Jan Rypka.* Eds. Felix Tauer, Vera Kubičková, and Ivan Hrbek. Prag: Nakl. Československé akademie věd, 1956. 374-386.

LEWIS, HENRY CLAY (fl. 1850-1858)
1602. Anderson, John Q. "Folklore in the Writings of *The Louisiana Swamp Doctor.*" *Southern Folklore Quarterly* 19 (1955): 243-251.

LIBANIOS (314-c. 393)
1603. Salzmann, Ernst. *Sprichwörter und sprichwörtliche Redensarten bei Libanios.* Diss. Tübingen, 1910. Tübingen: H. Laupp, 1910. 113 pp.

LIBEAUS DESCONUS (14th cent.)
1604. Whiting, Bartlett Jere. "Proverbs in Certain Middle English Romances in Relation to Their French Sources." *Harvard Studies and Notes in Philology and Literature* 15 (1933): 75-126, especially 122-125.

LIBERALITY AND PRODIGALITY (1567/1568)
1605. Whiting, Bartlett Jere. "*Liberality and Prodigality.*" *Proverbs in the Earlier English Drama.* Cambridge, Massachusetts: Harvard University Press, 1938; rpt. New York: Octagon Books, 1969. 136-138.

EL LIBRO DE BUEN AMOR (1330)
1606. Hernandez, José Luis Alonso. "Interprétation psychoanalytique de l'utilisation des parémies dans la littérature espagnole." *Richesse du proverbe.* Eds. François Suard and Claude Buridant. Lille: Université de Lille, 1984. II, 213-225.

LIBRO DE LOS BUENOS PROVERBIOS (13th cent.)
1607. Ariza Viguera, Manuel, and José Gonzáles Calvo. "Construcciones con infinitivo no preposicional en el *Libro de los buenos proverbios.*" *Boletin de la Real Academia Española* 56 (1976): 509-522.

1608. Bizzarri, Hugo Oscar. "Nuevo fragmento del *Libro de los buenos proverbios* contenido en el manuscrito BN Madrid 9248." *Incipit* 8 (1988): 125-132.

1609. Morgan, Frances Elnora Williams. "Proverbs from Four Didactic Works of the Thirteenth Century." Diss. University of Kentucky, 1968. 492 pp.

1610. Perry, Theodore A. "Judeo-Christian Forces and Artistic Tension in Medieval Letters: The Case of the *Libro de los buenos proverbios.*" *La Chispa '87: Selected Proceedings: The Eighth Louisiana Conference on Hispanic Languages and Literatures.* Ed. Gilbert Paolini. New Orleans, Louisiana: Tulane University, 1987. 251-256.

1611. Sturm, Harlan. *The "Libro de los buenos proverbios": A Critical Edition.* Lexington: University Press of Kentucky, 1970. 148 pp.

LIBRO DE LOS CIEN CAPITULOS (13th cent.)
1612. Bizzarri, Hugo Oscar. "Un testimonio mas papa tres capitulos del *Libro de los cien capitulos.*" *Incipit* 9 (1989): 139-146.

EL LIBRO DE LOS DOZE SABIOS (c. 1237)
1613. Bizzarri, Hugo Oscar. "Consideraciones en torno a la elaboración de *El libro de los doze sabios.*" *La Corónica* 18, 1 (1989-1990), 85-89.

1614. Walsh, John K. *"El Libro de los doze sabios" o "Tractado de la nobleza y lealtad": Estudio y edicion.* Madrid: Real Academia Española, 1975. 179 pp.

LIBRO DEL CAVALLERO ZIFAR (14th cent.)
1615. Piccus, Jules. "Refranes y frases proverbiales en el *Libro del Cavallero Zifar.*" *Nueva Revista de Filologia Hispánica* 18 (1965-1966): 1-24.

LICHTENBERG, GEORG CHRISTOPH (1742-1799)
1616. Fricke, Harald. *Aphorismus.* Stuttgart: Metzler, 1984. 14-17, 26-29, 61-64, 70-77, 153-160.

1617. Mautner, Franz H. "Der Aphorismus als literarische Gattung." *Zeitschrift für Ästhetik und allgemeine Kunstwissenschaft* 27 (1933): 132-175.

1618. Mautner, Franz H. "Maxim(e)s, Sentences, Fragmente, Aphorismen." *Actes du 4e Congrès de l'Association Internationale de Littérature Comparée, Fribourg 1964.* Ed. François Jost. The Hague: Mouton, 1966. II, 812-819.

1619. Mieder, Wolfgang. "'Regeln-Krieg, Sprüchwörter-Krieg': Zu den sprichwörtlichen Aphorismen von Georg Christoph Lichtenberg." *Lichtenberg: Essays Commemorating the 250th Anniversary of His Birth.* Ed. Charlotte M. Craig. New York: Peter Lang, 1993. 55-94.

1620. Riha, Karl. "Balla Balla, Balla Basta: Zur Poetik kleiner literarischer Formen." *Akzente* 21 (1974): 265-287.

1621. Rosenfeld, Hans-Friedrich. "Georg Christoph Lichtenbergs *Patriotischer Beytrag zur Methyologie der Deutschen* und die niederdeutsche Methyologie der Gegenwart: Ein Beitrag zur Ausdrucksfähigkeit und Bildkraft der niederdeutschen Sprache." *Jahrbuch des Vereins für niederdeutsche Sprachforschung* 78 (1955): 83-137.

LINCK, WENZESLAUS (1483-1547)
1622. Broek, Marinus A. van den. "Sprichwörtliche Redensart und sprichwörtlicher Vergleich in den Erbauungsschriften des Nürnberger Predigers Wenzeslaus Linck." *Leuvense bijdragen* 76, 4 (1987): 475-499.

LINDENER, MICHAEL (c. 1520-1562)
1623. Stambaugh, Ria. "Proverbs and Proverbial Phrases in the Jestbooks of Lindener, Montanus and Schumann." Diss. University of North Carolina, 1963. 381 pp.

1624. Stambaugh, Ria. "Proverbial Material in Sixteenth Century German Jestbooks." *Proverbium* No. 11 (1968): 257-267.

LINGUA (1607)
1625. Whiting, Bartlett Jere. *"Lingua." Proverbs in the Earlier English Drama.* Cambridge, Massachusetts: Harvard University Press, 1938; rpt. New York: Octagon Books, 1969. 164-167.

LION DE BOURGES (14th cent.)
1626. Picherit, Jean-Louis G. "Proverbial Material in *Lion de Bourges.*" *Olifant* 4 (1977): 244-258.

LION DE BOURGES (15th cent.)
1627. Fenster, Thelma S. "Proverbs and Sententious Remarks in the Octosyllabic *Lion de Bourges.*" *Neuphilologische Mitteilungen* 86, 2 (1985): 272-279.

LISPECTOR, CLARICE (1922—)

1628. Bohorquez, Elba. "Recours oraux employés par Clarice Lispector pour décrire la protagoniste d'*A hora da estrela*: Fondement cognitif de cette démarche." *Paremia* No. 2 (1993): 169-173.

LIVY [Titus Livius] (59 B. C.-A. D. 17)

1629. Crum, Richard Henry. "'Blood, Sweat and Tears.'" *The Classical Journal* 42 (1947): 299-300.

LLOYD, FRANCIS BARTOW (1861-1897)

1630. Figh, Margaret Gillis. "Folklore in the *Rufus Sanders* Sketches." *Southern Folklore Quarterly* 19 (1955): 185-195.

LOGAU, FRIEDRICH (1604-1655)

1631. Hess, Peter. *Epigramm*. Stuttgart: Metzler, 1989. 84-93, 98-102.

1632. Schnur, Harry C. "The Humanist Epigram and Its Influence on the German Epigram." *Acta conventus neo-latini Lovaniensis: Proceedings of the First International Congress of Neo-Latin Studies, Louvain 23-28 August 1971*. Eds. J. Ijsewijn and E. Keßler. München: Wilhelm Fink, 1973. 557-576.

LONGFELLOW, HENRY WADSWORTH (1807-1882)

1633. Monteiro, George. "'Eyes in the Glass'/'Head in the Glass.'" *Proverbium* No. 24 (1974): 955.

1634. Partridge, Eric. "Clichés." *A Charm of Words: Essays and Papers on Language*. New York: The Macmillan Company, 1961. 44-54.

LONGSTREET, AUGUSTUS BALDWIN (1790-1870)

1635. Tamony, Peter. "'To See the Elephant.'" *Pacific Historian* 12 (1968): 23-29.

LOPEZ DE AYALA, PERO (1332-1407)

1636. Bizzarri, Hugo Oscar. "Refranes, frases proverbiales y versos proverbializados en cuaderna via (el caso del *Rimado de Palacio*)." *Proverbium: Yearbook of International Proverb Scholarship* 9 (1992): 1-10.

1637. Ferro, Jorge Norberto. "Aproximacion al empleo de los proverbios en las *Crónicas de los Reyes de Castilla* del Canciller Pero Lopez de

Ayala." *Proverbium: Yearbook of International Proverb Scholarship* 9 (1992): 37-41.

LOW, SAMUEL (1765-c. 1810)

1638. Montgomery, Evelyn. "Proverbial Materials in *The Politician Out-Witted* and Other Comedies of Early American Drama 1789-1829." *Midwest Folklore* 11 (1961-1962): 215- 224.

LUCIAN [Lucianus] (c. 120-180)

1639. Prittwitz-Gaffron, Erich von. *Das Sprichwort im griechischen Epigramm.* Diss. München, 1912. Gießen: Alfred Töpelmann, 1912. 50-52.

1640. Rein, Theodor. *Sprichwörter und sprichwörtliche Redensarten bei Lucian.* Diss. Tübingen, 1894. Tübingen: H. Laupp, 1894. 104 pp.

1641. Schmidt, O. *Metapher und Gleichnis in den Schriften Lukians.* Winterthur, Zürich: Geschwister Ziegler, 1897. 138 pp.

LUCILLIOS (A. D. 1st cent.)

1642. Prittwitz-Gaffron, Erich von. *Das Sprichwort im griechischen Epigramm.* Diss. München, 1912. Gießen: Alfred Töpelmann, 1912. 43-45.

LUDUS COVENTRIAE (15th cent.)

1643. Whiting, Bartlett Jere. "*Ludus Coventriae.*" *Proverbs in the Earlier English Drama.* Cambridge, Massachusetts: Harvard University Press, 1938; rpt. New York: Octagon Books, 1969. 22-29.

LUDWIG, OTTO (1813-1865)

1644. Mieder, Wolfgang. "Das Sprichwort in den Prosaschriften Otto Ludwigs." *Das Sprichwort in der deutschen Prosaliteratur des neunzehnten Jahrhunderts.* München: Wilhelm Fink, 1976. 107-128.

1645. Schewe, Harry. "'Ihr gebt mir ja nichts dazu': Eine Redeformel der Volkssprache, ein Volkstanzlied und Goethes Ballade *Vor Gericht.*" *Beiträge zur sprachlichen Volksüberlieferung.* Eds. Ingeborg Weber-Kellermann and Wolfgang Steinitz. Berlin [East]: Akademie-Verlag, 1953. 28-38.

LUPTON, THOMAS (fl. 1578-1583)

1646. Whiting, Bartlett Jere. "Thomas Lupton's *All For Money.*" *Proverbs in the Earlier English Drama.* Cambridge, Massachusetts: Harvard University Press, 1938; rpt. New York: Octagon Books, 1969. 151-153.

LUTHER, MARTIN (1483-1546)

1647. Anderson, Sandra Mosher. "Words and Word in Theological Perspective: Martin Luther's Views on Literature and Figurative Speech." Diss. Northwestern University, 1973. 656 pp.

1648. Arnold, Katrin. "'Der Teufel ist den Sprichworten feind.'" *Neue deutsche Literatur* 31, 11 (1983): 155-158.

1649. Bambeck, Manfred. "Wenn einen der Teufel reitet." *Muttersprache* 92 (1982): 185-195.

1650. Bebermeyer, Renate. "'Ich bin dazu geboren, das ich mit rotten und teufeln mus kriegen': Luthers 'Teufel'-Komposita." *Muttersprache* 94 (1983-1984): 52-67.

1651. Berger, P.-R. "'Zum Huren bereit bis hin zu einem Rundlaib Brot': Prov. 6:26." *Zeitschrift für die alttestamentliche Wissenschaft* 99 (1987): 98-106.

1652. Brandt, Gisela. "Feste Wendungen." In Erwin Arndt and G. Brandt. *Luther und die deutsche Sprache.* Leipzig: VEB Bibliographisches Institut, 1983. 215-219.

1653. Brüllmann, Richard. *Lexikon der treffenden Martin-Luther-Zitate.* Thun: Ott, 1983. 248 pp.

1654. Bünker, Michael. "'Gebt dem Kaiser, was des Kaisers ist!'—Aber was ist des Kaisers? Überlegungen zur Perikope von der Kaisersteuer." *Kairos: Zeitschrift für Religionswissenschaft und Theologie* 29 (1987): 85-98.

1655. Cornette, James C. "Proverbs and Proverbial Expressions in the German Works of Luther." Diss. University of North Carolina, 1942. 225 pp.

1656. Cornette, James C. "Luther's Attitude Toward Wellerisms." *Southern Folklore Quarterly* 9 (1945): 127-144.

1657. Dithmar, Reinhard, ed. *Martin Luthers Fabeln und Sprichwörter.* Frankfurt am Main: Insel, 1989. 177-194, 231-233.

1658. Große, R., ed. *Martin Luthers Sprichwörtersammlung.* Leipzig: Insel, 1983. 100 pp.

1659. Haupt, Paul. "'Abraham's Bosom.'" *American Journal of Philology* 42 (1921): 162-167.

1660. Heuseler, J. A. *Luthers Sprichwörter aus seinen Schriften gesammelt.* Leipzig: Johann Ambrosius Barth, 1824; rpt. Walluf bei Wiesbaden: Sändig, 1973. 160 pp.

1661. Kroker, E. "Sprichwörter." *D. Martin Luthers Werke: Kritische Gesamtausgabe: Tischreden,* 6 vols. Weimar: Hermann Böhlau, 1921. VI, 666-677.

1662. Krumbholz, Eckart, ed. *Martin Luther: "Euch stoßen, daß es krachen soll": Sprüche, Aussprüche, Anekdoten.* Berlin: Buchverlag der Morgen, 1983. 255 pp.

1663. Kunstmann, John G. "And Yet Again: 'Wes das Herz voll ist, des gehet der Mund über.'" *Concordia Theological Monthly* 23 (1952): 509-527.

1664. Kurrelmeyer, William. "'Wes das Herz voll ist, des gehet der Mund über.'" *Modern Language Notes* 50 (1935): 380-382.

1665. Latendorf, Friedrich. *Hundert Sprüche Luthers zum Alten Testament in hochdeutscher, niederdeutscher und niederländischer Fassung.* Rostock: C. Hinstorff, 1883. 26 pp.

1666. Lemmer, Manfred. "Lutherdeutsch und Gegenwartssprache." *Sprachpflege* 32, 11 (1983): 161-166.

1667. Macintosh, A. "Note on Proverbs 25:27 [It is not good to eat much honey, so be sparing of complimentary words]." *Vetus Testamentum* 20 (1970): 112-114.

1668. Maess, Thomas, ed. *Dem Luther aufs Maul geschaut: Kostproben seiner sprachlichen Kunst.* Leipzig: Koehler und Amelang, 1982; Wiesbaden: Drei Lilien Verlag, 1983. 96-100.

1669. Mieder, Wolfgang. "Martin Luther und die Geschichte des Sprichwortes 'Wes das Herz voll ist, des geht der Mund über.'" *Sprachspiegel* 39 (1983): 66-74. Also in *Sprichwörtliches und Geflügeltes: Sprachstudien von Martin Luther bis Karl Marx.* Bochum: Norbert Brockmeyer, 1995. 13-22.

1670. Mieder, Wolfgang. "'Was Hänschen nicht lernt, lernt Hans nimmermehr': Zur Überlieferung eines Luther-Sprichwortes." *Sprachspiegel* 39 (1983): 131-138. Also in *Sprichwörtliches und Geflügeltes: Sprachstudien von Martin Luther bis Karl Marx.* Bochum: Norbert Brockmeyer, 1995. 23-32.

1671. Mieder, Wolfgang. "'Wine, Women and Song': From Martin Luther to American T-Shirts." *Kentucky Folklore Record* 29 (1983): 89-101. Also in *Folk Groups and Folklore Genres: A Reader.* Ed. Elliott Oring. Logan: Utah State University Press, 1989. 279-290.

1672. Mieder, Wolfgang. "'Wer nicht liebt Wein, Weib und Gesang, der bleibt ein Narr sein Leben lang': Zur Herkunft, Überlieferung und Verwendung eines angeblichen Luther-Spruches." *Muttersprache* 94 (Sonderheft, 1983-1984): 68-103. Also in *Deutsche Redensarten, Sprichwörter und Zitate: Studien zu ihrer Herkunft, Überlieferung und Verwendung.* Vienna: Edition Praesens, 1995. 10-45.

1673. Mieder, Wolfgang. "'Wine, Women and Song': Zur anglo-amerikanischen Überlieferung eines angeblichen Lutherspruches." *Germanisch-Romanische Monatsschrift* 65 ns 34 (1984): 385-403. Also in *Sprichwort—Wahrwort!? Studien zur Geschichte, Bedeutung und Funktion deutscher Sprichwörter.* Frankfurt am Main: Peter Lang, 1992. 169-190.

1674. Moser, Dietz-Rüdiger. "'Die wellt wil meister klueglin bleiben. . .' Martin Luther und das deutsche Sprichwort." *Muttersprache* 90 (1980): 151-166.

1675. Nelson, Timothy C. "'Ex abundantia cordis os loquitur': Ein Beitrag zur Rezeptionsgeschichte eines umstrittenen Sprichworts." *Proverbium: Yearbook of International Proverb Scholarship* 3 (1986): 101-123.

1676. Nelson, Timothy C. *"O du armer Luther. . ." Sprichwörtliches in der antilutherischen Polemik des Johannes Nas (1534-1590).* Diss. Uppsala Universitet, 1990. 305 pp. Bern: Peter Lang, 1992. 334 pp.

1677. Ottow, A. M. "Luther'sche [*sic*] Sprichwörtersammlung." *Deutscher Sprachwart* 4, 15 (1869): 236-237.

1678. Peil, Dietmar. "Beziehungen zwischen Fabel und Sprichwort." *Germanica Wratislaviensia* 85 (1989): 74-87.

1679. Pfeifer, Wolfgang. "Volkstümliche Metaphorik." *Zur Literatursprache im Zeitalter der frühbürgerlichen Revolution: Untersuchungen zu ihrer Verwendung in der Agitationsliteratur.* Eds. Gerhard Kettmann and Joachim Schildt. Berlin: Akademie-Verlag, 1978. 87-217.

1680. Reuschel, Karl. "*Luthers Sprichwörtersammlung*: Nach seiner Handschrift zum ersten Male herausgegeben und mit Anmerkungen versehen von Ernst Thiele (Weimar 1900)." *Euphorion* 8 (1901): 161-171.

1681. Schulze, Carl. *Die biblischen Sprichwörter der deutschen Sprache.* Göttingen: Vandenhoeck und Ruprecht, 1860. 203 pp.; rpt. with an introduction and bibliography by Wolfgang Mieder. Bern: Peter Lang, 1987. 203 pp.

1682. Schulze, Günter. *Pfeffernüsse aus den Werken von Doktor Martin Luther.* Berlin: Volk und Wissen, 1982. 110 pp.

1683. Seiler, Friedrich. *Deutsche Sprichwörterkunde.* München: C. H. Beck, 1922, 1967. 116-121.

1684. Stintzing, Roderich von. *Das Sprichwort "Juristen böse Christen" in seinen geschichtlichen Bedeutungen.* Bonn: Adolph Marens, 1875. 32 pp.

1685. Thiele, Ernst. *Luthers Sprichwörtersammlung: Nach seiner Handschrift zum ersten Male herausgegeben und mit Anmerkungen versehen.* Weimar: Hermann Böhlau, 1900. 448 pp.

1686. Thiele, Ernst, and O. Brenner. "Luthers Sprichwörtersammlung." *D. Martin Luthers Werke: Kritische Gesamtausgabe.* Weimar: Hermann Böhlau, 1914; rpt. Graz: Akademische Druck- und Verlagsanstalt, 1967. LI, 634-731.

1687. Weckmann, Berthold. "Sprichwort und Redensart in der Lutherbibel." *Archiv für das Studium der neueren Sprachen und Literaturen* 221 (1984): 19-42.

LYDGATE, JOHN (c. 1370-c. 1451)

1688. Duschl, Joseph. "Das Sprichwort bei Lydgate nebst Quellen und Parallelen." Diss. München, 1912. 99 pp.

1689. Walsh, Elizabeth. "John Lydgate and the Proverbial Tiger." *The Learned and the Lewd: Studies in Chaucer and Medieval Literature*. Ed. Larry D. Benson. Cambridge, Massachusetts: Harvard University Press, 1974. 291-303.

1690. Zupitza, Julius. "*The Prouerbis of Wysdom*." *Archiv für das Studium der neuren Sprachen und Literaturen* 90 (1893): 241-268.

LYLY, JOHN (c. 1554-1606)
1691. Frieser, Walter. "Das Sprichwort in den dramatischen Werken John Lylys: Zugleich ein Beitrag zur Geschichte des englischen Sprichworts." Diss. Leipzig, 1920. 205 pp.

1692. Pfeffer, Karl. *Das elisabethanische Sprichwort in seiner Verwendung bei Ben Jonson*. Diss. Gießen, 1933. Gießen: Richard Glagow, 1933. 29-32.

1693. Smith, Roland M. "Three Obscure English Proverbs [The game is not worth the candle; He that will swear will lie; Life is a pilgrimage]." *Modern Language Notes* 65 (1950): 441-447.

1694. Tilley, Morris Palmer. *Elizabethan Proverb Lore in Lyly's "Euphues" and in Pettie's "Petite Pallace" with Parallels from Shakespeare*. New York: The Macmillan Company, 1927. 461 pp.

LYNDSAY, Sir DAVID (c. 1490-1555)
1695. Kissel, Julius. *Das Sprichwort bei dem mittelschottischen Dichter Sir David Lyndsay*. Nürnberg: Monninger, 1892. 42 pp.

1696. Whiting, Bartlett Jere. "Sir David Lyndsay's *The Three Estates*." *Proverbs in the Earlier English Drama*. Cambridge, Massachusetts: Harvard University Press, 1938; rpt. New York: Octagon Books, 1969. 94-97.

M

MACEDONIOS (A. D. 1st cent.)

1697. Prittwitz-Gaffron, Erich von. *Das Sprichwort im griechischen Epigramm.* Diss. München, 1912. Gießen: Alfred Töpelmann, 1912. 61-64.

MACHADO DES ASSIS, JOAQUIM MARIA (1839-1908)

1698. M., A. "Rouge comme une pitangue.'" *Le Folklore Brabançon* 17 (1937-1938): 276.

MACHADO Y RUIZ, ANTONIO (1875-1939)

1699. O'Kane, Eleanor. "Antonio Machado, 'Aprendiz de saber popular.'" *Modern Language Notes* 87 (1972): 232-252.

1700. Sobejano, Gonzalo. "La verdad en la poesia de Antonio Machado: De la rima al proverbio." *Journal of Spanish Studies: Twentieth Century* 4 (1976): 47-73.

MACHAU[L]T, GUILLAUME DE (c. 1300-1377)

1701. Cerquiglini, Jacqueline, and Bernard. "L'écriture proverbiale." *Revue des sciences humaines* 41, 163 (1976): 359-375.

1702. Fehse, Erich. *Sprichwort und Sentenz bei Eustache Deschamps und Dichtern seiner Zeit.* Diss. Berlin, 1905. Erlangen: Universitäts-Buchdrucherei, 1905. 44. Also in *Romanische Forschungen* 19 (1906): 487-488.

MAHABHARATA (c. 4th cent. B. C.-A. D. c. 4th cent.)

1703. Hopkins, Washburn. "Proverbs and Tales Common to the Two Sanskrit Epics." *American Journal of Philology* 20 (1899): 22-39.

MAIMONIDES, MOSES (1135-1204)

1704. Bar-Sela, Ariel, and Hebbel E. Hoff. "Maimonides' Interpretation of the First Aphorism of Hippocrates." *Bulletin of the History of Medicine* 37 (1963): 347-354.

MAINTENON, FRANÇOISE D'AUBIGNÉ, Madame de (1635-1719)

1705. Brahmer, Miecyzslaw. "Le vicende del proverbio dramatico." *XIV. Congresso internazionale di linguistica e filologia romanza.* Ed. Alberto Várvaro. Naples: Macchiaroli, 1981. V, 509-511.

1706. Chaumeix, André. "La comédie proverbe." Rev. of *Je crois que je vous aime,* by G. d'Houville. *Revue des Deux Mondes* 40 (August 1, 1927): 698-708.

1707. Nikliborc, Anna. "Madame de Maintenon et ses proverbes." *Romanica Wratislaviensia* 9 (1973): 3-14.

MAL LARA, JUAN DE (1527-1571)
1708. Castillo de Lucas, Antonio. "Seleccion de refranes de interés, médico en la 'filosofia vulgar' de Juan de Mal Lara." *Revista de Etnografia* 16 (1972): 45-52.

1709. Sánchez y Escribano, F. *Los "Adagia" de Erasmo en "La Philosophia Vulgar" de Juan de Mal Lara.* New York: Hispanic Institute, 1944. 85 pp.

1710. Venier, Martha Elena. "Los proverbios domésticos de Mal Lara." *Actas del IX. Congreso de la Asociacion Internacional de Hispanistas.* Ed. Sebastian Neumeister. Frankfurt am Main: Vervuert, 1989. I, 681-686.

MALHERBE, FRANÇOIS de (1555-1628)
1711. Le Roux de Lincy, M. *Le Livre des Proverbes Français*, 2 vols. 2nd ed. Paris: A. Delahays, 1859; rpt. Genève: Slatkine, 1968. I, lxiii-lxiv.

1712. Sébillot, Paul. "Malherbe." *Revue des traditions populaires* 8 (1893): 453-454.

MALLARMÉ, STÉPHANE (1842-1898)
1713. Whiting, Bartlett Jere. "The English Proverbs of Stéphane Mallarmé." *Romanic Review* 36 (1945): 134-141.

MANKIND (c. 1475)
1714. Whiting, Bartlett Jere. *"Mankind." Proverbs in the Earlier English Drama.* Cambridge, Massachusetts: Harvard University Press, 1938; rpt. New York: Octagon Books, 1969. 73-75.

MANN, GOLO (1909-1994)
1715. Wandruszka, Mario. "Sprache aus Bildern." *Die europäische Sprachengemeinschaft:Deutsch—Französisch—English—Italienisch—Spanisch im Vergleich.* Tübingen: A. Francke, 1990. 51-76.

MANN, THOMAS (1875-1955)
1716. Mieder, Wolfgang. "Das Sprichwort als volkstümliches Zitat bei Thomas Mann." *Germanic Notes* 3 (1972): 50-53. Also in *Sprichwort, Redensart, Zitat: Tradierte Formelsprache in der Moderne.* Bern: Peter Lang, 1985. 11-14.

1717. Mieder, Wolfgang. "Sprichwörter im moderen Sprachgebrauch." *Muttersprache* 85 (1975): 65-88. Also in *Ergebnisse der Sprichwörterforschung*. Bern: Peter Lang, 1978. 213-238; *Deutsche Sprichwörter in Literatur, Politik, Presse und Werbung*. Hamburg: Helmut Buske, 1983. 53-76.

1718. Scheiber, Alexander. "'Er hätte sich vielleicht selbst in den kleinen Finger schneiden lassen.'" *Proverbium* No. 15 (1970): 528-529.

1719. Schmidt-Hidding, Wolfgang. "Deutsche Sprichwörter und Redewendungen." *Deutschunterricht für Ausländer* 13 (1963): 13-26, especially 13-14.

1720. Soler, Maria-Lourdes. "Locuciones idiomáticas en *Buddenbrooks*." Diss. Universidad de Barcelona, 1969. 670 pp.

1721. Soler i Marcet, Maria-Lourdes. "'Wenn das Haus fertig ist, so kommt der Tod': Sprichwörter und sprichwörtliche Redensarten in Thomas Manns *Buddenbrooks*." *Proverbium: Yearbook of International Proverb Scholarship* 10 (1993): 297-320.

1722. Uther, Hans-Jörg. "Machen Kleider Leute? Zur Wertigkeit von Kleidung in populären Erzählungen." *Jahrbuch für Volkskunde* (1991): 24-44.

THE MANNER OF THE CRYING OF A PLAY (c. 1503)

1723. Whiting, Bartlett Jere. "*The Manner of the Crying of a Play*." *Proverbs in the Earlier English Drama*. Cambridge, Massachusetts: Harvard University Press, 1938; rpt. New York: Octagon Books, 1969. 171.

MANNYNG, ROBERT (c. 1264-1340)

1724. Skeat, Walter William. "Robert Mannyng, of Brunne." *Early English Proverbs, Chiefly of the Thirteenth and Fourteenth Centuries*. Oxford: Clarendon Press, 1910; rpt. Darby, Pennsylvania: Folcroft Library Editions, 1974. 39-41.

MANSFIELD, KATHERINE (1888-1923)

1725. De Caro, Francis A. "Proverbs and Originality in Modern Short Fiction." *Western Folklore* 37 (1978): 30-38.

MANUAEL, Don JUAN (1282-1348)

1726. Ayerbe-Chaux, Reinaldo. "*El libro de los proverbios* del conde Lucanor y de Patronio." *Studies in Honor of Gustavo Correa.* Eds. Charles B. Faulhaber, Richard P. Kinkade, and Theodore A. Perry. Potomac, Maryland: Scripta Humanistica, 1986. 1-10.

MANZONI, ALESSANDRO (1785-1873)

1727. Fasani, Remo. "Un Manzoni milanese?" *Studi e problemi di critica testuale* 41 (1990): 51-66.

MARCABRU (fl. 1130-1150)

1728. Goddard, R. N. B. "Marcabru, *Li Proverbes au Vilain*, and the Tradition of Rustic Proverbs." *Neuphilologische Mitteilungen* 88, 1 (1987): 55-70.

MARIA DE JESUS, CAROLINA (1913—)

1729. Arrington, Melvin S. "Gnomic Literature from the *Favela*: The 'Provérbios' of Carolina Maria de Jesus." *Romance Notes* 34, 1 (1993): 79-85.

MARLOWE, CHRISTOPHER (1564-1593)

1730. Rusche, H. G. "Two Proverbial Images in Whitney's *A Choice of Emblemes* and Marlowe's *The Jew of Malta.*" *Notes and Queries* 209 ns 11 (1964): 261.

1731. Tilley, Morris Palmer, and James K. Ray. "Proverbs and Proverbial Allusions in Marlowe." *Modern Language Notes* 50 (1935): 347-355.

1732. Tkacz, Catherine Brown. "*The Jew of Malta* and the Pit." *South Atlantic Review* 53, 2 (1988): 47-57.

DER MARNER (c. 1231-c. 1267)

1733. Hofmeister, Wernfried. *Sprichwortartige Mikrotexte als literarische Medien, dargestellt an der hochdeutschen politischen Lyrik des Mittelalters.* Bochum: Norbert Brockmeyer, 1995. 278-282.

1734. Nicklas, Friedrich. *Untersuchung über Stil und Geschichte des deutschen Tageliedes.* Berlin: Emil Ebering, 1929; rpt. Nendeln, Liechtenstein: Kraus Reprint, 1967. 78-79.

MAROT, CLÉMENT (1496-1544)

1735. Le Roux de Lincy, M. *Le Livre des Proverbes Français*, 2 vols. 2nd ed. Paris: A. Delahays, 1859; rpt. Genève: Slatkine, 1968. I, lxii-lxiii.

1736. Sébillot, Paul. "Clément Marot." *Revue des traditions populaires* 26 (1911): 343-344.

THE MARRIAGE OF WIT AND SCIENCE (1569/1570)

1737. Whiting, Bartlett Jere. "*The Marriage of Wit and Science.*" *Proverbs in the Earlier English Drama*. Cambridge, Massachusetts: Harvard University Press, 1938; rpt. New York: Octagon Books, 1969. 138-142.

THE MARRIAGE OF WIT AND WISDOM (c. 1570)

1738. Tilley, Morris Palmer. "Notes on *The Marriage of Wit and Wisdom*." *The Shakespeare Association Bulletin* 10 (1935): 45-57, 89-94.

1739. Whiting, Bartlett Jere. "*The Marriage of Wit and Wisdom.*" *Proverbs in the Earlier English Drama*. Cambridge, Massachusetts: Harvard University Press, 1938; rpt. New York: Octagon Books, 1969. 143-147.

MARSTON, JOHN (1576-1634)

1740. Cross, Gustav. "Tilley's *Dictionary of Proverbs in England*, H 348, and Marston's *Antonio and Mellida*." *Notes and Queries* 206 ns 8 (1961): 143-144.

1741. Prager, Carolyn. "'If I Be Devil': English Renaissance Response to the Proverbial and Ecumenical Ethiopian." *Journal of Medieval and Renaissance Studies* 17, 2 (1987): 257-279.

1742. Rice, Warner G. "'To Turn Turk.'" *Modern Language Notes* 46 (1931): 153-154.

1743. Taylor, Archer. "Proverbs and Proverbial Phrases in the Plays of John Marston." *Southern Folklore Quarterly* 24 (1960): 193-216.

MARTIAL [Marcus Valerius Martialis] (c. 38-c. 101)

1744. Kuiper, Gerdien C. "An Erasmian Adage as 'Fortune's Fool': Martial's 'Oleum in auricula ferre.'" *Humanistica Lovaniensia* 39 (1990): 67-84.

1745. Schnur, Harry C. "The Humanist Epigram and Its Influence on the German Epigram." *Acta conventus neo-latini Lovaniensis: Proceedings of the First International Congress of Neo-Latin Studies, Louvain 23-28*

August 1971. Eds. J. Ijsewijn and E. Keßler. München: Wilhelm Fink, 1973. 557-576.

MARVELL, ANDREW (1621-1678)

1746. Cox, Philip. "Blake, Marvell, and Milton: A Possible Source for a Proverb of Hell." *Notes and Queries* 236 ns 38 (1991): 292-293.

1747. Cox, Philip. "Blake, Marvell, Milton, and Young: A Further Possible Source for a Proverb of Hell." *Notes and Queries* 238 ns 40, 1 (1993): 37-38.

MARX, KARL (1818-1883)

1748. Kann, Hans-Joachim. "Zu den Quellen von Spontisprüchen." *Der Sprachdienst* 29 (1985): 75-79.

1749. Mieder, Wolfgang. "'Proletarier aller Länder, vereinigt euch!' —Wozu? Geflügelter Abschied vom Marxismus." *Sprachspiegel* 47 (1991): 69-77. Also in *Sprichwörtliches und Geflügeltes: Sprachstudien von Martin Luther bis Karl Marx.* Bochum: Norbert Brockmeyer, 1995. 125-136.

1750. Seeger, Reinhart. *Herkunft und Bedeutung des Schlagwortes: "Die Religion ist Opium für das Volk."* Halle: Akademischer Verlag, 1935. 45 pp.

MASSINGER, PHILIP (1583-1640)

1751. Gaspary, A. "Allgemeine Aussprüche in den Dramen Philip Massingers." Diss. Marburg, 1890. 37 pp.

1752. "Glossary and Index to the Commentary: Proverbs." *The Plays and Poems of Philip Massinger.* Eds. Philip Edwards and Colin Gibson. Oxford: Clarendon Press, 1976. V, 328-330.

1753. Prager, Carolyn. "'If I Be Devil': English Renaissance Response to the Proverbial and Ecumenial Ethiopian." *Journal of Medieval and Renaissance Studies* 17, 2 (1987): 257-279.

1754. Rice, Warner G. "'To Turn Turk.'" *Modern Language Notes* 46 (1931): 153-154.

MATHER, COTTON (1663-1728)

1755. Whiting, Bartlett Jere. "Proverbs in Cotton Mather's *Magnalia Christi Americana.*" *Neuphilologische Mitteilungen* 73 (1972): 477-484.

MATTHEWS, HARRY (1930—)

1756. Everman, Welch D. "Harry Mathews's *Selected Declarations of Dependence*: Proverbs and the Forms of Authority." *The Review of Contemporary Fiction* 7, 3 (1987): 146-153.

MAUGHAM, WILLIAM SOMERSET (1874-1965)

1757. Schmidt-Hidding, Wolfgang. "William Somerset Maugham." *Englische Idiomatik in Stillehre und Literatur*. München: Max Hueber, 1962. 81-84.

1758. Shvydkaia, L. I. "Sinonimicheskie otnosheniia poslovits i aforizmov v angliiskom iazyke." *Leksikologicheskie osnovy stilistiki (Sbornik nauchnykh trudov)*. Ed. I. V. Arnol'd. Leningrad: Gosudarstvennyi pedagogicheskii institut im. A. I. Gertsena, 1973. 167-175.

MAXIMOS PLANUDES (c. 1260-c. 1310)

1759. Geisler, Eugen. "Beiträge zur Geschichte des griechischen Sprichwortes im Anschluß an Planudes und Michael Apostolius." Diss. Breslau, 1908; published as *Beiträge zur Geschichte des griechischen Sprichwortes (in Anschluß an Planudes und Michael Apostoles)*. Breslau: R. Nischkowsky, 1908. 40 pp.

MEDWALL, HENRY (c. 1462-1500)

1760. Whiting, Bartlett Jere. "Henry Medwall's *Nature*." *Proverbs in the Earlier English Drama*. Cambridge, Massachusetts: Harvard University Press, 1938; rpt. New York: Octagon Books, 1969. 77-80.

1761. Whiting, Bartlett Jere. "Henry Medwall's *Fulgens and Lucres*." *Proverbs in the Earlier English Drama*. Cambridge, Massachusetts: Harvard University Press, 1938; rpt. New York: Octagon Books, 1969. 210-212.

MEIER, GEORG FRIEDRICH (1718-1787)

1762. Strube, Werner. "Zur Geschichte des Sprichworts 'Über den Geschmack läßt sich nicht streiten.'" *Zeitschrift für Ästhetik und Allgemeine Kunstwissenschaft* 30 (1985): 158-185.

MELANCHTHON, PHILIPP (1497-1560)

1763. Sandvoss, Franz. *Sprichwörter aus Burkhart Waldis mit einem Anhange: Zur Kritik des Kurzischen B. Waldis und einem Verzeichnis von Melanchthon gebrauchter Sprichwörter*. Friedland: Richter, 1866. 159 pp.

1764. Stupperich, Robert. "Melanchthons Proverbien-Kommentare." *Der Kommentar in der Renaissance*. Eds. August Buck and Otto Herding. Boppard: Harald Boldt, 1975. 21-34.

MELEAGER [Meleagros] (c. 140-70)
1765. Prittwitz-Gaffron, Erich von. *Das Sprichwort im griechischen Epigramm*. Diss. München, 1912. Gießen: Alfred Töpelmann, 1912. 28-34.

MELVILLE, HERMAN (1819-1891)
1766. Babcock, C. Merton. "Melville's Proverbs of the Sea." *Western Folklore* 11 (1952): 254-265.

1767. Babcock, C. Merton. "Melville's World's Language." *Southern Folklore Quarterly* 16 (1952): 177-182.

1768. Babcock, C. Merton. "Some Expressions from Herman Melville." *Publications of the American Dialect Society* 3 (1959): 3-13.

MENANDER (c. 343-291 B. C.)
1769. Metzger, Bruce M. "'To Call a Spade a Spade' in Greek and Latin." *The Classical Journal* 33 (1938): 229-231.

MENNES, Sir JOHN (1599-1671)
1770. Newcomb, Robert. "Poor Richard and the English Epigram." *Philological Quarterly* 40 (1961): 270-280.

MENOT, MICHEL (c. 1440-1518)
1771. Neve, Joseph. "Proverbes et néologismes dans les sermons de Michel Menot." *Revue du Seizième Siècle* 7 (1920): 98-122.

MERWIN, WILLIAM STANLEY (1927—)
1772. Airmet, Douglas Elliot. 'How to Read a *Ballade of Sayings*.' "The Saying: Snatches for a Poetic." Diss. University of Iowa, 1985. 288-322.

MESCHINOT, JEAN (1422-1491)
1773. G., O. de. "Jean Meschinot." *Revue des traditions populaires* 20 (1905): 268-269.

MICHAEL CHONIATES (c. 1138-1222)
1774. Karathanasis, Demetrius. *Sprichwörter und sprichwörtliche Redensarten des Altertums in den rhetorischen Schriften des Michael Psellos, des*

Eustathios und des Michael Choniates sowie in anderen rhetorischen Quellen des XII. Jahrhunderts." Diss. München, 1936. Speyer am Rheim: Pilger, 1936. 128 pp.

MICHAEL PSELLOS (1018-c. 1078)

1775. Karathanasis, Demetrius. *Sprichwörter und sprichwörtliche Redensarten des Altertums in den rhetorischen Schriften des Michael Psellos, des Eustathios und des Michael Choniates sowie in anderen rhetorischen Quellen des XII. Jahrhunderts."* Diss. München, 1936. Speyer am Rhein: Pilger, 1936. 128 pp.

MIDDLETON, THOMAS (1580-1627)

1776. Holdsworth, R. V. "'Lie by It' in Middleton." *Notes and Queries* 226 ns 28 (1981): 242.

1777. Holdsworth, R. V. "Two Proverbs in Middleton and Some Contemporaries." *Notes and Queries* 226 ns 28 (1981): 172-173.

1778. Levin, Richard. "Proverbial Phrases in the Titles of Thomas Middleton's Plays." *Southern Folklore Quarterly* 28 (1964): 142-145.

1779. Taylor, Archer. "Proverbs and Proverbial Phrases in the Plays of Thomas Middleton." *Southern Folklore Quarterly* 23 (1958): 79-89.

MIKSZÁTH, KALMAN (1847-1910)

1780. Scheiber, Alexander. "'Er hätte sich vielleicht selbst in den kleinen Finger schneiden lassen.'" *Proverbium* No. 15 (1970): 528-529.

MILTON, JOHN (1608-1674)

1781. Cox, Philip. "Blake, Marvell, and Milton: A Possible Source for a Proverb of Hell." *Notes and Queries* 236 ns 38 (1991): 292-293.

1782. Cox, Philip. "Blake, Marvell, Milton, and Young: A Further Possible Source for a Proverb of Hell." *Notes and Queries* 238 ns 40, 1 (1993): 37-38.

1783. Doyle, Charles Clay. "Milton's Monolingual Woman and Her Forebears." *Proverbium: Yearbook of International Proverb Scholarship* 5 (1988): 15-21.

1784. Harman, Marian. "A Greek Proverb in Milton." *Classical Philology* 38 (1943): 259-260.

1785. Hedgeland, Philip. "Expressions in Milton." *Notes and Queries* 1st ser. 4 (1851): 394.

1786. Huttar, Charles. "Samson's Identity Crisis and Milton." *Imagination and the Spirit: Festschrift for Clyde S. Kilby*. Editor unknown. Grand Rapids, Michigan: Eerdmans, 1971. 101-157, especially 120-126.

1787. Knoppers, Laura Lunger. "'Sung and Proverb'd for a Fool': *Samson Agonistes* and Solomon's Harlot." *Milton Studies* 26 (1991): 239-251.

1788. Lansverk, Marvin Duane. "The Wisdom of Many, the Vision of One: The Proverbs of William Blake." Diss. University of Washington, 1988. 90-117.

1789. Nardo, Anna K. "'Sung and Proverb'd for a Fool': Samson as Fool and Trickster." *Mosaic* 22 (1989): 1-16.

1790. Nash, Ralph. "Milton, Jonson and Tiberius." *Classical Philology* 41 (1946): 164.

1791. Partridge, Eric. "Clichés." *A Charm of Words: Essays and Papers on Language*. New York: The Macmillan Company, 1961. 44-54.

1792. R. (a Reader). "Expressions in Milton." *Notes and Queries* 1st ser. 3 (1851): 241.

1793. Rosenberg, D. M. "*Samson Agonistes*: 'Proverb'd for a Fool.'" *The Centennial Review* 32, 1 (1988): 65-78.

LA MINISTRESSE NICOLE (1665)
1794. Desaivre, Léo. "*La ministresse Nicole*." *Revue des traditions populaires* 20 (1905): 303-304.

MISOGONUS (1560/1577)
1795. Whiting, Bartlett Jere. "*Misogonus*." *Proverbs in the Earlier English Drama*. Cambridge, Massachusetts: Harvard University Press, 1938; rpt. New York: Octagon Books, 1969. 225-230.

MITSCH, WERNER (1936—)
1796. Mieder, Wolfgang. "'Wahrheiten: Phantasmen aus Logik und Alltag': Zu den sprichwörtlichen Aphorismen von Werner Mitsch." *Muttersprache* 98 (1988): 121-132. Also in *Deutsche Redensarten, Sprichwörter*

und Zitate: Studien zu ihrer Herkunft, Überlieferung und Verwendung. Vienna: Edition Praesens, 1995. 127-138.

MIZAILLE (1662)

1797. Desaivre, Léo. "*Mizaille.*" *Revue des traditions populaires* 20 (1905): 305-312.

MÖCKEL, KLAUS (1934—)

1798. Militz, Hans-Manfred. "Phraseologische Wendungen in literarischen Texten." *Sprachpflege* 29, 5 (1980): 99-101.

1799. Militz, Hans-Manfred. "Kopfstand der Sprichwörter." *Sprachpflege* 32, 6 (1983): 83-84.

MOLIÈRE [Jean-Baptiste Poquelin] (1622-1673)

1800. Hudde, Hinrich. "'Conte à dormir debout': Eine Redensart als Bezeichnung für parodistische Märchen des 18. Jahrhunderts." *Romanische Forschungen* 97, 1 (1985): 15-35.

1801. Le Roux de Lincy, M. *Le Livre des Proverbes Français*, 2 vols. 2nd ed. Paris: A. Delahays, 1859; rpt. Genève: Slatkine, 1968. I, lxvi-lxvii.

1802. Le Roux de Lincy, M. *Le Livre des Proverbes Français*, 2 vols. 2nd ed. Paris: A. Delahays, 1859; rpt. Genève: Slatkine, 1968. II, 519-543.

1803. Pineaux, Jacques. "Molière." *Proverbes et dictons français*, 6th ed. Paris: Presses Universitaires de France, 1973. 62-65.

1804. Sébillot, Paul. "Molière." *Revue des traditions populaires* 5 (1890): 396-412, especially 407-412.

1805. Zholkovskii, Aleksandr K., and Iu. K. Tseglov. "Razbor odnoi avtorskoi paremii." *Paremiologischeskii Sbornik*. Ed. G. L. Permiakov. Moskva: Nauka, 1978. 163-210.

MOLINET, JEAN (1435-1507)

1806. Zumthor, Paul. "L'épiphonème proverbial." *Revue des sciences humaines* 41, 163 (1976): 313-328.

MONCRIEFF, WILLIAM G. T. (1794-1857)

1807. Bryan, George B., and Wolfgang Mieder. "'As Sam Weller Said, When Finding Himself on the Stage': Wellerisms in Dramatizations of Charles

Dickens' *Pickwick Papers.*" *Proverbium: Yearbook of International Proverb Scholarship* 11 (1994): 57-76.

MONTAIGNE, MICHAEL EYQUEM, Seigneur de (1533-1592)

1808. Bonnet, P. "Le 'souffler prou souffler' de Montaigne et son interprétation possible." *Bulletin de la société des amis de Montaigne* 3rd ser. 11-12 (1959): 33-43.

1809. Elaine, Sister M. Katherine. "The Moral Force of Montaigne's Proverbs." *Proverbium* No. 3 (1965): 33-45. Also published as "La force morale des proverbes de Montaigne." *Bulletin de la société des amis de Montaigne* 4th ser. 7 (1966): 49-59.

1810. Lafond, Jean. "Des formes brèves de la littérature morale aux XVIe et XVIIe siècles." *Les formes brèves de la prose et le discours discontinu (XVIe-XVIIe siècles)*. Paris: Librairie Philosophique J. Vrin, 1984. 101-122.

1811. Leake, Roy E. "Montaigne's Gascon Proverb Again." *Neophilologus* 52 (1968): 248-255.

1812. Newcomb, Robert. "Benjamin Franklin and Montaigne." *Modern Language Notes* 72 (1957): 489-491.

1813. Schmarje, Susanne. *Das sprichwörtliche Material in den Essais von Montaigne*, 2 vols. Diss. Hamburg, 1970. Berlin: Walter de Gruyter, 1973. 242 pp.; 161 pp.

1814. Screech, Michael. "Commonplaces of Law, Proverbial Wisdom and Philosophy: Their Importance in Renaissance Scholarship." *Classical Influences on European Culture, A. D. 1500-1700*. Ed. R. R. Bolgar. Cambridge: Cambridge University Press, 1976. 127-134.

1815. Tamony, Peter. "'To See the Elephant.'" *Pacific Historian* 12 (1968): 23-29.

1816. Wilcox, Stewart C. "Hazlitt's Aphorisms." *Modern Language Notes* 9 (1948): 418-423.

MONTANUS, MARTINUS (c. 1537-after 1566)

1817. Stambaugh, Ria. "Proverbs and Proverbial Phrases in the Jestbooks of Lindener, Montanus and Schuman." Diss. University of North Carolina, 1963. 381 pp.

1818. Stambaugh, Ria. "Proverbial Material in Sixteenth Century German Jestbooks." *Proverbium* No. 11 (1968): 257-267.

MONTFLEURY [Jacob d'Antoine] (1640-1685)

1819. Sébillot, Paul. "Montfleury." *Revue des traditions populaires* 10 (1895): 341-343.

MONTIGEL, RUDOLF (15th cent.)

1820. Hofmeister, Wernfried. *Sprichwortartige Mikrotexte als literarische Medien, dargestellt an der hochdeutschen politischen Lyrik des Mittelalters.* Bochum: Norbert Brockmeyer, 1995. 460-467.

MONTLUC, ADRIEN de (1589-1646)

1821. Le Roux de Lincy, M. *Le Livre des Proverbes Français*, 2 vols. 2nd ed. Paris: A. Delahays, 1859; rpt. Genève: Slatkine, 1968. I, lxxv-lxxviii.

MORANT UND GALIE (12th/13th cent.)

1822. Hofmann, Liselotte. *Der volkskundliche Gehalt der mittelhochdeutschen Epen von 1100 bis gegen 1250.* Zeulenroda: Bernhard Sporn, 1939. 78.

MORE, Sir THOMAS (1478-1535)

1823. Baird-Smith, David. "One Shrewd Wife in All the World." *Moreana: Bulletin Thomas More* 21, 83-84 (1984): 93-94.

1824. Cavanaugh, John Richard. "The Use of Proverbs and Sententiae for Rhetorical Amplification in the Writings of Saint Thomas More." Diss. St. Louis University, 1969. 476 pp.

1825. Doyle, Charles Clay. "The Popular Aspect of Sir Thomas More's Latin Epigrams." *Southern Folklore Quarterly* 37 (1973): 87-99.

1826. Doyle, Charles Clay. "John Webster's Echoes of More." *Moreana* 18, 70 (June 1981): 49-52.

1827. Doyle, Charles Clay. "Appendix D: Reports, Translations, and Adaptations of More's Latin Poems in the Sixteenth and Seventeenth

Century." *Thomas More, Latin Poems.* Ed. Clarence H. Miller et al. New Haven, Connecticut: Yale University Press, 1984. 697-709.

1828. Doyle, Charles Clay. "Looking Behind Two Proverbs of More." *Moreana* 23, 91-92 (1986): 33-35.

1829. Mauch, Thomas Karl. "The Role of the Proverb in Early Tudor Literature." Diss. University of California at Los Angeles, 1963. 126-184, 272-275.

1830. Pitts, Arthur William. "Proverb Lore in St. Thomas More's *Dyalogue of Comforte*." M. A. Thesis. Catholic University of America, 1960. 70 pp.

1831. Wilson, F. P. "English Proverbs and Dictionaries of Proverbs." *The Library* 4th ser. 26 (1945): 51-71.

MORETO Y CABANA, Don AUGUSTIN (1618-1669)
1832. Hayes, Francis Clement. "The Use of Proverbs in the 'Siglo de oro' Drama: An Introductory Study." Diss. University of North Carolina, 1936. 154-163.

MORGENSTERN, CHRISTIAN (1870-1914)
1833. Palm, Christine. "Christian Morgensterns groteske Phraseologie—ein Beitrag zur Rolle der Phraseologismen im literarischen Text." *Beiträge zur allgemeinen und germanistischen Phraseologieforschung.* Ed. Jarmo Korhonen. Oulu: Oulun Yliopisto, 1987. 221-235.

1834. Pape, Walter. "Zwischen Sprachspiel und Sprachkritik: Zum literarischen Spiel mit der wörtlichen Bedeutung von Idiomen." *Sprache und Literatur in Wissenschaft und Unterricht* 16, 56 (1985): 2-13.

MORITZ VON CRAON (c. 1215)
1835. Hofmann, Liselotte. *Der volkskundliche Gehalt der mittelhochdeutschen Epen von 1100 bis gegen 1250.* Zeulenroda: Bernhard Sporn, 1939. 78.

MOSCHEROSCH, JOHANN MICHAEL (1601-1669)
1836. Huth, Mari Luise. "Das Sprichwort bei Moscherosch." Diss. University of North Carolina, 1940. 121 pp.

1837. Seiler, Friedrich. *Deutsche Sprichwörterkunde.* München: C. H. Beck, 1922, 1967. 59-60.

1838. Stöber, August. "Sprichwörter und sprichwörtliche Redensarten aus Johann Michael Moscherosch's [sic] Schriften." *Alsatia* (1868-1872): 319-338.

MOSCHOS (2nd cent. B. C.)

1839. Baar, Adolf. *Sprichwörter und Sentenzen aus den griechischen Idyllendichtern.* Görz: Selbstverlag des Staatsgymnasiums, 1887. 41 pp.

MÜNCHENER OSWALD (c. 1170)

1840. Hofmann, Liselotte. *Der volkskundliche Gehalt der mittelhochdeutschen Epen von 1100 bis gegen 1250.* Zeulenroda: Bernhard Sporn, 1939. 76.

MÜNTZER, THOMAS (1489-1525)

1841. Pfeifer, Wolfgang. "Volkstümliche Metaphorik." *Zur Literatursprache im Zeitalter der frühbürgerlichen Revolution: Untersuchungen zu ihrer Verwendung in der Agitationsliteratur.* Eds. Gerhard Kettmann and Joachim Schildt. Berlin: Akademie-Verlag, 1978. 87-217.

MURFREE, MARY NOAILLES (1850-1922)

1842. Taylor, Archer. "Proverbs and Proverbial Phrases in the Writings of Mary N. Murfree." *Tennessee Folklore Society Bulletin* 24 (1958): 11-50.

MURNER, THOMAS (1475-1537)

1843. Fuchs, Eduard. "Thomas Murners Sprichwörter und ihre Quellen." *Beiträge zur Deutschkunde: Festschrift Theodor Siebs zum 60. Geburtstag.* Eds. Helmut de Boer et al. Emden: B. Davids, 1925. 76-84.

1844. Gruenter, Rainer. "Thomas Murners satirischer Wortschatz." *Euphorion* 53 (1959): 24-40.

1845. Harris, Amelia Johnston. "The Functions and Applications of the Proverb and Proverbial Expression in the German Poetry of Thomas Murner." Diss. University of North Carolina at Chapel Hill, 1991. 368 pp.

1846. Ischer, Rudolf. "Redensarten und Sittenschilderungen in den Schriften Thomas Murners." *Neuer Berner Taschenbuch auf das Jahr 1902* (1902): 54-56.

1847. Leffts, Joseph. *Die volkstüslichen Stilelemente in Murners Satiren.* Straßburg: Karl J. Trübner, 1915. 116-171.

1848.   Mezger, Werner. "Der Ambraser Narrenteller von 1528: Ein Beitrag zur Ikonographie der spätmittelalterlichen Narrenidee." *Zeitschrift für Volkskunde* 75 (1979): 161-180.

1849.   Pfeifer, Wolfgang. "Volkstümliche Metaphorik." *Zur Literatursprache im Zeitalter der frühbürgerlichen Revolution: Untersuchungen zu ihrer Verwendung in der Agitationsliteratur.* Eds. Gerhard Kettmann and Joachim Schildt. Berlin: Akademie-Verlag, 1978. 87-217.

1850.   Risse, Anna. "Sprichwörter und Redensarten bei Thomas Murner." *Zeitschrift für den deutschen Unterricht* 31 (1917): 215-227, 289-303, 359-369, 450-458.

1851.   "Schreiben an den Herausgeber, einige Spracherklärungen enthaltend, nebst Anhang einiger veralteten Sprüchwörter." *Deutsches Museum* (1779): 446-453.

1852.   Seiler, Friedrich. *Deutsche Sprichwörterkunde.* München: C. H. Beck, 1922, 1967. 55-56.

1853.   Uhl, Wilhelm. "Murner und das Sprichwort." *Thomas Murner, "Geuchmat."* Leipzig: Teubner, 1896. 261-263.

MUSIL, ROBERT (1880-1942)

1854.   Mautner, Franz H. "Maxim(e)s, Sentences, Fragmente, Aphorismen." *Actes du 4e Congrès de l'Association Internationale de Littérature Comparée, Fribourg 1964.* Ed. François Jost. The Hague: Mouton, 1966. II, 812-819.

1855.   Schmidt-Hidding, Wolfgang. "Deutsche Sprichwörter und Redewendungen." *Deutschunterricht für Ausländer* 13 (1963): 13-26, especially 14.

1856.   Wandruszka, Mario. "Sprache aus Bildern." *Die europäische Sprachengemeinschaft:Deutsch—Französisch—English—Italienisch—Spanisch im Vergleich.* Tübingen: A. Francke, 1990. 51-76.

MUSSET, ALFRED de (1810-1857)

1857.   Brahmer, Miecyzslaw. "Le vicende del proverbio dramatico." *XIV. Congresso internazionale di linguistica e filologia romanza.* Ed. Alberto Várvaro. Naples: Macchiaroli, 1981. V, 509-511.

1858. Brenner, Clarence D. *The French Dramatic Proverb*. Berkeley, California: Privately printed, 1977. 68 pp.

1859. Chaumeix, André. "La comédie proverbe." Rev. of *Je crois que je vous aime*, by G. d'Houville. *Revue des Deux Mondes* 40 (August 1, 1927): 698-708.

1860. Dessons, Gérard. "La parole du siècle dans les *Proverbes* de Musset." *Travaux de littérature* 4 (1991): 197-207.

1861. Hölz, Karl. "Mussets frühe *Proverbe*-Dichtung (1834-1836): Zum Wandel einer Gattung." *Zeitschrift für französiche Sprache und Literatur* 85 (1975): 128-144.

1862. Luce, Louise Fiber. "The Mask of Language in Alfred de Musset's *Proverbes*." *Romance Notes* 17 (1977): 272-280.

1863. Masson, Alain. "Eric Rohmer: Le Capricorne souverain de l'onde occidentale sur les *Comédies et proverbes*." *Positif* No. 307 (1986): 43-45.

1864. Shaw, Marjorie. "Les proverbes dramatiques de Carmontelle, Leclercq et Alfred de Musset." *Revue des sciences humaines* (1959): 56-76.

N

NADLER, KARL CHRISTIAN GOTTFRIED (1809-1849)

1865. Bräutigam, Kurt. "Volkstümliche Redensarten in Nadlers Mundartge-dichten." *Wie mer redde un schwätze: Mundarten zwischen Rhein und Tauber, Main und Murg.* Eds. Rudolf Lehr and Paul Waibel. Karlsruhe: Badenia, 1980. 14-22.

NASS, JOHANNES (1534-1590)

1866. Lukasser, N. 'Spruchweisheit des Volkes.' "Die Centurien des Johannes Nas, ihre Wurzeln und Formen, ein Beitrag zur Prosa des 16. Jhs." Diss. University of Innsbruck, 1953. 279-295.

1867. Nelson, Timothy C. "'Ex abundantia cordis os loquitur': Ein Beitrag zur Rezeptionsgeschichte eines umstrittenen Sprichworts." *Proverbium: Year-book of International Proverb Scholarship* 3 (1986): 101-123.

1868. Nelson, Timothy C. "*O du armer Luther. . .*" *Sprichwörtliches in der antilutherischen Polemik des Johannes Nas (1534-1590).* Diss. Uppsala Universitet, 1990. 305 pp. Bern: Peter Lang, 1992. 334 pp.

1869. Nelson, Timothy C. "Sprichwörtliche Polemik in der Gegenreformation: Zu Johannes Nas' *GAsinus Nasi BattimontAnus* (1571)." *Proverbium: Yearbook of International Proverb Scholarship* 7 (1990): 163-183.

1870. Nelson, Timothy C. "Die verkehrte Welt." *Europhras 90: Akten der internationalen Tagung zur germanistischen Phraseologieforschung, Aske/Schweden 12.-15. Juni 1990.* Ed. Christine Palm. Uppsala: Acta Universitatis Upsaliensis, 1991. 155-161.

1871. Schöpf, P. Johann B. *Johannes Nasus, Franziskaner und Weihbischof von Brixen (1534-1590).* Bozen: Jos. Eberle, 1860. 70-72.

NECULCE, ION (1672-1745)

1872. Bîrlea, Ovidiu. *Proverbes et dictons roumains—Proverbe si zicatori românesti.* Bucaresti: Editura didactia si pedagogica, 1966. 55 pp.

NEFFLEN, JOHANNES (1789-1858)

1873. Nefflen, Johannes. *Der Vetter aus Schwaben oder Schwabenbräuche aus dem Leben gegriffen von Johannes Nefflen.* Ulm: Lutz, 1842. 450-470.

NEGRUZZI, CONSTANTIN (1808-1868)

1874. Negreanu, Constantin. "O schita paremiologica: *Scrisoarea XII (Pîcala si Tîndala)* de C. Negruzzi." *Limba si literatura* 4 (1989): 527-537. Also in French as "Littérature et parémiologie chez François Villon et Constantin Negruzzi." *Proverbium: Yearbook of International Proverb Scholarship* 8 (1991): 113-119.

NEKRASOV, NIKOLAJ ALEKSEEVIC (1821-1878)

1875. Novožilov, I. A. "Poslovicy i pogovorki v poeme Nekrasova *Komu na Rusi zhit* xoroso.'" *Russkaia Rech'* No. 4 (1971): 41-48.

1876. Zhigulev, Aleksandr M. "Narodnye poslovitsy v tvorchestve Nekrosova" *Proverbium* No. 21 (1973): 788-795.

NEIDHART VON REUENTAL (c. 1190-c. 1246)

1877. Hofmeister, Wernfried. *Sprichwortartige Mikrotexte als literarische Medien, dargestellt an der hochdeutschen politischen Lyrik des Mittelalters.* Bochum: Norbert Brockmeyer, 1995. 209-239.

NEMCOVÁ, BOZENA (1820-1862)

1878. Grzybek, Peter. "Zur semantischen Funktion der sprichwörtlichen Wendungen in Bozena Nemcovas *Babichka.*" *Zur Poetik und Rezeption von Bozena Nemcovas "Babichka."* Ed. Andreas Guski. Wiesbaden: Otto Harrassowitz, 1991. 81-126.

1879. Mukařovský, Jan. "Přislovi jako součást kontextu." *Cestami poetiky a estetiky.* Praha: Edice Dilna, 1971. 277-359.

NESTROY, JOHANN (1801-1862)

1880. Hein, Jürgen. "Redensarten und Sprichwörter bei Johann Nestroy." *Sprache und Literatur in Wissenschaft und Unterricht* 16, 56 (1985): 14-17.

NEW CUSTOM (1559/1573)

1881. Whiting, Bartlett Jere. "*New Custom.*" *Proverbs in the Earlier English Drama.* Cambridge, Massachusetts: Harvard University Press, 1938; rpt. New York: Octagon Books, 1969. 130-132.

NGUGI WA THIONG'O, JAMES (1938—)

1882. Adeeko, Adeleke. "Words' Horse, or The Proverb as a Paradigm of Literary Understanding." Diss. University of Florida, 1991. 169-196.

NIBELUNGENLIED (c. 1200)

1883. Hofmann, Liselotte. *Der volkskundliche Gehalt der mittelhochdeutschen Epen von 1100 bis gegen 1250.* Zeulenroda: Bernhard Sporn, 1939. 78-79.

1884. Moelleken, Wolfgang Wilfried. "Gnomen im Nibelungenlied." Diss. University of Washington, 1965. 194 pp.

1885. Mone, Franz Joseph. "Zur Literatur und Geschichte der Sprichwörter." *Quellen und Forschungen zur Geschichte der deutschen Literatur und Sprache* 1 (1830): 186-214.

1886. Radke, Georg. *Die epische Formel im "Nibelungenlied."* Diss. Kiel, 1890. Fraustadt: L. S. Pucker, 1890. 62 pp.

NICARCH (A. D. 1st cent.)

1887. Prittwitz-Gaffron, Erich von. *Das Sprichwort im griechischen Epigramm.* Diss. München, 1912. Gießen: Alfred Töpelmann, 1912. 45-48.

THE NICE WANTON (1560)

1888. Whiting, Bartlett Jere. "*The Nice Wanton.*" *Proverbs in the Earlier English Drama.* Cambridge, Massachusetts: Harvard University Press, 1938; rpt. New York: Octagon Books, 1969. 196-198.

NIETZSCHE, FRIEDRICH (1844-1900)

1889. Brands, Hartmut. "*Cogito ergo sum*": Interpretationen von Kant bis Nietzsche. München: Karl Alber, 1982. 247-271.

1890. Fricke, Harald. *Aphorismus.* Stuttgart: Metzler, 1984. 119-126, 153-155.

1891. Kann, Hans-Joachim. "Zu den Quellen von Spontisprüchen." *Der Sprachdienst* 29 (1985): 75-79.

1892. Mautner, Franz H. "Der Aphorismus als literarische Gattung." *Zeitschrift für Ästhetik und allgemeine Kunstwissenschaft* 27 (1933): 132-175.

1893. Mautner, Franz H. "Maxim(e)s, Sentences, Fragmente, Aphorismen." *Actes du 4e Congrès de l'Association Internationale de Littérature Comparée, Fribourg 1964.* Ed. François Jost. The Hague: Mouton, 1966. II, 812-819.

1894. Pape, Walter. "Zwischen Sprachspiel und Sprachkritik: Zum literari-schen Spiel mit der wörtlichen Bedeutung von Idiomen." *Sprache und Literatur in Wissenschaft und Unterricht* 16, 56 (1985): 2-13.

NIVARDUS (12th cent.)
1895. Mann, Jill. "Proverbial Wisdom in the *Ysengrimus*." *New Literary History* 16, 1 (1984): 93-109.

1896. Singer, Samuel. "Nivardus von Gent, *Ysengrimus*." *Sprichwörter des Mittelalters*, 3 vols. Bern: Herbert Lang, 1946. I, 145-178.

NIZAMI (1141-1209)
1897. Rypka, Jan. "Das Sprichwort in Nizamis *Lajli va Magnun*." *Archiv Orientalni* 37 (1969): 318-325.

NJÁLS SAGA (13th cent.)
1898. Dopheide, Maria. "Sprichwörter in der Rede des Isländers dargestellt an ihrem Gebrauch in der *Njáls Saga*." Diss. Freiburg, 1973. 328 pp.

NOËL DE FAIL (c. 1520-1591)
1899. Philipot, Emmanuel. *Essai sur le style et la langue de Noël de Fail: La vie et l'oeuvre litteraire de Noël de Fail, gentilhomme breton*. Paris: E. Champion, 1914. Chapter 2.

NORTON, THOMAS (1532-1583)
1900. Whiting, Bartlett Jere. "Thomas Sackville and Thomas Norton's *Ferrex and Porrex*." *Proverbs in the Earlier English Drama*. Cambridge, Massachusetts: Harvard University Press, 1938; rpt. New York: Octagon Books, 1969. 279-281.

THE NORWICH PLAYS (16th cent.)
1901. Whiting, Bartlett Jere. "*The Norwich Plays*." *Proverbs in the Earlier English Drama*. Cambridge, Massachusetts: Harvard University Press, 1938; rpt. New York: Octagon Books, 1969. 35-36.

NOTKER III. LABEO (c. 950-1022)
1902. Burger, Harald. "Probleme einer historischen Phraseologie des Deutschen." *Beiträge zur Geschichte der deutschen Sprache und Literatur* (Tübingen) 99 (1977): 1-24.

1903. Jeep, John M. *Stabreimende Wortpaare bei Notker Labeo*. Göttingen: Vandenhoeck and Ruprecht, 1987. 172 pp.

1904. Redlich, Friedrich. "Grundsätzliches zum Sprichwort und seiner sozialen Ausprägung, besonders im Deutschen." *Wissenschaftliche Studien des Pädagogischen Instituts Leipzig* No. 2 (1971): 85-91.

1905. Seiler, Friedrich. *Deutsche Sprichwörterkunde.* München: C. H. Beck, 1922, 1967. 68-71.

1906. Singer, Samuel. "Sprichwortstudien." *Schweizerisches Archiv für Volkskunde* 37 (1939): 129-150, especially 129-137.

1907. Singer, Samuel. "Notker." *Sprichwörter des Mittelalters*, 3 vols. Bern: Herbert Lang, 1944-1947. I, 55-61.

NOVALIS [Friedrich Hardenberg] (1772-1801)
1908. Fink, Arthur-Hermann. *Maxime und Fragment: Grenzmöglichkeiten einer Kunstform: Zur Morphologie des Aphorismus.* München: Max Huber, 1934. 72-89.

1909. Fricke, Harald. *Aphorismus.* Stuttgart: Metzler, 1984. 88-97.

1910. Mautner, Franz H. "Der Aphorismus als literarische Gattung." *Zeitschrift für Ästhetik und allgemeine Kunstwissenschaft* 27 (1933): 132-175.

1911. Mautner, Franz H. "Maxim(e)s, Sentences, Fragmente, Aphorismen." *Actes du 4e Congrès de l'Association Internationale de Littérature Comparée, Fribourg 1964.* Ed. François Jost. The Hague: Mouton, 1966. II, 812-819.

NOVELLINO (13th cent.)
1912. Crespo, Roberto. "Una citazione di Matfre Ermengaud e il *Novellino*." *Lettere Italiane* 32 (1980): 232-234.

NYUGI, GERISHON (20th cent.)
1913. Eastman, Carol M. "The Proverb in Modern Written Swahili Literature: An Aid to Proverb Elicitation." *African Folklore*. Ed. Richard Dorson. Garden City, N. Y.: Anchor Books, 1972. 193-207.

O

OBRADOVIĆ, DOSITEJ (c. 1742-1811)
1914. Polenakovich, Kh. "Dve narodne poslovitse kod Dositeja i Vuka." *Stvaranje* 19 (1964): 1329-1331.

1915. Stojanović, Miodrag V. "Antička proverbijalna misao u delima Dositeja Obradovića." *Filološki Pregled* 8 (1970): 23-43.

O'CONNOR, FLANNERY (1925-1964)
1916. De Caro, Francis A. "Proverbs and Originality in Modern Short Fiction." *Western Folklore* 37 (1978): 30-38.

OCTAVIAN (13th cent.)
1917. Whiting, Bartlett Jere. "Proverbs in Certain Middle English Romances in Relation to Their French Sources." *Harvard Studies and Notes in Philology and Literature* 15 (1933): 75-126, especially 103-108.

ODOBESCU, ALEXANDRU (1834-1895)
1918. Negreanu, Constantin. "Valentele educative si stilistice ale expresiilor si proverbelor în limba literaturii artistice." *Scoala Mehedintiului* 3 (1978): 23-26.

ODOBLEJA, STEFAN (1902-1978)
1919. Negreanu, Constantin. "Cugetarile lui Stefan Odobleja despre stiinta." *Proverbium Dacromania* 4 (1989): 52-56.

OF GENTLENESS AND NOBILITY (c. 1530)
1920. Whiting, Bartlett Jere. "*Of Gentleness and Nobility.*" *Proverbs in the Earlier English Drama.* Cambridge, Massachusetts: Harvard University Press, 1938; rpt. New York: Octagon Books, 1969. 182-184.

O GRIANNA, SEAMUS [pseud. Maire] (1889-1969)
1921. O Corrain, Ailbhe. *A Concordance of Idiomatic Expressions in the Writings of Seamus O Grianna.* Belfast: Institute of Irish Studies, The Queen's University, 1989. 419 pp.

O'HARA, JOHN (1905-1970)
1922. Barrick, Mac E. "Proverbs and Sayings from Gibbsville, Pa.: John O'Hara's Use of Proverbial Materials." *Keystone Folklore Quarterly* 12 (1967): 55-80.

OLDYS, WILLIAM (1696-1761)

1923. Newcomb, Robert. "Poor Richard and the English Epigram." *Philological Quarterly* 40 (1961): 270-280.

O'NEILL, EUGENE (1888-1953)

1924. Bryan, George B., and Wolfgang Mieder. *The Proverbial Eugene O'Neill: An Index to Proverbs in the Works of Eugene Gladstone O'Neill.* Westport, Connecticut: Greenwood Press, 1995. 365 pp.

OPITZ, MARTIN (1597-1639)

1925. Angress, Ruth K. "The Epigram as a Genre." *The Early German Epigram: A Study in Baroque Poetry.* Lexington: University Press of Kentucky, 1971. 19-40.

1926. Schnur, Harry C. "The Humanist Epigram and Its Influence on the German Epigram." *Acta conventus neo-latini Lovaniensis: Proceedings of the First International Congress of Neo-Latin Studies, Louvain 23-28 August 1971.* Eds. J. Ijsewijn and E. Keßler. München: Wilhelm Fink, 1973. 557-576.

ORENDEL (c. 1190)

1927. Hofmann, Liselotte. *Der volkskundliche Gehalt der mittelhochdeutschen Epen von 1100 bis gegen 1250.* Zeulenroda: Bernhard Sporn, 1939. 75.

ORWELL, GEORGE (1903-1950)

1928. Schmidt-Hidding, Wolfgang. "George Orwell." *Englische Idiomatik in Stillehre und Literatur.* München: Max Hueber, 1962. 85-88.

ORZESZKOWA, ELIZA (1841-1910)

1929. Klosinski, Krzysztof. "Przyslowia." *Mimezis w chlopskich powiesciach.* Orzeszkowej, Katowice: Uniwersytet Slaski, 1990. 86-90.

OSOFISAN, FEMI (1946—)

1930. Adeeko, Adeleke. "Words' Horse, or The Proverb as a Paradigm of Literary Understanding." Diss. University of Florida, 1991. 197-220.

OSTROVSKIJ, ALEKSANDR NIKOLAEVIC (1823-1886)

1931. Grylack, Bevin Ratner. "The Function of Proverbs in the Dramatic Works of Aleksandr Nikolaevic Ostrovskij." Diss. New York University, 1975. 193 pp.

OSWALD VON WOLKENSTEIN (c. 1377-c. 1445)

1932. Hofmeister, Wernfried. *Sprichwortartige Mikrotexte: Analysen am Beispiel Oswalds von Wolkenstein.* Göppingen: Kümmerle, 1990. 307 pp.

1933. Hofmeister, Wernfried. *Sprichwortartige Mikrotexte als literarische Medien, dargestellt an der hochdeutschen politischen Lyrik des Mittelalters.* Bochum: Norbert Brockmeyer, 1995. 305-376.

OTERO, BLAS DE (1916—)

1934. Le Bigot, Claude. "La deconstrucción de la frase hecha en algunos poetas sociales." *Paremia* No. 2 (1993): 151-155.

OTFRID VON WEISSENBURG (c. 800-c. 870)

1935. Burger, Harald. "Probleme einer historischen Phraseologie des Deutschen." *Beiträge zur Geschichte der deutschen Sprache und Literatur* (Tübingen) 99 (1977): 1-24.

OTTE (12th/13th cent.)

1936. Hofmann, Liselotte. *Der volkskundliche Gehalt der mittelhochdeutschen Epen von 1100 bis gegen 1250.* Zeulenroda: Bernhard Sporn, 1939. 61-62.

OVID [Publius Ovidius Naso] (43 B. C.-c. A. D. 17?)

1937. Puccioni, Giulio. "Recupero di un'espressione proverbiale romana [Etiam capillus unus habet umbram suam (Even a hair has its shadow)]." *Maia: Rivista di Letterature classiche* 19 (1967): 176-178.

1938. Roos, Paolo. *Sentenza e proverbio nell'antichità e i "Distici di Catone": Il testo latino e i volgarizzamenti italiani.* Brescia: Morcelliana, 1984. 254 pp.

OWEN, GUY (1925—)

1939. Owen, Guy. "The Use of Folklore in Fiction." *North Carolina Folklore* 19 (1971): 73-79.

THE OWL AND THE NIGHTINGALE (c. 1250)

1940. Gee, Elizabeth. "The Function of Proverbial Materials in *The Owl and the Nightingale.*" *Parergor: Bulletin of the Australian and New Zealand Association for Medieval and Renaissance Studies* 24 (1979): 3-8.

1941. Schwingruber, Madeleine. "The Illocutionary and Perlocutionary Acts of the Proverbs in *The Owl and the Nightingale*." *Bulletin de la Section de Linguistique de la Faculté des Lettres de Lausanne* 6 (1984): 255-265.

1942. Skeat, Walter William. "*The Owl and the Nightingale*." *Early English Proverbs, Chiefly of the Thirteenth and Fourteenth Centuries*. Oxford: Clarendon Press, 1910; rpt. Darby, Pennsylvania: Folcroft Library Editions, 1974. 13-16.

P

PAIGE, SATCHEL (c. 1906-1982)

1943. Olinick, Stanley L. "On Proverbs: Creativity, Communication, and Community." *Contemporary Psychoanalysis* 23 (1987): 463-468.

PAINTER, WILLIAM (c. 1540-1594)

1944. Wright, Louis B. "William Painter and the Vogue of Chaucer as a Moral Teacher." *Modern Philology* 31 (1933): 165-174.

PALLADAS (A. D. 4th/5th cent.)

1945. Prittwitz-Gaffron, Erich von. *Das Sprichwort im griechischen Epigramm.* Diss. München, 1912. Gießen: Alfred Töpelmann, 1912. 52-59.

PALMA, RICARDO (1833-1919)

1946. Arora, Shirley L. *Proverbial Comparisons in Ricardo Palma's "Tradiciones Peruanas."* Berkeley: University of California Press, 1966. 205 pp.

PALMER, THOMAS (1540-1626)

1947. Manning, John. "Thomas Palmer and Proverbs: Antedatings and Additions to Tilley from *Two Hundred Poosees.*" *Notes and Queries* 234 ns 36 (1989): 427-429.

PALMERIN DE OLIVA (16th cent.)

1948. Garci-Gómez, Miguel. "La tradición del león reverente: Glosas para los episodios en *Mio Cid, Palmerin de Oliva, Don Quijote* y otros." *Kentucky Romance Quarterly* 19 (1972): 255-284.

PANDURO, LEIF (1923—)

1949. Holzapfel, Otto. "Stereotype Redensarten über 'den Deutschen' in der neueren dänischen Literatur." *Proverbium: Yearbook of International Proverb Scholarship* 4 (1987): 87-110.

PANN, ANTON (1794-1854)

1950. Negreanu, Constantin. "Valentele educative si stilistice ale expresiilor si proverbelor în limba literaturii artistice." *Scoala Mehedintiului* 3 (1978): 23-26.

PARMENIO (1st cent. B. C.-A. D. 1st cent.)

1951. Prittwitz-Gaffron, Erich von. *Das Sprichwort im griechischen Epigramm.* Diss. München, 1912. Gießen: Alfred Töpelmann, 1912. 36-37.

PARTONOPE OF BLOIS (13th cent.)

1952. Whiting, Bartlett Jere. "Proverbs in Certain Middle English Romances in Relation to Their French Sources." *Harvard Studies and Notes in Philology and Literature* 15 (1933): 75-126, especially 94-103.

PASCAL, BLAISE (1623-1662)

1953. Lafond, Jean. "Des formes brèves de la littérature morale aux XVIe et XVIIe siècles." *Les formes brèves de la prose et le discours discontinu (XVIe-XVIIe siècles).* Paris: Librairie Philosophique J. Vrin, 1984. 101-122.

PASOLINI, PIER PAOLO (1922-1975)

1954. Manacorda, Giuliano. "Espressioni proverbiali romanesche in *Ragazzi di vita* e *Una vita violenta.*" *Galleria-Rassegna bimestrale di cultura* 35, 1-4 (1985): 31-37.

PASTERNAK, BORIS (1890-1960)

1955. Liapunov, Vadim, and Savelii Senderovich. "Ob odnoi poslovitse i triokh funktsiiakh plana vyrazheniia poslovits." *Russian Literature* 19, 4 (1986): 393-404.

PASTON LETTERS (15th cent.)

1956. Jones, Kirkland Charles. "Proverbs, Proverbial Wisdom, and Medieval Topoi in the *Paston Letters.*" Diss. University of Wisconsin, 1971. 187 pp.

PATELIN, LA FARCE DE (15th cent.)

1957. Le Roux de Lincy, M. *Le Livre des Proverbes Français*, 2 vols. 2nd ed. Paris: A. Delahays, 1859; rpt. Genève: Slatkine, 1968. II, 499-500.

1958. Pineaux, Jacques. "La Farce de Patelin." *Proverbes et dictons français*, 6th ed. Paris: Presses Universitaires de France, 1973. 43-45.

1959. Walkley, M. J. "Une allusion au proverbe 'Il ne se tort pas qui va plain chemin' dans *Pathelin*, 284-290." *New Zealand Journal of French Studies* 10, 1 (1989): 52-55.

PAULHAN, JEAN (1884-1968)

1960. Paulhan, Jean. "L'expérience du proverbe." *Oeuvres complètes.* Paris: Cercle du Livre Précieux, 1966. II, 101-124.

1961. Syrotinski, Michael F. "Reinventing Figures: Jean Paulhan and the Critical Mystery of Literature." Diss. Yale University, 1989. 13-55.

PAULI, JOHANNES (c. 1455-c. 1530)

1962. Bambeck, Manfred. "'Weder Kuh noch Kalb': Zu einem Exempel bei Johannes Pauli." *Archiv für das Studium der neueren Sprachen und Literaturen* 221 (1984): 130-132.

1963. Schott, Clausdieter. "'Wer da kauft, der lueg, wie es lauft': Kaufrecht und Kaufmoral in Johannes Paulis *Schimpf und Ernst.*" *Alemannia: Landeskundliche Beiträge: Festschrift Bruno Boesch*. Bühl, Baden: Konkordia, 1976. 244-269.

1964. Seiler, Friedrich. *Deutsche Sprichwörterkunde*. München: C. H. Beck, 1922, 1967. 60-61.

1965. Stöber, August. "Sprichwörter und sprichwörtliche Redensarten aus Johann Pauli's [*sic*] *Schimpf und Ernst.*" *Alsatia* (1873-1874): 83-96.

PAULUS SILENTIARIUS (A. D. 6th cent.)

1966. Prittwitz-Gaffron, Erich von. *Das Sprichwort im griechischen Epigramm*. Diss. München, 1912. Gießen: Alfred Töpelmann, 1912. 59-61.

PEACHAM, HENRY (c. 1576-c. 1643)

1967. Manley, Lawrence. "Proverbs, Epigrams, and Urbanity in Renaissance London." *English Literary Renaissance* 15 (1985): 247-276.

PERCEFORÊT (12th/13th cent.)

1968. Flutre, L. F. "Les proverbes du roman de *Perceforêt.*" *Revue de linguistique romane* 31 (1967): 89-104.

PERCYVALL [Perceval], RICHARD (1550-1620)

1969. Selig, Karl-Ludwig. "The Spanish Proverbs in Percyvall's *Spanish Grammar.*" *Kentucky Romance Quarterly* 17 (1970): 267-274.

PÉRET, BENJAMIN (1889-1959)

1970. Éluard, Paul, and Benjamin Péret. *152 proverbes mis au goût du jour*. Paris: Bureau de recherches surréealistes, 1925; *152 Sprichwörter auf den neuesten Stand gebracht*. Ed. and translated and with an afterword by Unda Hörner and Wolfram Kiepe. Gießen: Anabas Verlag, 1995. 168 pp.

PERÓN, JUAN (1895-1974)

1971. Colombi, María Cecilia. "Clichés en el discurso de Perón." *Proverbium: Yearbook of International Proverb Scholarship* 12 (1995): 87-96.

PERRAULT, CHARLES (1628-1703)

1972. Hudde, Hinrich. "'Conte à dormir debout': Eine Redensart als Bezeichnung für parodistische Märchen des 18. Jahrhunderts." *Romanische Forschungen* 97, 1 (1985): 15-35.

PETAN, ŽARKO (1929—)

1973. Mieder, Wolfgang. "'Alles in bester Ordnung': Zu den sprichwörtlichen Aphorismen von Žarko Petan." *Sprachspiegel* 49, 3 (1993): 66-72. Also in *Sprichwörtliches und Geflügeltes: Sprachstudien von Martin Luther bis Karl Marx*. Bochum: Norbert Brockmeyer, 1995. 157-164.

PETERKIN, JULIA (1880-1961)

1974. Yates, Irene. "A Collection of Proverbs and Proverbial Sayings from South Carolina Literature." *Southern Folklore Quarterly* 11 (1947): 187-199.

PETRONIUS [Gaius Petronius Arbiter] (died A. D. 65)

1975. Jacobson, H. "Note on Petronius *Sat.* 31, 2: Vinum dominicum, ministratoris gratia est." *Classical Philology* 66 (1971): 183-186.

1976. Wagner, M. L. "Über die Unterlagen der romanischen Phraseologie im Anschluß an des Petronius' *Satyricon*." *Volkstum und Kultur der Romanen* 6 (1933): 1-26.

PETTIE, GEORGE (c. 1548-1589)

1977. Tilley, Morris Palmer. *Elizabethan Proverb Lore in Lyly's "Euphues" and in Pettie's "Petite Pallace" with Parallels from Shakespeare*. New York: The Macmillan Company, 1926. 461 pp.

PFAFFE KONRAD (12th cent.)

1978. Hofmann, Liselotte. *Der volkskundliche Gehalt der mittelhochdeutschen Epen von 1100 bis gegen 1250*. Zeulenroda: Bernhard Sporn, 1939. 76.

1979. Jäger, Dietrich. "Der Gebrauch formelhafter zweigliedriger Ausdrücke in der vor-, früh- und hochhöfischen Epik." Diss. Kiel, 1960. 35-41.

1980. Mone, Franz Joseph. "Zur Literatur und Geschichte der Sprichwörter." *Quellen und Forschungen zur Geschichte der deutschen Literatur und Sprache* 1 (1830): 186-214, especially 208.

PFAFFE LAMPRECHT (12th cent.)
1981. Jäger, Dietrich. "Der Gebrauch formelhafter zweigliedriger Ausdrücke in der vor-, früh- und hochhöfischen Epik." Diss. Kiel, 1960. 52-69.

PHANIAS (3rd cent. B. C.)
1982. Prittwitz-Gaffron, Erich von. *Das Sprichwort im griechischen Epigramm.* Diss. München, 1912. Gießen: Alfred Töpelmann, 1912. 27.

PHILIP OF MACEDON (382-333 B. C.)
1983. Metzger, Bruce M. "'To Call a Spade a Spade' in Greek and Latin." *The Classical Journal* 33 (1938): 229-231.

PHILIPPE DE MÉZIÈRES (c. 1327-1405)
1984. Picherit, Jean-Louis G. "Formes et fonctions de la matière proverbiale dans le *Songe di vieil pèlerin* de Philippe de Mézières." *La locution: Actes du colloque international Université McGill, Montréal, 15-16 octobre 1984.* Eds. Giuseppe Di Stefano and Russell G. McGillivray. Montréal: Éditions CERES, 1984. 384-399.

PHILLIP, JOHN (fl. 1566)
1985. Whiting, Bartlett Jere. "John Phillip's *Patient Grissell.*" *Proverbs in the Earlier English Drama.* Cambridge, Massachusetts: Harvard University Press, 1938; rpt. New York: Octagon Books, 1969. 236-239.

PHILODEMOS (c. 110-c. 40 B. C.)
1986. Prittwitz-Gaffron, Erich von. *Das Sprichwort im griechischen Epigramm.* Diss. München, 1912. Gießen: Alfred Töpelmann, 1912. 28-34.

PICHLER, ADOLF (1819-1900)
1987. Seiler, Friedrich. *Deutsche Sprichwörterkunde.* München: C. H. Beck, 1922, 1967. 64.

PICKERING, JOHN (1544-1596)
1988. Whiting, Bartlett Jere. "John Pickering's *The History of Horestes.*" *Proverbs in the Earlier English Drama.* Cambridge, Massachusetts: Harvard University Press, 1938; rpt. New York: Octagon Books, 1969. 282-285.

PIERCE, OVID WILLIAMS (1910–)

1989. West, Harry C. "Negro Folklore in Pierce's Novels." *North Carolina Folklore* 19 (1971): 66-72.

PIERRE DE BRETAIGNE (13th cent.)

1990. Diaféria, Michèle G. "Les Proverbes au conte de Bretaigne: A Critical Edition and Study." Diss. Florida State University, 1988. 80 pp.; published as *Li Proverbes au conte de Bretaigne: Critical Edition and Study.* New York: Peter Lang, 1990. 166 pp.

1991. Martin, Johannes. *Les Proverbes au Comte de Bretaigne.* Diss. Erlangen, 1892. Erlangen: Friedrich Junge, 1892. 22 pp.

PIETRASS, RICHARD (1946–)

1992. Grésillon, Almuth, and Dominique Maingueneau. "Polyphonie, proverbe et détournement, ou un proverbe peut en cacher un autre." *Langages* 19, 73 (1984): 112-125.

PIIRIKIVI, A. (1849-1916)

1993. Mustel, V. "A. Piirikivi—rahvaopetaja salmides." *Maanoored* 3 (1935): 103-104.

PINDAR (518-438 B. C.)

1994. Lasky, Edward D. "Note on Pindar's *Nemean* I, 24-25: To Pour Oil on Fire." *Classical Philology* 68 (1973): 219.

PLATEN, AUGUST (1796-1832)

1995. Novichkova, R. M. "Pro odnofrazovi teksti (na materiali nimets'koi movi)." *Movoznavstvo* 15, 3 (1981): 71-75.

PLATO (427-347 B. C.)

1996. Allen, Archibald. "Plato's Proverbial Perversion." *Hermes: Zeitschrift für klassische Philologie* 102 (1974): 506-507.

1997. Grünwald, Eugen. *Sprichwörter und sprichwörtliche Redensarten bei Plato.* Berlin: A. Haack, 1893. 15 pp.

1998. Jostforić, S. "Zu Platons Symposion." *Philologus* 91 (1936): 52-58.

1999. Lingenberg, Johann Wilhelm. *Platonische Bilder und Sprichwörter.* Köln: Franz Greven, 1872. 21 pp.

2000. Meichsner, Irene. *Die Logik von Gemeinplätzen: Vorgeführt an Steuer-mannstopos und Schiffsmetapher.* Bonn: Bouvier, 1983. 263 pp.

2001. Prittwitz-Gaffron, Erich von. *Das Sprichwort im griechischen Epigramm.* Diss. München, 1912. Gießen: Alfred Töpelmann, 1912. 6-8.

2002. Tarán, Leonardo. *"'Amicus Plato sed magis amica veritas': From Plato and Aristotle to Cervantes." Antike und Abendland* 30 (1984): 93-124.

2003. Tarrant, Dorothy. *"Colloquialisms, Semi-Proverbs, and Word-Play in Plato." Classical Quarterly* 40 (1946): 109-117.

2004. Tarrant, Dorothy. *"More Colloquialisms, Semi-Proverbs, and Word-Play in Plato." Classical Quarterly* 52 (1958): 158-160.

2005. Wilkins, Eliza Gregory. *"Know Thyself" in Greek and Latin Literature.* Diss. University of Chicago, 1917. Chicago: University of Chicago Libraries, 1917. 104 pp.

PLAUTUS [Titus Maccius Plautus] (c. 250-184 B. C.)
2006. Bebermeyer, Renate. *"Nomen est omen—Name ist stilmitteltaugliche Vorbedeutung." Sprachspiegel* 44 (1988): 7-9.

2007. Beede, Grace L. *"Proverbial Expressions in Plautus." The Classical Journal* 44 (1948-1949): 357-362.

2008. Pflügl, Franz Xaver. *Die lateinischen Sprichwörter bei Plautus und Terenz.* Straubing: A. Lechner, 1879/80. 44 pp.

2009. Roos, Paolo. *Sentenza e proverbio nell'antichità e i "Distici di Catone": Il testo latino e i volgarizzamenti italiani.* Brescia: Morcelliana, 1984. 254 pp.

2010. Schneider, Johannes. *De proverbiis Plautinis Terentianisque.* Diss. Berlin, 1878. Berlin: Kamlah, 1878. 53 pp.

2011. Wyss, Wilhelm von. *Die Sprüchwörter bei Römischen Komikern.* Diss. Zürich, 1889. Zürich: Friedrich Schulthess, 1889. 114 pp.

PLENZDORF, ULRICH (1934—)

2012. Higi-Wydler, Melanie. *Zur Übersetzung von Idiomen: Eine Beschreibung und Klassifizierung deutscher Idiome und ihrer französischen Übersetzungen.* Bern: Peter Lang, 1989. 335 pp.

2013. Smith, J. B. "'Mich streift ein Bus': A Dissenting View of Plenzdorf's 'Über den Jordan gehen.'" *New German Studies* 13, 2 (1985): 131-134.

PLUTARCH (c. 46-c. 120 B. C.)

2014. Borthwick, E. Kerr. "Bee Imagery in Plutarch." *Classical Quarterly* 85 ns 41, 2 (1991): 560-562.

2015. Crusius, Otto. *Plutarchi de proverbiis Alexandrinorum: Libellus Ineditus.* Tübingen: Fr. Fues, 1887. 34 pp. Also in *Corpus Paroemiographorum Graecum (Leutsch-Schneidewin) Supplementum.* Hildesheim: Georg Olms, 1961.

2016. Crusius, Otto. *Plutarchi de proverbiis Alexandrinorum: Libellum: Commentarius.* Tübingen: W. Armbruster and O. Riecker, 1895. 72 pp. Also in *Corpus Paroemiographorum Graecum (Leutsch-Schneidewin) Supplementum.* Hildesheim: Georg Olms, 1961.

POE, EDGAR ALLAN (1809-1849)

2017. Taylor, Archer. "Poe, Dr. Lardner, and 'Three Sundays in a Week.'" *American Notes and Queries* 3 (1943-1944): 153-155.

POIRTERS, ADRIAEN (1605-1674)

2018. Meertens, Pieter Jacobus. "Proverbs and Emblem Literature." *Proverbium* No. 15 (1970): 498-499.

POLLAK, FELIX (1909-1987)

2019. Grimm, Reinhold. "Ein Aphoristiker im Gehäus: Neues aus dem Nachlaß von Felix Pollak." *Modern Austrian Literature* 24, 3-4 (1991): 17-41.

2020. Mieder, Wolfgang. "'Sprichwörter leuchten ein: Aphorismen leuchten auf': Zu den sprichwörtlichen Aphorismen von Felix Pollak." *German Quarterly* 67, 4 (1994): 534-548.

POLYBIOS (c. 203-c. 120 B. C.)

2021. Scala, R. von. "Sprichwörtliches bei Polybios." *Philologus* 50 (1891): 375-377.

2022. Wunderer, Carl. *Polybios Forschungen: Beiträge zur Sprach- und Kulturgeschichte*, 3 vols. Leipzig: Dieterich, 1898-1899.

POMPADOUR, JEANNE ANTOINETTE POISSON, Madame de (1720-1764)

2023. Oesch, Will A. "Après nous le déluge." *Proverbium* No. 16 (1971): 575.

PONGE, FRANCIS (1899-1988)

2024. Higgins, Ian. "Proverbial Ponge." *Modern Language Review* 74 (1979): 310-320.

POPE, ALEXANDER (1688-1744)

2025. Schumacher, Meinolf. "'. . . ist menschlich': Mittelalterliche Variationen einer antiken Sentenz." *Zeitschrift für deutsches Altertum und deutsche Literatur* 119 (1990): 163-170.

POPESCU, D. R. (1935—)

2026. Constantinescu, Nicolae. "Structuri si expresii proverbiale în nuvela *Duios Anastasia trecea* de D. R. Popescu." *Limba si literatura* 4 (1989): 567-573; an abridgement in *Proverbium Dacoroamania* 4 (1989): 2-5.

POPOV, STALE (1903-1965)

2027. Kitevski, Marko. "Poslovitsite i pogovorkite vo deloto na Stale Popov." *Sovremenost: Literatura, Umetnost, Opstestveni Prasanja* 26, 4-5 (1976): 135-155.

PORIDAT DE LAS PORIDADES (13th cent.)

2028. Morgan, Frances Elnora Williams. "Proverbs from Four Didactic Works of the Thirteenth Century." Diss. University of Kentucky, 1968. 492 pp.

PORTA, GIOVANBATTISTA DELLA (1535-1615)

2029. Mulinacci, Anna Paola. "*Cercar Maria per Ravenna*: Da un proverbio, a un cantare, alla 'Fantesca' di G. B. Della Porta." *Italianistica: Revista di letteratura italiane* 19, 1 (1990): 69-77.

PORTER, HENRY (fl. 1596-1599)

2030. Hulme, F. Edward. "*The Pleasant Historie of the Two Angrie Women of Abington.*" *Proverb Lore*. London: Elliot Stock, 1902; rpt. Detroit, Michigan: Gale Research Company, 1968. 66-68.

2031. Morris, Alton C. "Proverbial Lore in *The Two Angry Women of Abington.*" *North Carolina Folklore* 13, 1-2 (1965): 25-35.

POWERS, JAMES F. (1917—)
2032. De Caro, Francis A. "Proverbs and Originality in Modern Short Fiction." *Western Folklore* 37 (1978): 30-38.

2033. Monteiro, George. "The Literary Uses of a Proverb." *Folklore* 87 (1976): 216-218.

PRÄTORIUS, JOHANNES (1630-1680)
2034. Müller, Curt. "Volkskundliches im *Spinrocken* des Johannes Prätorius." *Mitteilungen für sachsische Volkskunde* 7 (1917): 193-206.

PREMCAND [Dhampat Rai] (1880-1936)
2035. Jain, Sumat Prakasch. "Sprichwörter in Romanan Premcands und deren Vergleich mit den deutschen Sprichwörtern." Diss. Halle, 1967. 167 pp.

PRESTON, THOMAS (1537-1598)
2036. Whiting, Bartlett Jere. "Thomas Preston's *Cambyses King of Persia.*" *Proverbs in the Earlier English Drama.* Cambridge, Massachusetts: Harvard University Press, 1938; rpt. New York: Octagon Books, 1969. 289-294.

PRIDE OF LIFE (c. 1410)
2037. Whiting, Bartlett Jere. "*Pride of Life.*" *Proverbs in the Earlier English Drama.* Cambridge, Massachusetts: Harvard University Press, 1938; rpt. New York: Octagon Books, 1969. 67-68.

LI PROVERBES AU VILAIN (13th cent.)
2038. Goddard, R. N. B. "Marcabru, *Li Proverbes au Vilain,* and the Tradition of Rustic Proverbs." *Neuphilologische Mitteilungen* 88, 1 (1987): 55-70.

2039. Rattunde, Eckard. *Li Proverbes au Vilain: Unterschungen zur romanischen Spruchdichtung des Mittelalters.* Heidelberg: Carl Winter, 1966. 144 pp.

2040. Schulze-Busacker, Elisabeth. *Proverbes et expressions dans la littérature narrative du moyen âge français: Recueil et analyse.* Paris: Librarie Honoré Champion, 1985. 85-86.

2041. Schulze-Busacker, Elisabeth. "Les *Proverbes au vilain*." *Proverbium: Yearbook of International Proverb Scholarship* 6 (1989): 113-127.

2042. Singer, Samuel. "*Proverbes au Vilain*." *Sprichwörter des Mittelalters*, 3 vols. Bern: Herbert Lang, 1946. II, 97-152.

2043. Tobler, Adolph, ed. *Li Proverbe[s] au Vilain: Die Sprichwörter des gemeinen Mannes: Alfranzösische Dichtung, nach den bisher bekannten Handschriften herausgegeben*. Leipzig: S. Hirzel, 1895. 188 pp.

THE PROUERBIS OF WYSDOM (15th cent.)

2044. Zupitza, Julius. "*The Proverbs of Wysdom*." *Archiv für das Studium der neueren Sprachen und Literaturen* 90 (1893): 241-268.

PROUST, MARCEL (1871-1922)

2045. Riffaterre, Michael. "Fonction du cliché dans la prose littéraire." *Essais de stylistique structurale*. Paris: Flammarion, 1971. 161-181. Also in German as "Die Funktion des Klischees in der literarischen Form." *Strukturale Stilistik*. München: List Taschenbuch, 1973. 139-156.

PROVERBES EN RIMES (15th cent.)

2046. Frank, Grace, and Dorothy Miner. *Proverbes en Rimes: Text and Illustrations of the Fifteenth Century from a French Manuscript in the Walters Art Gallery, Baltimore*. Baltimore, Maryland: The Johns Hopkins Press, 1937. 117 pp. (text); 186 pp. (illustrations).

2047. Frank, Grace. "'Proverbes en rimes' (B)." *Romanic Review* 31 (1940): 209-238.

2048. Massing, Jean Michel. "Proverbial Wisdom and Social Criticism: Two New Pages from the Walters Art Gallery's *Proverbes en Rimes*." *Journal of the Warburg and Courtauld Institutes* 46 (1983): 208-210.

2049. Schulze-Busacker, Elisabeth. "Eléments de culture populaire dans la littérature courtoise." *La culture populaire au Moyen Ages: Etudes présentés au Quatrième colloque de l'Institut d'études médiévales de l'Université de Montréal 2-3 avril 1977*. Ed. Pierre Boglioni. Montréal: L'Aurora, 1979. 81-101.

PUBLILIUS SYRUS (1st cent. B. C.)

2050. Smith, Charles George. *Shakespeare's Proverb Lore: His Use of Sententiae of Leonard Culman and Publilius Syrus.* Cambridge, Massachusetts: Harvard University Press, 1963. 181 pp.

2051. Smith, Charles George. *Spenser's Proverb Lore: With Special Reference to His Use of the Sententiae of Leonard Culman and Publilius Syrus.* Cambridge, Massachusetts: Harvard University Press, 1970. 365 pp.

PUDUHEPA (13th c. B. C.)

2052. Fontaine, Carole R. "Queenly Proverb Performance: The Prayer of Puduhepa (KUB XXI, 27)." *The Listening Heart.* Eds. Kenneth Hoglund et al. Sheffield, United Kingdom: Journal of the Study of the Old Testament Press, 1987. 95-126.

PUSHKIN, ALEKSANDR S. (1799-1837)

2053. Schmid, Wolf. "Diegetische Realisierung von Sprichwörtern, Redensarten und semantischen Figuren in Pushkins *Povesti Belkina.*" *Wiener Slawistischer Almanach* 10 (1982): 163-195.

2054. Shakhnovich, Mikh. "Kratkaia istoriia sobiraniia i izucheniia russkikh poslovits i pogovorok." *Sovetskii fol'klor: Sbornik statei i materialov* 4-5 (1936): 299-368.

2055. Vorob'ev, P. G. "Poslovitsy i pogovorki v khudozhestvennom tvorchestve i pis'makh A. S. Pushkin." *Russkii Iazyk v Shkole* No. 4 (1949): 19-28.

2056. Zholkovskii, Aleksandr K., and Iu. K. Tseglov. "Razbor odnoi avtorskoi paremii." *Paremiologischeskii Sbornik.* Ed. G. L. Permiakov. Moskva: Nauka, 1978. 163-210.

PYNCHON, THOMAS (1937—)

2057. Workman, Mark E. "Proverbs for the Pious and the Paranoid: The Social Use of Metaphor." *Proverbium: Yearbook of International Proverb Scholarship* 4 (1987): 225-241.

Q

LA QASIDA DE MEALI (17th cent.)

2058. Rypka, Jan. *"La qasida de Meali*, composée sur les proverbes turcs."
Rocznik Orientalistsczny 17 (1953): 29-46.

QUEVEDO Y VILLEGAS, FRANCISCO GOMÉZ DE (1580-1645)

2059. Bergman, Hannah E. *"Los refranes del viejo celoso* y obras afines."
Nueva revista de filologia hispanica 24 (1975): 376-397.

2060. Fallows, Noel. "A Note on the Treatment of Some Popular Maxims in
the *Buscón*." *Romance Notes* 29, 3 (1989): 217-219.

2061. Krauss, Werner. "Die Welt im spanischen Sprichwort." *Studien und
Aufsätze*. Berlin: Rütten and Loening, 1959. 73-91.

2062. Krauss, Werner. *Die Welt im spanischen Sprichwort*. Wiesbaden: Limes,
1946. 3rd ed. Leipzig: Reclam, 1975. 117 pp.

QUINTILIAN [Marcus Fabius Quintilian] (c. 35-c. 96)

2063. Crane, Mary Thomas. "Proverbial and Aphoristic Sayings: Sources of
Authority in the English Renaissance." Diss. Harvard University, 1986.
464 pp.

LES QUINZE JOIES DE MARIAGE (c. 1420)

2064. Pineaux, Jacques. *"Les Quinze joies de mariage.*" *Proverbes et dictons
français*, 6th ed. Paris: Presses Universitaires de France, 1973. 48-50

R

RABELAIS, FRANÇOIS (1494-1553)

2065. Le Roux de Lincy, M. *Le Livre des Proverbes Français*, 2 vols. 2nd ed. Paris: A. Delahays, 1859; rpt. Genève: Slatkine, 1968. I, lxi-lxii.

2066. Maillet, Antonine. *Rabelais et les traditions populaires en Acadie*. Québec: Presse de l'Université Laval, 1971. 155-168

2067. 0'Kane, Eleanor. "The Proverb: Rabelais and Cervantes." *Comparative Literature* 2 (1950): 360-369.

2068. Pineaux, Jacques. "Rabelais." *Proverbes et dictons français*, 6th ed. Paris: Presses Universitaires de France, 1973. 55-57.

2069. Quinçay, B. de. "Les proverbes de Rabelais." *Revue des études rabelaisiennes* 7 (1909): 371-378.

2070. Rigolot, François. "Sémiotique de la sentence et du proverbe chez Rabelais." *Études Rabelaisiennes* 14 (1977): 277-286.

2071. Russell, Daniel. "A Note on Panurge's 'Pusse en l'aureille.'" *Études Rabelaisiennes* 11 (1974): 83-87.

2072. Russell, Daniel. "Some Observations on Rabelais's Choice of Names: Nazdecabre." *Romance Notes* 12 (1970): 186-188.

2073. Sainéan, L. "Proverbes et dictons." *La langue de Rabelais*. Paris: E. de Boccard, 1922. 343-448.

2074. Screech, Michael. "Commonplaces of Law, Proverbial Wisdom and Philosophy: Their Importance in Renaissance Scholarship." *Classical Influences on European Culture, A. D. 1500-1700*. Ed. R. R. Bolgar. Cambridge: Cambridge University Press, 1976. 127-134.

2075. Sébillot, Paul. "Le blason populaire dans Rabelais." *Revue des traditions populaires* 20 (1905): 98-102.

2076. Siewert, Gregg Hunter. "Proverbs and Language in Rabelais: Towards a Poetics of the Proverb." Diss. University of Iowa, 1991. 266 pp.

2077. Smith, W. F. "Les proverbes de Rabelais." *Revue des études rabelaisiennes* 7 (1909): 371-376.

RACINE, JEAN BAPTISTE (1639-1699)

2078. Le Roux de Lincy, M. *Le Livre des Proverbes Français*, 2 vols. 2nd ed. Paris: A. Delahays, 1859; rpt. Genève: Slatkine, 1968. I, lxxii-lxxiv.

2079. Sébillot, Paul. "Racine." *Revue des traditions populaires* 5 (1890): 242-243.

RAIMUND, FERDINAND (1790-1836)

2080. Gréciano, Gertrud. "Remotivierung ist textsortenspezifisch." *Europhras 90: Akten der internationalen Tagung zur germanistischen Phraseologie-forschung, Aske/Schweden 12.-15. Juni 1990.* Ed. Christine Palm. Uppsala: Acta Universitatis Upsaliensis, 1991. 91-100.

2081. Scheichl, Sigurd Paul. "Feste Syntagmen im dramatischen Dialog: Materialien zur Geschichte eines Stilmittels zwischen Goethe und Kroetz." *Tradition und Entwicklung: Festschrift Eugen Thurnher.* Eds. Werner Bauer, Achim Masser, and Guntram Plangg. Innsbruck: Institut für Germanistik der Universität Innsbruck, 1982. 383-407.

RAINE, WILLIAM MCLEOD (1871-1954)

2082. Loomis, C. Grant. "Folk-Language in William McLeod Raine's West." *Tennessee Folklore Society Bulletin* 24 (1958): 131-148.

RAMAYANA (A. D. 2nd cent.)

2083. Hopkins, Washburn. "Proverbs and Tales Common to the Two Sanskrit Epics." *American Journal of Philology* 20 (1899): 22-39.

THE RARE TRIUMPHS OF LOVE AND FORTUNE (1582/1583)

2084. Whiting, Bartlett Jere. "*The Rare Triumphs of Love and Fortune.*" *Proverbs in the Earlier English Drama.* Cambridge, Massachusetts: Harvard University Press, 1938; rpt. New York: Octagon Books, 1969. 266-270.

RASTELL, JOHN (c. 1475-1536)

2085. Whiting, Bartlett Jere. "John Rastell's *The Nature of the Four Elements.*" *Proverbs in the Earlier English Drama.* Cambridge, Massachusetts: Harvard University Press, 1938; rpt. New York: Octagon Books, 1969. 81-82.

RAVENSCROFT, EDWARD (c. 1650-1697)

2086. Ray, Robert H. "John Dunton and the Origin of 'A Penny Saved Is a Penny Earned.'" *Notes and Queries* 229 ns 31 (1984): 372-373.

RAWLINGS, MARJORIE KINNAN (1896-1953)

2087. Figh, Margaret Gillis. "Folklore and Folk Speech in the Works of Marjorie Kinnan Rawlings." *Southern Folklore Quarterly* 11 (1947): 201-209.

RECLUSE (14th cent.)

2088. Whiting, Bartlett Jere. "Proverbs in the *Ancren Riwle* and the *Recluse.*" *Modern Language Review* 30 (1935): 502-505.

REDFORD, JOHN (fl. 1535-40)

2089. Whiting, Bartlett Jere. "John Redford's *Wit and Science*." *Proverbs in the Earlier English Drama*. Cambridge, Massachusetts: Harvard University Press, 1938; rpt. New York: Octagon Books, 1969. 102-106.

REDING, JOSEF (1929—)

2090. Schaffner, Emil. "Spiel mit Wortfügungen und Wendungen." *Es rumpelt und stilzt im Sprach-Spülkasten*. Frauenfeld: Huber, 1982. 92-99.

RÉGNARD, JEAN-FRANÇOIS (1655-1709)

2091. Le Roux de Lincy, M. *Le Livre des Proverbes Français*, 2 vols. 2nd ed. Paris: A. Delahays, 1859; rpt. Genève: Slatkine, 1968. I, lxxv.

2092. Le Roux de Lincy, M. "Proverbes cités dans les comédies de Régnard." *Le Livre des Proverbes Français*, 2 vols. 2nd ed. Paris: A. Delahays, 1859; rpt. Genève: Slatkine, 1968. II, 543-546.

2093. Sébillot, Paul. "Régnard." *Revue des traditions populaires* 10 (1895): 286-292.

RÉGNIER, JEAN (c. 1390-1467)

2094. Heft, David. *Proverbs and Sentences in Fifteenth Century French Poetry*. Diss. New York University, 1941. Chapter 2. New York: Washington Square Press, 1942 (abridged to 12 pp.).

2095. Roques, Gilles. "'Sans rime et sans raison.'" *La locution: Actes du colloque international Université McGill, Montréal, 15-16 octobre 1984*. Eds. Giuseppe Di Stefano and Russell G. McGillivray. Montréal: Editions CERES, 1984. 419-436.

RÉGNIER, MATHURIN (1573-1613)

2096. Le Roux de Lincy, M. *Le Livre des Proverbes Français*, 2 vols. 2nd ed. Paris: A. Delahays, 1859; rpt. Genève: Slatkine, 1968. II, 501-505.

2097. Pineaux, Jacques. "Mathurin Régnier." *Proverbes et dictons français*, 6th ed. Paris: Presses Universitaires de France, 1973. 57-60.

REINAERTS HISTORIE (c. 1375)

2098. Sands, Donald B. "Reynard the Fox and the Manipulation of the Popular Proverb." *The Learned and the Lewd: Studies in Chaucer and Medieval Literature*. Ed. Larry D. Benson. Cambridge, Massachusetts: Harvard University Press, 1974. 265-278

2099. Sands, Donald B. "The Uses of the Proverb in the Middle Dutch Poem *Reinaerts Historie*." *Mediaeval Studies* 37 (1975): 459-468.

REINKE DE VOS (1498)

2100. Schröder, C. "Hundert niederdeutsche Sprichwörter, gesammelt aus mittelniederdeutschen und niederrheinischen Dichtungen." *Archiv für das Studium der neueren Sprachen und Literaturen* 43 (1868): 411-420.

2101. Schröder, C. "Aber hundert niederdeutsche Sprichwörter, gesammelt aus Mittelniederdeutschen und mittelniederländischen Dichtungen." *Archiv für das Studium der neueren Sprachen und Literaturen* 44 (1869): 337-344.

REINMAR VON ZWETER (c. 1200-c. 1260)

2102. Hofmeister, Wernfried. *Sprichwortartige Mikrotexte als literarische Medien, dargestellt an der hochdeutschen politischen Lyrik des Mittelalters*. Bochum: Norbert Brockmeyer, 1995. 240-254.

REJ, MIKOLAJ (1505-1569)

2103. Kuraszkiewicz, Wladyslaw. "Rad bywa smard, gdzie rajtarka." *Polski jezyk literacki: Studia nad historia i struktura*. Warszawa: Panstwowe Wydawnictwo Naukowe, 1986. 662-670.

RELJKOVIĆS, MATIJA ANTUN (1732-1798)

2104. Eismann, Wolfgang. "Phraseologismen in M. A. Reljkovićs *Satir*." *Studia Phraseologica et Alia: Festschrift für Josip Matešić zum 65. Geburtstag*. Eds. W. Eismann und Jürgen Petermann. München: Otto Sagner, 1992. 111-123.

RENNER, FELIX (1935–)

2105. Mieder, Wolfgang. "'Eine aphoristische Schwalbe macht schon einen halben Gedankensommer': Zu den Aphorismen von Felix Renner." *Sprachspiegel* 38 (1982): 162-167. Also in *Sprichwort, Redensart, Zitat:*

Tradierte Formelsprache in der Moderne. Bern: Peter Lang, 1985. 65-71.

2106. Mieder, Wolfgang. "'Ehrlich währt im Sprichwort am längsten': Zu Felix Renners sprichwörtlichen Aphorismen." *Sprachspiegel* 44 (1988): 41-47. Also in *Sprichwörtliches und Geflügeltes: Sprachstudien von Martin Luther bis Karl Marx.* Bochum: Norbert Brockmeyer, 1995. 63-70.

REPLY OF FRIAR DAW TOPIAS TO HIS LOLLARD INTER-LOCUTOR JACK UPLAND (c. 1420)
2107. Heyworth, P. L. "Notes on Two Uncollected Middle English Proverbs." *Notes and Queries* 215 ns 17 (1970): 86-88.

RESENDE, GARCIA de (1470-1536)
2108. Múrias de Freitas, Maria Constança. "Palavras e expressoes sobre vestuário no *Cancioneiro Geral* de Garcia de Resende." *Boletin de Filologia* 9 (1948): 121-149.

RESPUBLICA (1553)
2109. Whiting, Bartlett Jere. "*Respublica.*" *Proverbs in the Earlier English Drama.* Cambridge, Massachusetts: Harvard University Press, 1938; rpt. New York: Octagon Books, 1969. 110-115.

THE RESURRECTION OF OUR LORD (1530/1560)
2110. Whiting, Bartlett Jere. "*The Resurrection of Our Lord.*" *Proverbs in the Earlier English Drama.* Cambridge, Massachusetts: Harvard University Press, 1938; rpt. New York: Octagon Books, 1969. 46.

REUSNER, NIKOLAUS (1545-1602)
2111. Dittrich, Lothar. "Emblematische Weisheit und naturwissenschaftliche Realität." *Die Sprache der Bilder: Realität und Bedeutung in der nie-derländischen Malerei des 17. Jahrhunderts.* Eds. Wolfgang J. Müller, Konrad Renger, and Rüdiger Klessmann. Braunschweig: ACO Druck, 1978. 21-33. Also in *Jarbuch für Internationale Germanistik* 13 (1981): 36-60.

REUTER, FRITZ (1810-1874)
2112. Lawin, Clara Mary. "Proverbs and Proverbial Expressions in Fritz Reuter's Works: Addenda to Müller's *Der Mecklenburger Volksmund.*" M. A. Thesis. University of Chicago, 1945. 51 pp.

2113. Müller, Carl Friedrich. *Der Mecklenburger Volksmund in Fritz Reuters Schriften: Sammlung und Erklärung volkstümlicher Wendungen und sprichwörtlicher Redensarten im mecklenburgischen Platt.* Leipzig: M. Hesse, 1902. 132 pp.

2114. Neumann, Siegfried. "Das Sagwort in Mecklenburg um die Mitte des 19. Jahrhunderts im Spiegel der Mundartdichtungen Reuters und Brinckmans." *Deutsches Jahrbuch für Volkskunde* 12 (1966): 49-66.

2115. Raschen, J. F. "Slang: 'To Get Cold Feet.'" *Modern Language Notes* 27 (1912): 198-199.

REYMONT, WLADYSLAW STANISLAW (1867-1925)
2116. Plauszewski, Andrzej. "Funkcje stylistyczene przyslów w prozie Reymonta." *Prace Polonistyczne* 24 (1968): 82-90.

RIBEIRO, AQUILINO (1885-1963)
2117. Pinheiro Torres, Alexandre. "*O Malhadinhas*, visto através do seu adagiário." *Colóquio-Letras* 85 (1985): 50-56.

RICHARD OF CAMPSALL (1280/1290-1350/1360)
2118. Synan, Edward A. "Sixteen Sayings of Richard of Campsall on Contingency and Fore-Knowledge." *Mediaeval Studies* 24 (1962): 250-262.

RICHARDSON, SAMUEL (1689-1761)
2119. Newcomb, Robert. "Franklin and Richardson." *Journal of English and Germanic Philology* 57 (1958): 27-35.

RICHTER, CONRAD (1890-1968)
2120. Flanagan, John T. "Folklore in the Novels of Conrad Richter." *Midwest Folklore* 2 (1952): 5-14.

RIFBJERG, KLAUS (1931—)
2121. Holzapfel, Otto. "Stereotype Redensarten über 'den Deutschen' in der neueren dänischen Literatur." *Proverbium: Yearbook of International Proverb Scholarship* 4 (1987): 87-110.

RINSER, LUISE (1911—)
2122. Higi-Wydler, Melanie. *Zur Übersetzung von Idiomen: Eine Beschreibung und Klassifizierung deutscher Idiome und ihrer französischen Übersetzungen.* Bern: Peter Lang, 1989. 335 pp.

ROBERT, SHAABAN (1911-1962)

2123. Eastman, Carol M. "The Proverb in Modern Written Swahili Literature: An Aid to Proverb Elicitation." *African Folklore*. Ed. Richard Dorson. Garden City, N. Y.: Anchor Books, 1972. 193-207.

2124. Senkoro, F. E. M. K. "Ng'ombe Akivundika Guu: Preliminary Remarks on the Proverb-Story in Written Swahili Literature." *Design and Intent in African Literature*. Eds. David F. Dorsey et al. Washington, D. C.: Three Continents, 1982. 59-69.

ROBIN CONSCIENCE (c. 1550)

2125. Whiting, Bartlett Jere. "*Robin Conscience*." *Proverbs in the Earlier English Drama*. Cambridge, Massachusetts: Harvard University Press, 1938; rpt. New York: Octagon Books, 1969. 108-110.

ROBINSON, ROWLAND EVANS (1833-1900)

2126. Baker, Ronald Lee. "Robinson's Use of Proverbs and Proverbial Phrases." *Folklore in the Writings of Rowland E. Robinson*. Diss. Indiana University, 1969. 253-292. Bowling Green, Ohio: Bowling Green University Popular Press, 1973. 135-158.

ROETHKE, THEODORE (1908-1963)

2127. Galvin, Brendan. "Theodore Roethke's Proverbs." *Concerning Poetry* 5, 1 (1972): 35-47.

ROHMER, ERIC [Jean-Marie Scherer, a.k.a. Gilbert Cordier] (1920—)

2128. Masson, Alain. "Eric Rohmer: Le Capricorne souverain de l'onde occidentale sur les *Comédies et proverbes*." *Positif* No. 307 (1986): 43-45.

ROJAS, FERNANDO de (1465-1541)

2129. Cantalapiedra, Fernando. "Los refranes en *Celestina* y el problema de su autoria." *Celestinesca: Boletin Informativo Internacional* 8, 1 (1984): 49-53.

ROJAS, FRANCISCO de (1607-1648)

2130. Hayes, Francis Clement. "The Use of Proverbs in the 'Siglo de Oro' Drama: An Introductory Study." Diss. University of North Carolina, 1936. 163-170.

ROLANDSLIED

2131. Taylor, Archer. "'All Is not Gold That Glitters' and *Rolandslied,* 1956." *Romance Philology* 11 (1958): 370-371.

ROLLENHAGEN, GEORG (1542-1609)

2132. Richter, Roland. "Proverbs in Context: A Structural Approach." *Fabula* 15 (1974): 212-221.

2133. Richter, Roland. "Georg Rollenhagens *Froschmeuseler*: Struktur, Rhetorik und die Funktion von Sprichwort und Fabel." Diss. University of California at Los Angeles, 1970; published as *Georg Rollenhagens "Froschmeuseler": Ein rhetorisches Meisterstück.* Bern: Peter Lang, 1975. 139 pp.

ROMAN DE LA ROSE (1225/30-1275/80)

2134. Larsen, Judith Clark. "Proverbial Material in the *Roman de la Rose.*" Diss. University of Georgia, 1978. 140 pp.

2135. Schulze-Busacker, Elisabeth. "Eléments de culture populaire dans la littérature courtoise." *La culture populaire au Moyen Ages: Etudes présentés au Quatrième colloque de l'Institut d'études médiévales de l'Université de Montréal 2-3 avril 1977.* Ed. Pierre Boglioni. Montréal: L'Aurora, 1979. 81-101.

ROMAN DE RENART (1165-1205)

2136. Braet, Herman. "'Cucullus non facit monachum': Of Beasts and Monks in the Old French *Renart* Romance." *Monks, Nuns, and Friars in Mediaeval Society.* Eds. Edward B. King, Jacqueline T. Schaefer, and William B. Wadley. Sewa-nee, Tennessee: The Press of the University of the South, 1989. 161-170.

2137. Pineaux, Jacques. "Le roman de Renard." *Proverbes et dictons français,* 6th ed. Paris: Presses Universitaires de France, 1973. 45-48.

2138. Whiting, Bartlett Jere. "Proverbial Material from the Old French Poems on Reynard the Fox." *Harvard Studies and Notes in Philology and Literature* 18 (1935): 235-270.

ROMIEU, AUGUSTE (1800-1855)

2139. Siegel, Patricia J. "Political Proverbs and the French Revolution: The Landscape Observed by Théodore Leclercq and Auguste Romieu." *Re-*

Naming the Landscape. Eds. Jürgen Kleist and Bruce A. Butterfield. New York: Peter Lang, 1994. 159-175.

RONNER, MARKUS M. (1938—)

2140. Mieder, Wolfgang. "'Spaß muß sein,' sagte der Spaßmacher, aber. . . : Zu den Sagwörtern von Markus M. Ronner." *Sprachspiegel* 42 (1986): 162-170. Also in *Sprichwörtliches und Geflügeltes: Sprachstudien von Martin Luther bis Karl Marx*. Bochum: Norbert Brockmeyer, 1995. 51-61.

ROOSEVELT, FRANKLIN DELANO (1882-1945)

2141. Meichsner, Irene. *Die Logik von Gemeinplätzen: Vorgeführt an Steuermannstopos und Schiffsmetapher*. Bonn: Bouvier, 1983. 263 pp.

2142. Miller, Edd, and Jesse J. Villareal. "The Use of Clichés by Four Contemporary Speakers." *Quarterly Journal of Speech* 31 (1945): 151-155.

ROSEGGER, PETER (1843-1918)

2143. Seiler, Friedrich. *Deutsche Sprichwörterkunde*. München: C. H. Beck, 1922, 1967. 64-65.

ROSENPLÜT, HANS (c. 1400-c. 1470)

2144. Hofmeister, Wernfried. *Sprichwortartige Mikrotexte als literarische Medien, dargestellt an der hochdeutschen politischen Lyrik des Mittelalters*. Bochum: Norbert Brockmeyer, 1995. 430-459.

ROTIMI, OLA (1938—)

2145. Monye, Ambrose A. "The Use of Proverbs in Ola Rotimi's *The Gods Are not to Blame.*" *Proverbium: Yearbook of International Proverb Scholarship* 12 (1995): 251-261.

ROUSSEAU, JEAN JACQUES (1712-1778)

2146. Mieder, Wolfgang. "'Zurück zur Natur': Zum Weiterleben eines angeblichen Rousseau-Zitats." *Der Sprachdienst* 33 (1989): 146-150. Also in *Sprichwörtliches und Geflügeltes: Sprachstudien von Martin Luther bis Karl Marx*. Bochum: Norbert Brockmeyer, 1995. 71-78.

ROWLEY, WILLIAM (c. 1585-1626)

2147. Smith, Roland M. "Three Obscure English Proverbs [The game is not worth the candle; He that will swear will lie; Life is a pilgrimage]." *Modern Language Notes* 65 (1950): 441-447.

RÜCKERT, FRIEDRICH (1788-1866)
2148. Hilmi, Aladin. "Zum Problem der Übersetzung von Sprichwörtern und Redensarten." *Sprache im technischen Zeitalter* No. 96 (1985): 283-285.

RUDBECK, PETRUS (17th cent.)
2149. Klingberg, Av Göte. "Alphabetum proverbiale Bureanum-Rudbeckianum." *Arv* 17 (1961): 140-156.

RUDOLF VON BIBERACH (13th/14th cent.)
2150. Schmidt, Margot. "Zwillingsformeln als plus ultra des mystischen Weges." *Archiv für das Studium der neueren Sprachen und Literaturen* 223 (1986): 245-268.

RUEDA, LOPE de (c. 1510-1565)
2151. Hayes, Francis Clement. "The Use of Proverbs in the 'Siglo de Oro' Drama: An Introductory Study." Diss. University of North Carolina, 1936. 36-42.

2152. Recoules, Henri. "Refranero y entremés." *Boletin de la Biblioteca Menedez Pelayo* 52 (1976): 135-153.

RÜHMKORF, PETER (1929—)
2153. Riha, Karl. "Balla Balla, Balla Basta: Zur Poetik kleiner literarischer Formen." *Akzente* 21 (1974): 265-287.

RUFUS [Lucius Varius Rufus] (A. D. 1st cent.)
2154. Prittwitz-Gaffron, Erich von. *Das Sprichwort im griechischen Epigramm.* Diss. München, 1912. Gießen: Alfred Töpelmann, 1912. 48-49.

RUIZ DE ALARCON, JUAN (c. 1581-1639)
2155. Hayes, Francis Clement. "The Use of Proverbs in the 'Siglo de Oro' Drama: An Introductory Study." Diss. University of North Carolina, 1936. 105-117.

RUMELANT (VON SACHSEN), Meister (13th cent.)
2156. Hofmeister, Wernfried. *Sprichwortartige Mikrotexte als literarische Medien, dargestellt an der hochdeutschen politischen Lyrik des Mittelalters.* Bochum: Norbert Brockmeyer, 1995. 283-286.

RUXTON, GEORGE FREDERICK (1821-1848)
2157. Barrick, Mac E. "Ruxton's Western Proverbs." *Western Folklore* 34 (1975): 215-225.

S

SAAVEDRA FAJARDO, DIEGO de (1584-1648)

2158. Dittrich, Lothar. "Emblematische Weisheit und naturwissenschaftliche Realität." *Die Sprache der Bilder: Realität und Bedeutung in der niederländischen Malerei des 17. Jahrhunderts.* Eds. Wolfgang J. Müller, Konrad Renger, and Rüdiger Klessmann. Braunschweig: ACO Druck, 1978. 21-33. Also in *Jarbuch für Internationale Germanistik* 13 (1981): 36-60.

SACCHETTI, FRANCO (c. 1330-1400)

2159. Ageno, Franca. "Ispirazione proverbiale del *Trecentonovelle.*" *Lettere Italiane* 51 (1958): 288-305.

SACHS, HANS (1494-1576)

2160. Handschin, Charles Hart. "Das Sprichwort bei Hans Sachs." Diss. University of Wisconsin, 1902; published in *Bulletin of the University of Wisconsin Philology and Literature Series* 3 (1907): 1-153.

2161. Rosen, Heinrich. "Die sprichwörtlichen Redensarten in den Werken des Hans Sachs, nach Entstehung, Bild, Bedeutung, Vorkommen untersucht und sachlich geordnet." Diss. Bonn, 1922. 105 pp.

2162. Schweitzer, Charles. "Sprichwörter und sprichwörtliche Redensarten bei Hans Sachs." *Hans Sachs Forschungen.* Ed. Arthur Ludwig Stiefel. Nürnberg: Rau, 1894. 353-381.

2163. Seiler, Friedrich. *Deutsche Sprichwörterkunde.* München: C. H. Beck, 1922, 1967. 56-58.

2164. Seiler, Friedrich. "Sonst nicht belegte Sprichwörter aus Hans Sachs." *Germanisch-Romanische Monatsschrift* 13 (1925): 152-155.

2165. Stech, Svatopluk G. "A Remark on 'Goat in the Garden.'" *American Speech* 36 (1961): 139-140.

2166. Zahlten, Emil. "Sprichwort und Redensart in den Fastnachtspielen des Hans Sachs." Diss. Hamburg, 1921. 113 pp.

SACKVILLE, THOMAS, 1st Earl of Dorset (1536-1608)

2167. Whiting, Bartlett Jere. "Thomas Sackville and Thomas Norton's *Ferrex and Porrex.*" *Proverbs in the Earlier English Drama.* Cambridge, Massachusetts: Harvard University Press, 1938; rpt. New York: Octagon Books, 1969. 279-281.

SAINT GELAIS, MELIN de (1491-1558)

2168. Cohen, Helen Louise. "Proverbs and the Ballade." *The Ballade*. New York: Columbia University Press, 1915. 94-102.

SAINT LONG (17th cent.)

2169. Desaivre, Léo. "Saint Long, *Les amours de Colas*." *Revue des traditions populaires* 20 (1905): 312-313.

SAINTE-BEUVE, CHARLES AUGUSTIN (1804-1869)

2170. Forster, E. M. "The Ivory Tower." *The Atlantic Monthly* 163 (January-June, 1939): 51-58.

SALOMON UND MARCOLF (c. 1180/1190)

2171. Davis, Natalie Zemon. "Proverbial Wisdom and Popular Errors." *Society and Culture in Early Modern France*. Stanford, California: Stanford University Press, 1975. 227-267, 336-346 (footnotes). Also published as "Sagesse proverbiale et erreurs populaires." *Les cultures du peuple: Rituels, savoirs et résistances au XVIe siècle*. Paris: Aubier, 1979. 366-425; "Spruchweisheiten und populäre Irrlehren." *Volkskultur: Zur Wiederentdeckung des vergessenen Alltags (16.-20. Jahrhundert)*. Eds. Richard van Dülmen and Norbert Schindler. Frankfurt am Main: Fischer, 1984. 78-116, 394-406 (notes).

2172. Hofmann, Liselotte. *Der volkskundliche Gehalt der mittelhochdeutschen Epen von 1100 bis gegen 1250*. Zeulenroda: Bernhard Sporn, 1939. 76.

2173. Jones, Malcolm. "Marcolf the Trickster in Late Mediaeval Art and Literature or: The Mystery of the Bum in the Oven." *Spoken in Jest*. Ed. Gillian Bennett. Sheffield, United Kingdom: Sheffield Academic Press, 1991. 139-173.

2174. Lenk, Werner. "Zur Sprichwort-Antithetik im *Salomon-Markolf-Dialog*." *Forschungen und Fortschritte* 39 (1965): 151-155.

2175. Singer, Samuel. "Sprichwortstudien." *Schweizerisches Archiv für Volkskunde* 37 (1939): 129-150, especially 137-139.

2176. Singer, Samuel. "*Salomo und Marcolf*." *Sprichwörter des Mittelalters*, 3 vols. Bern: Herbert Lang, 1944-1947. I, 33-55.

SALVIATI, LIONARDO (1540-1589)

2177. Ageno, Fransa. "Le frasi proverbiali di una raccolta manoscritta di Lionardo Salviati." *Studi di filologia italiana* 17 (1959): 239-274.

SANCHEZ DE BADAJOZ, DIEGO (c. 1479-1549)

2178. Gillet, Joseph E. "'Las ochavas en cadena': A Proverb in Rodrigo Cota and Diego Sanchez de Badajoz." *Romance Philology* 6 (1952-1953): 264-267.

SAND, GEORGE [Amandine Aurore Lucie Dupin] (1804-1876)

2179. Brenner, Clarence D. *The French Dramatic Proverb*. Berkeley, California: Privately printed, 1977. 68 pp.

2180. Lucie, V. H. de. "George Sand." *Revue des traditions populaires* 16 (1901): 454-456.

SANDBURG, CARL (1878-1967)

2181. Mieder, Wolfgang. "Behold the Proverbs of a People: A Florilegium of Proverbs in Carl Sandburg's Poem 'Good Morning, America.'" *Southern Folklore Quarterly* 35 (1971): 160-168.

2182. Mieder, Wolfgang. "Proverbs in Carl Sandburg's 'The People, Yes.'" *Southern Folklore Quarterly* 37 (1973): 15-36.

SANTOB DE CARRIÓN (14th cent.)

2183. Alarcos Llorach, E. "La lengua de los *Proverbios Morales* de don Sem Tob." *Revista de Filologia Española* 35 (1951): 249-309.

2184. Arochas, Maurice. "Santob de Carrión's *Proverbios Morales* in Light of the Humanistic Trends of the Era." Diss. New York University, 1972. 249 pp.

2185. Barcia, Pedro Luis. "Sem Tob, proverbios y refranes." *Cuadernos del Idioma* 3 (1968): 47-70.

2186. Colahan, Clark, and Alfred Rodriguez. "Traditional Semitic Forms of Reversibility in Sem Tob's *Proverbios morales*." *Journal of Medieval and Renaissance Studies* 13, 1 (1983): 33-50.

2187. Joset, Jacques. "Opposition et réversibilité des valeurs dans les *Proverbios Morales*: Approche du système de pensée de Santob de Carrión." *Hommage au Professeur Maurice Delbouille*. Ed. Jeanne Wathe-let-Willem. Liège: Cahiers de l'A. R. U. Lg., 1973. 177-189.

2188. Joset, Jacques. "Quelques modalités du 'yo' dans les *Proverbios morales de Santob de Carrión*." *Etudes de philologie romane et d'histoire littéraire offertes à Jules Horrent*. Eds. Jean Marie d'Heur and Nicoletta Cherubini. Liège-Tournai: Gedit, 1980. 193-204.

2189. Klausner, Joel H. "The Historic and Social Milieu of Santob's *Proverbios Morales*." *Hispania* 48 (1965): 783-789.

2190. Kleinerman, Joseph. "The Phonology of Sem Tov's *Proverbios Morales*." Diss. University of Southern California, 1969. 307 pp.

2191. Lopez Grigera, Luisa. "Un nuevo códice de los *Proverbios morales* de Sem Tob." *Boletin de la Real Academia Española* 56 (1976): 221-281.

2192. Mettmann, Walter. "Spruchweisheit und Spruchdichtung in der spanischen und katalanischen Literatur des Mittelalters." *Zeitschrift für romanische Philologie* 76 (1960): 94-117.

2193. Perry, Theodore A., ed. *Santob de Carrión: "Proverbios Morales."* Madison, Wisconsin: The Hispanic Seminary of Medieval Studies, 1986. 233 pp.

2194. Perry, Theodore A. *The "Moral Proverbs" of Santob de Carrión: Jewish Wisdom in Christian Spain*. Princeton, New Jersey: Princeton University Press, 1987. 198 pp.

2195. Pienda, Jesús Avelino de la, and Clark Colahan. "Relativistic Philosophic Traditions in Santob's *Proverbios morales*." *La Coronica* 23, 1 (1994): 46-62.

2196. Zemke, John Max. "Critical Approaches to the *Proverbios morales* of Shem Tov de Carrión." Diss. University of California at Davis, 1988. 408 pp.

SARASIN, JEAN-FRANÇOIS (1614-1654)

2197. Sébillot, Paul. "Sarasin." *Revue des traditions populaires* 6 (1891): 470-473.

SARNELLI, POMPEO (1649-1724)

2198. Speroni, Charles. "I proverbi della *Posilecheata*." *Folklore* (Naples) 8 (1953-1954): 3-22.

SATYRE MENIPPÉE (1594)

2199. Sébillot, Paul. "*Satyre Menippée*." *Revue des traditions populaires* 10 (1895): 343-346.

SCARRON, PAUL (1610-1660)

2200. Sébillot, Paul. "Scarron." *Revue des traditions populaires* 8 (1893): 99-111, 182-193, especially 184-193.

SCHARPENBERG, MARGOT (1924—)

2201. Koch, Annegrete. "Der Redensart auf die Spur kommen: Ein Versuch über zwei Gedichte von Margot Scharpenberg." *Carleton Germanic Papers* 21 (1993): 21-30.

SCHEIDT, KASPAR (c. 1520-1565)

2202. Gallacher, Stuart A. "The Proverb in Scheidt's *Grobianus*." *Journal of English and Germanic Philology* 40 (1941): 489-508.

SCHENDEL, MICHEL VAN (1929—)

2203. Grandpré, Chantal de. "La poésie comme parole." *Voix et images: Littérature québécoise* 11, 2 (1986): 228-240.

SCHILLER, JOHANN CHRISTOPH FRIEDRICH VON (1759-1805)

2204. Bebermeyer, Renate. "'Geflügelte Zitate'—gestern und heute." *Sprachspiegel* 40 (1984): 66-70.

2205. Filtzinger, Philipp. "Die Sentenzen in Schillers Versdramen." Diss. Gießen, 1923. 58 pp.

2206. Garbe, Joachim. "Das also war des Pudels Kern! 'Geflügelte Worte' und ihr Ursprung." *Praxis Deutsch* 16 (July 1989): 30-32, 37.

2207. Guenther, Friedrich Joachim. *Entwürfe zu Vorträgen und Aufsätzen über 100 Sprichwörter und 100 Schillersche Sprüche für die oberen Klassen höherer Lehranstalten.* Eisleben: Reichardt, 1861; 2nd ed. by Carl August Peschel. Leipzig: George Reichardt, 1882. 450 pp.

2208. Kettner, Gustav, ed. "Russische Sprichwörter." *Schiller's* "*Demetrius.*" Weimar: Goethe Gesellschaft, 1894. 258-259.

2209. MacLean, James Beattie. "Use of the Proverb in Schiller's Dramas." Diss. University of Washington, 1952. 175 pp.

2210. Mieder, Wolfgang. "'Die Axt im Haus erspart den Zimmermann' (*Wilhelm Tell*, III, 1): Vom Schiller-Zitat zum parodierten Sprichwort." *Sprachspiegel* 40 (1984): 137-142. Also in *Sprichwort, Redensart, Zitat: Tradierte Formelsprache in der Moderne*. Bern: Peter Lang, 1985. 155-161; *Sprichwort—Wahrwort!? Studien zur Geschichte, Bedeutung und Funktion deutscher Sprichwört*. Frankfurt am Main: Peter Lang, 1992. 151-157.

2211. Mieder, Wolfgang. "'Zitate sind des Bürgers Zierde': Zum Weiterleben von Schiller-Zitaten." *Muttersprache* 95 (1984-1985): 284-306. Also in *Deutsche Redensarten, Sprichwörter und Zitate: Studien zu ihrer Herkunft, Überlieferung und Verwendung*. Vienna: Edition Praesens, 1995. 46-68.

2212. Mieder, Wolfgang. "'Wo neue Kräfte sinnvoll walten?' Zur Umformung Schillerscher Zitate zu Aphorismen und Graffiti." *Ethik und Ästhetik: Werke und Werte in der Literatur vom 18. bis zum 20. Jahrhundert: Festschrift für Wolfgang Wittkowski*. Ed. Richard Fisher. Frankfurt am Main: Peter Lang, 1995. 293-311.

2213. Niemeyer, Paul. *Die Sentenz als poetische Ausdrucksform vorzüglich im dramatischen Stil: Untersuchungen an Hand der Sentenz in Schillers Drama*. Berlin: Emil Ebering, 1934. 1-23.

2214. Novichkova, R. M. "Pro odnofrazovi teksti (na materiali nimets'koi movi)." *Movoznavstvo* 15, 3 (1981): 71-75.

2215. Reichel, Rudolf. "Zu Schillers *Tell* I, 1: Und mit der Axt hab' ich ihms Bad gesegnet." *Zeitschrift für den deutschen Unterricht* 6 (1892): 134-135.

2216. Riha, Karl. "Balla Balla, Balla Basta: Zur Poetik kleiner literarischer Formen." *Akzente* 21 (1974): 265-287.

2217. Scheichl, Sigurd Paul. "Feste Syntagmen im dramatischen Dialog: Materialien zur Geschichte eines Stilmittels zwischen Goethe und Kroetz." *Tradition und Entwicklung: Festschrift Eugen Thurnher*. Eds. Werner Bauer, Achim Masser, and Guntram Plangg. Innsbruck: Institut für Germanistik der Universität Innsbruck, 1982. 383-407.

2218. Seiler, Friedrich. "Das Sprichwort im Unterricht." *Zeitschrift für Deutschkunde* 31 (1920): 480-488, 524-533, especially 531-532.

2219. Skreb, Zdenko. "Die Sentenz als stilbildendes Element." *Jahrbuch für Internationale Germanistik* 13 (1981): 76-84.

2220. Taylor, Archer. "'In the Evening Praise the Day.'" *Modern Language Notes* 36 (1921): 115-118.

2221. Thümmel, Julius. "Über die Sentenz im Drama, namentlich bei Shakespeare, Goethe und Schiller." *Jahrbuch der deutschen Shakespeare Gesellschaft* 14 (1879): 97-114.

2222. "Uit Schiller's werken (7 spreekwoorden)." *De Toekomst* 21 (1877): 253.

SCHLEGEL, FRIEDRICH (1772-1829)

2223. Fink, Arthur-Hermann. *Maxime und Fragment: Grenzmöglichkeiten einer Kunstform: Zur Morphologie des Aphorismus.* München: Max Huber, 1934. 53-70.

2224. Fricke, Harald. *Aphorismus.* Stuttgart: Metzler, 1984. 51-54, 84-93, 155-159.

SCHMIDT, HELMUT (1918—)

2225. Meichsner, Irene. *Die Logik von Gemeinplätzen: Vorgeführt an Steuermannstopos und Schiffsmetapher.* Bonn: Bouvier, 1983. 263 pp.

2226. Mieder, Wolfgang. "'Die Hunde bellen, aber die Karawane zieht weiter': Zum türkischen Ursprung eines neuen deutschen Sprichwortes." *Der Sprachdienst* 32, 5 (1988): 129-134. Also in *Sprichwort—Wahrwort!? Studien zur Geschichte, Bedeutung und Funktion deutscher Sprichwörter.* Frankfurt am Main: Peter Lang, 1992. 203-210.

SCHOTTELIUS, JUSTUS GEORG (1612-1676)

2227. Höpel, Ingrid. "Sprichwort und 'Sinnbild' als moralisch verbindliche Zeichen bei Justus Georg Schottelius." *Emblem und Sinnbild: Vom Kunstbuch zum Erbauungsbuch.* Frankfurt am Main: Athenäum, 1987. 165-190.

2228. Mieder, Wolfgang. "Die Einstellung der Grammatiker Schottelius und Gottsched zum Sprichwort." *Sprachspiegel* 38 (1982): 70-75.

2229. Pape, Walter. "Zwischen Sprachspiel und Sprachkritik: Zum literarischen Spiel mit der wörtlichen Bedeutung von Idiomen." *Sprache und Literatur in Wissenschaft und Unterricht* 16, 56 (1985): 2-13.

2230. Schafferus, Ella. "Die Sprichwörtersammlung bei Schottelius." *Korrespondenzblatt des Vereins für niederdeutsche Sprachforschung* 45 (1932): 53-57.

SCHULZ, MAX WALTER (1921—)
2231. Kantola, Markhu. "Zum phraseologischen Wortpaar in der deutschen Gegenwartssprache." *Beiträge zur allgemeinen und germanistischen Phraseologieforschung: Internationales Symposium in Oulu 13.-15. Juni 1986*. Ed. Jarmo Korhonen. Oulu: Oulun Yliopisto, 1987. 111-128.

SCHUMANN, VALENTIN (c. 1520-c. 1559)
2232. Stambaugh, Ria. "Proverbs and Proverbial Phrases in the Jestbooks of Lindener, Montanus and Schumann." Diss. University of North Carolina, 1963. 381 pp.

2233. Stambaugh, Ria. "Proverbial Material in Sixteenth Century German Jestbooks." *Proverbium* No. 11 (1968): 257-267.

SCHUREK, PAUL (1890-1962)
2234. Lindow, Wolfgang. "Volkstümliches Sprachgut in der neuniederdeutschen Dialektdichtung." Diss. Kiel, 1960. Part I, 126-131.

2235. Lindow, Wolfgang. "Das Sprichwort als stilistisches und dramatisches Mittel in der Schauspieldichtung Stavenhagens, Boßdorfs und Schureks." *Niederdeutsches Jahrbuch* 84 (1961): 97-116.

SCHWITTERS, KURT (1887-1948)
2236. Riha, Karl. "Balla Balla, Balla Basta: Zur Poetik kleiner literarischer Formen." *Akzente* 21 (1974): 265-287.

SCOTT, Sir WALTER (1771-1832)
2237. Bouchier, Jonathan. "Local and Personal Proverbs in the Waverly Novels." *Notes and Queries* 10th ser. 1 (1904): 383-384, 402-403.

2238. G., M. N. "Local and Personal Proverbs in the Waverly Novels." *Notes and Queries* 10th ser. 2 (1904): 37.

2239. Lamont, Claire. "A Note on Gaelic Proverbs in *Waverley*." *Notes and Queries* 220 ns 22 (1975): 64-66.

2240. Mistletoe. "Local and Personal Proverbs in the Waverly Novels." *Notes and Queries* 10th ser. 2 (1904): 37.

2241. Pickford, John. "Local and Personal Proverbs in the Waverly Novels." *Notes and Queries* 10th ser. 2 (1904): 37.

2242. Raben, Joseph. "Proverbs in the Waverly Novels of Sir Walter Scott." Diss. Indiana University, 1954. 533 pp.

SCRIBE, EUGÈNE (1791-1861)
2243. Brenner, Clarence D. *The French Dramatic Proverb*. Berkeley, California: Privately printed, 1977. 68 pp.

SEALSFIELD, CHARLES (1793-1864)
2244. Robbins, Walter Lee. "A Hoffmann Influence on Sealsfield's *Die Prairie am Jacinto* (Wellerism: Aber Alles auf der Welt vergänglich, sagte immer mein alter Schulmeister)." *Germanic Notes* 6 (1975): 5.

SENECA [Lucius Annaeus Seneca] (4 B. C.-A. D. 65)
2245. Crane, Mary Thomas. "Proverbial and Aphoristic Sayings: Sources of Authority in the English Renaissance." Diss. Harvard University, 1986. 24-98.

2246. Roos, Paolo. *Sentenza e proverbio nell'antichità e i "Distici di Catone": Il testo latino e i volgarizzamenti italiani*. Brescia: Morcelliana, 1984. 254 pp.

2247. Skreb, Zdenko. "Die Sentenz als stilbildendes Element." *Jahrbuch für Internationale Germanistik* 13 (1981): 76-84.

SERDONATI, FRANCESCO (1540-1602)
2248. Speroni, Charles. "Wellerismi tolti dai proverbi inediti di Francesco Serdonati." *Folklore* (Naples) 4, 1-2 (1950): 12-31.

SERIFI (17th cent.)
2249. Macfie, A. L. and F. "A Turkish Proverb Poem by Serifi." *Asian Folklore Studies* 52, 2 (1993): 245-250.

SERLO OF WILTON (1109-c. 1207)

2250. Friend, A. C. "The Proverbs of Serlo of Wilton." *Mediaeval Studies* 16 (1954): 179-218.

SERVATIUS (1180/1190)

2251. Hofmann, Liselotte. *Der volkskundliche Gehalt der mittelhochdeutschen Epen von 1100 bis gegen 1250*. Zeulenroda: Bernhard Sporn, 1939. 77.

SEUSE, HEINRICH (1295-1366)

2252. Birlinger, Anton. "Sprüche aus H. Suso's *Büchlein von der ewigen Weisheit*." *Alemannia* 5 (1877): 56-57.

SHAKESPEARE, WILLIAM (1564-1616)

2253. Anderson, Ruth L. "'As Heart Can Think.'" *Shakespeare Association Bulletin* 12 (1937): 246-251.

2254. Andresen, Martha. "'Ripeness Is All': Sententiae and Commonplaces in *King Lear*." *Some Facets of "King Lear": Essays in Prismatic Criticism*. Eds. Rosalie L. Colie and F. T. Flahiff. Toronto: University of Toronto Press, 1974. 145-168.

2255. Asals, Heather. "'Should' and 'Would': Hamlet and the Idioms of the Father." *Genre* 13 (1980), 431-439.

2256. Barnum, Erika. "Translating Shakespeare's Proverbs: A Study of Seven German Versions of *Much Ado about Nothing*." Honors Thesis. University of Vermont, 1989. 100 pp.

2257. Brauscheid. "'Etwas ist faul im Staate Dänemark.'" *Zeitschrift des Allgemeinen Deutschen Sprachvereins* 19 (1904): 213-214.

2258. Bruster, Douglas. "The Horn of Plenty: Cuckoldry and Capital in the Drama of the Age of Shakespeare." *Studies in English Literature 1500-1900* 30, 2 (1990): 195-215.

2259. Carpenter, Sarah. "Lear's Fool: Another Proverb [Fools be fain to fight when wise men run away]." *Notes and Queries* 224 ns 26 (1979): 128-129.

2260. Champion, Larry S. "'A Springe to Catch Woodcocks': Proverbs, Characterization, and Political Ideology in *Hamlet*." *Hamlet Studies* 15, 1-2 (1993): 24-39.

2261. Cheatham, G. "Shakespeare's *The Taming of the Shrew*." *Explicator* 42, 3 (1984): 12.

2262. Cherry, Mary Jane. "A Classification and Analysis of Selected 'Sayings' in Shakespeare's Plays." Diss. The Catholic University of America, 1981. 192 pp.

2263. Clarke, Mary Cowden. *Shakespeare Proverbs: On the Wise Saws of Our Wisest Poet.* . . London: Chapman and Hall, 1848; New York: William J. Rolfe, 1908. 145 pp.

2264. Cook, Emmett Wayne. "Shakespeare's Use of Proverbs for Characterization, Dramatic Action, and Tone in Representative Comedy." Diss. Texas Technological University, 1974. 172 pp.

2265. Cross, Gustav. "Tilley's *Dictionary of Proverbs in England*, H 348, and Marston's *Antonio and Mellida*." *Notes and Queries* 206 ns 8 (1961): 143-144.

2266. Dent, Robert William. *Shakespeare's Proverbial Language: An Index.* Berkeley: University of California Press, 1981. 289 pp.

2267. Dickson, Bonnie Ethel. "The Proverbs in Shakespeare's Major Tragedies." M. A. Thesis. Duke University, 1938. 126 pp.

2268. Donker, Marjorie. *Shakespeare's Proverbial Themes: A Rhetorical Context for the "Sententia" as "Res."* Westport, Connecticut: Greenwood Press, 1992. 199 pp.

2269. Elam, Cecil. "Shakespeare's Old Saws." *Lippincott's Monthly Magazine* 58 (1896): 567-576.

2270. Engler, Balz. "*Othello*, II, 1, 155: 'To Change the Cod's Head for the Salmon's Tail.'" *Shakespeare Quarterly* 35, 2 (1984): 202-203.

2271. Falk, Doris V. "Proverbs and the Polonius Destiny." *Shakespeare Quarterly* 18 (1967): 23-36.

2272. Felhoelter, M. Clarita. "Proverbialism in *Coriolanus*." Diss. Catholic University of America, 1956. 161 pp.

2273. Felver, Charles S. "A Proverb Turned Jest in *Measure for Measure*." *Shakespeare Quarterly* 11 (1960): 385-387.

2274. Grabau, Carl. "Sprichwörter bei Shakespeare." *Jahrbuch der Shakespeare Gesellschaft* 55 (1919): 205.

2275. Green, Henry. "Emblems in Connexion with Proverbs." *Shakespeare and the Emblem Writers: An Exposition of Their Similarities of Thought and Expression*. London: Trübner and Company, 1870. 318-345.

2276. Halliwell, James O. *A Hand-Book Index to the Works of Shakespeare*. London: Bartholomew Close, 1866; rpt. New York: AMS Press, 1975. 390-395.

2277. Hofmann, Norbert. "Das Sprichwort in der literarischen Übersetzung." *Redundanz und Äquivalenz in der literarischen Übersetzung, dargestellt an fünf deutschen Übersetzungen des "Hamlet."* Diss. Tübingen, 1979. Tübingen: Max Niemeyer, 1980. 71-84.

2278. Holdsworth, R. V. "'Lie by It' in Middleton." *Notes and Queries* 226 ns 28 (1981): 242.

2279. Holdsworth, R. V. "Two Proverbs in Middleton and Some Contemporaries." *Notes and Queries* 226 ns 28 (1981): 172-173.

2280. Hulme, Hilda M. "Proverb and Proverb-Idiom." *Explorations in Shakespeare's Language: Some Problems of Lexical Meaning in the Dramatic Text*. New York: Longman, 1962; rpt. New York: Barnes and Noble, 1977. 39-88.

2281. Hulme, Hilda M. "On the Detail of Proverb Idiom, *King Lear*, II, iv, 65-88." *English Studies* 51 (1970): 529-537.

2282. Jente, Richard. "The Proverbs of Shakespeare with Early and Contemporary Parallels." *Washington University Studies (Humanistic Series)* 13, 2 (1926): 391-444.

2283. Jones, H. S. V. "A Proverb in *Hamlet*." *Modern Language Notes* 27 (1912): 210-211.

2284. Jorgensen, Paul A. "Valor's Better Parts: Background and Meanings of Shakespeare's Most Difficult Proverb." *Shakespeare Studies* 9 (1976): 141-158.

2285. Klein, Joan Larsen. "'What Is't to Leave Betimes?': Proverbs and Logic in *Hamlet*." *Shakespeare Survey* 32 (1979): 163-176.

2286. Klinck, Dennis R. "Shakespeare's 'Tameness of a Wolf.'" *Notes and Queries* 222 ns. 24 (1977): 113-114.

2287. Koch, Arne von. "A New Interpretation of 'Something Is Rotten in the State of Denmark.'" *Moderna Språk* 9 (1915): 157-160.

2288. Kuhl, E. P. "Shakespere's [*sic*] 'Lead Apes in Hell' and the Ballad of *The Maid and the Palmer*." *Studies in Philology* 22 (1925): 453-466.

2289. Kurikoma, Masakazu. "Shakespeare's Use of Proverbs." *Anglica* (Osaka) 4, 5 (1962): 36-57.

2290. Lever, Katherine. "Proverbs and Sententiae in the Plays of Shakespeare." *Shakespeare Association Bulletin* 13 (1938): 173-183, 224-239.

2291. Levine, Robert T. "Honesty and Beauty: An Emendation for *Hamlet*, III, i, 109-110." *Notes and Queries* 225 ns 27 (1980): 166-169.

2292. Lumpkin, Ben Gray. "Shaking the Dove-House Again." *Proverbium* No. 12 (1969): 322-323.

2293. Lyndon, C. *Apophthegms from the Plays of Shakespeare*. London: Simpkin and Marshall, 1851. 236 pp.

2294. Mair, James Allan. "Shakespearean Proverbs, Mottoes, Maxims, etc." *A Handbook of Proverbs, Mottoes, Quotations and Phrases*. London: George Routledge and Sons, 1873. 82-99.

2295. Marsh, John B. *Familiar Proverbial and Select Sayings from Shakespeare*. London: Simpkin, Marshall, 1863. 162 pp.

2296. Marx, Ludwig. "Die Sentenz in den Dramen Shakespeares." Diss. Gießen, 1915. 94 pp.

2297. Maxwell, J. C. "Charles G. Smith, *Shakespeare's Proverb Lore.*" *Notes and Queries* 210 (1965): 357-359.

2298. McCullen, Joseph T. "Iago's Use of Proverbs for Persuasion." *Studies in English Literature* 4 (1964): 247-262.

2299. Mieder, Wolfgang. "'Sein oder Nichtsein'—und kein Ende: Zum Weiterleben des Hamlet-Zitats in unserer Zeit." *Der Sprachdienst* 23 (1979): 81-85. Also in *Sprichwort, Redensart, Zitat: Tradierte Formelsprache in der Moderne.* Bern: Peter Lang, 1985. 125-130.

2300. Miller, Anthony. "A Reminiscence of Erasmus in *Hamlet*, III, ii, 92-95." *English Language Notes* 24 (1986): 19-22.

2301. Monitto, Gary V. "Shakespeare and Culmann's [*sic*] *Sententiae pueriles.*" *Notes and Queries* 230 ns 32 (1985): 30-31.

2302. Morgan, Aaron Augustus, ed. *The Mind of Shakespeare, as Exhibited in His Works.* London: Chapman and Hall, 1860. 321 pp.; London: George Routledge and Sons, 1876, 1880. 360 pp. (1st ed., pp. 296-302).

2303. Müller-Schwefe, Gerhard. "Sprichwörter als Übersetzungsproblem: Zum Beispiel in Shakespeares *Romeo und Juliet.*" *Die neueren Sprachen* 71 (1972): 341-351. Also in *Ergebnisse der Sprichwörterforschung.* Ed. Wolfgang Mieder. Bern: Peter Lang, 1978. 201-211.

2304. Nares, Robert. *A Glossary: or, Collection of Words, Phrases, Names, and Allusions to Customs, Proverbs, etc., Which Have Been Thought to Require Illustration in the Works of English Authors, Particularly Shakespeare and His Contemporaries*, 2 vols. London: R. Tripbook, 1822; Ed. James O. Halliwell. London: J. R. Smith, 1859. 584pp.; Eds. James O. Halliwell and Thomas Wright. London: George Routledge and Sons, 1905.; rpt. Detroit, Michigan: Gale Research Company, 1966. 981 pp.

2305. Needhan, Gwendolyn B. "New Light on Maids 'Leading Apes in Hell.'" *Journal of American Folklore* 75 (1962): 106-119.

2306. Norrick, Neal R. "Stock Similes." *Journal of Literary Semantics* 15 (1986): 39-52.

2307. Norrick, Neal R. "Semantic Aspects of Comparative Noun-Adjective Compounds." *Neuere Forschungen zur Wortbildung und Historiographie der Linguistik: Festgabe für Herbert E. Brekle*. Eds. Brigitte Asbach-Schnitker and Johannes Roggenhofer. Tübingen: Gunter Narr, 1987. 145-154.

2308. Obelkevich, James. "Proverbs and Social History." *The Social History of Language*. Eds. Peter Burke and Roy Porter. Cambridge: Cambridge University Press, 1987. 43-72. Also in *Wise Words: Essays on the Proverb*. Ed. Wolfgang Mieder. New York: Garland Publishing, 1994. 211-252.

2309. Orkin, Martin [R.]. "The Poor Cat's Adage and Other Shakespearian Proverbs in Elizabethan Grammar-School Education." *English Studies in Africa* 21 (1978): 79-88.

2310. Orkin, Martin [R.]. "Shakespeare's 'Clothes of Gold & Riche Veluet Weede': Proverb Allusions, Especially in *Othello*." *Unisa English Studies* 17, 1 (1979): 18-26.

2311. Orkin, Martin R. "A Proverb Allusion and a Proverbial Association in *1 Henry IV*." *Notes and Queries* 228 ns 30 (1983): 120-121.

2312. Orkin, Martin R. "A Cluster of Proverb Allusions in *Julius Caesar*." *Notes and Queries* 229 ns 31 (1984): 195-196.

2313. Orkin, Martin R. "'After a Collar Comes a Halter' in *1 Henry IV*." *Notes and Queries* 229 ns 31 (1984): 188-189.

2314. Orkin, Martin R. "Shakespeare's *As You Like It*." *Explicator* 42, 2 (1984): 5-7.

2315. Orkin, Martin R. "Shakespeare's *Henry IV, I*." *Explicator* 42, 4 (1984): 11-12.

2316. Orkin, Martin R. "Sir John Falstaff's Taste for Proverbs in *Henry IV, Part 1*." *English Studies* 65, 5 (1984): 392-404.

2317. Orkin, Martin R. "'He Shows a Fair Pair of Heels' in *1 Henry IV* and Elsewhere." *English Language Notes* 23, 1 (1985): 19-23.

2318. Orkin, Martin R. "Touchstone's Swiftness and Sententiousness." *English Language Notes* 27, 1 (1989): 42-47.

2319. Partridge, Eric. "Clichés." *A Charm of Words: Essays and Papers on Language.* New York: The Macmillan Company, 1961. 44-54.

2320. Pfeffer, Karl. *Das elisabethanische Sprichwort in seiner Verwendung bei Ben Jonson.* Diss. Gießen, 1933. Gießen: Richard Glagow, 1933. 32-35.

2321. Preis, A. "Shakespeare, Bacon, and English Proverbs." *Notes and Queries* 190 (1946): 146.

2322. Purcell, J. M. "*Antony and Cleopatra*, I, i, 42-43." *Notes and Queries* 203 (1958): 187-188.

2323. Purcell, J. M. "*Comedy of Errors*, II, ii, 57." *Notes and Queries* 203 (1958): 180.

2324. Purcell, J. M. "*Twelfth Night*, II, ii, 27-28." *Notes and Queries* 203 (1958): 375-376.

2325. Rendall, Vernon. "Proverbs and Popular Similes." *The Saturday Review* 148 (October 19, 1929): 443.

2326. Rice, Warner G. "'To Turn Turk.'" *Modern Language Notes* 46 (1931): 153-154.

2327. Schmidt-Hidding, Wolfgang. "William Shakespeare." *Englische Idiomatik in Stillehre und Literatur.* München: Max Hueber, 1962. 27-45.

2328. Segerström, Sigurd. "'Something Is Rotten in the State of Denmark.'" *Moderna Språk* 9 (1915): 199-203.

2329. Simonds, Peggy Muñoz. "Sacred and Sexual Motifs in *All's Well That Ends Well*." *Renaissance Quarterly* 42, 1 (1989): 33-59.

2330. Sjögren, Gunnar. "'Get Thee to a Nunnery.'" *Moderna Språk* 53 (1959): 119-125.

2331. Smith, Charles George. *Shakespeare's Proverb Lore: His Use of Sententiae of Leonard Culman and Publilius Syrus.* Cambridge, Massachusetts: Harvard University Press, 1963. 181 pp.

2332. Sprenger, R. "Eine Shakespearesche Redewendung bei Annette von Droste-Hülshoff." *Archiv für das Studium der neueren Sprachen und Literaturen* 115 (1905): 176-177.

2333. Stenhagen, Alfred. "'Something Is Rotten in the State of Denmark.'" *Moderna Språk* 10 (1916): 28-29.

2334. Stevenson, Burton, ed. *The Home Book of Shakespeare Quotations*. New York: Charles Scribner's Sons, 1966. 2055 pp.

2335. Taylor, Archer. "Shakespeare's Wellerisms." *Southern Folklore Quarterly* 15 (1951): 170.

2336. Thaler, Alwin. "'In My Mind's Eye, Horatio.'" *Shakespeare Quarterly* 7 (1956): 351-354.

2337. Thiselton Dyer, Thomas Firminger. *Folk-lore of Shakespeare*. London: Griffith, 1883; New York: Dutton, 1883; New York: Harper and Brothers, 1884. 416-444.

2338. Thümmel, Julius. "Über die Sentenz im Drama, namentlich bei Shakespeare, Goethe und Schiller." *Jahrbuch der deutschen Shakespeare Gesellschaft* 14 (1879): 97-114.

2339. Tilley, Morris Palmer. "'Good Drink Makes Good Blood.'" *Modern Language Notes* 39 (1924): 153-155.

2340. Tilley, Morris Palmer. "Pun and Proverb as Aids to Unexplained Shakespearean Jest." *Studies in Philology* 21 (1924): 492-495.

2341. Tilley, Morris Palmer. "*Much Ado about Nothing* (V, 1, 178)." *Modern Language Notes* 40 (1925): 186-188.

2342. Tilley, Morris Palmer. *Elizabethan Proverb Lore in Lyly's "Euphues" and in Pettie's "Petite Pallace" with Parallels from Shakespeare*. New York: The Macmillan Company, 1926. 461 pp.

2343. Tilley, Morris Palmer. "Unnoted Proverbs and Proverbial Allusions in *Twelfth Night*." *Philological Quarterly* 6 (1927): 306-311.

2344. Tilley, Morris Palmer. "'Twill Be Thine Another Day.'" *Modern Language Notes* 52 (1937): 394-397.

2345. Tilley, Morris Palmer. "Shakespeare Proverb Index." *A Dictionary of the Proverbs in England in the Sixteenth and Seventeenth Centuries.* Ann Arbor: University of Michigan Press, 1950. 803-808.

2346. Tuohy, Mother Paul Marie. "The Function of Proverbs in the First Two Scenes of *Hamlet.*" M. A. Thesis. Catholic University of America, 1962. 58 pp.

2347. Voigt, Hermann. *Gleichnisse und Metaphern in Shakespeares Dramen.* Straßburg: Müh, 1904. 115 pp.

2348. Wahl, Morris Callman. "Das parömiologische Sprachgut bei Shakespeare." *Jahrbuch der deutschen Shakespeare Gesellschaft* 22 (1887): 45-130; 23 (1888), 21-98.

2349. Walbran, C. J., ed. *A Dictionary of Shakespeare Quotations: Being a Collection of the Maxims, Proverbs, and Most Remarkable Passages in the Poems and Plays of Shakespeare.* London: Simpkin, Marshall and Company, 1849. 218 pp.

2350. Weekley, Ernest. "Proverbs Considered." *The Atlantic Monthly* 145 (April 1930): 504-512.

2351. Weinstock, Horst. "Die dramatische Funktion elisabethanischer Sprichwörter und Sentenzen bei Shakespeare (einschließlich der Sprichwortanspielungen)." Diss. München, 1956. 171 pp. Published as *Die Funktion elisabethanischer Sprichwörter und Pseudosprichwörter bei Shakespeare.* Heidelberg: Carl Winter, 1966. 227 pp.

2352. Whiting, Bartlett Jere. "'Old Maids Lead Apes in Hell.'" *Englische Studien* 70 (1936): 337-351.

2353. Williams, George Walton. "Shakespeare Metaphors of Health, Food, Sport, and Life-Preserving Rest." *Journal of Medieval and Renaissance Studies* 14, 2 (1984): 187-202.

2354. Wilson, F. P. "Shakespeare and the Diction of Common Life." *Proceedings of the British Academy for the Promotion of Historical, Philosophical and Philological Studies* (1941): 167-197. A "corrected and expanded" version in Wilson's *Shakespearean and Other Studies.* Ed. Helen Gardner. Oxford: Clarendon Press, 1969. 100-129.

2355. Wilson, F. P. "English Proverbs and Dictionaries of Proverbs." *The Library* 4th ser. 26 (1945): 51-71.

2356. Wilson, F. P. "The Proverbial Wisdom of Shakespeare." *Modern Humanities Research Association* 1 (1961) 1-24. Also in *The Wisdom of Many: Essays on the Proverb*. Eds. Wolfgang Mieder and Alan Dundes. New York: Garland Publishing, 1981. 174-189.

2357. Wilson, K. J. "Shakespeare's 'Tameness of a Wolf.'" *Notes and Queries* 223 ns 25 (1978): 149.

2358. Wurth, Leopold. *Das Wortspiel bei Shakespeare*. Wien: Braunmüller, 1895. 255 pp.

SHAW, GEORGE BERNARD (1856-1951)
2359. Barrick, Mac E. "[Let Justice Be Done] Though the Ceiling Fall." *The Shaw Review* 21 (1978): 31.

2360. Bryan, George B., and Wolfgang Mieder. *The Proverbial Bernard Shaw: An Index to Proverbs in the Works of George Bernard Shaw*. Westport, Connecticut: Greenwood Press, 1994. 286 pp.

2361. Schmidt-Hidding, Wolfgang. "Oscar Wilde und George Bernard Shaw." *Englische Idiomatik in Stillehre und Literatur*. München: Max Hueber, 1962. 71-76.

SHENSTONE, WILLIAM (1714-1763)
2362. Steensma, Robert C. "A Legal Proverb in Defoe, Swift, and Shenstone." *Proverbium* No. 10 (1968): 248.

SHIH NAI-AN (17th cent.)
2363. Eberhard, Wolfram. "Some Notes on the Use of Proverbs in Chinese Novels." *Proverbium* No. 9 (1967): 201-209. Also in *Studies in Chinese Folklore and Related Essays*. Bloomington: Indiana University Press, 1970. 176-181.

SHOLOKHOV, MIKAIL A. (1905-1984)
2364. Koltakov, S. A. "Poslovitsy i pogovorki v romane M. A. Sholokhova *Tikhii Don*." *Russkii iazyk v shkole* No. 1 (1987): 50-55.

SIDNEY, Sir PHILIP (1554-1586)

2365. Caldwell, Charles Barret. "Proverbs and Proverbial Phrases in Sidney's *Arcadia*, Books I-III." M. A. Thesis. Stetson University, 1937. 138 pp.

2366. Jordain, V. L. "Webster's Change of Sidney's 'Wormish' to 'Womanish.'" *Notes and Queries* 222 ns 24 (1977): 135.

2367. Libbey, Edwin Bissell. "Proverbs and Proverbial Phrases in the Original Version and in Books IV-V of the 1593 Edition of Sidney's *Arcadia*." M. A. Thesis. Stetson University, 1939. 92 pp.

SIDRAK (14th cent.)

2368. Burton, T. L. "Proverbs, Sentences and Proverbial Phrases from the English *Sidrak*." *Mediaeval Studies* 51 (1989): 329-354.

SIGEL, KURT (1931—)

2369. Mieder, Wolfgang. "'Aus de windische Schprich de Wind rauslasse': Bermerkungen zu Kurt Sigels redensartlicher Dialektdichtung." *Der Sprachdienst* 23 (1979): 145-149. Also in *Sprichwort, Redensart, Zitat: Tradierte Formelsprache in der Moderne*. Bern: Peter Lang, 1985. 45-51; Kurt Sigel. *Geifer-, Gift- und Suddelverse: Gedichte, Prosa und Spinnericks in Frankfurter Mundart*. Frankfurt am Main: Heinz Schutt, 1989. 68-73.

SIMONIDES (c. 556-468 B. C.)

2370. Prittwitz-Gaffron, Erich von. *Das Sprichwort im griechischen Epigramm*. Diss. München, 1912. Gießen: Alfred Töpelmann, 1912. 5-6.

SIR CLYOMON AND SIR CLAMYDES (c. 1578)

2371. Whiting, Bartlett Jere. "*Sir Clyomon and Sir Clamydes*." *Proverbs in the Earlier English Drama*. Cambridge, Massachusetts: Harvard University Press, 1938; rpt. New York: Octagon Books, 1969. 263-266.

SIR GAWAIN AND THE GREEN KNIGHT (c. 1370)

2372. Haines, Victor Y. "'Hony soyt qui mal pence': Can the Reader Sin?" *Revue de l'Université d'Ottowa/University of Ottawa Quarterly* 53 (1983): 181-188.

SIRACH, JESUS (2nd cent. B. C.)

2373. Bauckmann, Ernst Günter. "Die Proverbien und die Sprüche des Jesus Sirach: Eine Untersuchung zum Strukturwandel der israelitischen

Weisheitslehre." *Zeitschrift für alttestamentliche Wissenschaft* 72 (1960): 33-63.

SKELTON, JOHN (c. 1460-1529)

2374. Kinsman, Robert Starr. "Skelton's *Magnyfycence*: The Strategy of the 'Olde Sayde Sawe.'" *Studies in Philology* 63 (1966): 99-125.

2375. Kinsman, Robert Starr. "The Voices of Dissonance: Pattern in Skelton's *Colyn Cloute.*" *Huntington Library Quarterly* 26 (1963): 291-313.

2376. Mauch, Thomas Karl. 'Proverbial Material as a Weapon of Satire: John Skelton.' "The Role of the Proverb in Early Tudor Literature." Diss. University of California at Los Angeles 1963. 185-237, 265-269.

2377. Neuss, Paula. "Proverbial Skelton." *Studia Neophilologica* 54 (1982): 237-246.

2378. Neuss, Paula. "The Sixteenth-Century English 'Proverb' Play." *Comparative Drama* 18, 1 (1984): 1-18.

2379. Welsh, Andrew. "[John Skelton and the Proverb]." *Roots of Lyric: Primitive Poetry and Modern Poetics*. Princeton, New Jersey: Princeton University Press, 1978. 208-215, 217-219.

2380. Wentersdorf, Karl P. "Chaucer's Worthless Butterfly." *English Language Notes* 14 (1977): 167-172.

2381. Whiting, Bartlett Jere. "John Skelton's *Magnificence.*" *Proverbs in the Earlier English Drama*. Cambridge, Massachusetts: Harvard University Press, 1938; rpt. Octagon Books, 1969. 85-90.

SKUPY, HANS-HORST (1942—)

2382. Mieder, Wolfgang. "'Jedem das Sein.': Zu den sprichwörtlichen Aphorismen von Hans-Horst Skupy." *Sprachspiegel* 51 (1995): 137-144.

SLOWACKI, JULJUSZ (1809-1849)

2383. Kasjan, Jan Miroslaw. *Przyslowia i metaforyka potaczna w twórczości Slowackiego*. Torun: Praca wydana na zlecenie polskiej akademii nauk, 1966. 172 pp.

SLUNG, MICHELE (20th cent.)

2384. Wienker-Piepho, Sabine. "Sozialisation durch Sprichwörter: Am Beispiel eines anglo-amerikanischen Bestsellers." *Proverbium: Yearbook of International Proverb Scholarship* 8 (1991): 179-189.

SMILOVSKY, ALOIS (1837-1883)

2385. Mukařovský, Jan. "Přislovi jako součást kontextu." *Cestami poetiky a estetiky.* Praha: Edice Dilna, 1971. 277-359.

SMITH, JAMES (1605-1667)

2386. Newcomb, Robert. "Poor Richard and the English Epigram." *Philological Quarterly* 40 (1961): 270-280.

SMITH, THOMAS (1513-1577)

2387. Mauch, Thomas Karl. "The Role of the Proverb in Early Tudor Literature." Diss. University of California at Los Angeles, 1963. 148-162.

SMOLLETT, TOBIAS GEORGE (1721-1771)

2388. Boggs, W. Arthur. "Win Jenkins' Archaisms and Proverbial Phrases." *Language Quarterly* 4 (1965): 33-36.

2389. Taylor, Archer. "Proverbial Materials in Tobias Smollett, *The Adventures of Sir Launcelot Greaves.*" *Southern Folklore Quarterly* 21 (1957): 85-92.

SOCRATES (c. 497-c. 406 B. C.)

2390. Wilkins, Eliza Gregory. *"Know Thyself" in Greek and Latin Literature.* Diss. University of Chicago, 1917. Chicago: University of Chicago Libraries, 1917. 104 pp.

SOLZHENITSYN, ALEKSANDR (1918—)

2391. Kohan, John. "Peasants, Proverbs, and Problems of Historical Narrative in *August 1914.*" *Ulbandus Review* 2 (1979): 139-145.

SONGE DU VERGIER (c. 1370)

2392. Bar, Francis. "Langage familier et proverbes dans la première partie du *Songe du Vergier.*" *Études de langue et de littérature du moyen âge offertes à Felix Lecov par ses collègues, ses élèves et ses amis.* Eds. Gabriel Bianciotto, Joel Grisward, Geneviève Hasenohr, and Philippe Ménard. Paris: H. Champion, 1973. 7-17.

SOPHOCLES (c. 497-c. 406 B. C.)

2393. Harrison, Jane E. "Pandora's Box." *Journal of Hellenic Studies* 20 (1900): 99-114.

2394. Koch, Joh. Georg E. "Quaestionum de proverbis apud Aeschylum, Sophoclem, Euripidem." Diss. Königsberg, 1877. 92 pp.

2395. Wolf, Eugen. *Sentenz und Reflexion bei Sophokles*. Diss. Tübingen, 1910. Tübingen: H. Laupp, Jr., 1910. 177 pp. Leipzig: Dieterich, 1910. 145 pp.

SOTTIE DES SOTS TRIUMPHANS (1475)

2396. Dane, Joseph A. "Linguistic Trumpery: Notes on a French *Sottie* (Recueil Trepperel, No. 10)." *The Romanic Review* 71 (1980): 114-121.

SOYINKA, WOLE (1934—)

2397. Avery-Coger, Greta Margaret Kay McCormick. "Indexes of Subjects, Themes, and Proverbs in the Plays of Wole Soyinka." Diss. University of Colorado, 1980. 275 pp.

2398. Lindfors, Bernth. "Wole Soyinka and the Horses of Speech." *Essays on African Literature*. Ed. W. L. Ballard. Atlanta: Georgia State University, 1973. 79-87.

2399. Richards, David. "Owe l'esin òrò: Proverbs Like Horses: Wole Soyinka's *Death and the King's Horseman*." *The Journal of Commonwealth Literature* 19 (1984): 86-97.

SPENCER, HERBERT (1820-1903)

2400. Angenot, Marc. "'La lutte pour la vie': Migrations et usages d'un idéologème." *La locution: Actes du colloque international Université McGill, Montréal, 15-16 octobre 1984*. Eds. Giuseppe Di Stefano and Russell G. McGillivray. Montréal: Editions CERES, 1984. 171-190.

SPENSER, EDMUND (1552-1599)

2401. Adams, Gustav. "Proverb Lore in Spenser's Minor Poems." M. A. Thesis. Stetson University, 1935. 127 pp.

2402. Bevins, Lloyd Edward. "Spenser's Use of Proverbial Material in *The Faerie Queene*." M. A. Thesis. University of Virginia, 1940. 93 pp.

2403. Cincotta, Mary Ann. "Reinventing Authority in *The Faerie Queene.*" *Studies in Philology* 80, 1 (1983): 25-52.

2404. Doyle, Charles Clay. "Smoke and Fire: Spenser's Counter Proverb." *Proverbium* No. 18 (1972): 683-685.

2405. Doyle, Charles Clay. "Folklore." *Spenser Encyclopedia.* Eds. A. C. Hamilton et al. Toronto: University of Toronto Press, 1990. 311-312.

2406. Feeny, Sarah Jane. "The Aesthetics of Orality and Textuality in Spenser's *Faerie Queene.*" Diss. University of Missouri, 1991. 204 pp.

2407. Kinsman, Robert Starr. "Proverbs." *Spenser Encyclopedia.* Eds. A. C. Hamilton et al. Toronto: University of Toronto Press, 1990. 562-565.

2408. Maxwell, J. C. "Charles G. Smith, *Spenser's Proverb Lore.*" *Notes and Queries* 217 (1972): 80.

2409. Sessums, A. C. 'Spenser's Use of Proverbs.' "Proceedings of Dr. Greenlaw's Seminary 'C.'" No. 55 (1926-27): unpaginated. Unpublished student essays in The Johns Hopkins University Library (Baltimore, Maryland).

2410. Smith, Charles George. "Sententious Theory in Spenser's *Legend of Friendship.*" *A Journal of English Literary History* 11 (1935): 165-195.

2411. Smith, Charles George. *Spenser's Proverb Lore: With Special Reference to His Use of the Sententiae of Leonard Culman and Publilius Syrus.* Cambridge, Massachusetts: Harvard University Press, 1970. 365 pp.

2412. Tung, Mason. "Spenser's 'Emblematic' Imagery: A Study of Emblematics." *Spenser Studies: A Renaissance Poetry Annual* 5 (1984): 185-207.

STAVENHAGEN, FRITZ (1876-1906)

2413. Lindow, Wolfgang. "Volkstümliches Sprachgut in der neuniederdeutschen Dialektdichtung." Diss. Kiel, 1960. Part I, 131-133.

2414. Lindow, Wolfgang. "Das Sprichwort als stilistisches und dramatisches Mittel in der Schauspieldichtung Stavenhagens, Boßdorfs und Schureks." *Niederdeutsches Jahrbuch* 84 (1961): 97-116.

STEINBERG, WERNER (1913—)

2415. Kantola, Markhu. "Zum phraseologischen Wortpaar in der deutschen Gegenwartssprache." *Beiträge zur allgemeinen und germanistischen Phraseologieforschung: Internationales Symposium in Oulu 13.-15. Juni 1986.* Ed. Jarmo Korhonen. Oulu: Oulun Yliopisto, 1987. 111-128.

STEPNEY, WILLIAM (16th cent.)

2416. Selig, Karl-Ludwig. "Los refranes espanoles en *The Spanish Schoole-Master* de William Stepney." *Anuario de Filologia* 89 (1969-1970): 31-42.

STERNE, LAURENCE (1713-1768)

2417. Rogers, Pat. "Tristram Shandy's Polite Conversation." *Essays in Criticism* 32 (1982): 305-320.

2418. Ross, Ian Campbell, and Noha Saad Nassar. "Trim (-Tram), Like Master, Like Man: Servant and Sexton in Sterne's *Tristram Shandy* and *A Political Romance.*" *Notes and Queries* 234 ns 36 (1989): 62-65.

2419. Schmidt-Hidding, Wolfgang. "Laurence Sterne." *Englische Idiomatik in Stillehre und Literatur.* München: Max Hueber, 1962. 57-59.

STESICHORUS (640-c. 555 B. C.)

2420. Davies, M. "The Paremiographers on 'Ta tria ton Stesichorou.'" *Journal of Hellenic Studies* 102 (1982): 206-210.

STILL, JAMES A. (1906—)

2421. Roberts, Leonard. "Additional Notes on Archer Taylor's *On Troublesome Creek.*" *Kentucky Folklore Record* 8 (1962): 142-144.

2422. Taylor, Archer. "Proverbial Comparisons and Similes in *On Troublesome Creek.*" *Kentucky Folklore Record* 8 (1962): 87-96.

STIRLING, EDWARD (1807-94)

2423. Bryan, George B., and Wolfgang Mieder. "'As Sam Weller Said, When Finding Himself on the Stage': Wellerisms in Dramatizations of Charles Dickens' *Pickwick Papers.*" *Proverbium: Yearbook of International Proverb Scholarship* 11 (1994): 57-76.

STONEY, SAMUEL G. (born 1891)

2424. Yates, Irene. "A Collection of Proverbs and Proverbial Sayings from South Carolina Literature." *Southern Folklore Quarterly* 11 (1947): 187-199.

THE STONYHURST PAGEANTS (1610/1625)

2425. Whiting, Bartlett Jere. "*The Stonyhurst Pageants*." *Proverbs in the Earlier English Drama*. Cambridge, Massachusetts: Harvard University Press, 1938; rpt. New York: Octagon Books, 1969. 36-43.

STORM, THEODOR (1817-1888)

2426. Mieder, Wolfgang. "Die Funktion des Sprichwortes in Theodor Storms Werken." *Schriften der Theodor-Storm-Gesellschaft* 22 (1973): 95-114. Also in *Das Sprichwort in der deutschen Prosaliteratur des neunzehnten Jahrhunderts*. München: Wilhelm Fink, 1976. 168-187.

2427. Seiler, Friedrich. *Deutsche Sprichwörterkunde*. München: C. H. Beck, 1922, 1967. 65.

THE STORY OF KING DARIUS (1565)

2428. Whiting, Bartlett Jere. "*The Story of King Darius*." *Proverbs in the Earlier English Drama*. Cambridge, Massachusetts: Harvard University Press, 1938; rpt. New York: Octagon Books, 1969. 133-134.

STRABO (c. 63 B. C.-A. D. c. 19)

2429. Keim, J. "Sprichwörter uzd paroemiographische Überlieferung bei Strabo." Diss. München, 1909.

STRASSBURGER EIDE (842)

2430. Ewald, Konrad. "Formelhafte Wendungen in den *Straßburger Eiden*." *Vox Romanica* 23 (1964): 35-55.

STRATO (A. D. 2nd cent.)

2431. Prittwitz-Gaffron, Erich von. *Das Sprichwort im griechischen Epigramm*. Diss. München, 1912. Gießen: Alfred Töpelmann, 1912. 49-50.

STRITTMATTER, ERWIN (1912-1995)

2432. Mieder, Wolfgang. "Sprichwörter im modernen Sprachgebrauch." *Muttersprache* 85 (1975): 65-88. Also in *Ergebnisse der Sprichwörterforschung*. Bern: Peter Lang, 1978. 213-238; *Deutsche Sprichwörter in Literatur, Politik, Presse und Werbung*. Hamburg: Helmut Buske, 1983. 53-76.

2433. Spence, Hannelore Mueller. "Das Sprichwort in Erwin Strittmatters *Ole Bienkopp*." M. A. Thesis. University of Vermont, 1974. 121 pp.

STUART, JESSE (1907-84)
2434. Clarke, Mary Washington. "Proverbs, Proverbial Phrases, and Proverbial Comparisons in the Writings of Jesse Stuart." *Southern Folklore Quarterly* 29 (1965): 142-163.

2435. Clarke, Mary Washington. *Jesse Stuart's Kentucky*. New York: McGraw-Hill, 1968. 240 pp.

2436. Washington [Clarke], Mary Louise. "The Folklore of the Cumberlands as Reflected in the Writings of Jesse Stuart." Diss. University of Pennsylvania, 1960. 518 pp.

SUCKOW, RUTH (1892-1960)
2437. De Caro, Francis A. "Proverbs and Originality in Modern Short Fiction." *Western Folklore* 37 (1978): 30-38.

SÜSKIND, PATRICK (1949—)
2438. Wandruszka, Mario. "Contraintes instrumentales et liberté créatrice." *Europhras 88. Phraséologie Contrastive: Actes du Colloque International Klingenthal-Strasbourg, 12-16 mai 1988*. Ed. Gertrud Gréciano. Strasbourg: Université des Sciences Humaines, 1989. 453-458.

2439. Wandruszka, Mario. "Sprache aus Bildern." *Die europäische Sprachengemeinschaft: Deutsch—Französisch—English—Italienisch—Spanisch im Vergleich*. Tübingen: A. Francke, 1990. 51-76.

SUEVAS, SIGISMUND [a.k.a. S. Schwabe] (1527-1596)
2440. Broek, Marinus A. van den. "'Ein gut wort eine gute stat findet': Sprichwort und Redensart in Sigismund Suevus' *Spiegel des menschlichen Lebens*." *Diutscher Diute: Festschrift für Anthony van der Lee*. Eds. M. A. van den Broek and G. J. Jaspers. Amsterdam: Rodopi, 1983. 155-172.

SWEDENBORG, EMANUEL (1688-1772)
2441. Lansverk, Marvin Duane. "The Wisdom of Many, the Vision of One: The Proverbs of William Blake." Diss. University of Washington, 1988. 66-89.

SWIFT, JONATHAN (1667-1745)

2442. Bliss, Alan. "Irish Proverbs in Swift's *Polite Conversation.*" *Irish University Review* 9 (1979): 23-30.

2443. Carnochan, W. B. "Notes on Swift's Proverb Lore." *Yearbook of English Studies* 6 (1976): 63-69.

2444. Clark, John R. "Further 'Iliads' in Swift's Nut-shell." *Philological Quarterly* 51 (1972): 945-950.

2445. Jarrell, Mackie L. "The Proverbs in Swift's *Polite Conversation.*" *The Huntington Library Quarterly* 20 (1956): 15-38.

2446. Korkowski, Eugene. "Swift's Tub: Traditional Emblem and Proverbial Enigma." *Eighteenth-Century Life* 4 (1978): 100-103.

2447. Rogers, Pat. "Tristram Shandy's Polite Conversation." *Essays in Criticism* 32 (1982): 305-320.

2448. Schmidt-Hidding, Wolfgang. "Jonathan Swift." *Englische Idiomatik in Stillehre und Literatur*. München: Max Hueber, 1962. 45-52.

2449. Steensma, Robert C. "A Legal Proverb in Defoe, Swift, and Shenstone." *Proverbium* No. 10 (1968): 248.

SYLVAIN, GEORGES (1866-1924)

2450. Lang, George. "La Fontaine Transmogrified—Creole Proverbs and the *Cric? Crac!* of Georges Sylvain." *French Review* 63, 4 (1990): 679-693.

SYNESIOS (370-412)

2451. Sollert, Raphael. *Die Sprichwörter und sprichwörtlichen Redensarten bei Synesios von Kyrene*. Augsburg: Pfeiffer, 1910.

SZYMONOWICZ, SZYMONA (1558-1629)

2452. Swierczynska, Dobroslawa. "Przyslowia w *Sielankach* Szymona Szymonowica." *Ludowosc dawniej i dzis: studia folklorystyczne*. Eds. Ryszard Górski and Julian Krzyzanowski. Wroclaw: Ossolineum, 1973. 185-214.

T

TACITUS [P. Cornelius Tacitus] (c. 55-c. 120)

2453. Crum, Richard Henry. "'Blood, Sweat and Tears.'" *The Classical Journal* 42 (1947): 299-300.

2454. Jung, Paul. "Sprichwörter (Weisheit und Lüge)." *Sprachgebrauch, Sprachautorität, Sprachideologie.* Heidelberg: Quelle and Meyer, 1974. 99-109.

2455. Renehan, Robert. "A Proverbial Expression in Tacitus." *Classical Philology* 68 (1973): 114-115.

TALIAFERRO, HARDEN E. (c. 1818-1875)

2456. Whiting, Bartlett Jere. "Proverbial Sayings from *Fisher's River, North Carolina.*" *Southern Folklore Quarterly* 11 (1947): 173-185.

TALLEMENT DES RÉAUX, GÉDÉON (1619-90)

2457. Perrin-Naffakh, Anne-Marie. "Locutions et proverbes dans les *Fables de La Fontaine.*" *L'information littéraire* 31 (1979): 151-155. Also in *Proverbia in Fabula: Essays on the Relationship of the Fable and the Proverb.* Ed. Pack Carnes. Bern: Peter Lang, 1988. 285-294.

TAYLOR, BAYARD (1825-1878)

2458. Taylor, Archer. "Some Proverbial Expressions from Bayard Taylor's *Story of Kennett.*" *Keystone Folklore Quarterly* 6 (1961): 23-24.

TAYLOR, EDWARD (1642-1729)

2459. Arner, Robert D. "Folk Metaphors in Edward Taylor's *Meditation*, I, 40." *Seventeenth Century News* 31 (1973): 69.

2460. Arner, Robert D. "Proverbs in Edward Taylor's *Gods [sic] Determinations (Touching His Elect).*" *Southern Folklore Quarterly* 37 (1973): 1-13.

TAYLOR, JOHN (c. 1578-1653)

2461. Bruster, Douglas. "The Horn of Plenty: Cuckoldry and Capital in the Drama of the Age of Shakespeare." *Studies in English Literature 1500-1900* 30, 2 (1990): 195-215.

2462. Smith, Roland M. "Three Obscure English Proverbs [The game is not worth the candle; He that will swear will lie; Life is a pilgrimage]." *Modern Language Notes* 65 (1950): 441- 447.

TEPL, JOHANNES VON (1350-c. 1414)

2463. Mieder, Wolfgang. "Streitgespräch und Sprichwort-Antithetik: Ein Beitrag zur Ackerman aus Böhmen- und Sprichwortforschung." *Daphnis* 2 (1973): 1-32. Also in *Sprichwort—Wahrwort!? Studien zur Geschichte, Bedeutung und Funktion deutscher Sprichwörter.* Frankfurt am Main: Peter Lang, 1992. 113-149.

TERENCE [Publius Terentius Afer] (185-159 B. C.)

2464. Deutsch, Monroe E. "'Veni, Vidi, Vici.'" *Philological Quarterly* 4 (1925): 151-156.

2465. Pflügl, Franz Xaver. *Die lateinischen Sprichwörter bei Plautus und Terenz.* Straubing: A. Lechner, 1879/80. 44 pp.

2466. Roos, Paolo. *Sentenza e proverbio nell'antichità e i "Distici di Catone": Il testo latino e i volgarizzamenti italiani.* Brescia: Morcelliana, 1984. 254 pp.

2467. Wyss, Wilhelm von. *Die Sprüchwörter bei Römischen Komikern.* Diss. Zürich, 1889. Zürich: Friedrich Schulthess, 1889. 114 pp.

TEUSCHL, WOLFGANG (1943—)

2468. Kummer, Werner. "Die Sprüch-Wörter in Wolfgang Teuschls Bibelübersetzung *Da Jesus und seine Hawara.*" *Sprichwörter und Redensarten im interkulturellen Vergleich.* Eds. Annette Sabban and Jan Wirrer. Opladen: Westdeutscher Verlag, 1991. 128-138.

THACKERAY, WILLIAM MAKEPEACE (1811-1863)

2469. Mieder, Wolfgang. "'Wine, Women and Song': From Martin Luther to American T-Shirts." *Kentucky Folklore Record* 29 (1983): 89-101. Also in *Folk Groups and Folklore Genres: A Reader.* Ed. Elliott Oring. Logan: Utah State University Press, 1989. 279-290.

2470. Mieder, Wolfgang. "'Wine, Women and Song': Zur anglo-amerikanischen Überlieferung eines angeblichen Lutherspruches." *Germanisch-Romanische Monatsschrift* 65 ns 34 (1984): 385-403.

THEOCRITUS (c. 310-c. 250 B. C.)

2471. Baar, Adolf. *Sprichwörter und Sentenzen aus den griechischen Idyllendichtern.* Görz: Selbstverlag des Staatsgymnasiums, 1887. 41 pp.

THEOGNIS (c. 540-500 B. C.)

2472. Renehan, Robert. "An Unnoticed Proverb in Theognis." *Classical Review* 77 (1963): 131-132.

THERSITES (c. 1537)

2473. Whiting, Bartlett Jere. "*Thersites*." *Proverbs in the Earlier English Drama*. Cambridge, Massachusetts: Harvard University Press, 1938; rpt. New York: Octagon Books, 1969. 187-188.

THEYSBAERT, MICHIEL (16th cent.)

2474. "Spreekwoorden verzameld door Michiel Theysbaert 1594." *Vlaamsch Museum* 5 (1863): 367-376.

THOMASIUS, CHRISTIAN (1655-1728)

2475. Soliva, Claudio. "Ein Bibelwort in Geschichte und Recht [Alles nun, was ihr wollt, daß euch die Leute tun sollen, das tut ihr ihnen auch (So whatever you wish that men would do to you, do so to them); Was du nicht willst, daß man dir tu, das füg auch keinem andern zu (What you don't want one to do to you, don't do that to another)]." *"Unser Weg": Werkblatt der Schweizerischen Weggefährtinnen* Nos. 6-7 (1964): 51-57.

THOREAU, HENRY DAVID (1817-1862)

2476. Cameron, Kenneth Walter. "Emerson, Thoreau, *Elegant Extracts*, and Proverb Lore." *Emerson Society Quarterly* No. 6 (1957): 28-39.

2477. Loomis, C. Grant. "Henry David Thoreau as Folklorist." *Western Folklore* 16 (1957): 90-106.

2478. Moldenhauer, Joseph J. "The Rhetorical Function of Proverbs in *Walden*." *Journal of American Folklore* 80 (1967): 151-159.

2479. Reaver, J. Russell. "Thoreau's Ways with Proverbs." *American Transcendental Quarterly* 1 (1967): 2-7.

2480. Willis, Lonnie Leon. "Folklore in the Published Writings of Henry David Thoreau: A Study and a Compendium-Index." Diss. University of Colorado, 1966. 416 pp.

THURBER, JAMES (1894-1961)

2481. Carnes, Pack. "The American Face of Aesop: Thurber's Fables and Tradition." *Moderna Språk* 79 (1986): 3-17. Also in *Proverbia in*

Fabula: Essays on the Relationship of the Fable and the Proverb. Ed. Pack Carnes. Bern: Peter Lang, 1988. 311-331.

2482. Carnes, Pack. "The Fable and the Proverb: Intertexts and Reception." *Proverbium: Yearbook of International Proverb Scholarship* 8 (1991): 55-76.

TIRSO DE MOLINA [Gabriel Téllez] (1584-1648)
2483. Hayes, Francis Clement. "The Use of Proverbs in the 'Siglo de Oro' Drama: An Introductory Study." Diss. University of North Carolina, 1936. 227 pp.

2484. Hayes, Francis Clement. "The Use of Proverbs as Titles and Motives in the 'Siglo de Oro' Drama: Tirso de Molina." *Hispanic Review* 7 (1939): 310-323.

2485. Recoules, Henri. "Refranero y entremés." *Boletin de la Biblioteca Menedez Pelayo* 52 (1976): 135-153.

TOLKIEN, J. R. R. [John Ronald Reuel Tolkien] (1892-1973)
2486. Boswell, George W. "Proverbs and Phraseology in Tolkien's *Lord of the Rings* Complex." *University of Mississippi Studies in English* 10 (1969): 59-65.

TOLSTOY, LEV NIKOLAEVICH (1828-1910)
2487. Donskov, Andrew. "Tolstoj's Use of Proverbs in *The Power of Darkness.*" *Russian Literature* 9 (1975): 67-80.

2488. Hogan, Rebecca S. H. "The Wisdom of Many, the Wit of One: The Narrative Function of the Proverb in Tolstoy's *Anna Karenina* and Trollope's *Orley Farm.*" Diss. University of Colorado, 1984. 275 pp.

2489. Morson, Gary Saul. "Tolstoy's Absolute Language." *Critical Inquiry* 7 (1981): 667-687.

TOM TYLER AND HIS WIFE (c. 1661)
2490. Whiting, Bartlett Jere. "*Tom Tyler and His Wife.*" *Proverbs in the Earlier English Drama.* Cambridge, Massachusetts: Harvard University Press, 1938; rpt. New York: Octagon Books, 1969. 188-194.

TOMEO, JAVIER (1931–)

2491. Fournié, Sylvie. "Las expresiones fijas en una estética de la repetición: *Amado Monstruo* de Javier Tomeo." *Paremia* No. 2 (1993): 145-150.

TORRES NAHARRO, BARTOLOMÉ de (c. 1476-c. 1524)

2492. Hayes, Francis Clement. "The Use of Proverbs in the 'Siglo de Oro' Drama: An Introductory Study." Diss. University of North Carolina, 1936. 19-36.

THE TOWNELEY PLAYS [Wakefield Cycle of Mystery Plays] (14th cent.)

2493. Norrick, Neal R. "Der Vergleich im Mittelenglischen unter besonderer Berücksichtigung der *Towneley Plays*." *Neuphilologische Mitteilungen* 88 (1987): 256-267.

2494. Whiting, Bartlett Jere. "*The Towneley Plays*." *Proverbs in the Earlier English Drama*. Cambridge, Massachusetts: Harvard University Press, 1938; rpt. New York: Octagon Books, 1969. 11-22.

TRAVEN, BRUNO [a.k.a. Traven Torsvan and Ret Marut] (1890-1969)

2495. Baumann, Michael L. "The Question of Idioms in B. Traven's Writings." *German Quarterly* 60 (1987): 171-192.

THE TRIAL OF TREASURE (1567)

2496. Whiting, Bartlett Jere. "*The Trial of Treasure*." *Proverbs in the Earlier English Drama*. Cambridge, Massachusetts: Harvard University Press, 1938; rpt. New York: Octagon Books, 1969. 134-136.

TRIOLET, ELSA (1903–)

2497. Marsenac, Jean. "La canne blanche: Les proverbes d'Elsa Triolet." *Europe* 506 (1971): 82-85.

TRISTAN DE NANTEUIL (14th cent.)

2498. Sinclair, K. V. "Proverbial Material in the Late French Epic of *Tristan de Nanteuil*." *Speculum* 38 (1963): 285-294.

TROLLOPE, ANTHONY (1815-1882)

2499. Hogan, Rebecca S. H. "The Wisdom of Many, the Wit of One: The Narrative Function of the Proverb in Tolstoy's *Anna Karenina* and Trollope's *Orley Farm*." Diss. University of Colorado, 1984. 275 pp.

2500. Schmidt-Hidding, Wolfgang. "Anthony Trollope." *Englische Idiomatik in Stillehre und Literatur*. München: Max Hueber, 1962. 69-71.

TRUMAN, HARRY S. (1884-1972)
2501. Mieder, Wolfgang, and George B. Bryan. *The Proverbial Harry S. Truman: An Index to Proverbs in the Works of Harry S. Truman*. [forthcoming]. 254 pp.

TUCHOLSKY, KURT (1890-1935)
2502. Grésillon, Almuth, and Dominique Maingueneau. "Polyphonie, proverbe et détournement, ou un proverbe peut en cacher un autre." *Langages* 19, 73 (1984): 112-125.

TUTUOLA, AMOS (1920—)
2503. Ferris, William R. "Folklore and the African Novelist: Achebe and Tutuola." *Journal of American Folklore* 86 (1973): 25-36.

TWAIN, MARK [Samuel Langhorne Clemens] (1835-1910)
2504. Sinnema, John R. "The Dutch Origin of 'Play Hookey.'" *American Speech* 45 (1970): 205-209.

2505. West, Victor Royse. "Folklore in the Works of Mark Twain." *University of Nebraska Studies in Language, Literature, and Criticism* 10 (1930): 1-87.

TYNDALE, WILLIAM (c. 1490-1536)
2506. Mauch, Thomas Karl. "The Role of the Proverb in Early Tudor Literature." Diss. University of California at Los Angeles, 1963. 140-145, 163-179, 271-272.

2507. Whiting, Bartlett Jere. "Studies in the Middle English Proverb," 3 vols. Diss. Harvard University, 1932. 1386 pp.

U

UDALL, NICHOLAS (1505-1556)

2508. Whiting, Bartlett Jere. "Nicholas Udall's *Ralph Roister Doister.*" *Proverbs in the Earlier English Drama*. Cambridge, Massachusetts: Harvard University Press, 1938; rpt. New York: Octagon Books, 1969. 212-216.

UHLENBRUCK, GERHARD (1929—)

2509. Mieder, Wolfgang. "'Ein Aphoristiker dreht oft das Sprichwort im Munde herum': Zu den Aphorismen von Gerhard Uhlenbruck." *Sprachspiegel* 37 (1981): 66-75. Also in *Med: Schweizer Magazin für ärzliche Ökonomie* No. 10 (1981): 54-56, 59; *Sprichwort, Redensart, Zitat: Tradierte Formelsprache in der Moderne*. Bern: Peter Lang, 1985. 53-63.

ULRICH VON SINGENBERG [Truchseß von St. Gallen] (fl. 1209-1228)

2510. Hofmeister, Wernfried. *Sprichwortartige Mikrotexte als literarische Medien, dargestellt an der hochdeutschen politischen Lyrik des Mittelalters*. Bochum: Norbert Brockmeyer, 1995. 255-260.

ULRICH VON TURHEIM (c. 1195-c. 1250)

2511. Leitzmann, Albert. "Sprichwörter und Sprichwörtliches bei Ulrich von Türheim." *Beiträge zur Geschichte der deutschen Sprache und Literatur* 65 (1941-1942): 164-170.

ULRICH VON ZATZIKHOVEN (13th cent.)

2512. Hofmann, Liselotte. *Der volkskundliche Gehalt der mittelhochdeutschen Epen von 1100 bis gegen 1250*. Zeulenroda: Bernhard Sporn, 1939. 72-73.

2513. Mone, Franz Joseph. "Zur Literatur und Geschichte der Sprichwörter." *Quellen und Forschungen zur Geschichte der deutschen Literatur und Sprache* 1 (1830): 186-214, especially 204-207.

2514. Schütze, Paul. *Das volkstümliche Element im Stil Ulrich von Zatzikhovens*. Diss. Greifswald, 1883. Greifswald: Julius Abel, 1883. 42 pp.

ULSTER SAGAS (11th cent.)

2515. Bell, Alice M. "Proverbs, Sententious Language and Proverbial Phrases in the Ulster Sagas." M. A. Thesis, Radcliffe College, 1939.

USPENSKII, GLEB I. (1843-1902)
2516. Plotnikova, N. I. "Poslovitsy i pogovorki v tvorchestve G. I. Uspenskogo." *Vestnik Moskovskogo Universiteta, Seriia VII, Filologiia, Zhurnalistika* No. 7 (1976): 52-57.

V

VAENIUS, OTHO (1556-1629)

2517. Dittrich, Lothar. "Emblematische Weisheit und naturwissenschaftliche Realität." *Die Sprache der Bilder: Realität und Bedeutung in der niederländischen Malerei des 17. Jahrhunderts.* Eds. Wolfgang J. Müller, Konrad Renger, and Rüdiger Klessmann. Braunschweig: ACO Druck, 1978. 21-33. Also in *Jarbuch für Internationale Germanistik* 13 (1981): 36-60.

VALDÉS, ALFONSO de (c. 1490-1532)

2518. Morreale, Margherita. "Sentencias y refranes en los *Diálogos* de Alfonso de Valdés." *Revista de Literatura* 12 (1957): 3-14.

VALDÉS, JUAN de (c. 1500-1541)

2519. Andreotto, Miguel Angel. "Los refranes del *Diálogo de la Lengua*, de Juan de Valdés: explicación y confrontación literaria." *Boletin de filologia* 4 (1944): 95-115.

2520. Berkowitz, H. C. "The *Quaderno de refranes castellanos* of Juan de Valdés." *Romania Review* 16 (1925): 71-86.

VALDIVIELSO, JOSÉ de (c. 1560-1638)

2521. Arias, Ricardo. "Refranes y frases proverbiales en el teatro de Valdivielso." *Revista de Archivos, Bibliotecas y Museos* 81 (1978): 241-288.

2522. Arias, Ricardo. "Función de los proverbios en el teatro de Valdivielso." *Actas del Sexto Congreso Internacional de Hispanistas celebrado en Toronto del 22 al 26 de agosto de 1977.* Eds. Alan M. Gordon and Evelyn Rugg. Toronto: Department of Spanish and Portuguese, University of Toronto, 1980. 67-69.

VALÉRY, PAUL (1871-1945)

2523. Mautner, Franz H. "Maxim(e)s, Sentences, Fragmente, Aphorismen." *Actes du 4e Congrès de l'Association Internationale de Littérature Comparée, Fribourg 1964.* Ed. François Jost. The Hague: Mouton, 1966. II, 812-819.

VALLUVAR (6th/7th cent.)

2524. Sorrentino, Antonio. "Folkloristic Structures of Proverbs in the *Tirukkural.*" *Proverbium: Yearbook of International Proverb Scholarship* 6 (1989): 129-137.

VANCURA, VLADISLAV (1891-1942)

2525. Horalek, Karel. "Prislovi a aforismus." *Slovensky Národopis* 29 (1981): 557-561.

2526. Opelik, Jiri. "'Hrdelni pre' anebo prislovi cili k poetice jedneho titulu." *Česka Literatura* 18 (1970): 382-398.

VARGAS LLOSA, MARIO (1936—)

2527. Conca, Maria. "Sobre la semiòtica dels refranys." *Estudis de literatura catalana en honor de Josep Romeu i Fugueras*. Eds. Lola Badia and Josep Massot i Muntaner. Barcelona: Publicacions de l'Abadia de Montserrat, 1986. I, 345-355.

2528. Segura García, Blanca. "Las expresiones idiomáticas como medio para fingir oralidad en la novela de Mario Vargas Llosa." *Paremia* No. 2 (1993): 163-167.

VAUX, THOMAS, 2nd Baron Vaux of Harrowden (1509-1556)

2529. Landon, Sydney Ann. "Sundry Pithie and Learned Inventions": *The Paradise of Dainty Devices* and Sixteenth Century Poetic Traditions." Diss. University of Washington, 1986. 144 pp.

VAZOV, IVAN (1850-1921)

2530. Kostov, Marta. "Vergleiche im Roman *Unter dem Joch* von Ivan Vazov in konfrontativer Betrachtung ihrer deutschen und russischen Wiedergabe." *Linguistische Studien* ser. A. Arbeitsberichte No. 120 (1984): 138-174.

2531. Kostov, Marta, and Veselin Vapordzhiev. *Die Phraseologie der bulgarischen Sprache: Ein Handbuch*. Leipzig: VEB Verlag Enzyklopädie, 1990. 88-99.

VEGA CARPIO, LOPE FELIX de (1562-1635)

2532. Brown, Charles Barrett. "The Proverb Epigram in Lope de Vega's Plays." M. A. Thesis. Washington University, 1923. 159 pp.

2533. Canavaggio, Jean. "Lope de Vega entre refranero y comedia." *Lope de Vega y los origenes del teatro español*. Ed. Manuel Criado de Val. Madrid: EDI, 1981. 83-94.

2534. Hayes, Francis Clement. "The Use of Proverbs in the 'Siglo de Oro' Drama: An Introductory Study." Diss. University of North Carolina, 1936. 44-75.

2535. Hayes, Francis Clement. "The Use of Proverbs as Titles and Motives in the 'Siglo de Oro' Drama: Lope de Vega." *Hispanic Review* 6 (1938): 305-323.

2536. Morby, Edwin S. "Proverbs in *La Dorotea*." *Romance Philology* 8 (1954-1955): 243-259.

2537. Recoules, Henri. "Refranero y entremés." *Boletin de la Biblioteca Menedez Pelayo* 52 (1976): 135-153.

VERGA, GIOVANNI (1840-1922)
2538. Pappalardo, Salvatore. "Il proverbio nei *Malavoglia* del Verga." *Lares* 34 (1968): 19-32, 139-153.

2539. Wlassics, Tibor. "La poesia dei proverbi ne *I Malavoglia*." *Orpheus* 18 (1971): 19-31.

VERHAIM, KLAREN (1935-1966)
2540. Wexelblatt, Robert. "The Proverbs of Klaren Verheim: A Note from the Editor." *San Jose Studies* 10, 1 (1984): 97-104.

VICENTE, GIL (c. 1465-c. 1536)
2541. Hayes, Francis Clement. "The Use of Proverbs in the 'Siglo de Oro' Drama: An Introductory Study." Diss. University of North Carolina, 1936. 18-19.

2542. Joiner, Virginia, and Eunice Joiner. "Proverbs in the Works of Gil Vicente." *Publications of the Modern Language Association of America* 57 (1942): 57-73.

VIDAL, GORE (1925—)
2543. Monteiro, George. "Derisive Adjectives: Two Notes and a List." *Western Folklore* 34 (1975): 244-246.

VIGNALI, ANTONIO (1500-1599)
2544. Russo, Michele Dello, ed. *Lettera di Antonio Vignali arsiccio intronato in proverbii*. Napoli: F. Ferrante, 1864. 53 pp.

VILLON, FRANÇOIS (c. 1431-c. 1463)

2545. Céard, Jean, and Jean-Claude Margolin. "Rébus et proverbes." *Rébus de la renaissance: Des images qui parlent.* Paris: Maisonneuve et Larose, 1986. I, 135-162.

2546. Cohen, Helen Louise. "Proverbs and the Ballade." *The Ballade.* New York: Columbia University Press, 1915. 94-102.

2547. Demarolle, Pierre. "Autour de la *Ballade des Proverbes*: Aspects logiques de la poésie de François Villon." *Richesse du proverbe.* Eds. François Suard and Claude Buridant. Lille: Université de Lille, 1984. I, 75-85.

2548. Heft, David. *Proverbs and Sentences in Fifteenth Century French Poetry.* Diss. New York University, 1941. Chapter 2. New York: Washington Square Press, 1942 (abridged to 12 pp.).

2549. Le Roux de Lincy, M. *Le Livre des Proverbes Français*, 2 vols. 2nd ed. Paris: A. Delahays, 1859; rpt. Genève: Slatkine, 1968. I, lviii-lix.

2550. Negreanu, Constantin. "O schita paremiologica: *Scrisoarea XII (Pîcala si Tîndala)* de C. Negruzzi." *Limba si literatura* 4 (1989): 527-537. Also in French as "Littérature et parémiologie chez François Villon et Constantin Negruzzi." *Proverbium: Yearbook of International Proverb Scholarship* 8 (1991): 113-119.

2551. Paioni, Pino. "I proverbi di Villon." *Studi Urbinati di Storia, Filosofia e Letteratura* 45 (1971): 1131-1136, 1136a-1136b.

2552. Pineaux, Jacques. "Un poète du XVe siècle: François Villon." *Proverbes et dictons français*, 6th ed. Paris: Presses Universitaires de France, 1973. 50-52.

2553. Pinkernell, Gert. "Une réplique haineuse à la *Ballade des proverbes*, de François Villon, émanant du cercle de Charles d'Orléans." *Archiv für das Studium der neueren Sprachen und Literaturen* 224 (1987): 110-116.

2554. Schulz, Barbara. "Contribution à la sémiologie du discours proverbial: texte littéraire-texte pictural: Villon et Breughel." *Strumenti Critici: Rivista Quadrimestrale di Cultura et Critica Letteraria* 15 (1981): 359-377.

2555. Sébillot, Paul. "François Villon." *Revue des traditions populaires* 3 (1888): 465-473.

VINCENT DE BEAUVAIS (c. 1200-1264)

2556. Ruhe, Ernstpeter. *Les proverbes Seneke le philosophe: Zur Wirkungsgeschichte des "Speculum historiale" von Vinzenz von Beauvais und der "Chronique dite de Baudouin d'Avesnes."* München: Max Hueber, 1969. 121 pp.

VIRGIL [Publius Vergilius Maro] (70-19 B. C.)

2557. Puccioni, Giulio. "Recupero di un'espressione proverbiale romana [Etiam capillus unus habet umbram suam (Even a hair has its shadow)]." *Maia: Rivista di Letterature classiche* 19 (1967): 176-178.

VOITURE, VINCENT (1598-1648)

2558. Sébillot, Paul. "Voiture." *Revue des traditions populaires* 5 (1890): 712-716.

VODOVOZOY, V. I. (1825-1886)

2559. Barenbaum, I. "'Pravda v poslovitsakh'—Agitatsionnyi raek 60-kh godov XIX veka." *Russkaia literatura* 7 (1964): 178-181.

VOLTAIRE [François-Marie Arouet] (1694-1778)

2560. Calvez, Daniel Jean. "Le langage proverbial de Voltaire dans sa correspondance du 29 décembre 1704 au 31 décembre 1769." Diss. University of Georgia, 1980. 343 pp.; published as *Le langage proverbial de Voltaire dans sa correspondance (1704-1769)*. New York: Peter Lang, 1989. 312 pp.

VONDEL, JOOST VAN DEN (1587-1679)

2561. Chotzen, Theodor Max. "De 'wilde Yr' bij Vondel en elders." *Tijdschrift voor nederlandsche Taal-en Letterkunde* 53 (1934): 1-18.

2562. Maximilianus, Pater. "*Joseph in Dothan*, verses 1480-1481." *Vondelkroniek* 10 (1939): 34-36.

2563. Stoett, Frederik August. "*Joseph in Dothan*, verse 1481." *Vondelkroniek* 7 (1936): 77.

2564. Verdenius, A. A. "'Gods molen maalt langzaam.'" *Vondelkroniek* 10 (1939): 63-64.

VOSS, JOHANN HEINRICH (1751-1826)

2565. Mieder, Wolfgang. "'Wine, Women and Song': From Martin Luther to American T-Shirts." *Kentucky Folklore Record* 29 (1983): 89-101. Also in *Folk Groups and Folklore Genres: A Reader*. Ed. Elliott Oring. Logan: Utah State University Press, 1989. 279-290; *Deutsche Redensarten, Sprichwörter und Zitate: Studien zu ihrer Herkunft, Überlieferung und Verwendung*. Vienna: Edition Praesens, 1995. 10-45.

2566. Mieder, Wolfgang. "'Wer nicht liebt Wein, Weib und Gesang, der bleibt ein Narr sein Leben lang': Zur Herkunft, Überlieferung und Verwendung eines angeblichen Luther-Spruches." *Muttersprache* 94 (Sonderheft, 1983-1984): 68-103. Also in *Sprichwort—Wahrwort!? Studien zur Geschichte, Bedeutung und Funktion deutscher Sprichwörter*. Frankfurt am Main: Peter Lang, 1992. 169-190.

2567. Mieder, Wolfgang. "'Wine, Women and Song': Zur anglo-amerikanischen Überlieferung eines angeblichen Lutherspruches." *Germanisch-Romanische Monatsschrift* 65 ns 34 (1984): 385-403.

W

WACE, ROBERT (c. 1100-c. 1174)

2568. Brosnahan, Leger. "Wace's Use of Proverbs." *Speculum* 39 (1964): 444-473.

2569. Schulze-Busacker, Elisabeth. *Proverbes et expressions proverbiales dans la littérature narrative du moyen âge français: Recueil et analyse.* Paris: Librairie Honoré Champion, 1985. 87-93.

WAELKENS, D. (16th cent.)

2570. Meersch, D. J. van der. "*Kronyk der Rederykkamers van Oudenaerde* (Oude Spreekwoorden bij D. Waelkens)." *Belgisch Museum* 7 (1843): 68-69.

WAGER, LEWIS (fl. 1560/1567)

2571. Whiting, Bartlett Jere. "Lewis Wager's *Mary Magdalene.*" *Proverbs in the Earlier English Drama.* Cambridge, Massachusetts: Harvard University Press, 1938; rpt. New York: Octagon Books, 1969. 52-54.

WAGER, WILLIAM (fl. 1566)

2572. Neuss, Paula. "The Sixteenth-Century English 'Proverb' Play." *Comparative Drama* 18, 1 (1984): 1-18.

2573. Whiting, Bartlett Jere. "W. Wager's *The Longer Thou Livest The More Fool Thou Art.*" *Proverbs in the Earlier English Drama.* Cambridge, Massachusetts: Harvard University Press, 1938; rpt. New York: Octagon Books, 1969. 117-120.

2574. Whiting, Bartlett Jere. "W. Wager's *Enough Is as Good as a Feast.*" *Proverbs in the Earlier English Drama.* Cambridge, Massachusetts: Harvard University Press, 1938; rpt. New York: Octagon Books, 1969. 120-124.

2575. Whiting, Bartlett Jere. "W. Wager's *The Cruel Debtor.*" *Proverbs in the Earlier English Drama.* Cambridge, Massachusetts: Harvard University Press, 1938; rpt. New York: Octagon Books, 1969. 125.

WAIN, JON (1925-1994)

2576. Taylor, Archer. "How Nearly Complete Are the Collections of Proverbs?" *Proverbium* No. 14 (1969): 369-371.

WALDIS, BURKHART (c. 1490-1556)

2577. Sanders, Daniel. [Rev. of] *"Sprichwörterlese aus Burkhard Waldis mit einem Anhange von Franz Sandvoss." Archiv für das Studium der neueren Sprachen und Literaturen* 40 (1867): 188-199.

2578. Sandvoss, Franz. *Sprichwörter aus Burkhard Waldis mit einem Anhange: Zur Kritik des Kurzischen B. Waldis und einem Verzeichnis von Melanchthon gebrauchter Sprichwörter.* Friedland: Richter, 1866. 159 pp.

WALLACE, HENRY (1888-1965)

2579. Miller, Edd, and Jesse J. Villareal. "The Use of Clichés by Four Contemporary Speakers." *Quarterly Journal of Speech* 31 (1945): 151-155.

WALSER, MARTIN (1927—)

2580. Doane, Heike. "Zitat, Redensart und literarische Anspielung: Zur Funktion der gesprochenen Sprache in Martin Walsers Roman *Die Verteidigung der Kindheit.*" *Colloquia Germanica* 25, 3-4 (1992): 289-305.

2581. Mieder, Wolfgang. "Sprichwörter im moderen Sprachgebrauch." *Muttersprache* 85 (1975): 65-88. Also in *Ergebnisse der Sprichwörterforschung.* Bern: Peter Lang, 1978. 213-238; *Deutsche Sprichwörter in Literatur, Politik, Presse und Werbung.* Hamburg: Helmut Buske, 1983. 53-76.

WALTHER VON DER VOGELWEIDE (c. 1170-c. 1230)

2582. Hofmeister, Wernfried. *Sprichwortartige Mikrotexte als literarische Medien, dargestellt an der hochdeutschen politischen Lyrik des Mittelalters.* Bochum: Norbert Brockmeyer, 1995. 154-208.

2583. Lieres und Wilkau, Marianne von. *Sprachformeln in der mittelhochdeutschen Lyrik bis zu Walther von der Vogelweide.* München: C. H. Beck, 1965. Especially 1-29.

WANDER, KARL FRIEDRICH WILHELM (1803-1879)

2584. Dove, N. R. [pseud. of Karl Friedrich Wilhelm Wander]. *Politisches Sprichwörterbrevier: Tagebuch eines Patrioten der fünfziger Jahre, zur Charakteristik jener Zeit.* Leipzig: Wigand, 1872. 256 pp.; rpt. ed. by Wolfgang Mieder. Bern: Peter Lang, 1990. 296 pp.

2585. Mieder, Wolfgang. "'Gedanken sind zollfrei': Zu K. F. W. Wanders *Politischem Sprichwörterbrevier.*" *Einheit in der Vielfalt: Festschrift für*

Peter Lang zum 60. Geburtstag. Ed. Gisela Quast. Bern: Peter Lang, 1988. 326-342.

2586. Voigt, Günther. "Karl Friedrich Wilhelm Wander und sein *Politisches Sprichwörterbrevier*." *Deutsches Jahrbuch für Volkskunde* 2 (1956): 80-90.

WAPULL, GEORGE (fl. 1571/1576)
2587. Whiting, Bartlett Jere. "George Wapull's *The Tide Tarrieth No Man*." *Proverbs in the Earlier English Drama*. Cambridge, Massachusetts: Harvard University Press, 1938; rpt. New York: Octagon Books, 1969. 147-151.

WEALTH AND HEALTH (c. 1557)
2588. Whiting, Bartlett Jere. "*Wealth and Health*." *Proverbs in the Earlier English Drama*. Cambridge, Massachusetts: Harvard University Press, 1938; rpt. New York: Octagon Books, 1969. 84-85.

WEBER, KARL JULIUS (1767-1832)
2589. Weber, Karl Julius. "Sprichwörter." *Demokritos, der lachende Philosoph*. München: Winkler, 1966. 346-351.

WEBER, VEIT (15th cent.)
2590. Hofmeister, Wernfried. *Sprichwortartige Mikrotexte als literarische Medien, dargestellt an der hochdeutschen politischen Lyrik des Mittelalters*. Bochum: Norbert Brockmeyer, 1995. 468-477.

WEBSTER, JOHN (c. 1578-c. 1632)
2591. Doyle, Charles Clay. "John Webster's Echoes of More." *Moreana* 18, 70 (June 1981): 49-52.

2592. Jordain, V. L. "Webster's Change of Sidney's 'Wormish' to 'Womanish.'" *Notes and Queries* 222 ns 24 (1977): 135.

WEIDA, MARCUS VON (1450-1516)
2593. Broek, Marinus A. van den. "Sprichwort und Redensart in den Werken des Leipziger Volkspredigers Marcus von Weida." *Beiträge zur Erforschung der deutschen Sprache* 7 (1987): 168-181.

WEINHEBER, JOSEF (1892-1945)
2594. Hornung-Jechl, Maria. "Wiener Redensarten in Josef Weinhebers *Wien wörtlich*." *Muttersprache* 68 (1958): 142-147.

WEISE, CHRISTIAN (1642-1708)

2595. Mieder, Wolfgang. "Christian Weises *Bäurischer Machiavellus* als sprichwortreiches Intrigenspiel." *Daphnis* 13 (1984): 363-384.

2596. Schubert, Werner. "Sprichwort oder Zitat? Zur lateinischen Rede im *Bäurischen Machiavellus* von Christian Weise." *Weimarer Beiträge* 15 (1969): 148-166.

WEISSE, CHRISTIAN FELIX (1726-1804)

2597. Pape, Walter. "Der ästhetische Erzieher: Christian Felix Weiße oder die bürgerliche Utopie. 6d: Die moralische Anstalt für Kinder." *Das literarische Kinderbuch: Studien zur Entstehung und Typologie*. Berlin: Walter de Gruyter, 1981. 211-235.

WELTY, EUDORA (1909—)

2598. Blackwell, Louise. "Eudora Welty: Proverbs and Proverbial Phrases in *The Golden Apples*." *Southern Folklore Quarterly* 30 (1966): 332-341.

WERNHER, Bruder (c. 1190-c. 1250)

2599. Hofmeister, Wernfried. *Sprichwortartige Mikrotexte als literarische Medien, dargestellt an der hochdeutschen politischen Lyrik des Mittelalters*. Bochum: Norbert Brockmeyer, 1995. 261-272.

WERNHER DER GARTENAERE (late 13th cent.)

2600. Preuss, Richard. "Stilistische Untersuchungen über Gottfried von Straßburg." *Straßburger Studien: Zeitschrift für Geschichte, Sprache und Litteratur des Elsasses* 1 (1883): 1-75.

WEST, JOHN FOSTER (1918—)

2601. Abrams, W. Amos. "*Time Was*: Its Lore and Language." *North Carolina Folklore* 19 (1971): 40-46.

WESTCOTT, EDWARD NOYES (1846-1898)

2602. Glassie, Henry. "The Use of Folklore in *David Harum*." *New York Folklore Quarterly* 23 (1967): 163-185.

WETMORE, ALPHONSE (1793-1849)

2603. Montgomery, Evelyn. "Proverbial Materials in *The Politician Out-Witted* and Other Comedies of Early American Drama 1789-1829." *Midwest Folklore* 11 (1961-1962): 215-224.

WEVER, RICHARD (16th cent.)

2604. Whiting, Bartlett Jere. "Richard Wever's *Lusty Juventus.*" *Proverbs in the Earlier English Drama.* Cambridge, Massachusetts: Harvard University Press, 1938; rpt. New York: Octagon Books, 1969. 107-108.

WHETSTONE, GEORGE (c. 1544-c. 1587)

2605. Whiting, Bartlett Jere. "George Whetstone's *Promos and Cassandra.*" *Proverbs in the Earlier English Drama.* Cambridge, Massachusetts: Harvard University Press, 1938; rpt. New York: Octagon Books, 1969. 253-263.

WHITE, T. H. [Terence Hanbury White] (1906-1964)

2606. Redmond, Chris. "A Proverb in T. H. White [Four things not to trust: a dog's tooth, a horse's hoof, a cow's horn, and an Englishman's laugh]." *Notes and Queries* 220 ns 22 (1975): 209.

2607. Stewart, James. "A Proverb in T. H. White [Four things not to trust: a dog's tooth, a horse's hoof, a cow's horn, and an Englishman's laugh]." *Notes and Queries* 220 ns 22 (1975): 561.

WHITNEY, GEOFFREY (c. 1548-c. 1601)

2608. Rusche, H. G. "Two Proverbial Images in Whitney's *A Choice of Emblemes* and Marlowe's *The Jew of Malta.*" *Notes and Queries* 209 ns 11 (1964): 261.

WHYTHORNE, THOMAS (1528-1596)

2609. Eccles, Mark. "Words and Proverbs from Thomas Whythorne." *Notes and Queries* 219 (1974): 405-407.

WIBBELT, AUGUSTIN (1862-1947)

2610. Simon, Irmgard. "Sagwörter im plattdeutschen Werk Augustin Wibbelts." *Jahrbuch Augustin Wibbelt-Gesellschaft* 5 (1989): 24-45.

WIESNER, HEINRICH (1925—)

2611. Koller, Werner. "Redensartenspiel in der schönen Literatur." *Redensarten: Linguistische Aspekte, Vorkommenanalysen, Sprachspiel.* Tübingen: Max Niemeyer, 1977. 197-210, especially 197-199.

WILDE, OSCAR (1854-1900)

2612. Obelkevich, James. "Proverbs and Social History." *The Social History of Language.* Eds. Peter Burke and Roy Porter. Cambridge: Cambridge University Press, 1987. 43-72. Also in *Wise Words: Essays on the*

Proverb. Ed. Wolfgang Mieder. New York: Garland Publishing, 1994. 211-252.

2613. Schmidt-Hidding, Wolfgang. "Oscar Wilde und George Bernard Shaw." *Englische Idiomatik in Stillehre und Literatur*. München: Max Hueber, 1962. 71-76.

2614. Shvydkaia, L. I. "Sinonimicheskie otnosheniia poslovits i aforizmov v angliiskom iazyke." *Leksikologicheskie osnovy stilistiki (Sbornik nauchnykh trudov)*. Ed. I. V. Arnol'd. Leningrad: Gosudarstvennyi pedagogicheskii institut im. A. I. Gertsena, 1973. 167-175.

WILDER, THORNTON (1897-1975)

2615. Bülow, Ralf. "Stell dir vor, es gibt einen Spruch. . ." *Der Sprachdienst* 27 (1983): 97-100.

WILMOT, JOHN, 2nd Earl of Rochester (1647-1680)

2616. Adlard, John. "Plain-Dealing's Downfall." *Notes and Queries* 221 ns 23 (1976): 559.

WILSON, ROBERT (died c. 1600)

2617. Whiting, Bartlett Jere. "*The Three Ladies of London* by Robert Wilson." *Proverbs in the Earlier English Drama*. Cambridge, Massachusetts: Harvard University Press, 1938; rpt. New York: Octagon Books, 1969. 158-160.

2618. Whiting, Bartlett Jere. "*The Three Lords and Three Ladies of London* by Robert Wilson." *Proverbs in the Earlier English Drama*. Cambridge, Massachusetts: Harvard University Press, 1938; rpt. New York: Octagon Books, 1969. 160-164.

2619. Whiting, Bartlett Jere. "Robert Wilson's *The Cobbler's Prophecy*." *Proverbs in the Earlier English Drama*. Cambridge, Massachusetts: Harvard University Press, 1938; rpt. New York: Octagon Books, 1969. 277-278.

WIRNT VON GRAFENBERG (13th cent.)

2620. Hofmann, Liselotte. *Der volkskundliche Gehalt der mittelhochdeutschen Epen von 1100 bis gegen 1250*. Zeulenroda: Bernhard Sporn, 1939. 53-55.

WISDOM (c. 1460)

2621. Whiting, Bartlett Jere. *"Wisdom." Proverbs in the Earlier English Drama*. Cambridge, Massachusetts: Harvard University Press, 1938; rpt. New York: Octagon Books, 1969. 75-77.

WITTENWEILER, HEINRICH (14th/15th cent.)

2622. Keller, Martha. *Beiträge zu Wittenweilers "Ring."* Leipzig: Heitz, 1934. 156 pp.

2623. Wagner, Eva. 'Heinrich Wittenweiler (und das Sprichwort) als Vertreter einer späteren Zeit.' "Sprichwort und Sprichworthaftes als Gestaltungselemente im *Renner* Hugos von Trimberg." Diss. Würzburg, 1962. 179-188.

WOLF, CHRISTA (1929—)

2624. Militz, Hans-Manfred. "Das Antisprichwort als semantische Variante eines sprichwörtlichen Textes." *Proverbium: Yearbook of International Proverb Scholarship* 8 (1991): 107-111.

2625. Palm, Christine. "Die konnotative Potenz usueller und okkasioneller Phraseologismen und anderer festgeprägter Konstruktionen in Christa Wolfs Roman *Kindheitsmuster.*" *Europhras 88. Phraséologie Contrastive: Actes du Colloque International Klingenthal-Strasbourg, 12-16 mai 1988*. Ed. Gertrud Gréciano. Strasbourg: Université des Sciences Humaines, 1989. 313-326.

2626. Palm, Christine. "Fundgrube *Kindheitsmuster* und kein Ende: Zur semantischen Analyse einiger Phraseologismen im Text." *Europhras 90: Akten der internationalen Tagung zur germanistischen Phraseologieforschung, Aske/ Schweden 12.-15. Juni 1990*. Ed. Christine Palm. Uppsala: Acta Universitatis Upsaliensis, 1991. 163-179.

WOLFRAM VON ESCHENBACH (c. 1170-c. 1220)

2627. Hofmann, Liselotte. *Der volkskundliche Gehalt der mittelhochdeutschen Epen von 1100 bis gegen 1250*. Zeulenroda: Bernhard Sporn, 1939. 65-69.

2628. Jäger, Dietrich. "Der Gebrauch formelhafter zweigliedriger Ausdrücke in der vor-, früh- und hochhöfischen Epik." Diss. Kiel, 1960. 123-161.

2629. Jung, Paul. "Sprichwörter (Weisheit und Lüge)." *Sprachgebrauch, Sprachautorität, Sprachideologie.* Heidelberg: Quelle and Meyer, 1974. 99-109.

2630. Matz, Elsa-Lina. *Formelhafte Ausdrücke in Wolframs "Parzival."* Diss. Kiel, 1907. Kiel: H. Fiencke, 1907. 109 pp.

2631. Mone, Franz Joseph. "Zur Literatur und Geschichte der Sprichwörter." *Quellen und Forschungen zur Geschichte der deutschen Literatur und Sprache* 1 (1830): 186-214, especially 203.

2632. Nicklas, Friedrich. *Untersuchung über Stil und Geschichte des deutschen Tageliedes.* Berlin: Emil Ebering, 1929; rpt. Nendeln, Liechtenstein: Kraus Reprint, 1967. 78-79.

WOODES, NATHANIEL (fl. 1581)
2633. Whiting, Bartlett Jere. "Nathaniel Woodes's *The Conflict of Conscience.*" *Proverbs in the Earlier English Drama.* Cambridge, Massachusetts: Harvard University Press, 1938; rpt. New York: Octagon Books, 1969. 154-158.

THE WORLD AND THE CHILD (1522)
2634. Whiting, Bartlett Jere. "*The World and the Child.*" *Proverbs in the Earlier English Drama.* Cambridge, Massachusetts: Harvard University Press, 1938; rpt. New York: Octagon Books, 1969. 81.

WU CHING-TZU (1701-1754)
2635. Eberhard, Wolfram. "Some Notes on the Use of Proverbs in Chinese Novels." *Proverbium* No. 9 (1967): 201-209. Also in *Studies in Chinese Folklore and Related Essays.* Bloomington: Indiana University Press, 1970. 176-181.

WYATT, Sir THOMAS (1503-1542)
2636. Daalder, Joost. "Wyatt's Proverbial 'Though the Wound Be Healed, Yet a Scar Remains.'" *Archiv für das Studium der neueren Sprachen und Literaturen* 138 (1986): 354-356.

2637. Mauch, Thomas Karl. "The Role of the Proverb in Early Tudor Literature." Diss. University of California at Los Angeles, 1963. 269-271.

2638. Ross, Diane M. "Sir Thomas Wyatt: Proverbs and the Poetics of Scorn." *Sixteenth Century Journal* 18 (1987): 201-212.

WYCHERLEY, WILLIAM (1640-1716)

2639. Taylor, Archer. "Proverbs in the Plays of William Wycherley." *Southern Folklore Quarterly* 21 (1957): 213-217.

WYCLIF, JOHN (1320-1384)

2640. Skeat, Walter William. "John Wyclif." *Early English Proverbs, Chiefly of the Thirteenth and Fourteenth Centuries*. Oxford: Clarendon Press, 1910; rpt. Darby, Pennsylvania: Folcroft Library Editions, 1974. 127-129.

2641. Whiting, Bartlett Jere. "Studies in the Middle English Proverb," 3 vols. Diss. Harvard University, 1932. 1386 pp.

Y

YASAR KEMAL (1922—)

2642. Hess-Lüttich, Ernest W. B. "Sprichwörter und Redensarten als Übersetzungsproblem: Am Beispiel deutscher Übersetzungen spanischer und türkischer Literatur." *Mehrsprachigkeit und Gesellschaft: Akten des 17. Linguistischen Kolloquiums Brüssel 1982*. Eds. René Jongen, Sabine De Knop, Peter H. Nelde, and Marie-Paule Quix. Tübingen: Max Niemeyer, 1983. II, 222-236.

THE YORK CYCLE OF MYSTERY PLAYS (14th cent.)

2643. Whiting, Bartlett Jere. "*The York Plays*." *Proverbs in the Earlier English Drama*. Cambridge, Massachusetts: Harvard University Press, 1938; rpt. New York: Octagon Books, 1969. 8-11.

YOUTH (c. 1528)

2644. Whiting, Bartlett Jere. "*Youth*." *Proverbs in the Earlier English Drama*. Cambridge, Massachusetts: Harvard University Press, 1938; rpt. New York: Octagon Books, 1969. 90-92.

YWAIN AND GAWAIN (c. 1350)

2645. Whiting, Bartlett Jere. "Proverbs in Certain Middle English Romances in Relation to Their French Sources." *Harvard Studies and Notes in Philology and Literature* 15 (1933): 75-126, especially 115-118.

Z

ZATOCHNIKA, DANIILA (12th-13th cent.)

2646. Felitsyna, V. P. "Sopostavlenie tekstov *Moleniia* Daniila Zatochnika i sbornika poslovits XVII veka." *Voprosy teorii i istorii iazyka: Sbornik statei, posviashchennyi pamiati B. A. Larina.* Eds. N. A. Meshcherskii and P. A. Dmitriev. Leningrad: Izdatel'stvo Leningradskogo Universiteta, 1969. 119- 123.

ZESEN, PHILIPP VON (1619-1689)

2647. Meid, Volker. "Sprichwort und Predigt im Barock: Zu einem Erbauungsbuch Valerius Herbergers." *Zeitschrift für Volkskunde* 62 (1966): 209-234, especially 219-234.

ZIMMERSCHE CHRONIK (16th cent.)

2648. Birlinger, Anton. "Sprichwörter und sprichwörtliche Redensarten aus der *Zimmerschen Chronik.*" *Alemannia* 1 (1873): 304-307.

2649. Seiler, Friedrich. *Deutsche Sprichwörterkunde.* München: C. H. Beck, 1922, 1967. 54.

ZINCGREF, JULIUS WILHELM (1591-1635)

2650. Dittrich, Lothar. "Emblematische Weisheit und naturwissenschaftliche Realität." *Die Sprache der Bilder: Realität und Bedeutung in der niederländischen Malerei des 17. Jahrhunderts.* Eds. Wolfgang J. Müller, Konrad Renger, and Rüdiger Klessmann. Braunschweig: ACO Druck, 1978. 21-33. Also in *Jahrbuch für Internationale Germanistik* 13 (1981): 36-60.

2651. Schnur, Harry C. "The Humanist Epigram and Its Influence on the German Epigram." *Acta conventus neo-latini Lovaniensis: Proceedings of the First International Congress of Neo-Latin Studies, Louvain 23-28 August 1971.* Eds. J. Ijsewijn and E. Keßler. München: Wilhelm Fink, 1973. 557-576.

ZSCHOKKE, HEINRICH DANIEL (1771-1848)

2652. Vinken, P. J. "Some Observations on the Symbolism of 'The Broken Pot' in Art and Literature." *American Imago* 15 (1958): 149-174.

ZUCKMAYER, CARL (1896-1977)

2653. Kühn, Peter. "Phraseologismen: Sprachhandlungstheoretische Einordnung und Beschreibung." *Aktuelle Probleme der Phraseologie.* Eds. Harald Burger and Robert Zett. Bern: Peter Lang, 1987. 121-137.

2654. Mieder, Wolfgang. "Carl Zuckmayer und die Volkssprache." *Sprachspiegel* 32 (1976): 163-166. Also in *Sprichwort, Redensart, Zitat: Tradierte Formelsprache in der Moderne.* Bern: Peter Lang, 1985. 15-19.

INDEX OF SCHOLARS CITED
[Numbers refer to entries, not to pages.]

838, 841, 860, 866, 878-880,
891, 893, 906, 911, 912, 955,
960, 976, 1072, 1093, 1101,
1111, 1130, 1149, 1179,
1180, 1209, 1210, 1211,
1214, 1227, 1228, 1229,
1241, 1242, 1246, 1247,
1248, 1269, 1291, 1295,
1296, 1315, 1324, 1325,
1352, 1368, 1369, 1370,
1371, 1372, 1376, 1377,
1378, 1419, 1441, 1474,
1483, 1489, 1490, 1491,
1492, 1505, 1516, 1526,
1527, 1528, 1565, 1571,
1619, 1644, 1669, 1670,
1671, 1672, 1673, 1716,
1717, 1749, 1796, 1807,
1924, 1973, 2020, 2105,
2106, 2140, 2146, 2181,
2182, 2210, 2211, 2212,
2226, 2228, 2299, 2360,
2369, 2382, 2423, 2426,
2432, 2463, 2469, 2470,
2501, 2509, 2565, 2566,
2567, 2581, 2585, 2595, 2654
Militz, Hans-Manfred 159, 314,
872, 1500, 1514, 1798, 1799,
2624
Miller, Anthony 977, 2300
Miller, Clarence H. 978
Miller, Edd 756, 928, 2142,
2579
Miner, Dorothy 2046
Mistletoe 2240
Mittelstädt, Hartmut 922
Moelleken, Wolfgang Wilfried
1884
Mokitimi, Makali Isabella Phomolo 160
Moldenhauer, Joseph J. 2478

Molho, Mauricio 1120
Mone, Franz Joseph 161, 162,
1205, 1299, 1885, 1980, 2513,
2631
Monitto, Gary V. 2301
Monteiro, George 163, 321, 591,
774, 997, 1109, 1633, 2033,
2543
Montgomery, Evelyn 401, 1638,
2603
Montoto y Rautenstrauch, Louis
645
Monye, Ambrose A. 2145
Moran, William L. 349
Morawski, Joseph 164
Morby, Edwin S. 2536
Morel, Jacques 408
Morel-Fatio, Alfred 641
Morgan, Aaron Augustus 2302
Morgan, Frances Elnora Williams
165, 456, 1049, 1609, 2028
Morozova, L. A. 1587
Morreale, Margherita 2518
Morris, Alton C. 2031
Morson, Gary Saul 2489
Morton, Gerald W. 495, 1000
Moya, Ismael 166, 1340, 1341
Müller, Carl Friedrich 2113
Müller, Curt 2034
Müller, Gernot 1506
Müller-Salget, Klaus 1156, 1386
Müller-Schwefe, Gerhard 2303
Mulinacci, Anna Paola 2029
Mustel, V. 1993
Myrick, Leslie Diane 167

Nardo, Anna K. 1789
Nares, Robert 2304
Nash, Ralph 1450, 1790
Nassar, Noha Saad 2418
Needhan, Gwendolyn B. 2305

About the Compilers

Wolfgang Mieder is Professor of German and Folklore and head of the Department of German and Russian at the University of Vermont. In addition to editing *Proverbium: Yearbook of International Proverb Scholarship*, Mieder has written numerous books on paremiology and folklore, including *A Dictionary of American Proverbs* (1992), *Proverbs Are Never out of Season: Popular Wisdom in the Modern Age* (1993), *A Dictionary of Wellerisms* (1994), and *Wise Words: Essays on the Proverb* (1994).

George B. Bryan is Professor of Theatre History at the University of Vermont and has published several reference books on theatrical biography, the latest of which are *Stage Deaths: A Biographical Guide to International Theatrical Obituaries, 1850 to 1990* (2 vols., 1991) and *Ethel Merman: A Bio-Bibliography* (1992). In addition to *American Theatrical Legislation 1607-1900: Conspectus and Texts* (1994), Bryan also wrote *Black Sheep, Red Herrings, and Blue Murder: The Proverbial Agatha Christie* (Peter Lang, 1993).

Mieder and Bryan are the co-compilers of *The Proverbial Bernard Shaw: An Index to Proverbs in the Works of George Bernard Shaw* (1994), *The Proverbial Winston S. Churchill: An Index to Proverbs in the Works of Sir Winston Churchill* (1995), and *The Proverbial Eugene O'Neill: An Index to Proverbs in the Works of Eugene Gladstone O'Neill* (1995). *The Proverbial Harry S. Truman: An Index to Proverbs in the Works of Harry S. Truman* will soon be published.